The Tragedy of Almightiness

The Tragedy of Almightiness

Revaluing Ethical Life

SYBE SCHAAP

WIPF & STOCK · Eugene, Oregon

THE TRAGEDY OF ALMIGHTINESS
Revaluing Ethical Life

Copyright © 2016 Sybe Schaap. All rights reserved. Except for brief quotations in critical publications or reviews, no part of this book may be reproduced in any manner without prior written permission from the publisher. Write: Permissions, Wipf and Stock Publishers, 199 W. 8th Ave., Suite 3, Eugene, OR 97401.

Wipf & Stock
An Imprint of Wipf and Stock Publishers
199 W. 8th Ave., Suite 3
Eugene, OR 97401

www.wipfandstock.com

ISBN 13: 978-1-4982-3304-0

Manufactured in the U.S.A.   12/29/2015

First published in Dutch by Uitgeverij Damon, Budel (The Netherlands), 2006
Copyright ©Sybe Schaap, 2006
Translated by Diane Butterman, 2015

Cover: *Tower of Babel*, sand sculpture Thorn (2003)

To Marina

Contents

Preface • ix
Biblical References • xi

1 Introduction • 1
2 The Call for Justice • 18
3 Abraham's Belief • 30
4 Untruthful Atheism • 50
5 The Desire for Omnipotence • 58
6 Moses: Between Law and Promise • 97
7 Paul's Zeal • 113
8 Luther's Bitterness • 128
9 From God to Man • 142
10 The Imagination Unleashed • 160
11 The Messianic Unburdening • 183
12 The Stalinist Final Contest • 206
13 The Self-Conquest • 227
14 Faithful to the Earth • 242

Bibliography • 255

Preface

This book is about omnipotence. It addresses various questions pertaining to the origins of the longing for omnipotence, whilst at the same time explaining how such longing has been able to dominate belief and philosophy. The omnipotence theme harks back to a well-known and controversial concept dealt with in the philosophy of Nietzsche, that of the will to power. In the present book, the challenge that is taken up is that of further elucidating the power element of this whole concept in the spirit of Nietzsche's philosophical legacy. Examples are given to illustrate how thought relating to power has developed through the ages. Precisely how that arose in Hebrew and Christian thinking and was ultimately integrated into atheistic ideologies will be traced. Is it conceivable that in these different ideologies, man was seeking to fully come to terms with the old divine omnipotence? What was it that man was pursuing when the longing for omnipotence arose? What drove him, what was he seeking? And what has this single-minded attitude led to?

This book discusses the developments that have emerged in thinking that is related to power. It identifies the way it all began with Abraham and how it ended with the apparent loss of power-related thought in the communist experiment. But was that really where it all ended? Does it still perhaps simmer beneath the surface in, for instance, fundamentalist movements? The question posed is this: how does the idea of omnipotence affect the image of God, man himself and the way in which he evaluates his fellow man, and therefore also, ethical life? Monotheism suffers from being tempted to view God as omniscient, omnipotent, and utterly good. Even if in this way the image of God is not completely exhausted, the notion of omnipotence does have its dangerous facets. In this book it is these potential dangers and their consequences that are dealt with in depth.

One of the central questions is whether the longing for omnipotence opens up the way to allowing man's ethical meaning in life to be eroded. Is it not so that recently in atheism, but before that in religion, this personal privacy was robbed of its sacred core? The crucial question which that gives rise to is that of precisely how ethical life can be invested with renewed meaning. To that end, what is required of man? This requires the elucidation of two further concepts. Exactly what Hegel means when he refers to the atheism of the ethical world must be made clear, a matter referred to in this book as ethical atheism. Following on from that, one has to clarify what Nietzsche meant when he spoke of the death of God. Where, in both of these concepts, does the almighty stand?

The book draws on both the Bible and philosophy. Religion and atheistic ideologies are discussed from specific points of view. The perspectival approach does, however, carry the inherent risk of veering too much towards one-sidedness and exaggeration. This was the approach chosen so that as clear as possible of an idea of the theme referred to could be given. Even if this approach does not reveal the whole truth, what is asserted must be true. Merely the crucial space allowed in this book for the topic of truthfulness demands that this be the case.

What is narrated in these pages is, above all else, a story. Hence the reason that the quotations, references, and notes have been kept to the bare minimum.

Biblical References

The Bible used is the version that was translated in accordance with the stipulations laid down by the Dutch Bible Society. The books to which reference is made, together with their abbreviations, are the following:

- Genesis (Gen)
- Exodus (Exod)
- Numbers (Num)
- Deuteronomy (Deut)
- Nehemiah (Neh)
- Isaiah (Isa)
- Zechariah (Zech)
- The Letter of Paul to the Romans (Rom)
- The Letters of Paul to the Corinthians (Cor)
- The Letter of Paul to the Galatians (Gal)
- The Letters of Paul to Timothy (Tim)

1

Introduction

Eschatological expectations seem to be a constant, just like the call for justice. The longing for a promised land and for redemption from human suffering, for a new earth and for divine fulfillment are things that have always dominated the human spirit. The Old and New Testaments bear witness to this. The promise that God's kingdom will come on earth extends to the belief in an immortal heavenly life. Hope and expectation are not confined to religion. In modernity, *atheism* embraces such an eschatological heritage: man now thinks he is capable of recreating himself and his world. It is certainly conceivable that in the wake of failing revolutionary salvation, the torch will again be handed over to religion. Man seems to want to persistently live with the longing for the promise that, in whatever guise, justice will one day come to liberate him. This, however, is not all there is to the promise. What lies ahead of those who are not chosen and are not entitled to salvation? They too can expect a promise: that of retribution. They can expect to be confronted with the reverse side of *justice*: not in the form of salvation but in the form of the Last Judgment. They can expect avenging justice. There can be no eschatology without a belief in double-edged justice.

Does this mean that eschatological expectation inextricably links together hope and retribution? Can redeeming and avenging justice not be contemplated in isolation? Is there thus no salvation without judgment? This is the central question. But perhaps it should be further specified. Does another kind of pathos precede eschatological desire? Does man perhaps predominantly wish to do away with the existence with which he is familiar? Is there no hope and promise without a pathetic problem? This leads to a pressing question: a question concerning *omnipotence*. There can be no eschatological hope without the intervention of omnipotence and the omnipotent. Is the yearning for omnipotence really human? Must omnipotence offer man the certainty that the promise will be fulfilled? Does the call for justice lead to belief in omnipotence? Is the same true of the other component of salvation, avenging justice? Does omnipotence therefore also offer the certainty of retribution? These, then, are the questions pertaining to the origins of belief in the omnipotent, a faith that has to provide the certainty that, for the omnipotent, everything is possible. In a seemingly miraculous way, the call for justice brings together faith, hope, and omnipotence. If the facets *problem* and *promise* converge in man, is that something that is somehow embedded in the human condition? This is also a question we need to address. It is a question that is especially pertinent in the light of recent history, which underlines for us the full absurdity of the consequences of the problematic nature of man.

The call for justice and omnipotence is inherent in Nietzsche's interpretation of *man*. He refers to man as a *problem* and a *promise* all in one. This corresponds to man as characterized in the story of Creation in Genesis: there, man is depicted as the creature who can discern between what is *good* and *evil*. Thanks to this power of discernment, to consciousness and to willpower, to his perceptive and imaginative powers, man and human existence lose their innocence when compared with non-human creatures. Man distances himself from that which simply is. This human capacity is both promising and dangerous. This overwhelming question also arises. When contemplating omnipotence it must be made clear that the *problem* can drastically change course. The hazards that can arise must be made explicit if this problem is to become a standard for human existence. The extent to which this human standard may become a creative aspect of the imagination must be apparent. How powerful the imagination then becomes and just how it succeeds in labeling the problem of *evil*, and *the evil* also need to be made apparent. How was imagination able to get a grip on the call for justice and on omnipotence, that dangerous emergency measure that should have brought justice? First, hesitantly, there was divine omnipotence; later, more boldly, there was human omnipotence.

1.1 MAN AS A PROBLEM

It is in man that both the problem and the promise converge. Man is an open being; his capabilities and possibilities are not as firmly fixed as those of other living creatures. The openness facilitated by the problem also turns him into a promise. The openness provides him with a future dimension, with a forward-directed orientation, promising opportunities. However, that same openness has a backward dimension to it too, harking back to the past, to human memory, to a memory that cannot set itself free from what has happened and what has been done. Indeed, openness even enables man to be retrospectively creative: he can give himself a past and either invest it with a promise or a problem. That makes man dangerous.

1 Introduction

This *danger* occurs when man is seized by discomfort, by dissatisfaction with the reality he has been given, by his existence, by the world in which he lives. No satisfying answer is given to the existential question of whether this is all that there is. Dissatisfaction can thus grow into a strangling perception. Dissatisfaction cannot bear an existence that is perceived as dark and displeasing. Existence not only becomes darkened but darkness itself is given a name. *Evil* now reigns everywhere; everything is dominated by evil. Such discomfort summons up profound questions about the meaning of life. Why are things as they are and not *different*? Why is there no *better* existence? Why is there no peace and happiness? Having an *unhappy consciousness* gives the human capacity to distinguish a negative twist. It makes existence too dark to bear, evil too great to tolerate. The unhappy consciousness reveals the extent of the interminable perceptions and radical judgments of which man as a problem is capable. Discomfort does not stop at passive judgment: it becomes radical, it judges, it calls for action. Something snaps. What *is* disappears behind an obsessive prejudice: *what is cannot be true*. The unhappy consciousness wants to break *free* from this world, it does not want this world, it wants to be released from such an unbearable existence. Man as a problem creates a problem. What emergency measures will provide him with a solution?

Mirrored in this problem, the unhappy consciousness supplies a *longing*: a desire for that other, for the *possible* as opposed to the real. Discomfort leads to the temptation to take a radical turn. If what *is* cannot be true, could what is true not then point to what is not, to what *not yet* is? Could this be a way to tackle this too big of a problem? Could mere appearances, a comforting illusion, a hopeful promise, offer a way out? But then again there is *doubt*: is what is possible about this illusion enough? Can hope actually be fulfilled? Should not desire be supported by *certainty*? Should no certainty be offered that the possible will be fulfilled? Where is the liberating insight? Might it perhaps be possible to believe in the certainty of redemption? Such *belief* would open up a future; then true *light* would glimmer beyond darkness. This light would give hope to the unhappy consciousness during its unbearable existence. But where do faith and hope gain certainty of redemption? Then the need which is too great takes refuge in an imagined *emergency* measure: that of a *power* that surpasses all existing powers. This power must guarantee the unhappy consciousness that what exists is not only given a hopeful perspective, but that it can really be *made* to be different. And how creatively does the imagination support that which is virtually inconceivable? Somehow it must be possible to imagine a power that is capable of rediscovering or recreating the given world? Why not then place such power in a God? And if what was inconceivable has become conceivable, why then does man not appropriate this divine power? Steeled by the certainty of faith, man reaches for a power that should make the *totally different* possible. The problem that is too great finds a solution in redemption. It seeks refuge in a convenient emergency measure, in *omnipotence*.

There are many different ways in which the unhappy consciousness has given an interpretation to the longing for redemption. The evil in this world was always too great: too great to bear, too great to be a challenge. The unhappy consciousness has given evil an ingenious twist: it has made evil suspicious by requiring it to justify itself. Discomfort connected the *question of justification* to evil. That is how this consciousness seeks to pre-emptively defeat evil, if it cannot justify itself. Why this justification question? Because man is not capable of putting evil in context when making the age-old distinction between good and evil. It is no longer distinctive, it no longer challenges one to seek the good. If good and evil can no longer be held together in a distinguishing way, then both will be separated by a threatening abyss. The justification question is an emergency measure for the unhappy consciousness, an attempt to rid itself of evil. If it cannot be justified, then what is displeasing in this world may, indeed must, be combated under the one denominator of *evil*. And this, in turn, justifies the demand for redeeming and avenging *justice*. Does avenging justice secretly dominate redeeming justice? Is the unhappy consciousness not too easily tempted to vengefully judge unjustifiable evil?

Because of such unjustifiable evil, the world as we know it casts a strange and hostile gaze upon man. The world is strange, misleading, dark, full of deceptive appearances, untrue. The only escape, then, is to find the truth elsewhere, in a totally different world that makes possible a totally different existence. A totally different truth not only has to be discovered elsewhere but it also has to be truly *fulfilled*. Marx's eleventh *Thesis on Feuerbach* assumes that there is something liberating about fulfillment: "philosophers have merely *interpreted* the world, in various ways; the important thing is to *change* it." This says a lot about how we untruthfully deal with the truth. What *is* can merely be revealed as evil. So it has to be contested, turned into something different. Such interpreting is far removed from submissively *observing* what is: first of all, it is creative. As a cognitive creative activity, it is part of a practical creative activity, of *making something come true*. Behold the *world* of the unhappy consciousness: so permeated with evil that emergency measures have to provide the solution. And where do these emergency measures dwell: in the *theodicy*, the question of justification, the call for justice. How welcome that would be if justice could be connected to the *certainty* of providing an escape from evil. Could this justice not be *foreseen* and guaranteed by *providence*, divine, cosmic, historic, human? Could this providence be more powerful than evil?

All of this leads to a question of some enormity: the question of how this dangerous problem can be surmounted. Indeed, would not the question concerning the justification of evil and the envisaged escape constitute a *danger* in itself? Is it precisely this that makes man, as a problem, such a danger? Is this danger in fact the dark side of the promising nature of man? Must what is promising in man, therefore, keep itself far removed from justice?

1   Introduction

Man, with all his needs and emergency measures, is thus envisaged as a problem that is too great. Before the Lisbon earthquake, the theodicy did not lead to the perception of an emergency situation at all. The question pertaining to evil could be answered optimistically: it is not so bad, it is actually merely the apparent side of a world that is essentially good. This good is visible in all things, in cosmic and in human reality. The *interpretation* of the world therefore reveals meaning, despite the evil. Such interpreting makes the concealed order within or behind the manifest world known; it lays bare an existing order, determined by the laws of nature. Just as, in retrospect, the God of creation saw that everything was *good*, so man can also discover what is good in the world. The fact that the world manifests itself as coincidental, as contingent on us, is mere semblance. Everything is purposeful and thus rational and divine. God operates in the world as a law of nature, as purposeful rationality, as *common providence*. What seems to be mysterious or negative to man is nothing other than an illusory aspect of truth and goodness. This perspective has a reconciling effect on what appears, to man, to be evil. The *interpretation* makes everything different from how it seems. There is therefore nothing that still has to be fulfilled: things already have meaning or sense. After all, a benevolent creator does make everything essentially good, which eradicates what is—to man—any deceptive *appearance*. Science and history testify to this goodness. Thanks to providence, the cosmos can be construed as good.

Insight reconciles. In the presence of what is seemingly coincidental and evil, man *knows better*. To quote Leibniz: man knows that he has been given the best of all possible worlds and that this can be revealed to him. Insight therefore brings together the true and the good. The evil of this world cannot detract from the fact that the world is essentially good. Providence and insight, which is indebted to providence, *justify* existing evil: it is no real evil; it does not disturb what is good. Essentially, it can be explained by or understood from all that is good. Divine providence can be discovered and made visible. This frees man from a threatening unhappy consciousness. The justifying of evil is what makes existence bearable and meaningful; it means that nothing new has to be proven. Like providence, truth is also is more *powerful* than anything else in the world.

Providence and the truth that is founded in it work as a reconciling, and therefore as a redeeming power. This means to say that also in this case, the question concerning the justification of evil cannot be answered without the need for certain emergency measures, without the need for a power that surpasses appearances. This reconciling power of providence becomes complete when it not only applies to the natural cosmos but also to the human cosmos. Hegel points to the effectiveness of providence also in the *human* cosmos. He is referring in that way to the ethical order of such a cosmos. So the reconciliation with evil remains possible, even after the Lisbon earthquake. If the best of all possible worlds can no longer be identified in the natural world, then the alternative is the human cosmos. It is a world that is not yet complete but will become complete through this historical process. Also, this interpretation unites what is true and good. This interpretation can also provide an answer to the question of the justification of evil, human evil included. Because human evil is harder to tolerate than natural evil, the reconciling effect of this insight becomes even greater. Man *knows* that he is reconciled with his ethical world despite the apparent presence of what is negative and evil. Hegel's reconciliation theory is closely allied to Nietzsche's appeal to remain faithful to the earth and not find solace in interpretations that relate to other worlds or provide incentives to change the world.

But what if evil becomes too much for man to bear and can no longer be justified? Then the justification question, which had previously been so easy to answer, is soon given a radical twist. If evil demands justification but it cannot be found, then the question flounders. The appropriate justification question then has to seek an *emergency* exit. This is indeed what happens in the modern age, but what is most remarkable is the fact that providence accompanies such a trend. It should guarantee the prospect that change for the better will be *assured*. What was previously manifestly good is still *not yet*, but it is certainly imminent. Such certainty is the result of a *special* or personal kind of providence. It appears in the guise of a radical emergency measure, an assured escape from an irreconcilable world.

No matter how much the work of providence can be discovered through rationality and true insight, *interpretation* no longer suffices. Interpretation in isolation has a negative effect. After all, interpretation testifies that the true and good no longer converge. The true and good can only be united if there is a rigorous change in reality, including in the human world and in man himself. Since true insight can no longer discover good, here, in this world, good has to be attributed to a totally different world. Interpretation thus first and foremost unveils a problem: it detects too much evil. The justification question thus raised can, it emerges, be inflated to cosmic proportions: ultimately it is a cosmic question, it is about the whole world, about humanity, about history.

Why, then, pose this justification of evil question? Why not overcome evil and see it as a perpetual challenge as it is simply something that is intrinsic to man? Why is evil not given any differentiating appraisal? Does man *want* to pose this question because the call for justice demands that? Is it human unease that prompts this question?

Once the justification question has been radically posed, it becomes boundless. It then tempts one to perceive all that is displeasing, both human and natural, as *being* evil. There is then an irresistible urge to see all natural misery and shortcomings as *human* evil. Then the justification question—as a cause of this evil—also affects man. An ancient, mythical explanation takes on a more rational guise. The theoretical perspective declares that man is the *cause* of the evil, he is pronounced *guilty* in an ethical sense. Human deeds now have a detrimental effect on the once good creation or innocent natural world. In the beginning there was a human catastrophe, a fatal deed with cosmic consequences, a heinous deed that will forever repeat itself if no evasive action is taken. In this respect, whether or not the cause is to be sought in the Fall, in the destructive functioning of culture, in technology, or in any other cause is not so relevant. What is crucial is that *evil* is connected to human *guilt*. The justification question rationalizes a primitive reflex to make evil and guilt synonymous.

Whilst in the past the justifying of evil succeeded by embedding it in what is good and seeing it as the work of common, divine providence that now fails. There is a reversal: the evil of this world becomes impossible to *justify*. At best, it functions as a cunning ploy in the historicistic speech on the coming good. But even then evil is no mere semblance behind which the true and the good are to be discovered. The conclusion therefore is simple and far-reaching: this evil should not exist. Because of such evil, a world permeated with evil cannot be justified. This even accentuates the problem of discomfort and the unhappy consciousness: this world and this existence are unbearable. The cause of this unbearable evil cannot therefore be tolerated any longer. Unjustifiable evil leads to *accusations*. Adorno's verdict that this world is an irreconcilable conglomeration of guilt has radical consequences. There is no evil without human guilt and therefore those who are guilty. So human guilt and guilty man can no longer be justified. Precisely what all of this evokes will soon become clear.

The only remaining way to escape is by radically changing man and the world. There can be no change without external intervention, in other words, without emergency measures. Even if *history* offers an escape through redemption, the difference, when compared to the reconciling effect of general providence, is still fundamental. Not only is the justification of evil no longer sought *in* the historical process, but the redeeming deed has to come from elsewhere, from beyond man and the world that has fallen from grace. History is not a process of revealing the truth and discovering inherent good. For the sake of what is *good*, an essential settlement with universal evil is first required. Unjustifiable evil has to be destroyed, that is what has to be *done*. Only that will create space for the good that is still to come. Such good is not only a prospect but also something totally different from what present man and the world can offer.

The question of justification gives the ancient human *problem* a particular identity: evil is linked to guilt and good to redemption. The more intensely this problem is experienced, the stronger the need for assurance that the road from omnipresent evil to redeeming good can be successfully traversed will be. Is it miraculous that this certainty is placed in the hands of an *omnipotent* power? This immediately gives providence a specific, *special*, personal character. It no longer emanates from within, it intervenes instead from outside. Hence the reason that omnipotence has a personal character: that of the almighty. The omnipotent has to offer the certainty that it will guide the process of redemption. Because he can intervene with man, the world, and history, it can be trusted that good will eventually come.

This perspective of redemption moralizes in an unprecedented manner. The illusion of what exists and the present are as intimately connected with evil as is future good with what is true. This makes evil so omnipresent and unbearable that it no longer has the power to challenge in a distinguishing sense. If the emerging world were to reveal something else, then it would be deceptive *semblance*. From the point of view of an all-penetrating evil, the existing world is no longer justifiable either. That is why the omnipotent not only has to be more powerful than all evil, but also more powerful than everything else in this world. The fact that this foreseeing omnipotence has *control over* what is true and good will prove to have far-reaching consequences. A *truth* that is *mightier* than everything in this world is placed in the hands of an almighty one who turns himself, in his own name, *against* the existing world and its evil. The almighty one rises above the true and good. The question that thus arises is: what is this decreeing redeeming power capable of?

This does not answer the question concerning the *justification* of evil. To deal with the evil and the guilt of man and the world, evil returns in a different way. General providence can turn out to be fatalistic, but specific providence can prove to be *dangerous*. In fact evil returns, like something that is *needed* to make the transition from the old to the new world possible. After all, it is all about changing the world. So a battle has to be waged to eradicate the evil of this world, to nullify it. Beneficial *evil* is necessary if the unjustifiable *evil* of this world is to be defeated. Beneficial evil is required, and therefore justified. For the sake of redeeming *justice*, the omnipotent has at his disposal redeeming evil. This empowers the foreseeing omnipotent to wage a justified war against evil. No matter how mysterious the warlike deeds of the omnipotent are, the outcome will prove that the action was justified. In religion and modern atheist ideologies, certain matters do become clear about the work of such specific providence. What is demonstrated is what can happen if the omnipotent not only has access to what is true and good but also to beneficial evil. Twice it is a demonstration of a justified war against evil that cannot be justified. Time and time again people connect emergency measures to problems that are too big.

A little more should now be said about the bearing that the true and the good have on the question of justification. The great power of specific providence cannot be considered in isolation of the unhappy consciousness of man. This consciousness not only tends to turn away *from* the world as it is, but also to turn *against* it. It proves itself to be *reactive*. Will and consciousness are dominated by the word *no*. This *no* penetrates the knowledge, the will and the deed, the true and the good. The no *moralizes*. This no is a preoccupation, a prejudice that ruins the open mind. Prejudice ruins *truthfulness*, the will to see things as they are. If that which *is* can be not true, then that which is true will automatically be sought elsewhere: in a former, a coming, or a transcendent world. The notion of truth is separated from things as they are. The apparent, discomforting world thus becomes deceitful and evil. Moralizing interpretation turns away

1 Introduction

from the world as it is: it does not want this world, and therefore it does not want to see this world as it is either. However, what is supposedly true undergoes a moralizing metamorphosis: it is likened to the beckoning good, however one may interpret that.

Moralizing prejudice also affects man, the human world, and society as we know it. More to the point, moralizing judgment first and foremost affects the ethical environment. The moralist does not in the first place find unjustifiable *evil* in the physical cosmos, but rather in the human world. This turnabout in human judgment will also be extensively discussed. It is a change that robs the *good* of its *ethical* meaning. The question of how to treat the *other* virtuously is suppressed by the question concerning existential fulfillment in personal existence. It is not a particular form of ethical life but rather ethical life as such that is deprived of all meaning.

In the terms of Hegel, this reassessment of the ethically good can be called *atheistic*, atheistic in the ethical sense. Moralizing prejudice and the revaluation of the true, the good, and the evil accompany this ethically atheistic portent. The inherent danger of such atheism will become clear. What must also be made clear is the possible consequences if this reassessment not only turns against ethical heritage but also against the purpose of ethical life as such. Ethical atheism makes man *insincere*: he then ceases to seek good in his relation to the other. Sincere openness towards the other and the will to ethically order society are lost. The other becomes an object of the will to gain power. The direct link between dissatisfaction, unease, the unhappy consciousness, and the insincere desire to gain *power* will emerge. This will finds no peace. This will seeks justified war: not so much against evil but rather against its culprits. The call for justice also pulls in this direction as well.

So far, the focus has been on sketching man as the problem because man places faith in the redeeming omnipotence. In what respect, however, does Nietzsche also view man as a *promise*? He calls him a promise because man can also *overcome* this personal, all too human problem: the problem of the unhappy consciousness and the *turning away* from this life. Man can convert the *no* towards existence into a *yes*. The *no* can reside in a *yes* that is powerful enough to search the *true* in the given, apparent world, a yes that wishes to realize the *good* even without the emergency measures of randomness and omnipotence. Instead of constantly being *pursued* by an unhappy conscience, existence can also *challenge* man. Evil does not have to be experienced as unbearable but can instead be appreciated as a challenge.

This kind of self-conquest is also something that Nietzsche terms redeeming. This *redemption* does not free one *from* evil, nor does it seek such liberation. It does not want to justify evil but rather overcome it, time and again. This redemption seeks no justice either as redeeming or as avenging justice. Indeed, there is no need for it because man in the form of a promise also overcomes the question of the justification of evil. The prospect of man as a promise will henceforth play a perpetual role. What is so liberating about this point of view is the fact that the world does not have to be *interpreted* from the angle of the work of *providence*. Accordingly, it does not have to be *changed* from this perspective either. The world is too big and too much for such matters anyway. Only a *final*, profound question remains, that of how to overcome ethical atheism. This will prove to be impossible unless farewell is bidden to the omnipotent.

1.2 THE ATTRACTION OF OMNIPOTENCE

The desire to gain *omnipotence* has a long history. In religion, the yearning for this power is often typical of monotheism. It is a desire that cannot be seen in isolation of the turning of many gods to the one god. It might therefore be termed a *theological turn*. The desire for omnipotence *cannot* be gratified with many gods. In a certain respect, they are all equal, which is why they curtail each other's power. It can be stated that these gods—in accordance with the words of the God of creation—are equal to man. Gods and people have not, in this respect, become infinitely estranged from each other; man can walk with his gods. The desire for omnipotence leads to inequality between God and man. Man then has to conform to the will of the omnipotent. Man finds justification for this inequality in God's *justice*. As argued, justice has two interpretations: it can be avenging—a liberation *from*—and fulfilling, redeeming—a liberation *to*. The longing for omnipotence and justice brings with it a deterioration in people's ethical understanding of what is good: with increasing difficulty, man realizes and discovers what is good in his ethical social world. A new time horizon contributes to that. A door to the future opens; this stimulates man to leave the old existence behind and embrace the prospect of a new existence. No matter how religious the experience of all of this is, the theological twist is atheistic in the *ethical* sense. With ethical *atheism*, ethical life is robbed of its sacred core and so loses all significance. Ethical life loses its intrinsic value; it does not satisfy anymore, it provides man with too little happiness. Though it may well sound paradoxical, it is the demeanor of the one, almighty God, that is the cornerstone of the triumphal march of ethical atheism. The omnipotent has to be able to guarantee the human quest for another meaning, for alternative life's fulfillment.

In its religious form, too, this ethical atheism can be called *modern*: what is ethically distinguishable about good and evil flows over into an existential division between the two. That makes the justification of evil problematic. The fact that the desire for omnipotence has recently become more radical does not constitute a real break with religion. Man's present search for humanized, justified omnipotence might be termed an *ideological turnabout*. It is especially Marxism that provides a striking example of this. Whatever man ever lay in the hands of almighty God becomes rescinded. Simultaneously, he appropriates the fulfillment of justice. This change is all about the *incarnation of God*. Man starts to yearn for his own omnipotence; his imagination and credulity convince him that such omnipotence can be his. Once again, man prepares to liberate himself from the galling ethical bonds. The ethically atheistic spirit becomes activistic. Man interprets his world; he thinks he is able to change it.

The Old Testament provides some good examples of the *theological* turnabout. One example is the story of Abraham where one sees that God's power had to give him faith in the fulfillment of the divine promise. It is not a kind of *turning around* that should be viewed historicistically; in history there is no such thing as a starting point. In many ways, hesitantly and dispersed over long periods, it is future desire that has taken possession of the human spirit. In addition, ethics based on tradition has proven to lead to a tough life. This polymorphism is also apparent in *ideological* turnabout. Very many movements have expressed this, in many different ways. But this time, the toughness of the ethical life seems to be over.

The present book tells the story of the desire for *omnipotence*. It shows how man sees himself as the problem and how he maintains that through the emergency measure of power, he can free himself from that same problem. His dissatisfaction, unease, and unhappy consciousness all become too much for him. He encounters insurmountable, inherent problems in himself and so wants to free himself from them. The desire for omnipotence is an emergency measure that is all too human and one that should bring him justice: liberation from evil and fulfillment in life. The story that will be told is one of how in seeking justice the emphasis comes to lie more and more on avenging justice and on the repaying *of* evil. The call for justice is *reactive*. What first started with Abraham does, over the course of time, take on grotesque proportions. The plea for justice is finally channeled into justified repayment. It is a right that is transferred from God to man. The power attributed to God becomes *actual* omnipotence in man. Stalinism is the near-perfect *fulfillment* of this wish for power. This incarnated god demonstrates the ultimate urge for the rebirth of man and for the recreation of the world; this god fulfills the plea for justice, with the avenger taking the lead.

Stalinism is the apotheosis of the desire for power. That is also how Stalinism saw itself. However, one should be wary of attaching—for no apparent reason—a different interpretation of life to the failure of ideological religious zeal. Thinking purely in terms of power may reveal changes and developments, but it does not justify historicism. The many efforts to finally release man have therefore repeatedly failed and so the issue of man as the problem has not been resolved. The call for ultimate justice has not yet been satisfied. The desire for omnipotence can therefore always be aroused again in religious or ideological forms.

There is no providence that watches over human history. As long as man exists, he *remains* a problem and a promise all in one and will therefore think and act accordingly. Now he can at least endeavor to surmount his problematic status and become a promise. To that end, another interpretation of the *desire for power* will now be considered. It is not a desire that is directed at gaining as much power as possible, but it does give priority to the will and to the will's *active orientation*. The

Old Testament and Pre-Socratic Greek philosophy provide us with examples of man's actively wanting to be a *promise*. Instead of turning reactively against the world that has been given to him, he *actively* seeks his way within it. As Nietzsche asserts: man proves to be capable of remaining faithful to the world and to binding *challenges* to this earthly existence. In that mission he is led by two *virtues*: he proves himself to be truthful and sincere. Not afraid to see the world that has been given to him for what it is, he accepts the harsh reality as a challenge: he demonstrates that he is *truthful* in his understanding. He also turns out to be capable of *sincerity* in his contact with his fellow man and in the active quest to ethically interpret his existence. Both virtues are crucial to man as a promise.

If we are to gain more clarity on the change that leads to the power pathos, we should take a deeper look at the notion of *truth*. This idea also has its idiosyncrasies. Nietzsche called truth a difficult matter; for man the truth is not always easy to accept and to bear. It can therefore be difficult for man to be truthful, to accept things as they really are. For that reason, it is not strange that man so easily turns his back on reality and seeks truth elsewhere. The truth is something that is easier to cope with for those who have the courage to face up to their challenges and thus more akin to a risky undertaking. There are salient differences between the ways in which truth is interpreted in Pre-Socratic Greek philosophy and in the Hebrew tradition, so undoubtedly this helps to throw some light on the matter. Both traditions seek a specific relation to what is, to what is known, to reality, to the human and physical cosmos. In both cases, a specific *time horizon* is relevant, a time perspective that is decisive for the value and orientation underscoring the idea of truth.

The Greek philosophers' notions of truth were related to the *known* human and cosmic reality. In their thinking such ideas had to be *reflected*, revealed, and repeated. In such reflecting, man actually looks *back* and that, in turn, has to do with the specific character of the truth that has to be understood. Traditionally, it was a particular cosmos, a lively and living reality of natural and ethical powers. So the Greek philosopher reflected with a certain *respect* on what he had been given and on what he still had to learn and understand. In this sense, the oldest Greek philosophy does not really diverge much from its mythological roots. In its essence, the oldest philosophy retains a sacred core. The Greek thinker is guided by a time perspective that makes him look back. He has no real future, no prospect promising something different from what has always been. The expert cannot and does not really want to free himself from what must be discovered. Knowledge tells the story of what is; it repeats the tale of the world to which man is bound. Word and reality are in this respect *equal*: similarity discovers similarity. In what man verily knows and says, nothing new is revealed: that which is true contains no promise. From this point of view, *truthfulness* means being open and *wanting* to be open to what is known. As Hegel later reiterates, knowing is, in an almost literal sense, a matter of *discovering* or reproducing what already is. It demands openness with respect to what is known, even if this is a hard and frightening reality. That which is true comes first and last: it permeates the word. The Greek philosopher remains faithful to the earth, to his ethical environment. Hence the definition of man as *zoon politikon*, a political animal.

In the Hebrew tradition there is another time perspective that persists and which has consequences for the concept of truth. The notion of truth is rather more inclined to point *forward* to the future. That is why the relationship between the true and the real becomes slightly reversed. The true is open; it reveals a *forward-looking* objective for man. That then converts the appreciation of *truthfulness* into knowledge and knowing. That which is true also encapsulates that which not yet is; therefore it is associated with the possible, the other, the promise. That which is true incorporates the inherent promise that what has been promised will one day be given to man. It is this expectation that links truth to *faith*. Faith promises that truth will prevail: it is *more powerful* than anything in this world. This idea of what is true therefore binds together truth, faith, and power: how could truth otherwise ever triumph? While the gaze is fixed ahead, what *has been given* loses the sacred value recognized and adhered to by the ancient Greeks. The forward-oriented gaze seeks what is *still to be given*. This is what makes the Hebrew God a very different one from the Greek gods. While the latter all bind man to the given ethical world, the omnipotent is much more inclined to bind man to his promise and to oblige him to believe in him and in his promise.

The present book provides a *narrative* on omnipotence and thus on the faith that omnipotence requires. The central issue is that of the place occupied by the omnipotent in modern ideologies, but to examine this we need to return to biblical dogma. Key elements of these dogmas may be traced in the modern, atheistic perceptions of faith. What is explained is how man as a problem always wins from man as a promise and how man in his guise as a promise seems to become invisible. It is a miraculous but also dangerous *paradox*: that which is promised sets in like rot in man the promise.

The story begins with the calling of Abram, with him leaving behind his familiar environment and traditions and setting off for the Promised Land. The question is: how does this *journeying* change him as a *human being*. Why the new name Abraham? What is the significance of the fact that his *God* also changes? Does the name changing symbolize the belief in what man is promised? How does the omnipotent God differ from all the *traditional* gods? It is clear that future perspectives really do open up for Abraham and that he is able to believe that good will befall him. It is a perspective that repeats itself with Moses and the people of Israel. Again there is the promise of and the desire for certainty, again there is the belief in the omnipotent.

Whilst in the Old Testament faith has an earthly promise, this same promise takes a radical turn in the Christian faith. Faith then brings with it the promise of a heavenly life. But is that where things stop, with this heavenly justice that is allied to recreation and rebirth? Surely the other interpretation of justice, avenging justice, is also emphatically present? Is there a link with the old prophetic signs concerning the settling of old scores of the past with man and with the world? Is man of the past to blame for the evil that imprisons him and the old world? An assessment must be made of how vengeance comes into the picture, the avenging of evil since it can no longer be justified. Are the old and new dominated by good and evil? That would turn good and evil into *powers*, powers that have to fight to the bitter end in a fight that is apocalyptically charged; like a messianic *final battle*. Does almighty God have to guarantee victory? Does the final battle bring man *justice*, in both senses of the word? Would that not shackle redemption to an avenging kind of justice.

Apocalyptical doctrine undergoes a powerful revival in Protestantism. Luther reanimates the messianic perception of faith, but also simultaneously the call for justice. His ethical fatalism—this was incidentally also a feature of Paul's doctrine—will be discussed in depth. The question is whether the law still allows man to find what is good in ethical life. What does the law say about man's sinfulness? Is man actually *able* to live according to such a law? Or is it precisely this element of the doctrine that gives a powerful impulse to ethical atheism?

Modern philosophy somehow seems to incorporate these doctrinal elements. With atheistic religious zeal it transfers the omnipotence attributed to God to man. In Fichte's philosophy, it has to become clear how the *ideological* direction is prepared. To that end, his imaginative power is discussed together with the yearning for power which that feeds. This serves to clarify how Marxism elaborates on this. How does it make the ideological path revolutionary? What does this say about notions of truth? Does Marxism once again make truth mightier than anything else in the world? What is the significance of the fact that man now has to *fulfill* the promising idea himself? Revolutionary atheism seems to break away from faith in God while at the same time holding on to the promise made in God's name. Does this mean that the apocalyptic vision also remains effective? Does Marxism also expect to see a final battle between the powers of good and evil? That would mean that *atheistic Messianism* would consign this battle to man and his human omnipotence. Interestingly, that throws a new light on Stalin and Stalinism. Does Stalin seek to fulfill this Messianism? Does he unleash the final battle? Does imaginative power help him to do this? And is all of this done in the name of justice?

That would demonstrate how man's ethical view of life is sacrificed to this explosion of power and, with it, tradition and all the handed down *ethical values*. Is Marxism therefore especially atheistic in the ethical sense? Does this make Marxism a reflection of modernity, even if ideology ultimately loses its meaning? The early ethical life was sustainable in terms of sacred heritage. Culture gods protected this heritage. Gods did not promise, they *preserved*. They gave man a time perspective so that he could look back in awe at the source of the ethical heritage. Does faith in the omnipotent initiate a time horizon that gradually erodes the bond with the sacred origins of ethical life and its sustainability? If it does, faith will empower an ethical kind of atheism, *also within religion*. Does this mean that the gods of this ethical life will die? Have they died already, definitively? Does their death threaten the inherent ethical sense of what is good? Does this cause a deterioration in the lively, challenging distinction between good and evil leading to a dramatic separation? Does this distinction degenerate into a battle between good and evil, a battle waged in the name of justice? Let us consider again the *final* question that was posed earlier: is ethical life still possible after all the ethical gods have died? This has already been stated.

1.3 A FINAL QUESTION

Omnipotence is the perspective from which the story of ethical *atheism* will be told. The story has to clarify how ethical life loses its sacred heart and is robbed of its uniting power. It may sound paradoxical, but this atheism has its origins in religion. It is miraculous that the death-struggle of the ethical gods is heralded in religion and that modern atheism merely confirms this death-struggle. The plea for justice makes the ethical gods fade into the background. The biblical God also experiences a similar transformation: as the God of ethical life, he loses in the struggle with the God of justice. Gods and people exhibit great similarities. People who have an ethical outlook on life lose from those who seek justice. The call for justice really entangles people in unsolvable problems. This should really be put slightly differently: the call for justice *is* an all too human problem. The hope of being redeemed *into* the good life makes man grimly hope for redemption *from* unjustifiable evil. Justice has a fatally moralizing effect. The true is robbed of its cognitive sense, the good of its ethical sense. When reassessing the true and the good, man turns away from his world: leaving it in a *godforsaken* state.

I shall now just briefly elucidate the concept of *ethics* used throughout. It is a concept that relates to the whole range of morals and ethics, to ethical life and to jurisdiction, especially in sustainable, institutional contexts. The convention of summarizing ignores the many differentiations. The ethical outlook upon life focuses on the willingness of man to turn to the human world, to notice the other, to offer him something. In the fulfillment of ethical meaning, man *appreciates* the coexistence of people and the accompanying sustainable orientation of will and consciousness, acting and judging. In this appreciation, man displays his *sincere* attitude to his fellow man. This appreciation also renders ethical meaning to the gods and to religion. The matter of the existence of God or the gods is not important in this connection. The existence question actually ignores the essential meaning and value of religion. The ethical significance of gods emerges from their *effect*, which is a directional effect. In ethical atheism it is just as much about this effect, but it is equally about the significance of the omnipotent. God, who changes in form, value, and meaning, also derives his significance from the effect that it had upon man. In many ways, gods are images of man and an example for man, an ideal, a longing, a pathos. In atheism, too, the gods maintain an effect as an image and an example.

In this respect, the concept of *atheism* is not an indication that faith is disappearing but rather the opposite. Even if the existence and value of God or the gods can be denied or refuted, the specific meaning of gods and religion remains valid. The negative stance of *atheism* does not alter the fact that God and religion retain significance in atheism. Atheists, too, are attached to God, and are almost invariably more religious than the faithful—as borne out by Marxists. The reverse is also incidentally true—really to a similarly radical degree. This is what is meant by the concept of ethical atheism: it is a rejection of the sacred value and sense of ethical life. In religion, too, the ethical value of God and the gods can be rejected and refuge can be taken in another notion of god, another value of divine being. What is central to this book is the ethical meaning of atheism, also in religion. Modern ideology radicalizes this atheism but at the same time it adheres to the core of religion and the relevant professed values. This is most obvious in the call for justice. Ethical atheism therefore operates both in atheism *and* in religion: religiously and ideologically. In both forms of atheism, a reassessment of the true and good is in evidence. In both, the truth becomes more powerful than everything in this world. Where the incarnate god receives the *actual* power of decision about the true, the good, and justice, the danger of the desire for omnipotence becomes unmistakable.

The story of ethical atheism to be told in this book is accompanied by *final questions*, questions that cannot be ignored but which cannot be easily answered either. Can man bear the harsh reality if the sacred connection with the world that has been given to him is lost? Is a sincere life possible after the death of the ethical gods? Can man be receptive to ethical solidarity with his fellow man if he loses the sacred basis of ethical life? Hegel maintains that ethical life, no matter how rational it is, should be formed and anchored in older, deeper-lying religious essence. Nietzsche asserts that the death of the ethical God forces man himself to become the foundation of a truthful and sincere existence. Man will have to surmount his most dangerous problem: himself. He transfers the religious essence to mankind: to his ability to see the truth and to his will to do what is ethically good.

The present book is a narrative of the ethical atheistic change that man has undergone, both in religion and in terms of the relevant atheistic repercussions. The dangers are all mapped out. They are dangers that certainly have not disappeared in our day and age. In many guises ethical atheism festers on, spoiling the truthfulness and sincerity of man. As Nietzsche reminds us, man has definitely not overcome himself as the problem and it turns out that he is no random promise either. Can religion still provide an answer to this problem? Or does revived religion automatically activate the desire for redeeming omnipotence? Has the omnipotent permanently defeated the ethical gods? If this were true, then the question would naturally lead back to man: after all, he furnished himself with his gods. Can man surmount himself as the problem? Will he be able to conquer the yearning for justice? In that connection, does the omnipotent have to say goodbye to man? Or, over and above all of this, will man have to learn to bid the omnipotent farewell? The final questions remain unanswered. Let this, too, already be stated.

2

The Call for Justice

The question surrounding the *justification* of evil has dangerous implications. In two equivocal senses it asks too much. It furthermore makes it tempting to define evil in very broad outline by not only referring to human or moral unacceptability, but also to that which may be termed natural. That *which is* evil thus comes to imply all that is negative, all suffering and deficiency. Everything that is unacceptable is thus placed under the one denominator of that which is evil. It is a kind of latitude that makes the justification question grotesque.

The justification question seeks to do too much. It presumes that it can or should be possible to *justify* evil. The answering of the question must somehow provide an insight into evil or explain it. Gaining such insight into evil can be comforting but it can also be disquieting; the explanation can have a liberating but also a fatalistic effect. It may thus be asserted that all misfortune, including any suffering attributable to natural causes, must be interpreted as a *punishment*: a punishment visited upon humans from God or the gods for their sins, for human injustices, for human evil, for human guilt. It is an explanation that justifies evil by perceiving it as a legitimate punishment, a justification that has fatalistic implications and which threatens to make evil unbearably heavy. Then there is the consideration that evil may well be deserved but that one has to question whether the accompanying punishment serves any actual purpose. The suffering of man is deserved, thus justified, but otherwise pointless.

A more optimistic justification envisages evil as a negative manifestation of what is essentially a good cosmic order: the natural, human, and historic order of things. In its most profound sense, evil is really mere *semblance*, a directly visible, negative facet of a divine or rational order. Understanding such an order makes the negative facets relative in the positive sense of the word. The negative, or the evil, is explained and therefore justified. Justification does then reveal what is good, but does it preclude the drawing of fatalistic conclusions? In actual fact such justification implies that evil is not really of any great consequence, since that which is good prevails after all. Viewed in this light it certainly becomes more bearable. As a manifestation of a higher, good order, the burden of evil is lightened; this alleviation is reconcilable with existence. So *reconciliation* with evil, and thus with existence, is the most positive interpretation that the justification question has to offer. Once again, as punishment and as unreal manifestation, the justifying of evil leads to fatalism, be it understood and explained or not. That is all there is to it. Such fatalism is dangerous because all negativity is encompassed in that one conclusion. Man is doomed to coexist with evil. The distinguishing aspect disappears, that is all there is to it: evil provides no challenge.

The justification question can also lead to an antithetical conclusion, one that puts an end to resignation. This is, though, a more dangerous direction to follow. Understanding and explaining evil does at least make it indisputably clear that it *cannot be justified*. It is too much, too great, and it makes no intrinsic sense. Wherever it manifests itself, the justification question has the air of being rather *fateful*, of being something that befalls mankind while it should not. Here evil does not really count as punishment but the aspect of guilt does return, not as own guilt this time but rather as the guilt of the other, the instigator. Such evil lacks all sense. This forces one to draw the categorical conclusion: since evil cannot be justified it should not exist. If one then also yields to the temptation to see all that is negative as being somehow linked to evil or to guilt then the conclusion gains a broader more fatal tenor. Also the world and the reality in which this omnipresent evil fatefully abounds should not *be*. Having evil that cannot be justified burdens mankind with the insurmountable problem of having to seek good elsewhere.

What is so insurmountable about the justification problem is that it only provides man with the choice between fatalistic, nihilistic conclusions and things revolutionary. Once that which is distinguishing in evil no longer features in the picture it becomes impossible to deal with evil: it is rendered valueless, it does not challenge. Pursuing the justification of indistinguishable evil also taints the distinguishable in what is *good*. It thus turns into something entirely different that bears no relation to evil. Good and evil are completely forced apart; they become two separate worlds. The grotesque question pertaining to the justifying of evil should not therefore even be posed. It would be better to concretely treat the human and discriminatory aspects of evil like a challenge, like an opportunity to give a positive twist to things, *whatever* good and evil may be. The matter of *what* is actually good and *what* is evil can in that way remain open-ended. It remains both a distinguishing *and* a challenging question, one that invites people to value good and evil in concrete terms.

Yet mankind has posed the justification question. Was it abhorrence that drove man to do this? What merely remains then is emergency measures, an escape from eternal evil, the hope that justice will prevail. If this world cannot provide such justice then all that remains is an alternative world.

2.1 MEANING AND ABHORRENCE

Discontentment is a typical human trait; it may be termed an aspect of the human condition. If it constituted a reaction to some kind of deficiency, then this particular condition would deviate little from that of all life. But mankind reacts differently: with him unfortunate situations are prone to easily trigger his perception and imagination. Such a state of affairs can lead to an *unhappy state of consciousness*. As long as discontentment is concrete and directed, it remains within a person's powers to put an end to it. Otherwise, if the whole unhappy state of consciousness turns a person's entire existence into an issue, matters change. Existence is then viewed as meaningless and the consciousness starts to imagine a possibly totally different kind of life. Human powers of imagination have proved to be very susceptible to the phenomenon of an *existential longing* for a totally different kind of life. Hence the images of a promised land and a fulfilled life. Such kinds of images can then easily be supplemented by a plea for justice and the demand that mankind be treated fairly. How just would it not be to be liberated from unjustifiable discontentment? Could such longing not be linked to a *promise* and that same promise to guaranteed justice? In short, it is so very easy for the power of the imagination to fuel the fire of discontentment.

Discontentment, longing and imagination are the factors that force mankind to seek radical solutions to an existence that can no longer be justified: his *belief* will redeem him in the form of true justice. There is one final emergency measure in the form of a power that can somehow turn what has been promised into a reality. That is how the unhappy consciousness creates images for itself: of the possible, the justice, the pledge, and the power to which this justice can be entrusted. Discontentment and promise, belief and omnipotence: there is a *logical* kind of connectedness, albeit a *sinister* kind of logic that brings all of this together. It is sinister from the point of view that such logic is based upon a justification of discontentment. This logic in belief is not only very prevalent but also, so it seems, able to have a great effect. Exodus tells of the *awe-inspiring* acts of which God is capable (Exod 34:10). It is a faith that has moved mountains; it has set man and the world in motion. Faith makes everything different. It has *actually* proven to be mightier than anything in this world. It is not only a faith that brings with it the *promise* of miracles but it also *performs* miracles. It has set in motion an inconceivable imaginative power and has developed unprecedented vigor. To that end it has created its gods. Man created almighty God *in his image*. True belief permits as much as that. Not only does it offer guaranteed hope and firm trust but it also *activates* mankind, it allows imagination to seize power.

2 The Call for Justice

This lends unhappy consciousness its dark reverse side. It is moved by more than just a longing for light alone. Driven by discontentment it feeds on the experience of an unjustifiable and meaningless existence. The unhappy consciousness is therefore not so much driven by a longing for *purpose* as by aversion or *abhorrence*. This abhorrence amounts to darkness. Abhorrence creates an evil that cannot be justified and an existence that cannot be tolerated. Abhorrence whispers to consciousness that life should not be like that. It is abhorrence that precedes the yearning for purpose. The passionate longing for purpose is thus a longing born of abhorrence. Embedded in the justification question is the abhorrence of an unhappy consciousness that reveals itself as active. It is abhorrence that makes the longing for purpose an *obsessive* kind of longing. The search for purpose is driven by abhorrence, abhorrence that perpetually forces the consciousness to remain *retrospective* in its attitude. Abhorrence is dark and reactive. Can such darkness also become malignant?

The abhorrence couched in the longing and forward-looking glance is one that is formulated by prophets. Is there also something sombre in their credibility, which is more powerful than everything in the real world? Should not God's justice bring together salvation and *retribution*? Isaiah's redeeming God also shows his other side. It all begins in a very optimistic way: "Cease to dwell on days gone by and to brood over past history. Here and now I will do a new thing; this moment it will break from the bud" (Isa 43:18). In the first instance he profits from a redeemed, renewed existence in an existential and moral sense. After all, he surely implores people to turn their backs on the past with its doom, evil, and evil powers? Is there no abhorrence, no retribution, no justifiable punishing of evil? His words bear witness to the reverse. Alongside the prophetic prospect of a purposeful life, retribution is also given plenty of room for maneuver. The powerful truth is also driven by an aversion to the ubiquitous evil. Hence, the proclamation of judgment, of "revenge," of "the Powerful ones of Israel" against their opponents, their enemies. Justice reveals an innate close connectedness between redemption and "devastation" (Isa 1:24).

The effects of abhorrence can be so great that the distinguishing features of evil—in the form of good—virtually become *obliterated*. This is something that is almost literally demonstrated in neo-Marxist critical theory. The hope for a better life must be kept alive but it cannot and may not be concretely verbalized or visualized. Only evil can still be verbally expressed and explained. A vague, nostalgic experiencing of existential good is drowned by abhorrence at a kind of evil that is seen to be all-embracing. Obsessive abhorrence against evil that has become grotesque is extremely dangerous: such abhorrence creates darkness and, moreover, malignancy. Abhorrence *seeks* enemies, *creates* animosity and *justifies* an embittered view of *what* abhorrence conjures up and of *who* can be accused of this. The doctrine of redemption is too easily accompanied by a longing for deliverance *from* evil or even from the evildoers. Is also power, which seeks to be greater than everything else in this world, driven by such abhorrence? If so, the plea for redemption is just as *abyssal* as the perceived power of evil. It is the plea of an individual who is seized by abhorrence and can no longer rid himself of evil. The justification question is insufficient to conquer evil; what is fatal, though, is that the question does justify aversion.

Just a few thoughts about this *abyssal* aspect. Abhorrence and longing spoil the cohesion that man feels with the ancient own cosmos that has been given to him. This longing creates a *chasm* between what is handed down to him from the past and what the future has to offer. It creates a time perspective that transfers all sense of purpose to the future. It is a perspective that made antiquity shudder. In actual fact it signifies a rift with the traditional order. An *existential* longing for that which is totally different has a devastating effect upon the extant *moral* tradition. In its most radical guise it even ruins the purpose behind all moral life's fulfillment as such. Abhorrence and longing have an abyssal effect because they create a chasm between two divided worlds. The differentiating nature of good and evil is lost. Good and evil no longer represent distinguishing aspects of the same private world. The sought after purpose and the lived through abhorrence form the incomparable sides of the chasm. It is a chasm that divides two worlds. Reconciliation with the existing world and its evil is no longer possible. Evil no longer holds a challenge. The total lack of parity between good and evil, between life as it is and the promised salvation, situates man above an *abyss*, and that is what makes the experiencing of purpose and abhorrence so abyssal.

Just to elucidate: concrete evil can be combated, for instance by introducing more order to a failing society and by ensuring that it really does fulfill its own moral pretensions. Evil can be tackled by maintaining the legal order or by reinforcing the moral purpose and by striving to inculcate moderation and balance in people's behavior. Such measures will not free people from evil, but they will reduce the discernible level of evil. In this respect, the moral world may be said to form a collective social foundation, which helps good to concretely come into its own. In this same concrete respect, human life can also be improved from an existential point of view, such as by reducing poverty and providing better opportunities for people. Such kinds of improvements cannot be seen as salvation and that is not necessary either. Evil that can be concretely identified does not have to ruin connectedness with the human world. It is just as much a part of life as good. Evil demands no justification: it is merely the differentiating aspect of what amounts to actual and prevailing good. Evil reflects that which is good, thus making good a *criterion* for evil. By creating a division between good and evil and by seeking good elsewhere, a rift is ultimately formed which makes it impossible to deal with the evil that is thus rendered senseless. Such senseless evil gives way to abhorrence. It turns good into an *illusionary emergency measure* while making evil a *demonic reality*. The impenetrable inequality between good and evil prompts individuals to seek a bizarre escape in justification, salvation, and revenge. On the near side of the abyss, abhorrence seeks its justice by abandoning evil as an emergency measure in relation to vengeful justification. On the far side of the abyss, however, it is liberated existence that beckons. How, then, can one make the leap across such an abyss?

Does irreconcilable abhorrence make it possible to, in actual fact, survey the existing world in an open and honest way? Is such a person able to bear the truth or is it rather the case that abhorrence poisons the will to *honestly* deal with things as they really are? If the ethical world evokes such immeasurable abhorrence, is man still capable of sincere life fulfillment or does *zoon politikon* disappear? Hegel once called the ruined zest for life the atheism of the ethical world:[1] from an ethical point of view, society finds itself in a godforsaken, meaningless state. This has broader social implications. Feelings of responsibility *for* society, and thus for others, evaporate. It is sooner the case that the individual begins to demand that society make itself answerable *to him*. This provides another, yet again, dark twist to the whole question of justification. Just as evil that cannot be borne begs for justification, so now the ethical cosmos has to justify itself. Discontentment and abhorrence are transferred to the other. Evil holds that the other is its guilt, hence the dismal verdict of Sartre to the effect that hell has to be sought in the *other*. Evil that cannot be justified thus takes on an identity. The complaint about evil turns into an accusation whilst the judgment becomes a condemnation. It is therefore not strange to see that justification demands revenge, revenge upon the other because of the evil committed that cannot be justified.

2.2 THE TOO HARSH REALITY

There is an intimate link between the call for justification and the interpretation of the idea of truth. This becomes explicit when we further investigate the difference between the Old Greek and Hebrew notions of what constitutes truth.[2]

Pre-Socratic philosophy was accustomed to relating knowledge to the existing world. Since (because of the way the phenomenon appears to mankind) this world conceals itself from man, it is thought that has to strip the world of its secrecy. The Greek term *alètheia—lack of mysteriousness—*serves to express this sentiment. True knowledge seeks to understand what is and what, as such, must be conveyed in knowledge. In its most literal sense knowing thus has to do with *reflection*, with adhering to what is given. Thinking and knowing therefore brings with it little that is new, but this does not mean to say that thinking is a simple task. Indeed, lively phenomena make it difficult to establish truth. The process of making visible what was concealed is in keeping with the ancient orientation of mythical thinking because of its *retrospective* nature and the focus on what is already given to man. Much like mythical thinking, philosophy also looks back and contemplates the ethical cosmos that has been handed down to us. Religion and philosophy support ethical living *zoon politikon* in

---

1. Hegel, *Grundlinien der Philosophie*, 7.
2. Hejdánek, "Was ist Wahr."

the commemorating of his ethical cosmos, so knowing is also a kind of recognizing. If the gods die and religion can no longer come to people's rescue, then it is philosophy that binds mankind. Even the philosophical truth has nothing new to offer, only that which is long gone. Truth has to do with that which is *equal* recognizing what is equal. True knowledge has a meaning because it opens up a meaningful world. Knowledge reconciles. However, this must be correctly understood. Knowledge makes available the good that is present in the existing moral world. It reconciles with this good, it appreciates this good. It thus also recognizes the manifesting aspect of this truth and goodness, a phenomenon surrounded by what is negative and evil. Such recognition may be tragic but it does make it possible to bear the harsh reality. The essential question is not so much how to justify evil but how to discover, comprehend, and appreciate what is good. It is through getting to know and recognize good that inherent truth can help people to face the harsh reality.

This is also what Hegel has in mind when he formulates the philosophical task of coming to terms with the meaning of *what is*. Through this *what*, philosophical knowledge comes to focus upon what is general and meaningful in the actual world. In the first place, he takes it to mean the substantial, ethical core of the human environment. Gaining an insight into that reconciles one with the world. True insight values the ethical good in this world and is thus able to find reconciliation with the always coincidental, negative, manifesting aspect of what is. It sets out to ensure that philosophy, with all its ideas about truth, does not seek solace in transcendentalism or in deferring to another, better world. That which is good is here. It is up to philosophy to learn how to properly discover what is good; it must not occupy itself with what could be, with what can still happen. Here again, there is the retrospective glance. He literally proposes that philosophy in any case arrives too late to be didactic,[3] or to put it another way, that truth always comes *too late*. This is no diffidence. Openness to the inherent meaning of the existing ethical life makes the retrospective glance benevolent and blessed. It also makes it possible to bear the harsh aspect of reality.

The Hebrew notion of reality interprets truth as something that is *innovational*, also in the sense of being able to restore order. That which *is* true is really everything that is new or innovational. Truth offers an opening, not so much to the world as it is but more to the world as it could be and will become. Truth opens the door in a *forward* direction. It is an opening in time. Truth is an optimistic target for the existing world. The same degree of energy seems to be attributed to truth as that which the Greeks discovered in reality. What it is all about here is the authentic significance of the concept of energy with its etymon *ariston*, the superlative of *agathon*, the *good*. The Greeks maintained that moral reality was good, as an ethically ordered cosmos which itself *works on* in knowledge. In actual fact, Hebrew thinking reverses the relationship so that truth conceals in itself good, the good that still has to take place. Truth then propels man forward. It reveals what is to come, it hides and guarantees a promise, a

---

3. Hegel, *op cit.*, 17.

promise that man has to pay attention to already now (Isa 43:19) a promise in which he may believe. From this reality it already becomes possible to live: truth and belief, the route and the life are all interrelated. In its role as a forward galvanizing power, experience endows truth with energy. A certain inherent *power* is ascribed to truth, which is perceived to be more powerful than anything else in this world.

It is thus possible to believe in a triumphant truth. This connects the Hebrew God with the idea of truth to the effect that also God remains more powerful than anything else in this world. The power of the one truth corresponds to the power of the one God. Such power could not possibly have been ascribed to any of the very many Greek gods, each with their distinguishing ethical competencies. The transgressing of the various competencies led to conflict between the gods, hence the eternal efforts to restore the balance in the relations between the various gods. The highest justice resided in the restoring of balance. It was a kind of balance that would have been unthinkable without measure and thus also without moderation. This also defined the power of the will. A truth that is more powerful than anything in this world not only binds together truth and power but it also leads, via an inherent logic, to the dominion of one triumphant God, a God that gains dominion over the other gods. This forward-moving, beckoning *desire for power* makes it difficult to bear the harder aspects of traditionally accepted reality. Dissatisfaction with the tradition therefore threatens to emerge, with what is good about the ethical cosmos within which *zoon politikon* should feel comfortable. This gives rise to further far-reaching questions. Do the powerful truth and the power of the will make it possible to in fact feel at home in any world? Does this idea of truth not ruin veracity and does it not turn the evil of this world into an unbearable problem? Does not such powerful veracity force one to automatically pose the fatal question: how can evil still be justified? It is fatal because truth now dictates and creates discontentment with what is given. It is fatal because the good now moves too far away, *out of sight*.

One original feature of cultural religions is the way in which they are oriented to the ethical meaning of life. Religion directs itself towards knowing about and *recognizing* ethical obligations, to life's innermost motivation and to what is commanded. This ethical orientation helps individuals to order their existence. The basis of the ethical social order that has been passed down is sacred. Religion invests society with sustainable, intrinsic *purpose*, with an ethical kind of sense. In retrospect, the accompanying knowledge may be seen to consist, to a large degree, of figments of the imagination and of mistakes. Such knowledge may in reality be termed *true*, though this might sound strange. The image of reality encased in knowledge is actually limited, incorrect, and frightening. On top of that, there are also the fixed rituals and ceremonies that have to be considered which teach man to *become* a part of the ethical world, yet man does not *recoil* from this image of the world. No matter how terrifying all of this might seem, the cognitive facet of the religious revelation of the cosmos has a reconciliatory effect.

None of the fear, shock, and pain of the religious world picture detract from the fact that knowledge does not have a distancing effect. The religious image helps to bridge the gap; it prevents too much distance developing between man and reality. Insight helps people to adjust themselves to the ethical obligations. In religious wisdom man gets to *know* himself, his origins and his ethical reason for living. In this respect one may speak of such a thing as a *good life*. The good is given, it does not need to be found and it certainly does not need to be projected into the future! The harsh aspect of reality does not spur people on to become *untruthful* or to deliberately want to see things differently from the way they are.

If, with the death of the old cultural gods, an awareness arises that human existence could potentially be radically *different*, then this ethical orientation will also change. The orientation towards an ethical tradition thus loses the battle when pitched against an existential perspective of the future. Now that this ethical life has lost, in terms of intrinsic purpose, the harshness of this tradition becomes harder to bear. This life no longer satisfies. The perspective of the future lays bare a kind of *conviction* that taints the former truthfulness. Since conviction instructs and opens up another reality, it becomes even more markedly a *negative* interpretative framework of the existing world. It is only easy for this type of truth to confirm the harsh reality in this world. It is also only too easy for the insight into the existing world to get dragged down by what is negative. The forward-beckoning truth eclipses the retrospective glance. The notion that the truth might come too late can no longer be borne. The fact that things are sombre does not mean to say that life has *really* become harsher and that insight into it has *therefore* grown harder to bear. The sombre interpretation confirms an *experiencing* of reality, the experience of a believer. This experiencing does not so much *discover* evil that cannot be justified as reaffirm an *opinion* about it. It also confirms the view that good has to be sought elsewhere. Perpetual unrest thus threatens to emerge. So how can such unrest be assuaged?

Also here faith must come to the rescue. Believing in truth not only offers hope but it also provides certainty. True knowledge reaffirms certainty in belief. It is conviction that offers a guaranteed prospect of a new world. In terms of time this world is definitely not a reality. What *is* not yet true will certainly *become* true. Belief supports confidence in truth like a *promise*, *belief* provides the certainty that such promise will be *fulfilled*. Charitably reflecting on what *has been* given to mankind makes way for a restless anticipation of what mankind *will* in future receive. The more that what is real is suppressed by what is possible, the more the notion of truth allies itself to belief and how much stronger that belief must become. Hence the reason that the Heidelberg Catechism refers to real belief as *holding to be true* and as having *absolute trust*. Such holding to be true is what turns truth into a matter of belief. The intrinsic belief is therefore by definition true. Real belief is good; doubt is dangerous and thus evil. Belief moralizes about the truth: it transports good and evil to the world of belief.

2   The Call for Justice

Taking something to be true does in fact give way to an *amazing* kind of truthfulness that is not aimed at attaining an honest, true *knowledge* of what is the case, but which rather diverts the gaze to what is possible. In the most literal sense of the word the truth therefore becomes something amazing. Taking such amazement to be true does involve great danger. This danger does not even arise directly from the fantastic world that one hopes to one day conquer. The real danger lies in the *retrospective* glance that it activates, a glimpse of a world that does exist but which should not be there. The expectant holding to be true thus also applies to the given world and its evil. This is why such holding to be true can generate so much imaginative power. Conviction creates more than a meaningful image of the future, it also creates *abhorrence*: of evil that cannot be justified and of doers of evil that cannot be justified.

In that way, conviction also creates darkness; a sombre view of what is, existence, the cosmos, the ethical order. Hence the familiar reversal in the interpretation of the story of creation. The *Fall* amounts to a catastrophe that has plunged everything into destruction. It signifies a tragic turn of events. The God of creation could reflect happily on his activities and on the naming of good created by him. His work is, after all, significant. Benevolently, he is able to see things for what they are. He can really look back on the reality of things. He is also able to term the creation of mankind, the pinnacle of creation, good, in fact very good indeed. This assessment also applies to man after the Fall, man who has familiarized himself with the knowledge of good and evil. God gains joy from the person who resembles him, who is similar in the knowledge of good and evil and so also in the performing of good and evil. God's kindly judgment of creation evidences itself in his first act of creation—that of producing light. That light expelled the darkness that had been present on the wild and empty earth. Benevolently, God tackles the risky enterprise of creation and he genuinely looks back on what he has done. The evil that came with the Fall does not disturb his benevolence and truthfulness since good and evil both, after all, derive from God. Man has even familiarized himself with this divine perspective; he too now has good and evil at his disposal. This makes it possible to not only appreciate good but also evil.

It is the fatal turn taken in the interpretation that ruins the divine benevolence. The Fall is now viewed as a catastrophic victory on the part of evil. *Such* evil *is* now everywhere, man *is* evil and so he does not *act* otherwise, he cannot *do* otherwise. Now that he is no longer able to do good and to look kindly on matters, the *darkness* returns. Previously, darkness had covered the wild and empty earth. Now that the light of benevolence and authenticity has been dimmed, darkness returns as both an experience and an illusion. The once so finely created world now shrouds itself in darkness. This darkness is the reverse side of the coin concerning the hope that the story of creation will once again repeat itself, but then really properly. The recreation should really constitute a proper *miracle*. The old light did *distinguish* day from night and good from evil. The fatal turning point *divides* both. Hope is now vested on light that rests on the other side of darkness, upon the good on the other side of evil.

God himself is also carried along in the longed-for recreation, even now. The new God not only does good but *is* also unconditionally good. By attributing the power of the new truth to this God, he is able to offer the certainty of the new truth, that of realization. This truth dispels mankind from his world: man no longer feels at home in his world. What is visible in this world manifests itself as darkness, as evil. A wrong truth unveils a wrong world. The religious dogma is not able *to leave everything as it is*. Because this light likewise falls on the moral world the moral *integrity* of mankind also becomes tainted.

The Marxist thinker Adorno perfectly formulated the consequences of this religious belief: in a completely wrong world nothing good is possible. The apparently analytical proposition is totally dominated by a normative verdict, a verdict that shrouds everything in darkness. This verdict also eliminates the human capacity to gain knowledge of good and evil. In the totally wrong world there is in fact no single individual who is still capable of any morality, which means that the individual can only continue to live in such a way that *belief* convinces him that he has been a good creature.[4] A moral life is no longer possible. The omnipresent and impossible to justify evil forces him to seek good *elsewhere*, in a *recreated* world and an entirely new life. The retrospective glances serve only to reveal evil and guilt; the good that is to be realized beckons in the glance that is directed forward, the good that will befall the chosen ones. The will to possess *power* remains the factor upon which this dual orientation hinges. This power has a two-sided effect, it revenges and it promises. Religion places this power in God, and the later atheism in man. This power ruins what is true and good, the truth and the sincerity. As has already been mentioned, such obscuring is dangerous. It contains a sombre perspective, to which we shall return later, that of curative evil that turns against evil that cannot be justified. The obscured view of the world gives way to dark practices.

The history of omnipotence is long. The story of omnipotence can be repeatedly told. Here the story commences in the days when almighty God first makes himself known to us: at the time when he calls Abram and gives him the prospect of his promise. God's promise unites belief and omnipotence. The longed-for fulfilling of the promise and the belief in omnipotence have left their mark throughout human history in the form of imagination in combination with decisive action. Ultimately this belief justifies the most inconceivable: when people no longer expect this promise to derive from God, they then claim almightiness for themselves and go on to do what they have threatened to do. Belief can then literally move mountains. It justifies the war against evil, whatever this evil may be seen to imply. It would be incorrect to assert that the

---

4. Adorno, *Negative Dialektik und Jargon*, 294.

impossible then becomes a reality. God's becoming man is in fact proof of the achieving of the apparently impossible. The story that commences agreeably enough already bears the seeds of such darkness.

3

Abraham's Belief

The story of Abraham makes clear to us, in the broadest sense of the word, what renewed beginning and hope can entail. It demonstrates how the benevolent, retrospective glance can suddenly turn into a hopeful, forward-looking glance, how a new time horizon can make itself felt. It tells of the changing of godly and human names. Both God and man change: what was once equal becomes unequal. Though omnipotent God is able to promise man future salvation, much is expected in return. The new God expects from man firm belief, not only in the promise but also in him as God. Before it can be proved to exist, this faith really has to be put to the test. He who was once formed in God's image now embraces the virtue of humility.

3.1 THE ETERNAL CYCLE

The history of Abram commences with a radical change in his whole existence. "The Lord said to Abram, 'Leave your own country, your kinsmen, and your father's house, and go to a country that I will show you. I will make you into a great nation, I will bless you and make your name so great that it shall be used in blessings'" (Gen 12:1). It is a good indication of the new time horizon. At the same time, it constitutes a violation of the traditionally oriented outlook of man that prevailed in bygone times. It is all about attachment to tradition and kinship and the very foundations of people's ethical attitudes to life. Ethical life is firmly rooted in the already referred-to time horizon: that of retrospective contemplation on the origins of society. One is able to attribute everything that one has and *who* one is to those origins. The identity that is handed down is fixed in ethical rules on how to live that have to be rigidly observed. The heritage one possesses and the identity this gives are experienced as *good*, and so that

3 Abraham's Belief

is how they are recalled and passed on. That, then, was how life repeated itself, down the ages, from generation to generation in a never-ending pattern.

This good was ascribed to origins and to those who were responsible for such origins. Any real element of differentiation dwelt in virtues, in the ethical values and commandments that were passed down and which had to continue to be passed on. That which is ancient is passed on. The living memory of sacred origin supports the holding on to one's own *good* life. One is not so much happy in an existential sense; it is more that one possesses that which gives an ethical purpose to existence to which the experiencing of *happiness* is affiliated. It is not, therefore, as a sensing being that one finds happiness, but rather through the endurableness of a virtuous life. This happiness is what makes it possible to bear the harsh aspects of life as well as the harsh aspects of ethical compulsion. This life does not require rigorous changes, it is too balanced for that, it has too much ethical equilibrium.

The leaving of one's country does not, in itself, amount to a rift in such an existence. Within their tribal groups, or parts thereof, people have often gone from one *place* to another. That does not alter traditional life in the least: the endurable and unique, with kinship at its core, can obviously be perpetuated elsewhere in a similar fashion. The *rift* lies in the changing *experiencing of time*. The promise, the prospect of a promised land, opens up a future perspective. Man proceeds on his way and so experiences an open future. He is promised something new and that in itself is a new phenomenon. Abram breaks through the mythical cyclic experiencing of time with its wariness of anything that represents change, its aversion to the unknown future. He fixes his gaze on what lies ahead in the hope of something different, something new. That which is new is not so much another environment but rather another, now truly for the first time, purposeful life. The God that offers him this perspective and who guides him in this respect is the God of the promise, the God who provides a prospect of what is still to come. This changing God also changes mankind and his attitude to life. The glance that is turned towards the future also touches on attachment to the future, on tradition and on life being organized in that light. Such experience will have been reciprocal: a changing view of the sacred origins and the pressure of the tradition will have stimulated mankind to overcome his wariness of the future and different circumstances.

The story does not explicitly mention this reciprocal nature of things. Nevertheless, Abram's changing time horizon embraces more than just a forward oriented and hopeful glance. The retrospective gaze must also have changed. Has a certain *dissatisfaction* developed within him concerning what has been handed down to him from the past? Has dissatisfaction become his *motive* in his longing for a changed life? Does this dissatisfaction lie enveloped in the promise? Does Abram want to be blessed? Does he want to receive blessing from others, not just God's favors and mercy but also that of his fellow man? He does not want to give; he wants to receive. He who blesses him, he who is beneficial to him, will also himself be blessed whilst he who curses him will in turn be cursed. In all those matters his God goes before him (Gen 12:3). This is no longer the benevolent God. Dissatisfaction seeks change, something better. Since the world of old that was bestowed upon him offers no more satisfaction, man develops hope and orients himself towards the future, towards a better future.

What dissatisfaction signifies is that the legacy that has been given to him—the sacrosanct that should be preserved—no longer provides satisfaction. It is no longer seen as *good*, virtuous, valuable, or meaningful. The experiencing of deficiency becomes normative. Hence the departure from his *father's house* and the prospect of a promised land: a land where life will bring another kind of fulfillment. What is therefore essential to the exodus is not only the time perspective but also the other facet of what has been promised, the prospect of a fulfilled life. There is more at stake than simply the fact that the *good* of the present, of the ancient ethical life is freed and projected into the future. Also the very essence of what is *good* becomes subject to change. The new good is different from the previous good. The longed-for blessing no longer corresponds to ethical existence. The new experiencing of time also opens up a new experiencing of *meaning*.

The open future is marked by yearnings, expectations, hope, the possible. It is an openness that also makes things unreliable, uncertain. Is man really given what is good? Does God really fulfill his promise? Without having faith in what is to come, the bold venture of future and change becomes virtually unimaginable. Is it something that can really be believed in? Can God seal the promise of this future with absolute certainty?

In conjunction with how time is experienced and how interpretation is given to what is good and meaningful, a revolution may be said to occur with Abram. Traditional peoples are especially familiar with cyclic perceptions of time: they live in accordance with the perennial return of *the equal*. This equal aspect is founded on a perception of time that binds man to what is essentially unchanging in the passage of things and daily occurrences. It is an equal quality that also characterizes the developments in his society: in reality nothing changes. The cyclic perception of time is crucial to the maintaining of the traditional ethical order. The cyclic perception of time justifies the solidity of the ethical order. This justification ensures that the harsh aspect of ethical order is not experienced as evil, not to mention as evil that cannot be justified. With the help of rites and ceremonies man learns to hold on to what is simply the order of things, the cosmos, society. If all of that is to be made possible, there is only one inherent opening in cyclic time: a retrospective opening. It is an opening that points to the beginning, the source, the origins of society, and the then given ethical order. The source is endowed with sacred value by attributing a divine guise to the founder of the ethical order. Mankind thanks gods for the source and thereby also for the existence of society. This sacred certainty is commemorated and transmitted in rites and ceremonies. By sanctifying the origins of the ethical order, society can be held together.

The only perspective that therefore escapes from the uniquely cyclic experiencing of time is that of backward-looking orientation. It is a perspective that links the eternally equal with the sacred value of order. But what of the forward-oriented perspective, the future? The only future that man knows is that of the similitude that is to be eternally repeated. What belongs to the future, in the sense of change and renewal, is predominantly feared. Anything that is of the future in the sense of being new and not similar is experienced by people as threatening, dark, indeed as an abyss. That which is dissimilar gives rise to fear. There is thus no longing for a future that brings change or renewal. So there is no hope, no cry for salvation from the everywhere-manifest deficiency, from the pain of repression. Suffering can be explained; it is not without purpose. Man is contented with what he possesses in an ethical sense. The sacred order is adhered to with much effort, harshness, and cruelty. Just as the God of creation reflects benevolently on what he had done, so traditional man can look back in satisfaction at what has been bestowed upon him. One sees that all of this is *good*, ethically good.

What is thus so characteristic of traditional society is its ethical order; the morality of ethics is something that permeates every facet of life. Man experiences it as worthwhile and good to be a part of society. The individual as such has no value, does not exist as a meaningful entity. In an ethical sense man is *zoon politikon*. In much the same way, ethical *good* serves as a focus for knowledge, for the *true*. From the backward-oriented perspective man receives knowledge of the established reality. It is therefore useless to afterwards interpret such knowledge as being *factually* true or untrue. After all, it is not so much about factual as *ethical* insight: the comprehending of the cosmos from an ethical perspective. In retrospect there is much that can be said about the concrete cognitive content of the insight pertaining to morality. This does not, however, alter the fact that man is in possession of a reality perspective that deals respectfully with what is given. Through that man proves his authenticity. Man can be open to reality, even if it is harsh. The ethical order is also harsh, but that does not detract from its purpose. Ethical life is hard but satisfactory.

Openness to what is certain emerges, for instance, from the expelling of man from paradise. Without any bitterness the harshness of human existence is described. Not only is there no hope for a better life but the route to that better life is also cut off. The eternal recurrence of what is similar offers no utopian outlook, no prospect of a new beginning. For the individual, there is only the prospect of returning to the face of the earth from whence man originally sprang. It is not about separate individuals. The fact that man returns to being dust does not alter the fact that, in the ethical sense of things, man is in possession of an enduring, eternal life. It is in this ethical reality that gods and people meet up. That is why the God of creation is able to sanctify harsh reality, the coexistence of good *and* evil: after all, it is an existence that has purpose, ethical purpose. That is why for God and man there is no prospect of something that is possible and new, no longing for a perfect life. Man *is* already in possession of a blessing, namely that of the ethical good. He does not need to be comforted with the promise of a future blessing.

Hence the reason that the change of direction that occurs with Abram is one that particularly affects the intrinsic aspect of what is *good*. The essence of what is truly ethically good is diverted to the meaning behind longed-for, existential good. The expected fulfillment now has to bestow blessings. The change about in the time horizon cannot be considered in isolation of the *revaluation* of what is experienced as good.

3.2 THE PROMISED LAND

Abram lives in the hope of the good that is still to come. He looks ahead in the hope of a better future. He comes to terms with the old fear of the changing, the dissimilar. It is therefore not so much a case that he seeks his salvation *elsewhere* as that he seeks *another* salvation. It is not *leave your country* that is decisive for the complete change, but rather the repercussions in the form of the order to leave his *kindred* and his *father's* house. By being open to this task and seeing it through, blood ties and tradition are in danger of being lost. The emphasis upon the father figure is weakened. At the same time, the value of the father as a guarantee for the tradition that is to be hallowed, inherited, and protected decreases; the tie becomes looser. From this time onwards the sacred is in danger of becoming less central. The attention shifts to what still has to be obtained. The predicted *blessing* is no longer strongly linked to blessed ethical inheritance; the attention surrounding blessing moves to the promised wealth. This wealth has another significance and gives rise to a different experience than that attached to the old ethical order. The nature of that which is *good* changes. Indeed, it is with Abram that the change in the nature of what is *good* becomes visible, and after him it will gain in strength. The experiencing of what is good in ethical life is ousted by the longing for a fulfilled existence. Mankind *learns* to live on the basis of longing, with hope; he *forgets* how to preserve what was so long fulfilled.

Belief itself is based upon the hope of blessing; it is a belief in God who makes a promise and keeps it. Hope, too, becomes meaningful. The prophets give this hope a radical interpretation; it turns into the hope of *deliverance*. Isaiah learns to believe in a God who provides hope, who brings the prospect of deliverance and salvation. It is a prophetic message which, possessed with yearning, attaches itself to a future perspective and ceases to cleave to the legacy of the past. Why make such a legacy holy? If there is anything that is still held on to, it is the past promise. This does not mean to say that the ethical legacy is immediately lost. What is crucial is the fact that there is a certain tension between the ethical *good* and the promised *better*, between law and

3   Abraham's Belief

salvation: between the old and the *new* life and that echoes in the words of Isaiah: "Cease to dwell on days gone by and to brood over past history. Here and now I will do a new thing; this moment it will break from the bud" (Isa 43:18).

As already asserted, the *good* which is now hoped for is something of a very different nature from the ethical good that has to be carefully preserved. Ethical good keeps society together like a binding factor and creates peace. It is, after all, a possession. The same cannot be said of the new good. It speaks of a promised land, a promised fulfillment, a reward that *will* be great (Gen 15:1). It is the *not yet* aspect of this longing and this promise that makes people restless. The *good life* that is now hoped for is a life of *existential* longings that are still to be fulfilled. What is now so amazing is that the intrinsic aspect of these longings promises peace, the peace of fulfillment, a fulfilled existence. It seems to move in the direction of the description ultimately given by Habermas: that of the *Befriedigung* and *Befriedung* of human *existence*. He has in mind the satisfying of human needs, the freeing of people from poverty and want, the peaceful living together of people in universal consensus. What one may question is whether this peace *at the end* of the process of fulfillment can actually be achieved. It is thinkable that the referred-to satisfaction might lead to what Hegel termed the *bad infinity* of human desire. The achieved fulfillment can only too easily be ruined by ever-increasing and newly-developing forms of desire. Unrest thus comes to supplant the promised peace. More to the point, is it conceivable that absolute peace and universal consensus could represent anything other than totalitarian agreement between individuals, thus having been firmly imposed and internalized? It is a question that will return when the atheistic realization of the omnipotent is considered. It should be borne in mind that this *peaceful* life is something quite separate from the ethical order that is experienced as meaningful. The peace of fulfillment not only demands emancipation from the traditional ethical order but also from all ethical purpose. Ethical life is, after all, experienced as a compulsion that stands in the way of new happiness.

But what if the promised peace and satisfaction do not materialize? What if the experiencing of such deficiency does not cease? What if all that is longed for is not satisfied and there is no way of freely achieving a state of living in harmony? What will then have become of the ethical solidarity that prevents people from becoming each other's enemies? Will the cursing then be justified (Gen 12:3)? The dispute between Abram and Lot could turn out to be significant regardless of how explicable the cause might be. That would then force apart even the few who had managed to stay together as their solidarity would not be sufficient to surmount such disagreement. It should be noted that the discontentment between the two was a direct result of their respective wealth, of a kind of blessing that was excessive to start with. Do they decide to go their separate ways because they expect even greater prosperity? How easy it is for the experiencing of a lack of blessings to lead to envy and conflict. Does the yearning for fulfillment correspond to a benevolent attitude to life? Those who are allied easily go their separate ways; the bond is easily broken when the land that lies before them has to promise more. All that is good about their mutual alliance then proves to be fragile. That which is good yields to the longing for that which is better. Unrest is their final motivating force.

Unrest is not, however, something that only manifests itself at the end as flawed fulfillment. Already at the *beginning* the spirit is disturbed by unrest. Though Abram might be in possession of the promise, his hopes and desires are permeated with unrest. He perpetually falls prey to doubt. Will the promise really be fulfilled? Will that which is promised really be given to him? The desire for certainty cannot then fail to present itself. He wants confirmation that the hope for what has been promised will not be accompanied by shame. The old *fears of* the future may well have disappeared, but they have been replaced by *doubts about* the future.

He who promises another something in ethical *sincerity* appreciates it if the promise is respected, even if that is hard to honor. Such a promise creates a bond as it involves placing trust. A *sincere promise* give rise to solidarity, not so much because the one who makes the promise *has* to give something but more because he has something to give and *wishes* to give it. It is that desiring to give that lies at the heart of the sincerity of promising. He who wishes to sincerely give receives trust from the other: he is granted belief in the promise. The promise *has*, after all, been made. For the other, it is therefore a certainty. As far as the bond is concerned, it is not necessary to wait until the promise has been met or concretely fulfilled. The promise itself binds. Hence the reason that, for Nietzsche, the ethical question is eminently that of whether a person is equipped to promise another something and to subsequently keep that promise. *Can* and *does* a person give to another what is his? The promise binds the individual who makes the promise, who gives his word. This therefore makes promising a *bestowing* virtue.

    How different is the attitude of one who longs to receive something from another, who *longs* for something to be given to him, and who subsequently demands certainty that what he longs for will be *given* to him. This kind of longing fuels the inclination to distrustingly wonder if the other will do what is longed of him. There is constant doubt: *can* the other meet the promise, does he *want* to do that, is he to be trusted, was it *sincerely promised*? Can that which has been promised really be fulfilled? What has been promised has not yet taken place—it still has to happen. And if part of that is fulfilled, is that then all there is? Is it the true fulfilling of what has been promised? Is it not insufficient? Does the *other* not fall short? This is the kind of unrest that comes to the fore if the emphasis shifts in two respects: from the one who makes the promise to the one to whom the promise is made, and subsequently also from the *promise* to what *has been promised*. Ethical benevolence succumbs to unrest and distrust. That is why people demand *certainty*, so that which has been promised can be lived up to.

3 Abraham's Belief

For Abram, it is therefore not enough that God continually promises that what has been promised will come to him. It is the perpetual doubt that adds to the need for certainty. How can he be reassured that God will keep his promise (Gen 15:8)? How can Abram's belief be sufficiently substantiated? How can his belief give him certainty?

This does not come about without a radical change in the God that has to be believed in. A new God rewards the series of above-mentioned changes: the time perspective that controls human life, the interpretation of what is experienced as good, the attitude that people have to life. The previous God and man were each other's equals in the matter of distinguishing between good and evil. If good and evil change their guises though, will God and mankind remain the same, or will they too change their guises? Is it not seemingly natural for the one who has to be given so much to become further removed from the one from whom certainty is desired? How far does the distancing go?

3.3 THE OMNIPOTENT

The path of history demonstrates how Abram is always filled with doubt about whether God will honor his promise about future blessings. That is when God appears to him in a fundamentally different guise, in the guise of that of the *omnipotent*. "I am God Almighty . . . so that I may set my covenant between myself and you and multiply your descendants . . . Your name shall no longer be Abram, your name shall be Abraham" (Gen 17:1). Together with God, man also undergoes rigorous change, expressed in a change of name. The new name given to man is linked to that which is to come, to the fulfilling of what has been promised. The country where Abraham still dwells like a stranger will be given to him and to his descendants in perpetuity. It is not only so that man longs to *be given* something, but he also places the *fulfilling* of this promise entirely in God's hands. For the certainty of fulfillment signs alone are not enough. If adequate certainty is to be provided, then God himself also has to undergo change. It is not sufficient to know that God *is prepared* to give what is promised, it must also be certain that he *can* give what is promised. A sincere promise is no longer enough. Sincerity bows to the demand for absolute certainty. Everything must therefore be possible for God. Sincerity is too relative, which is why *unlimited* divine capacity is required: only that will provide sufficient certainty. Only upon that basis can the promise be believed in and can belief hold the promise of fulfillment *to be true*.

To that end, *omnipotence* is ascribed to God. The new God is able to do awe-inspiring things. However, such almightiness has a reverse side to it that cannot be ignored. God's omnipotence may give mankind certainty about what has been promised, but it is a certainty that makes man totally dependent upon God. The result is that the basis of faith that exists between God and man becomes characterized by humility, by meekness. Almightiness and humility give shape to the growing *inequality* in the relationship between God and man. It is the inequality of those who demand certainty and the one who is credited with having the capacity to realize that promise. The alliance between God and man is one of unequal parties. There is a high price to pay for God's omnipotence.

The difference when compared to the God of the story of creation is great. The way in which that God resembled the first people was reflected in the knowledge of good and evil. For both everything in this life lies open. What is good and what is evil is not firmly and unconditionally established for either party. Knowledge really highlights just how *relative* good and evil are. Hence the eternal question, which asks which differentiating verdict is actually correct, and precisely how that can be converted into dealing in a responsible and ethical fashion. There is also another respect in which God and man represent all that is relative in ethical life: they are both interested in the relationships that exist between individuals. What one of the two perceives as good in all of that immediately has repercussions for others: there is no definite point of reference. Or, to put it another way, there is no such thing as unconditional good. That which is relative forces people to realize that there is no clear-cut answer to the question concerning good and evil. No matter how many answers are given, it is always the recurrent relative question that is finally reiterated. Even ethical gods are unable to ignore everything that is relative about society. The question of good and evil thus becomes an endlessly returning challenge. It is something from which man cannot be freed but that is not necessary either. It is not a challenge that needs to unsettle people or to make them become fatalistic. Since it always remains possible to seek and to do good, ethical life becomes something meaningful in itself. It offers ethical happiness. Deliverance from such a challenge is just as unnecessary as any other kind of life's fulfillment. Those who do seek to be delivered from this challenge will have to give another interpretation of good and bad and seek a different kind of life's fulfillment. In that way, both God and man will change.

    All of this happens in the story of Abraham. God and man change just as much as do notions about good and the experiencing of what has meaning. Do God and man still have a feel for the relative nature of what is good and evil? Now that a changed individual seeks the guaranteed fulfillment of a different way of life, so his God also changes; he is now known as the *omnipotent*. What is new is that Abraham prostrates himself before this God who, to him, is totally unequal: a humble man experiences the converse to omnipotence. He recognizes his dependence upon God and accepts his subordinate status. He finds a God who *must* and who, thanks to his omnipotence, *is able to* fulfill the promise. The assurance that the hope will not be in vain comes at a price. Man wants to already be able to *believe* in the keeping of the promise, but for his part the omnipotent demands of his subordinates unconditional belief in him. That is how far the inequality goes on both sides. Those who want to definitely believe in what should be possible must believe in the omnipotent. Unfailing belief offers a solution if

3 Abraham's Belief

doubt perpetually threatens hope. For the time being, man attributes all omnipotence to God: he maintains that it is a status that is unattainable for himself. This does not, however, detract from the fact that the *will to be omnipotent* and the belief in that has been awakened. The omnipotent has to justify human desires. The omnipotent has to put an end to the relative nature of good and evil that can no longer be tolerated. God has to bridge the gap between longing and fulfillment, between what could be and reality. It is that chasm between the two worlds that makes the omnipotent impossible to comprehend. It will become clear exactly where this will lead.

Genesis shows how far-reaching the transformation of God and man is. It is fascinating to compare this change with the previous recognition of the omnipotent. That is what is described in *the Tower of Babel*. Mankind prepares to build a tower, the top of which reaches as far as heaven. God acknowledges this and draws his conclusions: "See it is one people and they have one language. This is the start of their struggle; now nothing of what they plan to do will be feasible" (Gen 11:6). One language, one tongue for mankind united as one people. God assesses this from the point of view of human omnipotence and deeds founded on that perspective. The angle of language, people and power encourages mankind to become a *hubris*. Man then wants to translate into deeds what he *thinks* he is able to do. God thus intervenes and disperses mankind. Apparently God sees the idea of human unity and the yearning for human omnipotence as something undesirable. The whole notion of omnipotence is distasteful to him: that is the deeper significance of the confusion of tongues imposed by him. It constitutes an ironic anticipation of Habermas' universal communicative consensus, and the practical purpose thereof is unmistakable: mankind has been forewarned.

The omnipotent is a completely different entity from the God that intervenes in overconfident human striving. The new God now *himself* opens up the perspective of the omnipotent. The *new* belief has to eradicate the uncertainty surrounding what *not yet* is. In what cannot yet be verily known, what may merely be hoped for as an *idea* can surely only be believed. No matter how ornate and convincing the evidence of what is still to come, it is not yet a fact. When it comes to this kind of bearing witness, it is all about something that still has to be proved. Belief and authenticity cannot be reconciled with each other. No matter how earnestly man seeks the realization of belief, it will remain something unknown. The certainty provided by belief is not to be found anywhere in the vicinity of truth. This belief not only ruins the relativity of good and bad but it also spoils authenticity.

Whenever belief and truth are brought together, this always has far-reaching consequences for the notion of truth and thus also for truthfulness or authenticity. The belief in *what-is-not-yet* connects the idea of truth to what is not. This therefore converts the truth into a speculative kind of *holding-to-be-true* or even into an activated *truth-making*. This idea of truth makes everything thinkable, everything possible. On the basis of this notion it should be possible to speak of a real faith, were it not for the fact that it is precisely this idea that ruins authenticity. The cognitive respect for what is loses ground in the battle concerning the longing for what not yet is or for what simply is not.

The cognitive truth is connected to something that is known in the sense of being a fact, being actually the case, and thus, in essence, knowable. Truth is the correspondence that is to be realized between what one thinks is the case and what really is the case. Knowledge *follows*. Knowledge takes the existing world as its target and touchstone. There is nothing negative about this degree of *relativity* within the notion of truth. Such relativeness binds and directs human knowledge. The relative demands of man a certain *virtue*: the virtue not to give up orienting oneself to what is given, no matter how obscure it may be—how difficult to know, how hard to bear.

Knowing within the time-honored definition of ethical reality gives a fairly good idea of this virtue. It is a kind of knowing that is oriented towards a certain cosmos, a good order, an ethical home base. This ethical reality must be known before its full value can be recognized and before that value can be endorsed. Since the content of what is true is a sacred reality, this same sacral element may be said to extend to knowledge. Indeed, people have respect for what is known; knowledge is a result of that which deserves *respect*. It should be remembered that the cosmos is not so much experienced as a strict actual entity, but rather as a world that is meaningful to inhabit. The truth has more to offer than an empirical repetition of something strictly factual. The truth unveils purpose, it discovers the significance of what is given, it feels thankful. The *true* representation of what is a fact and what is known reveals the inherent *good* thereof. Since what is known deserves respect, the question surrounding verity is also treated with much respect. In this sense, the gods are also knowable; they are familiar to man. The *equal*—man—is thus able to know his *equal*—the gods and the divine cosmos. The notion of truth unites two like factions. The submissive nature of knowledge, of thinking *about*, just like the respect that such knowledge conjures up, helps man to remain faithful to the world. Truthfulness demands that this respect for that which is recognized in what is known is also retained when it is not simply possible for the given world to be identified with what is good.

As soon as the idea of truth starts to concentrate upon what is not, upon something that is not at all, or at least not yet, a reality—in something that can only be testified to and can only be believed in—then this virtue is spoilt. Knowing no longer automatically follows; it no longer links two similar certainties. That which *is not* is, in fact, the other or *dissimilar*, it belongs to what is not recognizable to man. Since that which is not is placed in the hands of God, it is also passed on to a dissimilar God. Anything dissimilar that cannot be recognized can only, at best, be taken to *be true* and what is taken to be true still has to be realized. All that is relative and provisional about knowing is converted into the unconditional decisiveness of omnipotent God. It is he who has to provide the certainty that what is dissimilar can be held to be possible and will one day become a reality. The omnipotent thus presents a *vérité à faire*, a constructible truth. The cognitive respect for what is turns into a respect for belief in what is to be substantiated.

As this notion of truth merges with what is possible, it is inevitable that the certain earthly reality will come to lose its sacred sense and make way for aversion. Having a knowledge of what is certain no longer satisfies and so it comes to be seen as a negative omen, like some kind of deceptive appearance. The world of ideas that had once been held to be true may still be instrumental to what is good, but this good does not dwell in the conventional order of things. *Ethical atheism* does not therefore only lead to a *reassessment* of ideas of what is good but also of the idea of truth: truth is no longer an understanding between two equals. The God who withdraws from the given ethical reality is no longer man's equal and so he is not recognizable to man. The omnipotent becomes infinitely elevated and can merely be believed in. The fact that the omnipotent and the elevated is at the same time *unfathomable* only serves to reinforce the inequality between man and God, moreover, it produces an *unconditional* kind of belief: belief that goes against the grain. Indeed, this is what emerges when Abraham's belief is put to the test by God. That which is true consists of little more than the certainty of intrinsic belief. It is belief that is directed towards the possibility of what is possible. The omnipotent ensures such realization. What else can the omnipotent consider to be true and thus also possible?

3.4 DIVINE ARBITRARINESS

Belief in the omnipotent does not diminish the fact that man can always doubt the willingness of the omnipotent to honor his pact. Is the all-powerful one in fact sincere? It is thus no surprise that Sarah, who is elderly, has doubts about her promised motherhood. The reaction of the omnipotent is, however, totally as one might expect: "Could anything be too miraculous for the Lord?" (Gen 18:14). That which is thought by mankind to be virtually impossible might be viewed as a miracle by mankind, but not by the omnipotent. The fact that man perceives it as a miracle once again underlines for us how infinite the distance is between God and man.

For God, however, there is a certain element of risk attached to the seemingly so obvious aspect of doubt. The lack of certainty in belief does not only affect mankind; it is also an unstable situation that makes the position of God in relation to man vulnerable. Omnipotence requires an unconditional degree of human belief in God: belief determines the extent to which both are connected. Belief that is uncertain makes the inequality between God and man also inconceivable for God. No wonder that the omnipotent so rapidly becomes despondent about man, his weaknesses, his proneness to doubt, and his lack of certainty with regard to the matter of belief. Yes, for mankind who is so humble and dependent it is easy to doubt! Is the omnipotent really prepared to perform the promised miracle? Does he really want to enter into the already so one-sided covenant with man? Will he keep his promise? Is he sincere in that? Can he really be trusted? He is, after all, unfathomable, is he not? It is not so much God's omnipotence but rather the *position* of the omnipotent in relation to man that can so easily be eroded by human doubt. Whilst man asks for certainty, God asks for belief. That is why human faith has to be so deep, great enough to eradicate all doubt. Hence the reason that the Heidelberg Catechism labels true belief a definite knowledge of and an unshakable trust in God's authenticity. What is meant here is the solidity of the *vérité à faire*. This is more than simply a trust in the *manipulability* of truth; it is a firm religious trust in its *actual* substantiation. God demands unconditional human belief in him, his position, and his promise. Can such a relationship between the humble and the omnipotent ever be completely sincere?

Trust can easily be eroded by doubt: where faith is concerned, merely having trust is not enough. True, unshakable belief in omnipotent God involves having so much trust that even when his ways are unfathomable there will be no doubt, even when he bestows evil upon mankind.[1] Hence the reason for the demand for *unquestioning acceptance*. Such belief is not only great but also, in terms of its consequences, *blind*. The trust in faith must, after all, also remain when nothing of the God who—to mankind—is so unfair, is understood or *can* any longer be understood. Full of inner trust, man must want to follow God's most wondrous paths. Unconditional belief furthermore makes man compliant as far as divine *arbitrariness* is concerned. Does man's humility really extend so far? Can faith stand firm if God's arbitrariness is really so impossible to fathom? Can belief really make the faithful so subservient to God's word and will?

The omnipotent is only able to maintain his position in relation to man if he is certain of the unconditional trust that man places in him. Even the omnipotent therefore requires the *certainty* of belief. It must also be possible to count upon the compliance of man if God asks the utmost of him, if all *meaning* behind what God intends with man seems absent, if God bestows evil upon man. This goes further than simply recognizing God's divine providence or in trusting in God when man no longer comprehends anything about his ways. It goes beyond Job's sustained trust in the justice of God, even when he has been struck by incomprehensible plagues. It is therefore about more than recognizing that for God, *nothing* is too wondrous and nothing is without ultimate purpose. That fact that nothing should detract from human trust in the providence of God is one thing. There is also the matter, though, of man *actually* wanting to go along with what God asks of him. This not only applies to the fulfilling of the promise, to wishing to go along with the *vérité à faire*. The

---

1. *The Heidelberg Catechism*, article 26.

element of willingness must also remain in cases when God asks people to do things that conflict with his own ethical commandments or with what he has promised. This goes much deeper than just not understanding what it is that the omnipotent wishes to achieve with man. There is ultimately so much that man does not understand but which can be explained through his faith. It becomes more complicated, though, when God's *arbitrariness* apparently seems to lack all purpose. Omnipotence is then suddenly inseparably allied with arbitrariness: without complete freedom of the will to determine, there can be no omnipotence. What if God asks man to do something that apparently contradicts everything for which the name of God stands? Then one will see if there is really evidence of humility, humbleness, and compliance on the part of man. Then it will become clear to what extent faith *justifies* everything that God desires. Then it will be apparent that the last remnants of virtue are sacrificed to humility and compliance. People will then see how devastating justification by means of faith can really turn out to be. Unconditional faith teaches mankind to obey, to not only blindly *do* that which is seemingly pointless but to also *want to* do that. In other words, that which God desires has already been justified beforehand.

To convince himself that this meek will of mankind really exists, God puts Abraham's faith to the test. He demands that he offer up his child. It is something that seems to be totally incomprehensible, utterly senseless. Apart from anything else, we are dealing here with the sacrificing of the very son that had been given to Abraham as confirmation of God's *covenant* with him. This is true benevolent faith. Here God threatens to break his own promise, a promise that was sealed in a covenant. Surely, then, such a demand for sacrifice contravenes this pact? Is such a God still plausible? The testing of Abraham goes beyond the covenant. In effect, God's order puts the *relationship* entered into through the covenant to the test, a relationship founded on a totally *unequal* footing. The pact has neither been entered into from two sides nor from positions of equality. Even *within* the covenant the omnipotent stands opposed to his subordinate. The omnipotent is always able to act in an arbitrary fashion, he is able to make and break a covenant. Through God's incomprehensibility, the covenant lacks any type of reciprocity. This is already evident from the way in which the omnipotent describes the covenant: it is, after all, *his* covenant that is made between the two of them (Gen 17:2). Even though it serves to reinforce the other in his belief, the covenant is entered into entirely from the side of the omnipotent.

The omnipotent *cannot* offer mankind certainty, as that would erode omnipotence itself. The other party therefore remains permanently subordinate and is expected to display this through his humility and compliance. For his part, the subservient one is expected to substantiate this. God must really make sure *that* Abraham fulfills this promise. Does Abraham really recognize what the divine position entails? Does he truly appreciate what humility encompasses? Is he not assailed by doubt when God reveals this most incomprehensible side of himself and asks so much of man? That is what the omnipotent wants to know. He wants to eradicate all possible doubt! So that is why he wants to know, indeed *must* know if Abraham is prepared to take his faith to the limits. He is not only required to literally hear God's orders (Gen 22:18) but to also *act in accordance* with what he is told. Behold the totalitarian implications of omnipotence. It is the same situation as that in which the protagonist in Orwell's *1984* finds himself: it is the blind recognition that all is good, regardless, that no single distinction counts. By unconditionally feeling affection for and serving *big brother*, the victory becomes his.

So too with Abraham. When given the order to make the sacrifice, he does not make the slightest protest, he asks no questions. Only when his faith proves so deep that both his deeds and his will bear testament to that is God satisfied and ready to intervene: "Now I know that you are a God-fearing man. You have not withheld from me your son, your only son" (Gen 22:12). The believer has proved that God's vulnerable position is no longer under threat. In order to confirm this, God reaffirms the covenant made previously with Abraham. Once again there is the promise of future blessings, the *reward* for recognizing God's power. "I swear: inasmuch as you have done this and have not withheld your son, your only son, I will bless you abundantly" (Gen 22:17). It almost seems like a repetition of the previously made pact but with one subtle variation. This time Abraham has not only recognized the *inequality* of the two parties involved in the covenant, but he has also proven that he is *able* and *willing* to abide by that. There is utter humility: rather than simply being subservient to God, his faith has now made him one with the omnipotent's power to influence his will. Now that it emerges that man knowingly bends to God's desire to determine man's will, the position of the omnipotent is ensured. The fact that Abraham's faith has been able to withstand this heaviest of tests is something that marks and seals such omnipotence.

Abraham has thus exhibited his belief. His God-fearing nature has emerged from his total submission to God's will. Plentiful blessings therefore become the prospect to which he can look forward. He is thus *rewarded* for his submissiveness, for being God-fearing to an absurd degree.

How, then, do things go with those who are less God-fearing, with those who even go as far as to defy God's will? In the Bible there is a striking story that serves to exemplify the lot of those who do not abide by God's commandments and who therefore live in sin. It is the tale of Sodom and Gomorra, the cities in which virtually all the inhabitants are guilty of great sins. What is so fascinating in this connection is the dialogue that Abraham has with God when the latter reveals his plans to destroy Sodom. Abraham's repeated plea to save the city by forgiving its inhabitants was not directed at those who lived ungodly lives but at the possible righteous: because they should not be allowed to perish, the sinners ought to be forgiven. It was not thus a matter of true forgiveness because in such a case the godlessness would have to be forgiven. For that matter, God himself does not show true forgiveness. The omnipotent cannot in fact

3 Abraham's Belief

tolerate the notion of people shrinking from his will. In order to establish and confirm his omnipotence, he is therefore required to intervene so that the cities in question and all their inhabitants are turned inside out and wiped from the face of the earth.

This is no longer the God known from the time of the *Flood*. At that time, the wrath of the people was sufficient for that God to eradicate virtually all of creation from the face of the earth. It was as though he wanted to redo creation. But in the case of creation it was surely all about an individual having a knowledge of good *and* evil? Such a person cannot therefore be blamed for the fact *that* he sins? God seems to realize this in retrospect: he shows regret for his own overreaction. That is why he makes a promise to mankind: he will never again in the future curse the face of the earth because of mankind. Anger is, after all, a typical human trait (Gen 8:21). To underscore that, God enters into a covenant with one man, his descendants, and with all living creatures. He promises to never again eradicate any living sort by means of a flood. He furthermore promises to always commemorate this pact so that it becomes an eternal bond between God and all living creatures. Herein lies the essence of the promise: it entails *promising* the other something and abiding by and *wanting* to abide by that promise. It is a promise that is made in all *sincerity*.

Such sincerity towards the other is necessary in view of the fact that gods must also want to adhere to their own promises. The gods of the past could fall short. They also therefore had to be able to demonstrate authenticity and sincerity: they had to be able to triumph over themselves, over their own struggle with fallibility. There was thus certainly good sense in confirming the promises made to the other, to mankind. This also applied to the God of Abraham. He was not yet omnipotent, he was still the God of creation, the God who actually openly recognized that he was man's equal both in terms of being good and evil. Both possessed the capacity to gain a knowledge of good and evil, both would therefore have to deal with that. That meant that both parties would have to recognize the relative facets of existence. Such recognition demands of both the capacity to perpetually *want to know* about good and evil. God and man must therefore be truthful, striving ceaselessly to gain true insight. Dealing with good and evil requires of both parties that they recognize the other: so God and man must both demonstrate and *want to* demonstrate *sincerity*. It was a situation to which the gods and the people of the past were committed. Being truthful and sincere was an eternal, perennial challenge.

This God can teach man to find peace with this perpetual challenge and therefore also with the relative facets of existence. That is what lies at the heart of creation and the Fall of man. It is the essence of the covenant after the Flood. There is no prospect, therefore, of a totally different life, no yearning for a promised land in which all will be good. This good is no blessing or reward but rather a virtuous, ethical life. Equally, the ultimate fate of man to return to the earth as dust, is no punishment. Neither is this fate the last which remains for man. The good, the inherent harvest of a good life, comes to the other *after* his own individual life has ended. It comes in ethical values that are to be inherited. An upright life is *less finite*, less coincidental, less contingent. Righteousness dwells within the perspective of higher values, in ethical wealth. Righteousness builds on the foundation of communities of people. This good is no reward that can be looked forward to, but rather something that has intrinsic meaning. Hence the covenant made between a sincere God and man in his likeness after the time of the Flood.

The story of Abraham shows how unrest and distrust, suspicion and envy start to gain the upper hand. Whilst people have to continually look to God to preserve the prospect of being blessed, God has to keep a suspicious eye on man. Is his position not under threat? Does man completely bend to his will? Do other gods challenge his power? In reward for the recognized omnipotence man expects to receive God's blessings. In both cases it is unrest that prevails, both parties perpetually feel pressurized. As the notion of ethical good is ruined, so the satisfaction found there is also lost. Man expects to receive the satisfaction of blessings in reward for true belief.

3.5 SINFULNESS

The omnipotent and mankind have become each other's antitheses. There is a great chasm that divides them. As a matter of fact, this inequality is perpetuated in the world as it is at present and as it should be. In the process, such inequality also affects man as he now is and as he should be. Everything that is becomes entangled in sharp contrasts. Good and bad become, in everything, each other's irreconcilable and diametrical opposites. Moralizing about truth also gives rise to questions concerning what is true and what is good. This not only invests truth with new value, but also good and evil. Good and evil come to appreciate what now exists and what should be: the environment, human existence, mankind itself. The ethical division between what is good and what is evil tells us something about the consequences of the human will and human deeds in terms of life and society. This differentiation defines the human capacity to *do* good and evil; knowing about this then prompts mankind to explore these two central ideas. The fact that it is not completely obvious *what* precisely good and evil *are* makes it just that much more challenging to establish the difference. It is the relative nature of good and evil that also makes it an intensely interpersonal matter.

The moralizing revaluation of good and evil pulls man and the world apart in their given and desired existence. Since evil becomes an inherent component of existence, the world as we know it becomes a reality in which mankind no longer feels at home. This world is permeated with a kind of evil that cannot be justified. In a similar way, evil becomes a feature of man as he is: man *is* inherently evil or sinful which is why he commits evil, he cannot do otherwise. In relation to his fellow man but especially in relation to God, he falls short no matter how one views the matter. It is not so much *what* he does that is so concretely and demonstrably *sinful* that counts, but the very fact *that* he is *sinful*. And instead of seeking an *ethical* problem and challenge in the concrete sins committed, the *sinfulness* of man is viewed as a problem in itself, as an *existential* problem. Sinfulness is part and parcel of existence as it is. Any irresolvable and crippling problem is in fact no real challenge but rather a curse.

Here, too, vengeance must be sought for the inequality between omnipotent God and humble, dependent man. What sinfulness really means is that man fails to live in faith and according to God's will. That is something different to the evil witnessed in people's individual ethical lives and in their social lives. Even then, the evil is of this world, but it is nothing other than the reverse side of the coin pertaining to good, which is also of this world and can also be done. Ethical evil or sinfulness is an indication of the *state of being* of man. Such evil reveals man as he is. This state of being is, in a fatal sense, decisive for his thinking, will and actions. In the words of Heidegger, sinfulness could be termed *existential* because it exposes something of the essential existence of man. Up to a point, man is able to resist this evil but, because of his state of being, it is a shortcoming that pursues him in a fatal way. In the final instance, this can only be recognized or persistently ignored. Belief in a good God simultaneously encapsulates an acknowledging of human deficiency; refusal to acknowledge this amounts to a perpetuating of sinfulness. After this recognizing or persisting follows again something like the blessing or the curse, because it is, in fact, all about recognizing or persisting in the presence of God. Once again, the evil of sinfulness underlines for us the inequality which exists between God and man.

This inequality between God and man also clarifies the story of Abraham just as much as its implications. He who persists with evil and in refusing to recognize his own sinfulness can be sure that the omnipotent will ultimately intervene. He can expect to receive the punishment of revenge. This revenge is not so much meted out for committing demonstrable evil but more for having sinfully expressed a turning away from God or, in other words, godlessness. Living in sin is something that can ruin human society, but turning away from God has more serious consequences. Showing *godlessness* actually threatens to make his omnipotence relative. Persisting in a life of sin therefore means withdrawing from God's will and defying his omnipotence. It is particularly that which distinguishes the godless from the god-fearing Abraham, not his deeds. Abraham is prepared to comply with the absurd request to murder his son if God asks this of him. What it involves, though, is a deed which in ethical terms is sinful, a sin that can be *justified* if it is God who requests that of man. Again, it is not because of his deeds but rather because of his faith that the god-fearing Abraham is blessed whilst the godless can expect revenge. The avenging justice that befalls him serves again to confirm God's omnipotence. This once again makes visible how good and evil can be ethically separated into *the* good and *the* evil; into the believers and the godless. Formerly, God and man were each other's equals in terms of good and evil.

Now the interminable contrast between good and evil extends to the distancing of God from man. This separation reveals again the vulnerability of God's omnipotence. Over and over again the subordinate status of man must be concretely demonstrated. Omnipotence makes God restless and suspicious, envious and revengeful. There is always the latent threat of inadequacy, on the part of man and God.

How can God still find joy in mankind, his creation? Every time that human belief falters, the vulnerability of the omnipotent's position is once again laid bare. Omnipotence turns God into a restless entity: he has to perpetually ascertain that man reaffirms his omnipotence. If the omnipotent wants to find peace then man has to be completely one with his will. That not only demands of faith a complete and ultimate conquering of evil, but it also puts an end to what is specifically human in man, to the differentiating between good and evil and to freely acting in accordance with that. In the story of Abraham, this facet does not yet come to the fore. It is all about a consequence of justice that resides in God's omnipotence and which will emerge from the sequel story. It is not without reason that the Heidelberg Catechism speaks of God's endless wrath about man who is ever disobedient.[2] This wrath will only disappear if the sinfulness recedes, if it is conquered. The moralized anger has dangerous implications. This anger demands justice, an abolition of evil. Just like the evil of faithlessness, this affects sinful man and his very existence. In conquering evil, the omnipotent is forced to dispense with persistent disbelievers. In switching from ethical evil to sinning man there is another twist that lies embedded *ad hominem*. In the interests of securing his position, the omnipotent is driven towards triumph, as a logical consequence, by something called *final judgment.* This judgment completely ignores the struggle against evil or the sins that disrupt ethical life. In this judgment, what counts is the omnipotent himself. Together, omnipotence and sinfulness threaten all that is human in mankind.

Even though it is the position of God that is central to the story of Abraham, the story is also about a growing human yearning for omnipotence. This longing is translated into an *image of God* and man subjects himself to this image, but essentially the whole thing is about the human desire to gain *power*. The story of Abraham reveals how much this yearning is linked to the hope of being blessed with a better existence. What also already becomes clear is that there is another side to this hope in the form of the obsession surrounding sinfulness and evil.

The quest for omnipotence is one with a long history. It is Abraham who starts the trend linked to dissatisfaction and yearning, to evil that cannot be justified and to the justice that arises from sustained *ethical atheism*. The doctrine conflicts with the ethical essence of religion. Ethical atheism has its origins *in* religion. Over the course of time it becomes more powerful, first within religion but later outside religious circles.

2. *The Heidelberg Catechism*, article 7, 10.

3 Abraham's Belief

In order to be able to further tell this story within the context of religion, more first has to be said about the significance of ethical atheism. This exploration will simultaneously throw more light on precisely what is included in the notion of God's omnipotence. By gaining insight into the atheistic implications behind this idea, just what has been passed on to modern atheism will also emerge.

4

Untruthful Atheism

In modern times faith has, ostensibly, lost all significance. The hold that religion has on public life and on ethics seems to be diminishing. Increasingly, ultimate authority is being ascribed to man and, in the process, the image of god is becoming ever more vague. Often little other remains than a residue of non-devotional religiosity. What significance might such a situation have for society? Modernity has, in effect, rigorously abolished God from cultural and institutional life. Religion, it seems, is no longer a public matter but rather a *private* affair. But this is not where it ends. The atheistic sensationalism of Feuerbach is also being enthusiastically disseminated. People count the once-promised blessings that are still partly the lot of sensual desire. There is, though, an ironic side to this brand of atheism, namely that of the naïve *credulity* upon which such sensationalism is founded. Indeed, one has to be credulous to expect to gain true life's fulfillment and happiness from such construed satisfaction. There is a tempting type of *faith* that is active within private religiosity and sensationalism: a kind of faith that radically dispenses with the original ethical effect of religion. It would therefore appear that the belief in existential fulfillment begun with Abraham did, after all, have a future.

Does this then mean to say that *faith* may well outlive region? Is it now a sort of religiousness with a distinct atheistic character? This would be a strange turn of events, were it not for the fact that this kind of credulity is already latently present in religion. Since time immemorial, this religiousness has contributed to the hollowing out of the ethical meaning of religion. Modern atheism only undermines the remnants of morality to which religion and public ethics seek to cleave. Atheistic credulity also therefore has its roots in religion itself. That is where the attack launched by existential good was made upon ethical good. There is another way of expressing this: *aesthetics* and *ethics* may be said to have become each other's adversaries. Ethical atheism gives a dangerously large amount of free rein to credulity.

Many sustained attempts have, however, been made to give morality a different kind of foundation; one may, for instance, point to Pre-Socratic philosophy and to the first enlightenment. The modern enlightenment, though, and Romanticism have undermined these endeavors. In modern ideologies, the opposition to the traditional ethical order gains a radical, moralizing impetus. God's will and support are no longer needed in the struggle between good and evil. Man himself looks for the omnipotence required to tackle evil, to wage a *battle* against the powers of evil. During this battle an old and creative sentiment becomes active, an only too human sentiment in the form of *resentment* which lacks all naïve credulity. The yearning for justice has taken possession of the spirit; modernity also seeks salvation. In that connection, it not only seeks the terrestrial version of *heavenly* justice but it also becomes apparent that God is taking *avenging* justice out of people's hands. There is therefore a dark side to desire as well. The urge to seek life fulfillment also demands retribution. As the evil of this world can no longer be justified it may, and indeed must, be combated. Again, then, the amazing paradox arises: in order to diffuse the evil that cannot be justified, the evil required for this battle is treated as justifiable. What therefore becomes relevant is a justified war.

4.1 A PHILOSOPHICAL DILEMMA

In terms of the atheistic opposition to God and belief in God, there is something ironic about the fact that faith demonstrates various parallels in monotheism and in atheism. Much of what the name of God stands for is actually preserved in atheism. The diminishing value of ethical life's fulfillment has already been mentioned, as has the call for justice and the yearning for power so that justice may triumph. It is only the *subject* of omnipotence that changes: man takes the place of God. It is in conjunction with such obstinate cleaving to this core of faith that Nietzsche speaks of *untruthful* atheism. This atheism sketches one of the major problems facing man, a problem described by Nietzsche as *the death of God*. It was a kind of *death* viewed in relation to the ethical significance of God and religion. In referring to the death of God, what he really meant was that people no longer gain any pleasure from their ethical life's fulfillment. Since man is unable to remain faithful to the world this makes him false, and the fact that an ethical attitude to life can no longer please him makes him insincere.

This leads one to question whether there is any future in ethically oriented religion. Is religion nothing other than a relic from bygone times, undoubtedly still something private, but something that is no longer capable of having an influence upon morals and institutions? Is religious fundamentalism not proof of this? Surely it offers little more than a vindictive and nihilistic resistance to all that is experienced as disagreeable? Is religion perhaps doomed to share the same fate as that which previously befell art by ceasing to be a source of truth, by no longer being a foundation supporting the ethical coexistence of people. Is this God therefore dead, also *within* religion?

In times past, religion played a big part in people's social lives. Religious establishments provided a basis for culture, ethics, and institutions. Cultural religions played a big part in the construction of an ethical life. One pressing question that was in fact already posed earlier is then the question of how close this alliance is. Is ethical life able to outlive the death of God? Is a well-founded ethical life without gods and without religion thinkable? The experience had with modern, ideological atheism makes this question only more urgent. Can atheism be reconciled with sincerity? The fact that ethical atheism also flourished greatly in religion makes this question even more weighty.

In reality, though, the atheistic ideologies of the last few centuries have led to little more than catastrophe, they therefore mobilize hardly any support. Amid such a fiasco, religion is not easily given a second chance. The failing of ideologies is not something that rapidly resurrects the ethical significance of religion. The rigorous morality to which *fundamentalism* resorts is something of a bygone era that does not intrinsically bind people. Ecclesiastical ethical concern and doctrine are especially directed towards the peripheral areas of public order. Evangelical and postmodernist religious introspection has little else to offer than an entirely individual and private kind of religiosity, accompanied by an occasionally exciting but generally vague inner emotional life intended to convince one that there really is more than the not so enthralling daily reality. Such religiosity offers little ethical meaning. Even if the church does not shrink, religion will certainly decline. One may then question whether the modern believer can really be distinguished from the *untruthful* atheist. This leads back to the earlier posed and to be answered question pertaining to the degree to which modern atheism links up with the ethical atheism present in belief in God. It is thinkable that atheism keeps those who are credulous glued to the essential element of belief that was also connected to the name of almighty God.

This question produces a philosophical dilemma, a dilemma that forces philosophy to be cautious when launching any criticism upon religion. As far as the ethical effect is concerned, we must wait to see if *philosophy* can be equated with early forms of religion. Is philosophy able to offer man intrinsic ethical meaning? Is it able to arouse inner respect for what has been commanded while possessing no further sacred value? How can one make sure that such doctrinal excursions do not culminate in some type of philosophical fundamentalism? The underlying problem with philosophy is that it is primarily directed towards knowledge and so has to learn how to deal with truth. Its insight reflects on what is the case, on what has happened, on what has been done. It is all about truth and therefore also about true insight into the good, into what is ethically good. It thereby also relates to the insight into the humiliating reality of what religion, faith, and philosophy itself have, with quasi-religious credulity, held to be true and have declared to be good. The philosophical *premise* is different from that supported by religion. Philosophical wisdom has its roots in true insight. By contrast, religious wisdom is certainly not founded on what is true but rather on what is good. Can philosophy reconcile in itself these two kinds of wisdom? Is it able to give man what is good? Or can it do little else than teach man how to *seek* what is good? For the time being this dilemma will remain.

4.2 FAITH THAT LIVES ON

It has already been stated that amid all the significance and effects of the old cultural religions, the aspect that was probably most important was the ethical one. Religion gave shape to human coexistence by generating a whole host of ethical rules, commandments, and laws. It was religion that endowed society with identity and inner cohesion. Furthermore, it was the sacred nature of that alliance that made society sustainable. Thanks to that sacred character, religion was able to bestow upon man spirituality and culture. In this respect religion was also, in itself, a form of human joy, an expression of thankfulness.

This was the ethical core to which Christianity held, even though that was more apparent in ecclesiastical institutions than in religious doctrine. Especially the Catholic Church saw itself as a guardian of a tradition that was still essentially experienced as sacred. Religious *doctrine* and institutional *life* have perpetually served to internally divide Christianity. After all, the doctrine of redemption diverts the temporal experience from the matter of sacred origins to the issue of anticipated salvation. The obligatory aspect of what has been handed down begins to *vie* with what has been promised and is still to come. All of this was to finally culminate in the biggest *dilemma* with which Paul had to wrestle: that of holding on to the values of the Jewish laws while simultaneously also upholding the belief in messianic expectations. It will slowly become clear how, for him, it was future expectations that would come to dominate and how it was that the Christian God thus had to forfeit ethical significance and effect. The belief in the promise and in justice thus wins in the contest with values and an ethical life. In modernity, the ethical bedrock of traditional institutions becomes so tainted that Hegel is prompted to speak of the *atheism of the ethical world* while Nietzsche declares the *death of God*. Here, neither is alluding to the disappearance of belief from public life but rather to something else. The reference is to people's loss of cultural and institutional connectedness. And it is the inherent danger lurking there that is worse than the void precipitated.

So belief lives on after the death of God. In this respect God might be said to have survived ethical atheism and the God of faith can also be said to have survived modern atheism. The often triumphant deathblow was not all that telling: atheism was invariably not true enough for this deed. In reality, many of those who asserted that they did not believe in God and who denied his existence remained faithful to him. One can vehemently deny the *existence* of the one and omnipotent God whilst believing with as much conviction in the significance of such omnipotence. That is how Nietzsche is able to assert that God lives on, even under circumstances when people no longer believe in him. It is through this *living on* that he draws attention to the heart of religious belief, the attractive atheistic meaning that can so easily be transferred to radical atheists. The Marxist Adorno bears testimony to this in an unsurpassed fashion. He maintains that real believers cannot *truly* believe in God, that is to say in the full implications of such belief; only those who do not believe in God can adhere to that for which the divine name really stands.[1]

The belief in God therefore lives on, even after the death of God. It has cast in front of itself a shadow that falls also on modern, predominantly ideological atheism. Over the course of time, the story of Abraham takes on a more radical identity. The subsequent question is, how has the belief in the omnipotent and in the possibility founded in that been able to spread with regard to what is possible. What must be elucidated is how—in Nietzsche's words—Christian values could become intertwined with politics, revolution, and resentment. What still has to be explained is how atheism builds on the Christian doctrine of redemption whilst, in the process, not only incorporating eschatology, but also attaching to it an own kind of Messianism. What is so radical about it is that it seeks to put an end to the dilemma faced by Paul and Christianity: the dilemma of the division between doctrine and life together with the devotion to the promise *and* the holding on to ethical values. Atheism puts an end to the dual value that Christianity attributes to what is *good*: the facets of ethical and existential good. What is so radicalizing about atheism is that ethical good does not so much disappear from view as become passionately contested.

Atheism can hold on to the very core of religion by translating religious doctrine into rational and, for modernity, more *credible* terms. Sensual, worldly fulfillment as the final stage in an historical process would seem to be more rational than the spiritual, heavenly fulfilling of God's promise. This point was to clearly emerge from Marx's critical appraisal of religion. In his fight against the illusory happiness promised by religion he does not reject the illusion as such, but rather the illusion in a mistaken guise. In his own way, he clamps on to the Christian doctrine of redemption and to Messianism. His redemption dogma sees that which is good in ethical order as the root of all evil, which is why he demands that it be destroyed. Abraham with his revolutionary ways not only leaves behind his father's house and kin, but he also breaks away from all of that. Only such a radical breaking with the past will open up the way to the promised fulfillment. The route followed without God must make atheism plausible. Through this credibility a convincing faith can be maintained, a faith

---

1. Adorno, *op. cit.*, 393.

that asserts that the possible really *can* come about, a faith that in fact *made* possible what had previously been thought impossible.

On the matter of the effect and after-effects of gods, there is one more thing to be said. Gods are man's very own creation; they have a human origin. This origin does not detract from their value and effect; it does the reverse. When rounding off the creative process, man leaves what is human about his creative deed behind him: it is afterwards the case that he actually comes to see these gods as his predecessors, as more original and divine than himself. This is what gives the gods their deep-rooted authority. This moreover makes it possible for them to do something in return, to give something back to man. They become an image for man, an *example*; they become a creative force. In their turn, they contribute to the creation of man, their man. This *exemplary* effect was something that the gods were able to sustain for a long time; it gave them an immortal quality and it made them tough and enduring. Such an exemplary effect is something that can also continue long after gods have died. Even after the death of the ethical God, the God of faith continued to have an effect. This makes it fascinating to trace what the divine name really represents and how man is able to reinstate the example that was first with God while seeing how man once again takes possession of the divine name. The humanizing of God clearly demonstrates how man becomes master of his divine example.

The question concerning the significance of God and God's becoming man is one that ignores the matter of God's actual *existence*. It is all about the significance of God and how he operates, it is about the exemplary nature of God and what the name of God encompasses. The atheistic opposition to a belief in the existence of God is nonsensical. Whilst the *intrinsic* aspect of the divine being is frequently too lightly dismissed, the atheist shackles himself to his God. The rejected God does not therefore disappear out of the life of the atheist at all. That is the direction in which the amazing, negative nature of such atheism leads one: it does not live *without* God but turns itself instead obsessively *against* God. In a negative respect, such atheism is God's prisoner. It derives its identity from what does not exist or from what should not exist. Instead of functioning without God it becomes enmeshed in activism against God. Such activism may be termed *reactive* because it does not extricate itself from its object. The atheist shackles himself in a retrogressive direction. Why have such a negative constraint, why not an active and forward-looking outlook? Is the obsessive attachment to something that does not exist not *ironic*? Perhaps it is. More to the point, such an obsession has dangerous implications.

The question concerning whether or not God actually *exists* is not a very fruitful one. Apart from anything else, it is a question that ignores the significance and value of a concept of God and religion. At the very heart of many convictions and accompanying conceptual frameworks, it is first and foremost all about the perspective that opens up and the effect which this has. Incidentally, this not only applies to religions but also to the worlds of ethical and metaphysical ideas. The nature of the *idea of freedom* or *justice* is enough of a motivating force to rank such ideas highly and make people active. This also applies to categories of apparently empirical relevance, the existence of which is indistinct. The *will* or the *I* factor are unclear categories in empirical terms and yet they form targets for human thinking and operations. They offer a meaning perspective; they "live" in a conceptual sense. Or, to put it another way, they are *actual* in the active and creative sense of the word; they exert an effect on human existence. That which does not *exist* in a strictly empirical sense can *work* in an extremely powerful way both in the interests of good and evil. The significance of religion is not then anchored in God's existence either. The real value of God lies in his name and in the effect that his name has upon man, his will and actions, his life and society. The name of God is value-generating. This does not deviate from metaphysical or ethical values that may or may not be denoted as religious. The ethical and metaphysical interpretation of the name of God makes it possible for man to endow things with value. A reactive kind of atheism much too easily dismisses such meaning and value.

The fact that gods have little more significance in cognitive, natural, scientific respects and that they are no longer useful when it comes to explaining amazing events or phenomena, is of less relevance. Although, in olden times, the close affinity that God and religion had with the *idea of truth* was of major importance, it is not, as has been established, absolutely essential to religion. To put it another way: the scientific refuting of religious explanations does not, by definition, touch on the more concrete significance of religion. It must, however, be acknowledged that God and his word have been wielded as rivals in scientific insight in a big way. Holding on to that has done religion no good. Indeed, if such competing with science were abandoned, that might well do good religion some good. The proper significance and meaning of religion lies beyond the question pertaining to truth: that is precisely where an element of challenge could be found. Religion should not so much seek to be *truthful* as to be *sincere*.

This does not, however, give one grounds to brand atheism nonsensical and cast it aside. Its pathos is reactive. It harbors, too, within it, a danger that has become manifest in the twentieth century. Covertly—or else openly and radically—modern, ideological atheism has held on to the ethical atheistic sediment of belief in religion. What once occurred under the umbrella of religion was later perpetuated within atheism. With revolutionary élan, the tale of Abraham was picked up and further pursued. After Abraham's omnipotent God had managed to inspire religion, his heirs were also inspired by religious doctrine. That is what makes it so important to follow this particular story as it unfolds in the narrative of the people of Israel, Christianity, and modern atheism. It is not a story that will be related here in any great detail but just enough will be told to highlight the exact danger that lurks in the name of the almighty and in omnipotence.

4 Untruthful Atheism

If this story is to be told, then the matter of what God's omnipotence precisely entails has to be somewhat clarified. What is the significance of the notion of God's omnipotence? What is the atheistic motive underscoring all of this? What is the exact effect of this idea?

5

The Desire for Omnipotence

The idea of almighty God cannot be contemplated in isolation of monotheism. In this respect the atheistic reaction to this phenomenon is also linked to monotheism. In the Old Testament there is plenty of evidence of the tendency to adopt a monotheistic approach to God; it finds its apotheosis in Christianity. The longing for omnipotence activates the route to the one God. That one God is no longer willing to be placed alongside the many other gods.

What we shall now endeavor to do is to distill the essence of that one particular God. There is nothing at all random about his distinguishing features: they belong explicitly to him. As soon as one speaks of the *one*, awe-inspiring, *omnipotent* God, it is logical that other distinguishing characteristics automatically fall in place. These are fascinating in themselves, but what is even more fascinating is a number of the *aporia* and contradictions that the concept of that one omnipotent being unavoidably brings with it. This forces one to wonder why, despite all else, this image is so consistently retained. Why is God not perceived differently? Why does *aporia* not make one think? Now there is no alternative than to recognize that this God reflects what image man who believes in him and serves him has of himself, an image to which man will stubbornly hold on at all costs. It is therefore thinkable that logical *aporia* will be tolerated. It is also thinkable that such *aporia* will stimulate activistic hope: the hope of conquering them in a practical way.

Omnipotent God may be seen as an *idealized image* projected by man himself, an image that he as an individual *cannot* yet make his own and which he would not openly *dare* to appropriate. Even openly manifested *humility* does not alter the fact that the image of God is a human ideal and desire, an ideal which, for the time being, is kept at a distance. This detachment did not prevent many rulers and prophets

5   The Desire for Omnipotence

from maintaining that in the name of their God they had to endeavor to bridge the gap between God and man. Many connected their theistically expressed desires with surrogate human actions. The passionate desire to *realize* God's will is something of all ages. Even though the omnipotence lies with God, his name lends itself to human use. Even the openly confessed incomprehensibility of God's ways has not prevented man from wanting to explore them and discover their special character. This does not alter the fact that the name of God also makes man modest, reserved; after all, man himself does not readily have at his disposal all the possibilities attributed to God.

In the light of the modern realization that it was not God who created man in his image but rather man who created his gods, *humility* disappears. Something radical changes in man who was once created in God's image. It is atheism that exposes human longing in the name of God. However it is God that is refuted, not that longing. Not only does man think that he *can* now do more, but it also turns out that he *dares* to do more. The time-honored longing triumphs over humility and modesty. The divine *ideal* does not just turn into a human ideal, but also into a reputed human *capacity*. God becomes man. Modern atheism seeks to make omnipotent God disappear from view but his being does not disappear at all. Man who has become a god cleaves stubbornly to the image of his so violently opposed predecessor; he covets that divine image and makes it his own.

The distance between God and man that had once seemed like a great abyss now appears to have been so completely bridged that man can continue without God. At least, the new, human representatives of omnipotence maintain that they can carry on without God. They maintain the massive distance from those whom the gods who have become man now believe they are able to hold sway. Or, to put it another way: the humble longing of the past turns *brazen*. This boldness proves just how dangerous the idea of omnipotence is. Since the idea of God's omnipotence precedes the modern, atheistic assumption of power, it is important to elucidate this idea and its implications. This automatically makes one wonder if another image of God might not be preferable. Why not a more moderate image of God? Why not a more modest ideal and modified yearning? Would the previous, more ethical value of the gods not be more preferable?

Just another remark needs to be made about the image of omnipotent God. Hume asserted that honest, logical reasoning about the nature and effect of God would inevitably lead to polytheism. Though that might be so in theory, the common present-day notion that there is only one God is virtually undisputed, but it is not a view that is adhered to because logic leads to the conclusion that there is simply one omnipotence. There is clearly evidence of a *preconceived notion*, one that precedes all others. Through longing, necessity, or hope, man is driven to believe in the dominion of just *one God*. The representations that ensue from that leave no space for other gods. Though the images that people have of this God are diverse, there is a general recognition that in this diversity of images it is the one or same God that shines through. The former abundance of gods has faded away completely. With modern atheism things are no different: even those who deny the existence of God base their thoughts of denial on one God. Atheistic preconceived notions are also fairly fixed, and that is not merely because religion offers the image of one God—that one God in fact lingers on in the imagination—and there is good reason for that.

There are a number of other characteristics that are ascribed to this one God and which have logical consequences. There is more to God's uniqueness than first meets the eye. The most important thing being his already mentioned omnipotence: he is capable of all that is thinkable; his will can really engineer all that is possible. In this respect he is a creator without a source, he is the basic cause: everything originates from him. As he is himself eternal, unending, and not begun, he stands at the commencement of what has come into being and is thus finite. The omnipotent reaches further: alongside unity and universality, a time and space spanning omnipresence, there is also omniscience incorporated in his omnipotence. Hence the reason for also clinging to God's providence even if all his paths seem incomprehensible. He is furthermore perfect in all respects: perfect goodness is what characterizes him. Every feature, though, necessitates further explanation, and each of these features tells us something about man. Or, to put it another way, if the idea of God's omnipotence arises and gains ground it is not only God that changes but also man. It is therefore a logical consequence that omnipotence does something with people. Every feature gives rise to questions and focuses on aporia. They are questions of a logical and intrinsic nature. Such questions may elicit amazement or hesitation but they will be overruled by a powerful reaction: the reaction of religious conviction, an untruthful *holding to be true*.

In modern times, such holding to be true is trumped by a further-reaching reaction, that of the deed. Decisiveness is used in the battle to suppress doubt and unbelief. The *verité à faire* is the *final*, extreme, and untruthful guise that the omnipotent assumes. Even the untruthfulness of the deed is a logical implication of the restlessness and brutality that shelters in the wish for omnipotence. Indeed, omnipotence *cannot* find peace and balance. Omnipotence is inherently reactive: it is allergic to everything that can threaten omnipotence. The fact that the omnipotent tolerates no other gods is an openly confessed point of envy. Omnipotence condemns to jealousy, and this jealousy takes on an obsessive identity in the modern God that has become man. This, in turn, throws light on the final messianic struggle. This final battle is really a logical consequence of the wish to gain omnipotence, a kind of omnipotence that is propelled onwards, perpetually feeling it is under threat and therefore forced to admit to that uncomfortable position.

5 The Desire for Omnipotence

5.1 GOD'S UNIQUENESS

Believing in *one single God* is, in itself, a fairly amazing phenomenon. Why not have more gods? All in all, it is a remarkable image of God, a God who furthermore tolerates no other gods, a God who wants to be the only one. How could the idea of many gods be supplanted by the concept of that one God?

Throughout human history, religion has often been polytheistic. Peoples and cultures of the past not only possessed whole hoards of their own gods but they also freely tolerated that in each other. It was what made such cultures so colorful. There is not only something pleasant and stimulating about having an abundance of gods, but it also has a *moderating* effect. It almost automatically demands a certain division of power, competences, and influence. It demands of the gods the capacity and the willingness to behave in a restrained fashion, taking into consideration their own limitations and respecting the domains of others. However, no illusion of harmonious unity, of utterly friction-free balance, should be attached to this diversity. In view of the fact that it is frequently not possible to sharply cordon off an own domain, there are always boundary issues that inevitably arise which have tragic consequences. Indeed, having a multitude of gods also means that there will be *competition*. Creating a border automatically tempts people to want to cross such a border and that, in turn, compels others to have to defend such a border. Greek mythology shows us just how creative something like this can turn out to be: there one sees gods who had to give each other leeway but who at the same time could not resist interfering with each other, and so began to challenge and even threaten each other.

Harsh as it may be, this provides a striking impression of human reality, of the *ethos* demanded by social interaction. Whilst everyone is able to challenge and be challenged by others, everyone must at the same time learn to be accommodating and give others the space they need. This, in turn, involves refining the art of knowing how to *strike a balance* while not pushing the challenge too far. Ancient Greek ethics formulated the complexity of what constitutes what is *good* as illustrated by the various gods and disseminated in society. Such ethics not only justifies challenges but it also seeks a balance and the necessary amount of insight and moderation. All that is *competitive* in myth and philosophy invites people to go far whereas the *ethos* in fact cautions people to be wary of what is *too* much, *too* far-fetched, and *too* extreme.

Adopting an accommodating stance in relation to others requires a certain degree of openness and courtesy, also when others unexpectedly put in an appearance. Having various gods opens up the way for new gods, hence all the openness, selflessness, and hospitality. Such openness and hospitality was very apparent in Paul's demeanor at the Areopaag in Athens when he became engaged in discussion with Greek sages. The Hellenistic respect for many gods is evidenced in the altar devoted to an unknown

God. They showed interest in Paul's talk about his "unknown" God and only distanced themselves from him when he referred to resurrection from the dead, which was impossible for them to grasp. The inviting, challenging lives of the Greek Gods reflected coexistence with *ethos*, as well as an eye for the ethical and for public virtues. Not only in the lives of Greek gods was this openness manifest, but the Roman pantheon also reflected something similar: there are always more gods included in the divine *pax Romana*. The Book of Job in the Old Testament provides a somewhat similar example of such an openhearted and divine life. There mention is made of the sons of God, including Satan. It emerges that God is even prepared to charitably tolerate having Satan at his side even as a challenge. This instantly leads to exciting competition concerning Job's person.

The Old Testament teaches monotheism, at least in the religion of the people of Israel. The compelling monotheism changes slightly in the spirit of the one God: a good sense of openness and constrained competition turns into *envy*. It is not only the case that the one jealous God is unable to tolerate other gods besides himself, but he is also ill-equipped to deal with injustice towards himself; he wants to be loved (Exod 20:5). The fact that he, as God of his own people, tolerates no other gods in his presence creates an awkward situation with the gods of other peoples. The way in which this image finally affected man is clear: after all, it is the image in which man recognizes himself, in which he reflects himself. In turn, this specific image that man has of himself has consequences for human relationships. This does not mean to say that the relationships between tribes or groups in the era of many gods was fundamentally friendly or peaceful. Now, however, animosity and envy are theologically justified and become part and parcel of divine justice.

The one jealous God does not leave man in peace either. He demands that man unconditionally chooses to be for or against him. He wants to be loved and rewards that with clemency, with blessings. There are no more barriers, no more boundary-crossing tensions, no unity in challenge, moderation or balance. Seemingly automatically, the one God then goes a step further, he not only expects man to *opt for* him but also to *devote* himself to him. The image of God works. If man does not opt for God he becomes wrathful. Especially at such times, human devotees feel justified to display decisive action. It is all about devotees who not only have to lead others back to God but who also have to take revenge upon the unfaithful in his name. In effect, this God permits nothing, tolerates little, and is particularly oriented to maintaining his own, unique position. He *wants* to be a unique being; that makes him overzealous, impatient, restless, quickly angered. The yearning for uniqueness makes him suspicious and embittered. He seeks release from the guaranteed unconditionality. The envious God does not therefore want to share anything with other gods, he does not tolerate them in his presence, he is not prepared to enter into benevolent competition with them. Contact with that which is alien is classified as evil, as something that leads to curses and necessitates purification. A jealous God tolerates little. The capacity to put

5   The Desire for Omnipotence

things in perspective is foreign to him; he is enraged by the slightest infringement of what he commands. This destroys all zest for life. An envious God demands subjugation and—when things go wrong—conversion. If people serve him then he is merciful, but if that does not happen he proves to be wrathful and vengeful. It is an image that is also *exemplary*. Those who believe in him know that their own overzealous behavior is justified.

The prophets bear witness to the inherent perspective of God's uniqueness and unbridled wrath, which, apparently, is not confined to his own people. Some are eager to gain more and so seek to extend their realms beyond their own particular boundaries. It is a perspective that embraces—in a seemingly natural fashion—all peoples, all nations, and the entire world (Isa 25:6, 26:11). The beckoning stance is the ultimate establishment of the *universal kingdom* of that one God. It is a view that is ruled by an atmosphere of animosity and strife. The sense of challenge is thus replaced by intolerance. If other gods are endured then that is temporarily at the very most, but they are definitely classified as enemies. The obsessive attitude towards the own people extends to others too. Also then, there can be no talk of charitable competition, nothing is relative, and hostility is everywhere. It would even seem that other gods and other peoples are *pursued* so that they can be conquered and eliminated. Such uniqueness is relentless until the Lord becomes king "over all the earth; on that day the Lord shall be one Lord and his name the one name" (Zech 14:9). The one jealous God cannot find peace until his name has been established as that of the only one and all have subjugated themselves to him. The envy destroys any kind of satisfaction. Can such ultimate dominion over the whole world offer any true peace? Surely it will have to be perpetually *maintained*?

    A crucial question to ask is whether this jealous striving for dominion and unity is imperatively inherent to the notion of uniqueness. If that is so, then one *cannot* do otherwise than *want* to be unconditionally in agreement. This would have something fatal or really paradoxical about it, like the one God not being able to do otherwise than *want to be able*. Is God, in his quest for uniqueness therefore doomed to remain envious? Does the uniqueness so sought by him force him to want, in effect, to be a world God? Is he *unable* to rest until he has become lord of all the peoples of the world? Does that restless urge to secure uniqueness fatally deprive him of the ability to accept things external to himself with a certain sense of equanimity? Does it take away his ability to exercise moderation and display good-humored irony?

The aspect of uniqueness of the one God also lies at the core of the radical metamorphosis that Paul undergoes. It is all about switching from being an ardent defender of the Jewish law to being an equally fervent proclaimer of the eternal kingdom of God for the entire world. The death of Jesus is something he places in the context of the entire old, divided world, whilst his resurrection promises to bring the realization of a new world, a world that is *united*. God's salvation now applies explicitly to all peoples. It is a kind of salvation that is directed at making people devote everything to him. It is thus the salvation of universal bowing to the one God. The notion of having just the one God furthermore gives rise to an idea that there is just one *humanity*, one *world*, and one *history* of fulfillment. God's previous promise to Abraham that encompassed all races of the world (Gen 12:3) now has to be fulfilled. At the same time the realization of the perspective accompanying just one God, the entire world history, and all of mankind, opens up.

Attention is perpetually given to the matter of gaining dominion over the entire world and the whole of mankind. Is there really evidence here of two parties, of God and man? Is the dominion related to the uniting of two parties that have to be brought together? Does it not amount to an infringement upon God's uniqueness and the unity to which this is directed and must be directed? Such unity could indeed amount to a sham and be something that conflicts with God's unity. The dominion of God now requires that this God be *accepted* by all nations and people. This will provide space for two parties operating in mutual alliance. Does God's uniqueness really allow for the existence of another party?

In this connection, what is significant is the fact that there seems to be constant talk of a possible *reconciliation* between God and man. The more dominant the evil powers and sin are, the more obsessive the envy that such evil evokes will be. God also claims to represent love, which, incidentally, is an amazing thought if one considers that the God of jealousy also wants to be a God of love. But is this really all about real reconciliation and *love*? Is it about love for the *other* in his other guise? Does the one party truly accept the other so that he is able to coexist alongside him *as the other*? Or is it about a different kind of love with consequences for being different? The situation is as follows: God's love is not so much love for man and it is no real reconciliation with man with all his differences. The love of God seeks surrender from man, total conversion. Nehemiah may well have lucidly explained the ambiguity of the love of this one God (Neh 13:29). He asks God to *remember* how others have tainted the bond, to remember in the sense of to *not forget*: it is a type of recalling that demands cleansing from all that is strange and evil. God must remember this. It has something compulsive about it as a result of his uniqueness and inherent jealousy. God may not forget this most private being, God may not tolerate what is different. Hence Nehemiah's own specific: "Remember me for my good, O God." That *is* the way he is, he fully experiences the one God; his whole *existence* is devoted to the will of the one God. He therefore maintains that he has a right to receive God's love and so it is in this context that he asks God to remember him. The *my good* is nothing other than the utter subservience of one to another: he no longer wants to be another, he is no more the other. The love of the one party is no *giving* love but rather a kind of love that *claims*, a love that makes things its own property. The one God wants to be so unconditionally loved that everything else is consumed in him.

5 The Desire for Omnipotence

What is fascinating to consider is whether ideological atheism takes over the notion of God's uniqueness or whether it is more a case that it elaborates on this idea. Does uniqueness then also lead to envy? Does this idea offer man parallel love? Does the god-made-man entity become imprisoned in a restless, intolerant strife? Does the uniqueness then want to govern all people and humanity, the whole world and history? It may once again be reiterated: the image of God can, in the most literal sense, *live on*. God-made-man could indeed once again make it practically and lucidly clear what the idea of uniqueness and unity and the therein encompassed envy means once such an idea becomes a *vérité à faire*. This point will be addressed later. First there are other features of the one God to be examined, features that cannot be seen in isolation of uniqueness and envy.

5.2 GOD'S INFINITY

To start with, there is the *infinity* and *omnipresence* of God in terms of the dimensions of time and space. From this point of view, God is not subject to any kind of boundaries or constraints; he is elevated above such things. What exactly this *way of being* entails is obscure and can really be nothing other than obscure as the concept *infinite* is negatively formulated.

Infinity in terms of *time* indicates that God has always been there and will always remain. In terms of time, God is not bound to a finite existence. It is a finiteness that applies to everything in the cosmos: to things, living creatures, and also to man who is finite in a physical sense. The fact that God is of all time or, in other words, exalted *above* such a thing means that he does not dwell *in* time in the sense of being subjected to it. That is not, however, the case for all that has been created: it has become, it changes, is transient, and thus finite *in* time. There is a huge chasm between what is infinite and what is finite.

Being infinite, from the point of view of the dimension of time, also means that God is not subject to what happens either in a forward-looking or in a backward-looking respect: to what has been, what changes, or what is to come. He is thus not so much passively elevated above time—above in a dative sense—as actively. The *active* infinity aspect means that he is able to move around in time to an unlimited extent while freely having at his disposal all the things that are subjected to time. This is what lies at the core of Ockham's conviction: God is in no single way subjected to his own creation, not even to his creation of time. Viewed from this angle, it means that God is able to instantly change everything related to the *present*. That thus means that he is likewise able to determine what is to come or the *future*. This notion means that he can even change what was; he can therefore also make the *past* bend to his will. His omnipresence and infinity in time therefore encompasses the present, the future, *and* the past. Though the concrete significance of God's infinity may extend beyond human powers of imagination, it is an idea that can be grasped in an abstract sense. It can be believed in.

The notion of infinity in a *spatial* sense is one that is easier to comprehend: it is all about God being present immediately and everywhere, or at least having the capacity for that.

No matter how obscure and incomprehensible God's infinity is, it is an idea that must surely be very attractive to people. Why otherwise should this feature, this capacity, be attributed to God? The thought that he in some way or another actually exists, yet is not subject to that which is limiting, to the finiteness of time and space, is not only an incredible but also a paradoxical concept. Though infinity and omnipresence may be conceivable as concepts, how can this limiting notion really be given actual, concrete substance? The idea not only spawns the question of *how* the infinite can *exist* but also how it can operate, how the different can affect the different.

The paradoxical aspect of the infinite is really automatically conjured up by the *negative* nature of the concept: it in fact reveals nothing but that God is *not* finite. But what is he *then*? Is it not impossible to give positive content to the negative without simultaneously again putting an end to the infinite? God is *not*-finite, what awaits him is an utterly not-finite existence. The Old Testament therefore demands, in a logical sense, a justifiable forbidding of imagery. Every depiction constitutes an attack upon infinity. But *then* who or what *is* that infinite quality? The assertion supposes that God *is*, which is something slightly different from a metaphysical idea or people's abstract thought. If, then, real existence and infinite being is attributed to him, what way of being is that? God's infinity merely gives rise to quandaries. As soon as the abstract, negative concept of the *not*-finite is departed from and a positive interpretation is given, the infinite is violated. The profound divide between the finite and the infinite cannot be bridged. All interpretations of the infinitive made in a not-negative respect lead to logical contradictions. Every further description, every qualification, is simultaneously a constraint, a boundary which therefore makes the infinite finite. This, in turn, makes the strictly infinite above all else a yearning, a hankering, a form of escapism that must *liberate* from the gravity and tragedy of finiteness. But does this longing not seek a little too much; is it not *excessive*?

There is also an aporetic component to the infinity of God and the *finite* nature of *man*. How can finite man in fact draw any conclusions about infinite God? How can anything be asserted without violating God's infinity? Every word spoken is that of a finite human and thus something that taints the infinite. As Wittgenstein stated, it should be concluded that one cannot talk about the infinite and so one should simply remain silent on the matter. The reverse is equally true. How can a being that is unconditionally elevated above and is different from what is finite have contact with or exert

5   The Desire for Omnipotence

an influence upon this finite factor? How—in the words of the ancient Greeks—is it possible for that which is different to know about the different or have an effect upon it? No matter how many alternative routes are construed there is an irresolvable aporia that comes to the fore.

In the interests of maintaining an open relationship between God and man, would it not be better to surrender the idea of an existing or even of a fabricated infinity? What possible purpose can a negative concept of limitations that can only be abstractly applied have? Such a concept can only create unrest. Once again, it is the expression of a *yearning* that can never be fulfilled: an endless yearning. But that is not where it ends. As will emerge, it is also about a *dangerous* kind of longing. That will become evident when man himself becomes consumed by this longing and, as a finite being, develops for himself the prospect of infinite fulfillment. Imagine that he then goes on to seek to be the *equal* of *this* God and so demands the realization of an infinite *existence*. Imagine that man or mankind, or else a human representative, would wish to freely have control over the present and the future. Even worse, imagine that he might also wish to have control over the past; that he would want to *undo* what has been done. And if such longing were to prove stronger than the possibility to realize it, what solutions would man then become entangled in? The temptation attached to this excessive longing will be discussed at length.

Here, too, the antithesis of a *mythical* concept of time and all the related gods again imposes itself. The many gods are all limited, tied to a specific domain, to a specific space; none of them are therefore omnipresent. Neither are they endlessly elevated above time. Just like everything else, they too have come into being, in their case among the Greeks where they were born of the difficult struggle against the virtually indomitable forces of nature. The fact that it is concretely possible to speak of the derivation of the gods in terms of historical time provides liberation from an irresolvable logical kind of dilemma. The idea of there having concrete origins brings peace. The attachment to a cyclic concept of time also releases people from the longing to be elevated above the dimension of the future. Cyclic thinking knows no liberating, redeeming future: nothing and no one stands above time in terms of a prospect of the future, not even the gods. Also, the gods are tied to the *eternal* recurrence of the equal, to what is in an essential sense eternally not changeable. As a matter of fact, the eternally recurrent also has an infinite quality to it from the point of view that it remains eternally the same. This infiniteness has no *power over* time but is inescapably a *captive* of time. This latter phenomenon is also what is *fatal* for the gods. Much as they are also able to play with their limitedness, that same limitedness challenges them, much as the inevitable chain of events prompts them to introduce change to the eternally recurring it does not free them from that. They cannot elevate themselves above time; they have no power over that. *Hybris*, the temptation to take self-exaltation too far, evokes counter forces and thus the comforting awareness of one's own limitations.

The idea of eternal equality confers a certain degree of peace. The gods cannot have command of time freely or in freedom. They cannot forge ahead unlimitedly; they certainly cannot go back. They cannot *undo* what was done in the past and they cannot mold the future to suit their wishes. They are limited in their possibilities, in what is *possible*. Why should these limitations be a problem? Why should a limited capacity have an obsessive effect? Why should a *limitation* not be a challenge? Surely that is preferable to the obsessive, but at the same time crippling, effect of *incapacity*?

As ever, gods and people mirror each other. The image that man has of his gods says something about his own self-image. In the story of creation told in Genesis there is little that emerges about the notion of God's infinity. The incarnation of the living beings created by God instantly makes God and man *equal*. There is no reference to equality, though, in terms of infinity. The similarity between the two parties is indicative of the image that man may have of himself. This image enters into the internalized concept of time: that of an eternal consistent existence.

That is something God makes quite clear after the expulsion from paradise. There is no road back to paradise, to the natural state from which—in the beginning—man had freed himself through the Fall: such access is forbidden to man. A *backward* longing for what in another way could be good is in every way closed off. The same applies to the *forward* directedness. Man is offered no single prospect of ever being able to attain a new paradise. Man is doomed to passing his life in a purposeful way in a finite world until such a time that he returns to the face of the earth from whence he came. All that is human about him does not alter the fact that he remains dust and will return to being dust. There is absolutely no kind of *curse* inherent in this. The return gives peace, the peace of eternal unity with time and the finiteness of things situated *in* time, human existence included. Why then long for an infinite existence? So he no longer needs to eat from the tree of life. Regarding the relative nature of existence, this is something that is *easy* to live with, for God and man.

But is it not so that what lurks in the process is a lapse into the relative nature of things, into pure transience? Not necessarily. Instead of longing for what is absolutely infinite and thus, in the process, creating an irresolvable and restless contrast between what is infinite and finite, it is possible to distinguish in a more moderate way between what is *more and less finite*. Even what is *in* time does not necessarily have to be immediately finite and transitory. The finiteness of things may well make the changeableness and *ultimate* transience thereof unavoidable but it is a very gradual process. From the angle of time it is all about what is more and less rapidly *transient*, less or more sustainable; in terms of time and space there is evidence of limited or wider validity.

The relative nature of what *is* has another significance alongside the limited and the negative. *Relative* also means: having a relation to, having connectedness with

5 The Desire for Omnipotence

other matters, with the other, even if that changes. In terms of *time*, all that exists has come into being from something else, carries that within it, and passes it on. Everything that exists has, in a *spatial* sense, an outward working, towards the other, to what surrounds it. In this relative sense, what is can also be perceived as good or evil: as either being or not being courteously, constructively, challengingly related to the *other* and, thus, also the other. What *is* gains, in this relative sense, broader and more enduring significance. In this relative way it, is therefore possible to meaningfully discuss *good and evil*.

In this relative sense, good and evil are invested with ethical significance as far as involvement with others goes. Something that only exists in itself cannot be good. Viewed in this light, the idea of infinity might be seen as a *ruining* of what is relative, including the accompanying ethical significance thereof. The notion of infinite good deprives it of all that is relative. By experiencing the relative side of matters with gratification, man is not only released from dangerous longing but he is also offered an exciting challenge. The confined nature of things in terms of time and space invites people to extend long and far beyond the boundaries, but not *too* long and far. As challenging as that which is relative can be, the contrast between all that is finite and infinite can be depressing and paralyzing. The absolute infinite makes what is totally opposite equally and utterly finite and, *in being* finite, perfectly hopeless. All feelings of own value are lost and perpetually there is an awareness of *futility*. It is precisely this that makes people restless and tempts them to pursue a *mistaken* kind of longing: they long to know how it is to be the only one who is *not* subjected to absolute finiteness, whatever such infinity may entail. The infinity of God creates the illusion of such redemption; that which accompanies an own kind of finiteness and futility. The *antithesis* is ruination. It condemns both the finite and the infinite to a fatal struggle. The contrast condemns the infinite to a battle against all that threatens the perspective of infinity. It condemns the finite to a fatal longing for salvation from its own finiteness, and therein lies the *futility* of this longing and this struggle.

Might *atheism* be inclined to simply surrender the notion of an infinite being? Even those who reject the idea that God exists are capable of cleaving, in their own way, to the idea of infinity. Why should they not have a yearning to be freed from the lack of prospect offered by what is finite? Why is there no atheistic longing to be released from a finite type of existence? Why should it not be possible to transfer the atheistic core of God's infinity to man? The illusion that the infinite, despite all possible aporia, could after all be seen in a positive light or concretely realized is attractive enough for that. Such an illusion can become an obsession, an obsessive *dissatisfaction* with the always-impending shortfall or lack, with the not being good enough factor. The obsession can also provoke a *struggle* against everything that stands in the way of infinity. Even man can imagine that he is or that he wants to be an infinite being: the temptation to want to turn this notion into a reality is great. What is *not*—or at least not *yet*—can undoubtedly be substantiated. The atheistic longing could perhaps underline just how dangerous such an image of God is. The disappearance of God can make the contrast between that which is finite and that which is infinite unbearable, and so also the experiencing of restlessness and futility. That can have a fatal effect upon the actual *relative* nature of things: also the endurable comes to be experienced as useless and lacking in purpose, as transient, as being only worthy of going to wrack and ruin or at least of aiming in that direction.

The idea of God's infinity also erodes the relative facet of ethical life. This will be further elucidated. What will also be discussed is how atheism pins onto to that an irreconcilable battle. The escape from the paralyzing contrast can only be a leap, a leap over the unbridgeable chasm. Religion flees into a spiritualized solution to escape from the futility of a finite existence. The unequal hopes to still find equality with God in an immortal existence after this finiteness. Hope is fixed on redeeming infinity in terms of time. Atheism gives its own interpretation to such leaps as that of the ceaseless satisfaction found in physical needs. Adorno even makes mention of a physical, bodily "resurrection of the flesh." In so doing he not only draws attention to the possible satisfying of physical needs but also to a conceivable abolition of physical death.[1] He believes that physical liberation from the limitations to which existence has up until now been subjected is possible. This converts the infinite into a quantitative, endlessly expanding finiteness. The belief that man will find here satisfaction and salvation thus has to be great. Such a kind of believing is dangerous because it clamps man between addiction and feelings of futility. Hence the reason that Hegel speaks of the futility of a *bad infinity*. What will emerge is that the greatest danger in the *backward* oriented aspect of infinity dwells in the matter of time: in the belief in the possibility of being able to undo what was once done. What will be explained is just how, in all of this, the yearning for avenging justice finds its way.

5.3 OMNISCIENCE

It is highly probable that there is yet another human longing that is reflected in a capacity that is attributed to the omnipotent: that of his *omniscience*. Does also this image of God harbor a secret image created by man himself? Does man place in the hands of his God a kind of power that is still unattainable for him? Is it again the divine emerging as a projection of human longings? That is how it would seem. After all, it is modernity that passes on this endless capacity of God to man. In the first place it starts as an *idea*. The next step comes from modern ideologies because they declare the idea to be a realistic human possibility. Man himself then has omniscience at his disposal or at least simply makes that idea come true in the form of *vérité à faire*.

---

1. Adorno, *op cit.*, 207, 518.

5   The Desire for Omnipotence

At some point in the past, omniscience was ascribed to the one God as a capacity. The one and only omnipotent and infinite one knows everything. There is nothing that stands in the way of his knowledge. Nothing escapes from his all-seeing eye, for him nothing is impenetrable. Everything that is and everything that happens is known about beforehand by the creator, even developments that have been initiated by man. There is a certain implication inherent in the notion of omniscience that even elicited an explicatory appraisal from Nietzsche. If all knowledge resides in God then all truth will also dwell in him. At the end of the day, an omniscient God cannot lie about what occurs. He cannot hide himself from the things that are completely open to him, nor from all the things that are within him. In this respect omniscience seems to equate with honesty. An omniscient God should therefore honestly defend all that lies within his knowledge. An omniscient God should be *truthful*, open about what is, also about the true insight into matters. Such a situation would link omniscience to a higher order of value and virtue. The question that arises, though, is whether omniscience and truth can really exist side by side. The notion of omniscience does in fact bring with it various reservations, questions surrounding the justifying of God's position in relation to his own omniscience, and also questions pertaining to man's position in all of that. One important aporia is the problem of the providence of the omniscient.

God's omniscience cannot be considered in isolation of his infinity in terms of time or, in other words, his unlimited backward and forward shooting insight into matters. The omniscient not only knows every single detail of what has happened in the past but he also knows what is going to happen in the future. This, then, is where the problem of divine *providence* resides. Also, God's own deeds and interventions fall first and foremost under the umbrella of his complete insight. For him everything is transparent; everything can be explained beforehand. He must have been aware of what took place within the context of his own creation. He must also therefore have known about the evil: he must even have incorporated it. Whenever he intervenes in what he has created, such a thing must have been pre-known: the intervention must thus have been integral. All later interventions are clear to him beforehand; all that comes later has been planned in advance and is thus transparent from the start. He reigns over all that is subject to change as the first and only one, as the original one, also as the complete and *transparent* reason itself. This is what leads to the never-ending and oft repeated justification question. How can the omniscient and also omnipotent *justify* the evil present in his creation? How can he reconcile his cognitive conscience with his moral conscience? The justification question leads to an irresolvable aporia. There is only really one way of resolving this particular aporia and that is by not posing the justification question at all; by making sure that it does not have to be asked. Not ascribing omniscience to God is one way of making this possible.

There is another more pressing question that cannot be considered in isolation of the first one. God's omniscience is hard to reconcile with the notion of such a thing as a free, conscious human *will* and with human responsibility. How can his complete insight and providence be rhymed with even a minimal degree of freedom in terms of human will? For the omnipotent, the outcomes of apparently free human expressions of will must not only be known beforehand but they must be integrated into creation. Where God's *providence* is concerned, there can surely be nothing that occurs that is unforeseen? If he wants to allow space for the unforeseen then even he has to wait and see what happens so that he, too, is left to stand and watch in amazement. Without omniscience he will only know about what has happened *retrospectively* so that insight into such matters could also become a difficult issue for him as well. In this respect, the idea of omniscience puts paid to the virtue of truthfulness. What is so typical of the truth is, of course, its property of being able to *look back on* what has occurred. The truth can never *pre*dict. Truthfulness is the quality of being open to the truth, of openly looking back on what is and on what has arisen. Truthfulness recognizes this *relative* nature of things. The whole idea of omniscience instantly dispenses with such a relative and dependent perspective: the knowledge anticipates the action; it is foreseen. The omniscient knew about the occurrence beforehand, which is the only possible explanation if one thinks that he, the omnipotent, had incorporated all of this. The truth of the omnipotent is a fulfilled kind of truth. Again the *vérité à faire* robs the omnipotent of the earlier suggested truthfulness.

It is a predicament that also touches on the relationship between the omnipotent and man. God's omnipotence is something that is diametrically opposed to human freedom, to the freedom of the human will to determine. The omnipotent and omniscient has created and foreseen everything, even the reputed evil *of man*. If, therefore, the omniscience and thus the providence of God is adhered to then there is little that can be blamed on man. An amazing and furthermore tormenting point of irritation is that it is, once again, a consequence of the utter *inequality* that exists between God and man. God's omnipotence is not compatible with man being equal to him. God's omnipotence degrades man thus reducing him to an incarnation of his providence, which means that man is innocent of what he thinks and does. This, in turn, makes God's justice absolutely impossible to comprehend.

If, however, man were to become God's equal and if man also had the capacity to distinguish things in complete freedom then God would be forced to wait and see how man would cope with such a situation. That would then refute God's omniscience. It is God's unbridled providence that makes man inherently irresponsible in all that he thinks and does. A *"person"* who must in the first place completely bend to God's will and knowledge is, in effect, robbed of all that makes him human. Ultimately this forces him to return to the state of natural innocence from which, through the Fall, he had just managed to escape. God's omniscience is therefore something that does not correspond to what makes man human. The omniscient does not tolerate another equal: he is an *only knowing* one. This makes the omniscient lonely and even

5 The Desire for Omnipotence

reserved towards himself. It is good to be aware of this when God's atheistic heirs present themselves.

There is yet another aporia to which God's omniscience leads, to that of the disappointing *theodicy*. The question is, how was an omniscient and omnipotent God able to make that which was created in the way that it was: imperfect, full of suffering and anger, full of human imperfection? If he was able to foresee everything why, then, did he create such an imperfect world, why did he make evil possible? It is unthinkable that this could have come as a surprise to an omniscient God. The thought that the omniscient might have consciously wished for all the imperfection of creation and all the suffering and evil involved is hard to justify. A *cause* of evil *not* intended by God is unthinkable because in such a case he would not be omnipotent. The only explanation is to conclude that there must be a *good reason*, an ultimate good cause underlying all of this. The theodicy posits that the good cause, which is beyond man's understanding, *justifies* evil. A moderating variation upon this theme is the notion that by increasing his insight man will eventually come to comprehend this objective. The theodicy forces man to adopt a dangerous type of *fatalism*, the conclusion being that he will either blindly or not, submit to the anticipated will of God and resign himself to what happens because that is how God wants things to be. Even if it was possible to find a *concrete* explanation for all the evil in God's creation, the justification would still remain dubious: if everything could have been created differently why should all of this have been necessary? Even then it would still only be possible to surrender to the impenetrability of God. The dubious aspect of the theodicy also has a very dangerous side to it: what simply occurs is always justified. An omniscient and provident God forces man to *abstractly* justify *before* everything takes place, also including what is done by man together with the evil committed by him. Little imagination is required to *predict* what would happen if man were to take God's place and, in a similar way, justify his will and deeds beforehand.

The whole idea of God's omniscience leads to a dangerous kind of *fatalism*. The theodicy extends *beyond good and evil*. That is something different from the observation that viewed *retrospectively*, evil might be seen to have a purpose, that it challenges, that it can lead to something good. In the end, good and evil are relative views. A retrospective view is something different from justifying something beforehand. Evil can challenge and can bring a change for the better. This is not a *preliminary* justification, nor is it a carte blanche to carry out evil on the basis that it will always somehow lead to good. *Afterwards*, when what has happened has come to pass, it might be possible to assert that some good or something positive has come out of it. Living *in* the knowledge of good and evil demonstrates that even evil can have a purpose. But true insight gained retrospectively is diametrically opposed to any kind of providence that is expected to be able to justify everything beforehand. The paths of the omniscient go *beyond good and evil*; they are not only curious and impossible to fathom but they also give the omniscient a dangerous position in relation to mankind. The infinite and omniscient God not only stands above man but also *above* the truth. Everything is foreseen by him, known beforehand, justified in advance. The cognitive conscience is, in an ethical sense, unscrupulous. God's omniscience places man *below* the truth: all that remains for him is to follow the incomprehensible will of the omniscient. No insight into the situation can alter matters. All of this therefore makes God and man fundamentally *unequal*. Once again, what is dangerous about this emerges when this legacy is taken over by atheistic ideologies. Then it becomes clear where the inequality in the position above and below the truth leads; then it becomes evident what the justification beyond good elicits.

As has been asserted, providence also places the conscience in an awkward position. God's omniscience is linked to what is still to come, to what lies concealed in the future and to what man has no notion of. How can omniscient God bear all the doom and evil that awaits man and of which he already has prior knowledge? How can this *cognitive conscience*, this knowing *beforehand* be reconciled with a *moral conscience*? God cannot stand cognitively above the truth *and* at the same time be conscientiously above good and evil. Surely he cannot accept with a clear conscience all the divine and human evil foreseen by him? He must place himself totally *beyond* good and evil if he is to situate man *below* good and evil. Ultimately man does nothing other than what lies encompassed in God's knowledge. The argument that it is man who commits this evil and so brings the consequences upon himself does not dispel the aporia. If God knew about this beforehand, why, then, did he allow it to happen in the first place? The idea of providence is incompatible with an ethical conscience because it puts an end to that. Omniscient providence is atheistic in an ethical sense.

The backward-looking time dimension of omniscience also leads to an absurdity. The omniscient God knows of everything that has already taken place. His *memory* is perfect; everything is retained. He therefore remembers everything that has happened, even the most dreadful evil. He forgets nothing—he is unable to *forget*! How is it possible to live with that? The past never lets him go. He cannot free himself from the burden of *what was*. The oppressive burden of so many memories must eat away, like a corrosive, at what Nietzsche calls a *good conscience*, in other words: the capacity to open oneself up to the future, to what lies concealed in one's own deeds. The cognitive conscience does not give the omniscient a moment's peace. Or is it more the case that the burden of so much *not being able to forget* pushes him towards a forced redemption of the, always in pursuit, backwardness? Does this lead to a forced position *above* good and evil? That is how the omnipotent God will free himself from the ethical testing in which the God of creation did dare to participate. This non-omniscient God was still able to regret that history unfolded as it did. He did not

5 The Desire for Omnipotence

stand above the truth, nor did he stand above good and evil. He was unable to predict beforehand what would become of man but did not need to do that either. He was therefore also surprised by the situation arising that preceded that of the Fall. This God subsequently also showed himself to be truthful enough to afterwards provide an explanation for what he had precipitated through the Fall. What then emerged was that he also possessed an ethical conscience. His deed, the Fall, makes him remorseful in retrospect so that he may be said to repent. The not omniscient God can be *truthful* and *sincere* which is something that the omniscient God leaves behind him, or rather, must leave behind him.

The idea of omniscience not only leads to aporia and absurdity but also to fatalism and unscrupulous justification. The theodicy does not therefore provide a solution. Absurd as it may seem, this idea proves to be very attractive to man. None of the accompanying absurdity dissuades him from the idea, from the longing to elevate himself above the truth and the ethical conscience. The notion of omniscience thus lays bare a human yearning that will outlive the belief in God. Even if it is all about an incomprehensible and impossible to grasp idea of belief, such faith remains extremely powerful and alluring. The fact that such an idea leads to moral unscrupulousness does not prevent people from aspiring towards it.

Omniscience therefore also has its attractions, but the belief in an omniscient God fades. In *A Brief History of Time*, Hawking sketches the perimeters of a perfect scientific theory, one that embraces the macro and the micro cosmos. This complete theory comprehends and explains everything, not only *what* occurs in the empirical world but also *why* it is like it is and not otherwise. The attainability of this knowledge goal is near at hand and gives rise to optimism. The hope of Leibniz is fulfilled. The triumph of human reasoning leads to knowledge of "the mind of God."[2] Thanks to scientific knowledge, man is able to occupy the position of omniscient God. His all-explaining reason reveals what is divine in omniscient man and so God is made redundant. Omniscience recruits. With the death of God, though, man is far from bidding farewell to his being.

Even though the stance adopted by Hawking may come across as naïve, totalitarian ideologies prove how dangerous the yearning for omniscience is. Without any reservation it is claimed that an all-embracing insight into man, society, and history has been realized or will be realized. The kind of unprincipled activism to which this pretension leads can be proven. There is, however, one aspect of this activism that should be highlighted. Omniscience not only pretends to have unravelled all secrets, but it also tolerates no further secrets, a fact which incidentally undermines the pretension. Complete insight must also be completely predicted so that it can rule out all that might be unexpected and deviant. The position adopted above the truth strangulates

---

2. Hawking, *Brief History of Time*, 179, 185.

and at the same time excludes. Does this not make the notion of omniscience inherently *totalitarian*?

Ultimately, it is difficult for the natural sciences to ignore failed predictions and therefore also surprises—aside from the fact that the unexpected can be suppressed or dishonestly reinterpreted. Natural scientific explanations always, in fact, pertain to given *reality* and not to a reality fabricated by man. In the end, it is always a given reality that is adhered to in science that describes and explains what is already the case, what occurs. Theories constitute an interpretive framework but they do not create an own cosmos. Such science knows no *vérité à faire*. This is what makes it inherently open, honest, and truthful: it does not create or recreate, such a divine attribute is not set aside for such theories.

Such creative pretensions would be more likely to manifest themselves in the sciences linked to man, society, and history. Epistemology and scientific theory have fanatically endeavored to justify such a praxis. In the human world, a description, explanation, or prediction can in fact be *fulfilled*, for instance, through praxis, by intervening in reality or by adapting the deviating reality to the compulsion of the theory. Where such adaptation does not go smoothly, propaganda and terror can offer support: the facts are adjusted to fit the theory. Such a theory does not stick to what exists but instead creates; it makes what is recreated fit the requirements. The theory is more important than the truth; it fulfills itself. In the interests of truth and truthfulness, Thomas Masaryk goes as far as to call Kant's knowledge-*a priorism* redundant.[3] The idea of truth demands a virtually sacred respect for what is given and for what thus precedes knowledge. The truth demands a submissive kind of *reflection*, a recognition that the truth always comes *too late*; that is something from which truthfulness does not recoil. Truthfulness therefore conflicts with the longing for omniscience; it conflicts with the dangerous escape route of realization.

This *realization* also bridges the gap between the yearning for omniscience and the evidence of omnipotence. *Realization* is the emergency measure towards which the restless and futile facets of the longing for omniscience push.

5.4 OMNIPOTENCE

The notion of God's omniscience and providence cannot be sustained without holding on to that of his omnipotence. Omniscience and omnipotence need each other. From an historical point of view, the idea of God's omnipotence appears to precede all the other related features. A *new* God reveals himself as omnipotent to a *new* kind of man. It is a notion that has already been explored. For the almighty God everything is

---

3. Čapek, *Gespräche mit Masaryk*, 303.

5   The Desire for Omnipotence

possible, purely and solely at his command (Isa 45:5). Nothing can exist or can even be conceived of that is beyond his power. *Nothing* furthermore means *nobody*. God's omnipotence is exclusive and that is the way is *must* be: in logical terms omnipotence is something that is indivisible. The fact that the omnipotent tolerates no other gods alongside himself is also a condemnation: because of his omnipotence he is *unable* to tolerate any other equals in his spheres. The omnipotent puts paid to the notion of equality, and that means equality with other gods and with man. Any other power has to be completely subordinate to his. Hence such referrals as "the one and only Lord" and "the King of kings" (1 Tim 6:15). Having another *omnipotence* would therefore constitute, in logical terms, a *contradictio in terminis*. God's omnipotence is the most specific feature of monotheism, if other gods were to claim their own sovereign power then that would constitute a threat to the omnipotence. The fact that everything lies within God's power means that not only *everything* is his, but also *everyone*.

It is not about a sovereign power that can be exclusively wielded in the present. In such a case, omnipotence would merely have a forward oriented kind of power, but omnipotence also extends backward. It is not only what he does and is going to do that falls within his domain, but also what he has already done. His is thus able to have a retrospective influence to an unlimited degree. In both directions there is no power that can oppose him. Not only the future, but also the past lies entirely in his hands. It has already been asserted that God's omnipotence has the capacity to rise above good and evil whether that be natural misfortune or injustice perpetrated by man. All evil issues from his doings, is anticipated from him, or is assentingly tolerated by him. Omnipotence implies that the earlier referred to ethical unscrupulousness is in evidence. Were the evil to be viewed as external to his power or agreement then this would instantly put his omnipotence in perspective. Such unscrupulousness also comes into the picture when one contemplates the nature of what is good. The fact that God has not done or produced good is something of a mystery. Why did he not or does he not do good if that lies within his immediate power? The only possible justification that remains is the theory that he is instantly able to engineer possible good but that he is stalling before actually doing that. For whatever reason then, the withheld good is temporarily deposited, *by him*, in a future perspective that is kept open. The good that fails to materialize really only leaves open to man two possible options. Either he can hope and believe that it will one day still come about, or he can resign himself to God's impenetrability. Omnipotence presumes that there is total freedom of will. For God everything is possible, but what he actually does with his position of power is entirely subject to his *will*. Just as omniscience places him above the truth, so omnipotence lends him unconditional freedom, access to unlimited *arbitrariness*. The free will of the omnipotent bows to nothing and knows absolutely no constraints. That is something that believers will have to recognize and accept.

Recognition does not detract from the fact that God's omnipotence and arbitrariness give rise to colossal questions concerning justification. How can his all-powerfulness be reconciled with his omnipotence and with the truthfulness that underlies it? The entire reality is, after all, a matter of God's own free will, for him it is therefore a fact of life. If there is evidence of truth for the omnipotent then this is completely a *vérité à faire*, an utterly random, already *created* or still to be created type of reality. Just like omniscience, omnipotence and the presence of free will elevate God above the truth. What he does is by definition unconditionally true. It is the truth of the almighty; he *is*, himself, the truth. This thus renders the idea of truth nonsensical and God's paths implausible—which is a step further than being impenetrable. When one comes face to face with imperfect reality, the *vérité à faire* of the omnipotent becomes an absurdity.

There is another explanation for why man, in the first place, needed to create for himself an image of an omnipotent and omniscient god. This creator is himself driven by a longing to rise above the truth and to thus become truth incarnate. What lingers in this image is an own longing for omnipotence, freedom, and arbitrariness. The yearning to be above the truth gives rise to notions of omnipotence and free will. It is a longing that takes reservations and questions surrounding justification for what they are. The image of *omnipotence*, unconditional freedom of will, and the power to create all issue from an all too human longing for such creative power. What lies buried in the idea of omnipotence is a yearning for unconditional freedom, a longing not to be subjected to something that is precedential or to any kind of pre*conditions*. If a world is to be won, then freedom, arbitrariness, and omnipotence have to be obtained. The question that remains, though, is that of the price that has to be paid for such omnipotence.

One thing that has to be surrendered is the loss of credibility of the omnipotent himself. Not only does he elevate himself above the truth of the external reality that is there to be explored, but also above himself as a being that is to be explored. The omnipotent is also utterly false in relation to himself. His desire for omnipotence prevents him from, as it were, becoming thoroughly conversant with himself, from seeking and becoming acquainted with himself, in effect: he *does not seek himself*. In the interests of unconditional freedom of will, he refuses to gain insight into himself. This means that the ways of the omnipotent are not only impenetrable to others but also to himself. His knowledge can be no *self*-knowledge because no facts can precede his freedom of will. The basic principle, *know thyself*, underlying all wisdom does not apply to the omnipotent. Everything that might conceivably come before almighty God would ruin his omnipotence. He therefore also needs to be liberated from him*self*, he must be elevated above himself, close himself off to all that is unique to him. The basis of a virtuous kind of wisdom lies in a truthful attitude towards himself. The almighty is not capable of such virtue and wisdom. This touches on the longing for omnipotence. Those who become obsessed with such longing ruin a great virtue, that

5   The Desire for Omnipotence

of wisdom and self-knowledge. The yearning for omnipotence makes people untruthful, deceitful, and blind.

As soon as the desire for omnipotence demonstrates decisiveness, it becomes entwined in insurmountable diffidence. More to the point, as soon as the unconditional free will has at its disposal something that is concrete, it gets entangled in relative matters and thus in self-restrictions. As soon as omnipotence starts to take action it is no longer itself. Above all else, the discriminatory demonstrates that omnipotence is not everything. Whichever way one looks at it, concretely thinking up and wanting something is restricting. Everything that the omnipotent thinks, wants, or does, everything from which his omnipotence should emanate, limits him. Everything that he does lays bare the limits of his omnipotence. Through all of this he simultaneously discovers what he has not done, what he is not. It all shows the finite aspect of his infinite omnipotence. How can this leave him in peace? It is precisely through his deeds, through the realization of his omnipotence, that what he has *done* does not let him go but binds him instead to the longing for omnipotence.

He is only able to endeavor to avoid the finite and relative aspects of what has been done by escaping into the *restlessness* of infinite motion. The desire for omnipotence forces him to perpetually rescind all the finite aspects of what has been done by him. The desire for omnipotence condemns him to a restless striving, to the fatality of the infinitely possible, to the seeking of ever-new roads and new possibilities. This fatal compulsion is diametrically opposed to the freedom that the omnipotent longs for. The only solution that lies open to the desire for omnipotence is *hopeless infinity*. The selfless being has thrown off all his shackles and has condemned himself to fatality with no prospects, to a world that has to be retrieved. God's aesthetic heirs will prove how the battle against the constricting nature of other powers is felt in the struggle against all that is relative in people's own deeds.

In this restlessness the same deceitfulness comes to the fore as in the denial of oneself. Omnipotence pretends that everything that the omnipotent possesses is captured in its free will and providence. God may never be forced to *react* to what arises, nor to what he himself has done. That would ultimately place him in a dependent position in relation to what arises and that, in turn, would make his omnipotence relative. At the same time, the longing for omnipotence is really the most radical and uncompromising *reaction* to the world as it is and to man as he is, the omnipotent self included. The yearning for omnipotence becomes strong when the world as it is no longer is accepted, when existence is experienced as a *shackle*, as a prison from which one wants to be freed. Omnipotence has to free people from the existing situation; omnipotence offers the ensured promise of that, the assurance that the possible is possible. While the origin of the omnipotent is maximally *reactive*, its pretension keeps this secret and the illusion of unlimited *activity* is sustained. It is in this paradox of lies that the omnipotent enmeshes himself.

This can culminate in the most amazing kind of argumentation. Even though such reasoning is unusual in Christian theology, the radical nominalism of Ockham provides certain instances of this, which must, indeed, have inspired Stalin. Thus, the omnipotent in his omnipotence must even be able to go backward in time. Ockham declares the omnipotent to be free of the pressure of time and from the past. God is freely able to change the past; even this power is included in his omnipotence. The retroaction is not of a reactive nature: after all, providence pretends that it is not about an *enforced* subsequent intervention. The intervening in the past may not be a reactive subsequent action, an unforeseen correction, an act of recovery concerning what was not, in retrospect, desired. Pure *arbitrariness* needs to react to nothing. The omnipotent will accepts no natural laws, no institutions, no human laws. It is not disturbed by the justification question related to why the world was created as it is. He has wanted everything, intended it all to be as it is, beforehand and in retrospect. Nothing and nobody can bindingly affect his will and deeds, not even him*self*. Neither can he be, for himself, the other, the being that has to be known. Naturally, man is not able to steer or even influence almighty God either. But can man then, in line with the previous image of God, possess free will?

The matter of the relationship between God's unconditional free will and the will of man; the element of freedom in man's will, is an extremely difficult point. The idea of omnipotence prohibits people's own human freedom, their will, and their actions; such freedom of will would make God's freedom and arbitrariness perfectly relative. Even human *will* has to correspond to all that emanates from God's will. Man cannot make the omnipotence of God relative; man cannot force God to react to him. Is it then possible to speak of a free human kind of will if it always has to correspond to that of God? The logic of the omnipotent, which leads to absurd conclusions, is a consequence of contradicting what the God of creation asserted about man, namely that he was his equal. Both the omnipotence and the providence of God force a situation to arise in which man is not allowed even the slightest *actual* freedom of will. In conjunction with the position of God, nothing that man thinks and does can result from an own kind of free will and capacity to discern. God's omnipotence exempts man in advance from responsibility and guilt. Every inch of freedom given to man represents a fatal invasion of God's omnipotence. His providence and omnipotence make him totally *unequal* to any others, gods and people. If this God cannot even deal truthfully with himself how can he sincerely deal with others?

The belief in omnipotence emanates from a dangerous human longing. The image of the omnipotent imagines a human dream, that of an own inherent capacity to escape from imprisonment, throw off the shackles and turn into reality what is believed to be possible. Though the human coveting of *power* may be ancient, the desire for *omnipotence* may be labeled modern. That which man once invested in the image of God is revoked by modern atheism. The totalitarian ideologies bear witness to a revived belief in the omnipotent and to the justice which may, in that way, be realized. The irony is that this humanized longing is also of an envious nature: even human omnipotence tolerates no omnipotence alongside of it. Virtually automatically, the longing for omnipotence leads to an embittered conflict between the one and the other. The profound inequality between God and man is repeated in the ceaseless conflict between man and man, between the one and the other. The only comforting aspect of the humanized desire for omnipotence is that the absurdities, aporias, and paradoxes of omnipotence are now unmistakably made visible. Could this lead to any sort of *repentance*, to *wisdom* that makes people more modest, more moderate, more balanced? Does this wisdom also liberate people from another absurd notion, that of the utter goodness of God?

5.5 COMPLETE GOODNESS

God's utter goodness is also linked, as an indisputable feature, to his name. How could he be envisaged as anything other than good? How could he really *be* anything other than good? Even God's punishing justice is unable to spoil this image of goodness. His goodness cannot be separated from his justice: the deliverance *from* the inherent imprisonment of an existence that cannot be borne and the deliverance *to* a good, fulfilled life. Without omnipotence there can be no goodness and justice. In that way, omnipotence leads to a moralizing development in the experiencing of good and evil.

If this is to be understood, two interpretations have to be given to the notion of what constitutes good: there is *being* good and there is *doing* good. It all has to do with the difference between an existential and an ethical interpretation of the good and the evil from which it has to be distinguished. Ethical good is directed at interpersonal communication, at correct relations between people. Such good demands something from the orientation of individual human will and from ensuing actions. Ethical good is directed outwards, to the *other*, it thus demands something from the individual person and gives balance and order to life and society. With existential good, individuals or larger entities ask for something precisely in connection with their *own* way of existence: this has to be good in the sense of freeing from deficiencies and satisfying needs. In a certain respect, it is all about the differentiation between egoism and altruism, between wanting and being able to give as opposed to wanting to receive. In this ethical respect, good and evil cannot be contemplated in isolation of each other: good has to be established and maintained against the backdrop of always threatening evil. In the existential sense, the fulfilling of a completely good existence is dreamed about. How can such fulfillment be achieved, how can it be given to man, how will it become possible? Hence the reason that omnipotence is introduced as a sufficient condition for this good. The omnipotent operates as a guarantee for this justice; to that end he also redeems from evil, from everything that stands in the way of what is good. In this sense omnipotent God himself is already the mirror of that good: he is seen to be implicitly good. This could not be said of the ethical gods.

This notion of complete goodness is also something that leads again to reservations, to irresolvable justification questions. Such questions not only touch on God's utter goodness, but also on the notion of utter goodness itself. In addition, there is the consideration that the whole idea of existential good spoils the ethical meaning of good and evil.

God's goodness is a broad concept. In the first place there is the consideration that God himself is perfectly good. The fact that he *is* perfectly good should be taken to mean that nothing evil or bad clings to him: he *is* in himself formed from perfect good, evil *is* not in him. Can this really be upheld? Does he in fact *do* good and nothing other than that? Does his goodness also direct itself towards the other? Does this also emerge in an *ethical* sense? It is something that is, after all, encapsulated in his name. The way he is is also the way in which he should appear to the outside world. His goodness dictates this unequivocally. In his complete goodness he also *does* good in everything; his goodness is felt in everything that lies outside him, in his creation, in man. In everything that is of God and in everything that he does his goodness shines through.

That gives an ethical slant to God's complete goodness. The fact that there is nothing bad and nothing evil in him makes omnipotent God identical to all the good contained in the cosmos, also all the good in human existence. Wherever it is apparent, all good must be attributed to him. The radical consequence of this is the conclusion that no good can exist outside of God: it only emanates from him. God's goodness therefore says still more about him, about his love, his benevolence, justice, mercifulness, and charitability. This means that he truly wants his goodness to reach out to others even if it is not reciprocated—for instance because that other one turns against God. Hence the reason that God's goodness must also make people thankful, really beforehand, for whatever he does.

But then comes the question of justification: if the omnipotent is really good, how is evil then possible? Then there is the matter of the relationship with ethical good and evil: if he is the reflection and promise of a good life, can that still then be reconciled with good and evil in an ethical sense? Such good is surely relative?

The original significance of *good* is that it is, before all else, *ethical*. What is good is relative. It says something about the way in which gods and people should behave towards each other. In their lives and actions they are, of course, involved with each other. He who goes forth and takes action meets the other: this demands in a literal sense *answer*ability. This also means that living and living together in all possible forms and connections is not definitely established beforehand, not even in close

5   The Desire for Omnipotence

traditional structures. All of this could be different, though. Such *openness* in human life and coexistence gives rise to ethical questions: *as man*, man has to organize, which is something that is not automatically laid down. In so doing, he must bear the other in mind, he must be prepared to accept the other as having been *given* to him and to *give* something himself: this is where *good* comes into the equation. That which is good has a cohesive effect on people; it makes living together possible. Together these things do not put individuals out of the picture at all. One has to *want* to do good and not lapse into the reverse, into the disintegrating forces of evil. To *be able* to do good and to be able to give something to fellow man, man has to elevate and enrich himself. In this respect, man has to be able to love himself so that he is also able to love the other. That which is good *elevates*, also in an ethical sense. It gains an ethical guise in the shape of morals and rules, institutions and culture. No matter how elevated it is, it remains an open business, an eternal challenge.

In this ethical respect, the differentiation between good and evil extracts man *as man* from natural existence. Ethical good cannot be conceived of without the *evil* component. Evil is also an ethical concept; it says something about the interaction with the other. It lies differentiatingly encapsulated in what is good. Good and evil imply each other; they are interconnected human opportunities, which means that man also contributes to good and evil. Indeed, man *is* not *naturally* good or evil: natural existence knows no evil. Also, evil is connected to consciousness, will, and actions. Through that which is evil, man ruins that which is elevated. In what is evil man does not *give*, but rather *takes* instead. Evil ruins the own elevating and that of society. Ethical gods invested good and evil with significance. These gods were human *ideals*: in them man bestowed upon himself images and examples. In many respects ethical good and evil are *relative*. The content is not established beforehand, the ethical dimension says something about people's involvement with each other and that which differentiates cannot be separated. As an eternal challenge, ethical good offers no redeeming future dimension. The *eternal* challenge holds for the choice of concrete content and for wanting and doing this.

The omnipotence of God lends good and evil an ever-changing and moralizing guise: they must tell us something about what God and man *are*. Instead of being connected with the order of human *co*existence, good and evil are allied to the *experiencing* of existence, to human *life*. This not only ruins the relative facet, but also the invested *value*. What the ethical idea once perceived to be impending evil now becomes a beckoning perspective. It is now seen as good to seek oneself, not in order to be able to *give* in a better way but so as to be able to receive in a better way, if not to *take*. The good becomes a desirable life. *Ethical* meaning shifts to *aesthetic* significance. Where existence falls short man now sees evil. Moralizing turns good and evil into categories of being. It is all too easy to now bracket together with such moralized evil that which was formerly good, ethical rules for living, culture and institutions. Where they are experienced as irksome in terms of life fulfillment, the relevant judgment does not focus on intrinsic improvement but on alternative ways of living.

Good and evil no longer stand distinguishingly *side by side* but are rather divided, abyssal, and in *opposition* to each other. That which is relative is spoilt. In the existence that is permeated with good and evil there is a massive gaping chasm. On the far side of the chasm, good implies that an existence free of evil is conceivable. This turns good into a beckoning promise, one that can be believed in. In this interpretation of what is good, God is also moralized about as an utterly good God, the God who *is* good and who also promises such good to man. This also places God on the far side of the chasm. God's goodness thus also implies that a judgment is made about human existence, a judgment that entices people towards an optimistic future dimension, a deliverance from evil. God's goodness implies that there is a hopeful promise: it concerns more than God alone. Now we return to the earlier-mentioned reservation. The thorough goodness of the omnipotent makes the *existence* of evil an irresolvable problem. How can God who is completely good tolerate evil let alone commit evil himself? How can the origins and the existence of evil be explained? If God is utterly good how can his redeeming justice also be a repayment, a judgment?

The notion of the *perfectly* good is a concept that is untenable. Whilst that which is good distinguishes and is therefore unavoidably relative, the whole idea of complete goodness seeks to break down this relative facet. Even in a *logical* sense this idea is untenable: *perfect* good is a logical contradiction. Good cannot be thought of without taking into consideration the differentiating side—that of what is evil, bad, or whatever, and in whatever sense of the word. Each concept intrinsically implies that something differentiates; in other words, when one talks of good, one automatically refers to what differentiates; conceptually that is included. Good also unleashes evil so that it, in principle, also becomes possible. By referring to what is good, one automatically simultaneously refers to what is evil and to what is thus also included. In this opening up sense, he who seeks good also therefore seeks evil. In seeking good, one must thus be prepared to also accept the possibility of inherent evil. This is, therefore, the good side of the freed up evil.

It is for this reason that good can never, by definition, be seen as perfect: the differentiating aspect is always at any rate intrinsic. It is therefore appropriate that in paradise there is mention of the tree of knowledge, of good *and* evil, and that good is therefore brought within reach, together with evil. Absolute good is inconceivable; it is an empty concept, a *contradictio in terminis*. *Omnis determinatio est negatio*. If one goes in search of what is *completely* good then that which differentiates must be eliminated and that, in turn, means that it then becomes impossible to refer to anything being solely good. In order to be freed from what is negative, determination must be forbidden. Hence the escape route, the attempt to situate good somewhere else in another or future dimension and view evil as transient. The logical nonsense of this

5 The Desire for Omnipotence

notion also renders the idea of perfect good a *contradictio in terminis*: it simply cannot be contemplated without giving rise to aporia. The mere entertaining of the notion gives rise to unrest and conflict. Here it is not simply about the battle between good and evil, but also about the struggle with the differentiating self. The whole notion of utter good ruins the capacity to deal with that which differentiates: the good divides, judges, and destroys everything that is different. That is why the perfectly good God is unable to cope with what is relative. He seeks himself and wants only himself. He ruins his old ethical being and thus also his capacity for balance and moderation.

Since man sees himself reflected in the image of his God, the goodness of God therefore also has dangerous consequences for man and for his self-recognition. From an ethical point of view, that which is good says more about the relative side of people's thinking and the will or actions of man. Whether a person *is* actually good or bad is not of any relevance. *Doing* good is a totally different matter from *being* good. By moralizing about good and evil, man is not so much presented as a being who does good or evil as a being that *is* good or evil. The moralizing evaluation is basically directed at man as an existing entity. Such a re-evaluation is incorrect and dangerous. It is in his *deeds* that a criminal does things that are evil but that does not mean to say he *is* evil as a person. In an ethical sense, there *is* no such thing as good and evil people. In an ethical sense it is not the individual who is condemned but his actions. Even the biggest criminal remains, in this sense, a human being. The *being* status recoups such deeds from man. The translation of *ad hominem* is a dangerous consequence of the moralizing about good and evil. In this respect, the moralizing re-evaluation of good and evil is an extremely detrimental *deed*; it is, as it were, a truly fatal *Fall*. The re-evaluation mirrors the divine example. The notion of God being completely good is anything but an innocent idea, let alone a sanctifying thought. The whole idea bears witness to an ethical kind of atheism with dangerous consequences. What is dangerous about following this path is the way in which good and evil are wielded *ad hominem*. One then starts to speak in terms of good and evil individuals in isolation of human deeds: man as such is then termed good or evil. History shows us precisely where such re-evaluation can lead.

There is a previously addressed point of reservation that once again puts God's justice in the picture. Will a God that *is* utterly good also *do* that which is completely good? An irresolvable theodicy is unavoidable. And this is not only in conjunction with the question of how a completely good God can accept that evil is done by others. It also has to do with the evil committed by the good God himself. How can such evil be justified? A thoroughly good God will surely virtually automatically only do what is good? By committing evil or by tolerating it he then becomes, by definition, not completely good. How could a God that is completely good unleash evil? How could he burden man with the ethical problem of good and evil? The fact that he even considers the possibility of that makes him complicit in the actually committed evil. The evil is therefore also in him and so he is not utterly good.

One could then go on to argue that God who is good knows about such evil and that he has, in principle, triggered it but that he does not actually commit such evil himself. There resides no evil in him in the sense of his own thoughts, intentions, and deeds. This does not, however, detract from the fact that he consciously and deliberately *allows* it; he lets evil happen. The good and omnipotent God allows his creatures and creation to be weighed down by evil. He stands by and watches as people commit evil and become victims of evil. How can a good God put up with such evil without feeling a need to intervene? It is a diabolical dilemma: either God's goodness is not perfect or his *omniscience* and *omnipotence* must be confined. The assertion that the evil done might have a deeper significance or serve a higher goal does not resolve the justification problem. The omnipotent and good one could achieve such significance and such an aim without the need for evil. A certain kind of absurdity lurks here. Is there a conceivable justification that retains the goodness and omnipotence of God?

Desperate measures offer no solution. One could reason that good and evil both lie within God's power and are matters affiliated to his providence. What happens and what is done is therefore entirely his affair. If good and evil both ensue from God, if his arbitrariness has to justify both those things then the matter of good and evil has nothing to do with man: all that then remains for man is fatality. A more sophisticated solution to the aporia might indeed be to attribute some kind of deeper significance to evil. Evil is committed, even by God, but ultimately it serves a higher goal. And all of this is once again built into God's providence.

This justification on the basis of God's providence can also be made effective by terming God's paths incomprehensible to man. The justification of evil is then projected into a time dimension in the interests of an ultimate change for the better. This latter matter might be concealed from man but not from God. Now there is finally really evidence of *justified* evil, justified for the sake of the anticipated and promised good. It is thus all about *doing evil* for the sake of ultimate *good*. This solution totally destroys the ethical significance of good and evil. Now it is possible to commit evil because it is not really evil as such but rather a precursor of the good to follow. Such ruination becomes even greater if this sort of justification of evil gains an *ad hominem* status. It can take the shape of justified evil that may and must be deployed against evil that can no longer be justified, against the existence of people in whom evil predominates. This makes the justifying of evil absurd and extremely dangerous. The own evil is now justified by being seen as a battle against and a settling of scores *with those* who are evil, a precondition in the struggle to secure the good to which those who are good are entitled. What is dangerous is that *in his goodness*, not only the good God deals like that with evil and with the evil ones, but man also goes on to copy his example. The justification offers an image and an example of a God who intends what

5   The Desire for Omnipotence

is best for those whom he has singled out as good, so that he is therefore justified to deal with those who are evil. It is this justification that underlies the punishing, avenging, and redeeming justice. The justifying of such ominous evil comes within reach when the omnipotent and completely good God takes over from the ethical God. This ominous evil becomes overt when modern atheism begins to avail itself of such attractive justifications.

The whole notion of the concept of utter good gives rise to yet another problem from the point of view that it is used as a *substantive*. In *abstracto* or like *the good* in a general sense, that which is good points to something acceptable. In what sense of the word though? *What*, precisely, is the essence of such good? Much the same can, of course, be argued concerning *the* evil. To start off with, it is not at all clear what should concretely be understood by the terms good and evil. As soon as good and evil are qualified they begin, in various respects, to become relative. In concrete terms what is good not only distinguishes itself from what is seen as evil but also from other views about what is good in itself. That which is good is not unequivocal. That which is true has a point of focus, it is namely the correct reflection of what is simply a fact; hence the reason that it is possible to speak of *the* truth, even if the final interpretation of that is unattainable. Good and evil are really no open matters, one can at best merely give a certain direction to what they imply.

A state of peace between people may be referred to as good, but what should peace be taken to mean? Does it mean that there is an absence of armed or unarmed conflict, or is it more about universal and complete agreement between people? Does this latter view exclude conflict or does it also extend to competition? Is a state of peace without competition really desirable? This can surely also evoke its own kind of harm such as diminishing resilience and mobility in people and society. Much the same applies when recognizing good as a state of universal and utter happiness. What does such happiness consist of, what does utter actually mean? Can a description pretend to be universal? Once again, good and evil are, inevitably, relative concepts. They are a matter of what a person wants, of what he chooses, and they are affiliated to the orientation of his actions. The element of freedom in all of this, of further determination, cannot be ignored. This relative aspect certainly does not imply that there is unbridled relativism or uncontrollable arbitrariness. The nature of this idea, of the inherently relative, is what really makes relativism or arbitrariness impossible. With good and evil it is also all about the relationships between individuals and how involved they are with each other. It would be absurd to talk of firm individual ethics or morality. No matter how open the question concerning ethical good is, the answer includes reciprocity, relativeness, a divided opinion about the orientation of will and actions. This divided opinion is nothing less but also nothing more than an incitement to generality. Without such orientation towards generality the whole purpose of good is lost. Without freedom, the openness and nature of good are lost. Universality is able to ruin the openness and thus the freedom couched in the eternal returning question concerning ethical good.

It is a danger that is encompassed in both the idea of the *perfect* good and the *perfectly* good. Ascribing the notion of *perfect* goodness to *the* one, omnipotent, and perfectly good being means that the relative is replaced by arbitrariness. The good takes possession of the content of that which is good. As the *perfectly* good one he knows all about perfect good, in his omnipotence he is furthermore able to *realize* this. That which is completely good is something that nobody can tolerate, neither gods nor people. All openness towards others leads to relativeness and so spoils the state of perfection. The idea of perfect goodness gives rise to endless distancing from and inequality with the other. As soon as the idea of the one and perfect good breaks through, there is no other possibility than that this *one* goes on to determine what is unconditionally good. That which is good lies in him, he knows it, does it, and bestows it upon those who are not his equals. That which is good is a matter of arbitrariness emanating from the one who is good. Those who are unequal are therefore left with no alternative than to *believe* that this is *what is* good, no matter what it entails. This then makes man completely subordinate to and dependent upon his utterly good God. It is only through *mercy* that the unequal party is able to participate in the divine good. Human good has to be withheld from him. Even just the hint of an own interpretation would ruin the goodness of God: it would then, after all, become relative. An own, free, human involvement in that which is good signifies evil in the eyes of God. The tragic paradox is this: when forced to seek that which is good, man proves unable to be allowed, or even able, to find it. The unequal can only in one way hope to attain anything approximating God's goodness and that is by, as a believing group, totally subjugating themselves and losing themselves in his goodness, *whatever* such goodness might entail. All that remains for them is to be *humble* to an absurd degree. In that respect, he not only has to display that he is God's absolute unequal but he must also *be* completely unequal. The notion of absolute goodness being the property of that which is completely good is atheistic in an ethical sense. It is an idea that strips man of his own worth, a value that he had gained from his own ability to distinguish between good and evil. Such devaluing becomes practical when modern atheism takes over this idea.

The perspective of the *perfect* good forces man to hope that *the* good and provident God will bestow such good upon him. All that remains for him is to hope for mercy, for a kind of clemency that will deliver him from the evil of his own will, his own judgment, his own choices. Meanwhile this unequal status taunts both God and man. The inequality negatively condemns both parties to each other. For God, who is good, human intractability is something intolerable, for man, God's goodness is unfathomable.

5 The Desire for Omnipotence

The good for which man hopes and which God must give is linked to the redeeming of inequality. It is a kind of hope that is latently coercive: God and man must *want* to dispense with each other's different natures. However, they become each other's equals through the complete unification of the one with the goodness with the other. The redeeming of man's otherness means that he becomes indistinguishably one with his God. God's goodness is unthinkable without his justice. Redeeming justice has two sides to it, the aspect of mercy and the aspect of revenge. God in fact has to put an end to what his goodness opposes, to what wants to remain different. The completely good God therefore turns against the God of creation and the equality created between God and man. The completely good God is forced to recreate God and man. The recreated God and man are no longer entities with a capacity to distinguish: the recreation makes them indistinguishably one.

In that way, God's goodness opens up a future perspective in which that which is good triumphs as justice. Seemingly automatically, this perspective turns radically against that otherness and against evil, its cause. Evil is now the domain of those who *are* not only different from their God but who also *want to be* different in that respect. Man is thus blamed for being different: it is turned into a human fault. Evil is given an *ad hominem* twist: it becomes the possession of the guilty, bad, angry, as opposed to the good. The moralizing that surrounds good and evil presses towards a pay off with evil and those who are evil; it enlists punishing, avenging justice. The redeeming of such being different is therefore unthinkable without the converse facet of mercy, namely: justice that settles matters with evil and with the evil. God's goodness leads to conflict, to a final conflict. God's goodness evokes *Messianism*. The distinguishing between good and evil changes into an immeasurable division between the two and a final battle in which the good must triumph. The final battle between good and evil is a basic stipulation for a recreation that redresses everything.

This where the extreme consequences of the moralizing about good and evil are revealed, and therefore also the consequence of the loss of ethical meaning. No redeeming justice without retribution. The final contest has the character of a justified war. It is a war that demonstrates something incredible which is really paradoxical. The war waged against evil that cannot be justified justifies the perpetrators' own evil. It is in fact deployed from the viewpoint of that which is completely good.

5.6 THE MESSIANIC CONSEQUENCE

The whole idea of divine goodness and omnipotence does betray a certain uncontrollable human unrest and discontentment. The ability to deal with that which is relative is ruined, nothing leaves man in peace, he has to react to everything. That which is relative does not disappear. Inevitably man is confronted with the other, with barriers that he is unable to raze. The idea of perfect good works like something that *ruins* human interaction with the world as he knows it, in which omnipotence creates the illusion that this can be *compensated*. The idea of utter good is abyssal. On the one side of the great chasm reigns unrest, the experiencing of the evil of an imperfect existence, whilst on the other side the illusion of the opposite, the totally different, beckons. Between the two poles lies the promise, the hope that the other side can be reached. Between the two extremes lies also the belief that the other side can be *made* attainable. The two sides of the contrast can no longer be differentiatingly held together, the gap cannot be bridged. All that remains is the hope that it might be possible to leap to the other side. But who is capable of making this leap, who has the chance to reach the other side? Man who is chained is unable to do that; the power of evil is too strong. He therefore has to put himself in the hands of the omnipotent, at the disposal of his will and justice.

The idea of utter good gives free rein to the power of unrestrained *illusion*. Man creates for himself the image of a completely good God and a perfect existence attributable to him that will one day be achieved. By contrast, there is the image of irreconcilable evil and man who is trapped in that. Man chains himself to evil, he experiences his existence as a kind of imprisonment. He imagines that he can reach the other side of the chasm the moment that a fatal human flaw in creation is resolved. Hence the whole idea or re-creation of a reconstruction effort that will *restore* everything. This brings moralizing *fulfillment* into the picture again, now in the sense of making *good*. This recovery is only possible after a radical end has been put to the power of evil. The image of a catastrophic finish is therefore added to the image of a catastrophic beginning of history. Moderation and balance disappear *from view*. It is the whole idea of perfect good that gives a new and radical impetus to the imagination. Hence the notion of a climax, the *eschatological view* of a decisive final battle between good and evil, between the power of good and the power of evil.

Gods who pretend not to *be* completely good are able to deal with the relative nature of good and evil. They do not know what is good *to start off with*, which is why the open question as to what is good and what is evil does not lead to an irreconcilable conflict between the two. The relative nature of good and evil is reconciled to the eternal identity of evil in a general sense, and can therefore always be activated to instigate good: in relative evil resides also, in fact, a challenge and a change for the better! What if good is seen, can it then be shared by people and sought after and done? The opinion that gods and people must *be* good or bad does not fit in here: they do good or evil in a differentiating and thus a relative sense.

Ethical evil torments much less. Ethical life seeks the good, without *hoping* that it will ever be complete and without too much *desperation* concerning evil. With a somewhat archaic but nonetheless well-chosen word, evil may also be termed that which occurs *perforce*.[4] It comes, of necessity, with man, and it does not have to

---

4. Translator's note: the Dutch word used here is "*noodwendig*" (cp. the German "*notwendig*"),

5 The Desire for Omnipotence

signify disheartening need but can be seen as a *change* for the better in terms of a challenge. The opportunity to *do* good is not affected by the eternal presence of evil, on the contrary! In an ethical sense, good and evil cannot be contemplated in isolation of each other. Hence the reason that in the story of creation, the relationship between God and man is not ruined by the Fall, on the contrary. Neither does the Fall represent a fabrication mistake or some kind of catastrophe that requires recreation. The prospect of a new kind of person, of a new heaven and earth, is rightfully omitted in this story. There is no gaping chasm between God and man, so no completely good God is needed to save man who has lapsed into evil. The ethical distinction between good and evil gives man a kind of freedom and offers him a challenge. Differentiation is a human *value* and, as such, a precondition to man's human existence. Man must not *want* to be delivered from this kind of value. Such value provides reconciliation in a general kind of way with the imperfection of existence. This general human fact of life does not force people towards acceptance or fatalism at all, and it leads even less to fantasies of redemption. Every special manifestation of what is experienced as evil challenges, like a new excuse for a change for the better.

As soon as good gains a concrete *being* perspective, evil threatens to take on the guise of unfulfilled existence. Already this makes it harder to bear. Introducing an additional facet to *delivering* from such evil, to freeing *from* suffering and loss, makes it even harder to bear. Such evil becomes irreconcilable if it is converted to a power, if it is demonstrable, if it gets an identity. It is really only then that it becomes clear precisely *what it is* that people want to be delivered *from*. It is only then that man starts to feel trapped and chained: imprisoned by another, tied down by guilt. The prospect that it could all have been so different, like in a promised land with a new, fulfilled existence, makes this negative aspect even more sensitive. *What* exactly is promised is secondary. The mere fact *that* everything could be different stimulates the powers imagination and draws attention to the negative, the causes, the guilt, the guilty. The mere fact *that* this is quite thinkable and that evil is apparent turns the complaint into an accusation. Discontentment makes the imagination creative and sows bitterness. Evil no longer challenges; it takes on a weightiness from which man wants to be redeemed. The imagination therefore instigates an irreconcilable fight *against* this evil.

The active freedom *to do* something gives way to a reactive longing to be freed *from*. It is no longer possible to deal with evil and so it must disappear, it must be destroyed. Being released from being chained to evil is not enough either. The obsession is not so much to do with being chained to *evil* as to do with being chained to the guilty, to *the evil*. That which is good is unthinkable without redemption. The casting off of the chains *unleashes* the justified crusade against *evil* and the settling of scores

---

which, very literally translated, means "necessary turn." The word "perforce," though not perhaps archaic is certainly old-fashioned and definitely comes very close to the essential meaning of "*noodwendig*."

with *the evil*. This, too, is incorporated into the whole idea of God's goodness. God's utter goodness forces *enmity* to arise and enemies to be created. The abyssal division between good and evil extends to the equally great divide between those who have to suffer defeat and those to whom good is bequeathed. The God of love makes way for the God of justice. His love is valid for those who are able to love *him*. He cannot forgive; he cannot give. If the God of love deals in such a restrictive way with the notion of *neighborliness*, how then can man in his image be expected to simply love his neighbor? How can man who has become so evil still be able to love *himself*?

One should not forget that the gods of the past were also just as reactive. They, too, punished, avenged, settled old scores with evil. A certain degree of *hybris* was not alien to them: they invariably went to extremes. The story of the Flood shows how God reacted to man's anger. He wiped wicked man from the face of the earth and eradicated the earth that had been ruined by man. Such extreme behavior was merely displayed in the interests of initiating a new beginning. This renewed beginning had nothing to do with recreating, with fulfilling creation or with triumphing over complete good. The *renewed* beginning changed nothing about the origins of mankind instigated by the Fall. Man who survived the Flood remained the being known for his ethical discrimination between good and evil. After the Flood, there is thus no other perspective; there is no perfect world or fulfilled existence. There is, however, God's hope that man will not again fall prey to intense anger, that there will be no total ethical downfall and that man will once more walk with God (Gen 6:9).

It is no devastation, therefore, to permanently abolish evil and to allow perfect good to prevail. God was merely *remorseful* about what had happened to man: there was no animosity towards him, no justice, no revenge. Redemption is not thus needed, nor a new earth, nor the rebirth of man. It appears that God is able to repent and to promise temperance. God himself also remains the same familiar God and in that way man's equal; he is no omnipotent, perfect God. Hence the reason that the permanent ethical alliance between God and man is expressed through a *covenant* with man, which is a totally different covenant from the one made with Abraham. What omnipotent God promises to Abraham is future salvation; what God promises in the covenant made after the Flood is to not again *react* so angrily to man's anger. Never again the likes of the Flood; never again a new beginning. In effect he presents matters slightly differently. He will not again behave in such a reactionary fashion. He will no longer be *remorseful* about how he has created man with equal capacities for good *and* evil. The God of ethical life therefore recognizes his own weaknesses and knows, when challenged, how to overcome such challenges. It is as if God himself needed time to get used to the man that he had created; it was as if he needed time to realize that things are simply no different with man, his equal. God recognizes his equality with

5 The Desire for Omnipotence

man. Only *equals* can be sincerely ethically allied. In equality, people are able to make the necessary promises to each other in word and deed and abide by such promises.

As soon as evil becomes irreconcilable, one is instantly forced to question how the omnipotent can tolerate the existence of such evil, how he is able to justify it. The *justification question* emanates from an inability to deal with evil, to tolerate it and to allow oneself to be challenged by it. This inability precipitates a *justified* struggle against evil and the struggle becomes the pre*condition* for future salvation. It is an incredible turnabout: irreconcilable animosity and conflict in the interests of peace and salvation.

The consequences can certainly be felt. Since evil no longer resides in God and cannot therefore be justified by God, the question shifts to man. Evil must then emanate entirely from man in a general sense, but also as far as actually committed evil goes. Hence the reason for the overpowering aspect of human *sinfulness* and guilt. This does not so much have to do with guilt surrounding people's own deeds and the recognition that man has consciously committed such deeds, but rather with the *moralized* guilt of man as such. Such guilt does not mean that—alongside all the great good—man also *commits* evil: it is a kind of guilt that points to man *being* evil! Man is thus condemned to *commit* sinful acts because he *is* evil. Since man *is*, in essence, sinful he brings upon himself *justified* judgment in the form of vengeance. The evil of sinfulness leads to the justified evil of avenging punishment. Man legitimately falls under God's avenging justice.

The question surrounding justice changes God. The God who was able to repent for his *own* deeds is replaced by a God who is no longer able to detach himself from the evil of the *other*. For this God, it is no longer possible to reconcile with evil. He, too, has to be freed from it. He not only has to be released from the sinfulness of man but also from *man* who has been tainted by sinfulness. As God is no longer able to reconcile himself to the man who he has created he also wants to see a new, reborn kind of man. God also suffers from moralized evil, he is also unable to justify it. He is just as chained to evil as man. He is man's prisoner and so he has to be freed from man. He is therefore also condemned to the future perspective of the final battle.

The dogma of redemption gives rise to apocalyptical visions. The spirit becomes obsessed with the prospect of the completion of history, which is close at hand, with the conquering of evil, with the leap over the abyss in the direction of salvation. The old creation and the old mankind have to make way for something new and entirely different. In a *new* creation, a new man will share in God's perfection. In the *renewed* beginning after the Flood, everything had remained essentially the same; in the renewed beginning after recreation everything must become essentially different. Ever since the time of the prophets apocalyptical visions have taken possession of the human spirit, which has trusted in the expectation that God will intervene in history.

The abyssal division between good and evil leaves no other alternative than redemption, than the total triumph over evil.

The abyssal division between good and evil, God and man, present and future, thus gives rise to a major problem. How can God and man again be brought together, how can the gap between the two be narrowed? How can the reason for this division, this evil, be dispelled? How can powerless man be freed from being fettered to evil? How can the battle be fought if the one who is shackled has been rendered powerless? More to the point, how can such a battle possibly be staged in a sinful world?

Enter the *Messiah*. His task as savior and redeemer is to secure a radical and definite triumph over the all-prevailing evil. Only through his final strife can the deep-seated problem be resolved and can God and man be united. There can be no salvation without resisting evil, the evil powers, those who represent evil. It also amounts to a battle against the sinfulness of man, and thus, also against old-style man who has lapsed into sinfulness. Man who has fallen into sinful ways and has been shackled to evil cannot himself be expected to lead such a battle. God therefore has to intervene. To that end he will send the Messiah at the end of time. As God's representative this incumbent will have to stage a battle that will be a matter of life and death. He will establish a *messianic kingdom* and under his dominion evil will be banished. The messianic kingdom thus represents an interim phase with a transition figure on the road to God's eternal kingdom. The interim phase is a *catharsis*, a cleansing, a deliverance from the old world and from the old kind of human, a liberation that will make the leap over the abyss possible. During the course of this struggle it will also become clear who will witness this leap, who falls under God's redeeming justice and will be entitled to a reborn existence.

Small wonder that many saw in Jesus the Messiah. Small wonder that there was general disappointment when he failed to fulfill that role. It is a status that was thus attributed to him after his death. In that way, the historical *Jesus* faded behind the dead, resurrected, and returned *Messiah*. All Jesus' doctrines concerning brotherly love and forgiveness as well as inner peace and enduring living *together*, actually stand in the way of this messianic re-evaluation. In messianic religious dogma, it is no longer in fact about walking with an ethical God who is equal to man. It is all about God's representative dispelling God's wrath. This is what makes man's salvation possible. It is a salvation that will become a reality at the time of the Last Judgment when the crucified and resurrected Messiah returns as the redeemer *of* evil and the *judge* of evil people. Only then will the condition be fulfilled of redeeming *to* that which is new and establishing unity with God. Now it becomes fully clear what the two facets of the divine justice of God entail. The justice conferred by salvation, love, and peace only comes into the picture after the storm of avenging justice has abated and culminated in the Last Judgment, the final day. The old covenant with Abraham has a radicalized

5   The Desire for Omnipotence

messianic sequel. No promised land without first settling matters with evil. Hope is confronted with the reverse side of the coin of justice.

In messianic faith, the goodness of God conquers the ethical God long before the final strife commences. With the prospect of final judgment and redemption it is justice that wins brotherly love: evil is transferred from the *deed* to the perpetrator. Revenge wins from ethical love. The forgiving of *sins* switches to the directing of *sinners*, a thing which forces sinners to acknowledge their own sinfulness, to recognize how far removed they are from good and from elevated God. Now *new* person can come about without confirming the futility of ethical life.

The various aporia emanating from the omniscience, omnipotence, and goodness of God therefore only leave open the road to one possible solution, that of the *deed*, the redeeming battle, the practical answers to the logical riddles. Even the religious disposition situates the logical mysteries in the dimension of the practical solution. This feeling still in fact leaves the deed with God and with the one appointed to deputise for him. The actual say that he has in the final battle will demonstrate that, for the omnipotent, nothing is too miraculous. This real miracle once again demands omnipotence. It is the omnipotence of God that gives those who believe certainty in the possibility to conquer evil and in the *manipulability* of what is good. Omnipotence provides the certainty that what had apparently seemed impossible is in fact possible and that people and the world really can be *changed*. This practical miracle justifies more than just the final strife against the old type of person and the world. It also justifies avenging justice and *resentment* towards all in whom evil resides, the evil that stands in the way of the possible and what can be manipulated. How is it possible for a good and omnipotent God to be fettered to his wrath? How can he justify such shackling? The real problem lies in the chaining of such resentment to what is evil and to evil-doers. It is the fact *that* there is evil that is more exasperating than *what* the evil itself is. *Who* it can be attributed to produces more creativity than *how* evil actually manifests itself. The signaling of evil is a more creative deed than all the good that is still to be realized. The justifying of such resentment also amounts to a stain on ethical life.

At the end of the day, there is something only too human that creeps into this messianic perspective, an all too human longing. Is there perhaps a certain hankering alive in Messianism to become, in a certain respect, God's equal? Does Messianism constitute an endeavor to justify an all too human yearning for revenge? In that way the evil of resentment is not only accepted, but it also becomes part and parcel of the great eschatological miracle, the miracle of the redeeming deed, the deed that has to resolve mysteries. The messianic perspective is above all else a human *opiate* and one that indices a dangerous kind of pathos. The messianic orientation reveals and imagines a creative human *deed*. The theological horizons do not stop at the expectation of heavenly happiness. Revenge also comes into the picture.

Time and again man creates for himself gods who give back to him what is theirs. Even the omnipotent and good God imagines and reinforces a human longing. It is not only in secrecy that man seeks to *make* this image *his own*. Just think of how often he rushed to help his God and of how often he led the way. If only he could move his mountains *himself*. If only he could undo what had in the past been done to him. If only he *himself* could make the impossible possible.

It is not only in religion that Messianism has become prominent; it has also penetrated into modern thinking, into certain mainstream ideologies. The ideological path demonstrates how God becomes man and how man annexes the divine and makes it his own. The divine being assumes an instantly human form. In the process of God's becoming man the atheist takes back what man had once lain in the hands of God. The messianic final judgment is brought within human reach. Zealous leave is now taken from something that is unique to the old type of religion, the guarding of the ethical solidarity of people. Ideological atheism transforms the inequality of God and man into a radical kind of *inequality* between human beings. That justifies its own brand of Messianism. A human messiah seizes the imagination, in justice, in arbitrariness, in justification. More than being able to determine *who* are the chosen ones, this messiah imagines that he is able to dispense with *evil* and with *evil-doers*. The offloading of this into the twentieth century has demonstrated how *this* fantastical human creature has been able to become a reality.

Does this story prompt one to pose a final question? Does the radical nature of ethical atheism compel one to return once more to the original ethical value of God? Is there a future for religion that extends beyond the death of this ethical God? The story that will be able to elicit this question must first be told.

6

Moses: Between Law and Promise

What now has to be explored is the story of the gradual seizure of power on the part of the omnipotent. It is simultaneously the story of how ethical atheism managed to make its effect felt. What began with Abraham was to continue with Moses, the prophets, Paul, and with Christian eschatology. It is definitely no one-dimensional story. The stronger call for redeeming justice does not detract from the fact that both the Hebrew and the Christian traditions allow space for a striking kind of duality. They are traditions that have an eye for ethical order, for the retaining of an old-style creation—no matter how finite that might be—and for the responsibilities of present-day man, no matter how far he may have lapsed into sin. The traditional faith of religion endeavors to sustain a *dual perspective* in relation to *dogma* and *life*. The longing for recreation cannot instantly release religion from all the concerns pertaining to creation. The new, radical religious doctrine does not exclude the old, ethical value of religion. That remains intact, for a long time. No matter how *untruthfully* faith influences the existing world, religion bids no radical farewell to a *sincere* attitude to life. To put it another way, the biblical tradition operates in *two worlds*: eschatological religious doctrine is entangled in competing with concern for the ethical regulating of life.

The eschatological perspective thus leaves room for the *law*. Nevertheless, the *promise* also serves to make this law *relative* in the wrong kind of way. That which is ethically good is insufficiently satisfying; in the final instance it is *to no avail*. The *experiencing* of futility undermines the ethical meaning of life. The question pertaining to meaning shifts more and more as it veers towards the eschatological perspective, towards redemption and the relevant final battle against evil. Tunneling away like a mole, the *doctrine* of redemption slowly erodes sacred ethical *life*. Doctrine operates like an agent of *decay*. The final upshot is that it becomes increasingly more difficult to hold together religious dogma and ethical life. Luther's eschatological *doctrine* confirms this religious decay—though, there too, the *church* again allows space for the ethical providing of *substance* to life. Does the futility of ethical meaning really leave any space for ethical life's enjoyment? This will be the central question in the next few chapters. Behind the image sketched lurks a subsequent question, a question which asks how modern atheism is able to radically take advantage of the triumphal insertion of ethical atheism into religion. It leads to the conclusion; that of the fulfillment of the promise—on the part of man himself.

6.1 THE EXODUS

In a most evocative fashion, the exodus of the people of Israel reveals the tension referred to that is perceptible in modern religion. The story of the exodus from Egypt and the prospect of the Promised Land does, in many respects, resemble the story of Abraham. One might even see it as an elaboration of the earlier narrative. Again there is an exodus, this time in the form of an escape from an oppressive, unbearable existence. Again there is an omnipotent God who has to vouch for the promise of a new and fulfilled existence. And once more, the omnipotent demands that there be *unfaltering* faith in him and in his promise.

Yet there are various things that change. In part, the Promised Land becomes Abraham's inheritance, albeit with an altered name. The promise does not require an absolute revival in all respects. The people of Israel undergo more than a mere name change and so redemption becomes, in a radical sense, also a redeeming *from*. Suddenly there is clearly evidence of a chasm between old and new, a chasm that makes it necessary to take a leap. Before the Promised Land can be entered and made suitable for the promise, it is *man* who has to change. To that end, it is not only necessary to embark on a long journey through the wilderness but the people of Egypt also have to be repressed. Old-school man must, as it were, depart from the stage; the old human identity has to be radically reviewed. There can be no Promised Land and new life without man undergoing radical change. From that point of view, the story provides a basis for the modern revolutionary process. Indeed, that is also what emerges from another aspect of the revolutionary upheaval: the aspect of unceasing unrest and perpetual progressive movement. To make such a process possible, the *God* of Israel more emphatically takes on the guise that he had already shown to Abraham: that of the omnipotent partner in the whole covenant. More than ever before, God becomes the Lord who is in charge of his people.

The story starts at a time when the people of Israel were slaves in Egypt. The people came to see the oppression as something unbearable. As soon as God notices the misery of his people, he is forced to recall his covenant with Abraham and so he decides to intervene. The covenant is revitalized. Once more the God of Israel presents himself as the God of *redemption*, but that is not where it ends. It turns out to revolve around something else, and to be more than a liberation from a state of repression. The deliverance takes on a radical significance.

Because of the desperate existence, God decides to rescue his people "from the power of Egypt, and to bring them up out of that country into a fine, broad land . . . a land flowing with milk and honey" (Exod 3:8). Ultimately, the rescuing amounts to something more than simply putting an end to repression. It is not so much about giving the people *autonomy* or independence in a political or ethical sense. In Egypt, there is no evidence of an equal administering justice, nor is there such a thing as autonomous ethical identity elsewhere. What is much more readily of central significance is having a *good* country and a *good* life. Moses is given the task of guiding the people through the process of redemption. It becomes his duty to free the people from all their misery and lead them to a country where they will have a good life. God connects with his people and that is confirmed by the covenant with a utopian *future* perspective. Once again it is a covenant with that which is good in the form of a promise. Again there is the *time dimension* that radically divides good and evil, now also in terms of historical time. If man is to enjoy a new life then the old existence will have to be relinquished.

Such radical reform does, however, give rise to one big *problem*. Do the people want that which has been promised? Are they really prepared to give up everything in exchange for this new existence? Are these people able to bridge the gap between that which exists and that which has been promised? Are they truly aware of the promised salvation? Do the people really want such salvation? Do they really want to undertake the journey to the Promised Land? In this connection what is important is the fact that the effect of the promise is, in the first instance, *negative*. The promise leads to a situation in which the distance from the present existence is only magnified. But that is also the purpose of the promise. In other words, the promised salvation casts an extra dark shadow over the given situation. God's promise of salvation and the prospect he offers of a future *good* life, are things that contrast sharply with the *evil* of the given reality. The promise accentuates the experiencing of the world of repression and shortcomings as well as the imperfection of existence. But is it sufficient to activate the people?

Such a radical turnabout of events in human existence demands a great deal from man. If they really want to go ahead with the exodus, the Israelites will have to be prepared to withstand the many moments of hardship during their journey to the Promised Land. Are the people of Israel sufficiently aware of the *meaning* of the promise? Or, to put it another way, is the intensity of their misery enough for them to want to radically *say farewell* to their old existence? Does the misery provide grounds enough for an unshakable belief in what is yet to come, and is there, indeed, sufficient faith in omnipotent God who has to guarantee this? The necessity of the departure from the present life and from its evil must therefore be *radically* appreciated. Man has to be severed from his old roots. The *belief* in the good of future existence should not really give rise to any uncertainty whatsoever and that is also something that God beseeches of man. The promise therefore confronts the people with the radical divide between salvation and ruin, between good and evil. The promise is unfathomable; it creates a radical breach between past and future. There is no way back: that, at least, must be clear before the exodus can commence. That is the end to which evil, the misery of existence as it is, must be lived through to its full potential.

God thus examines the way in which *exaggeration* works. Accentuating the misery must, of necessity, lead to *estrangement*. The exaggerating of misery must evoke an experience, one that—in later times—will similarly be adopted by the romantic, Marxist, and existentialist movements to justify their respective causes. Not only must the existing situation be found to be negative, it must also be experienced as unbearably *evil*. It is to that end that God intervenes. He intervenes in the status quo. He piles on the actual pressure, makes things even more oppressive. To convince the Israelites of the necessity and purpose of their exodus, their existence is made even more arduous: in the short-term there is more repression, in the short-term there is an increasing of the suffering, an intensifying of the evil.

The inherent evil of present existence has to be experienced in its *totality*. It therefore has to be devoid of everything that is relative. The presence of so much evil makes reconciliation with existence impossible. Such a kind of existence is no longer bearable. The way in which God gives substance to *exaggeration* has another curious side to it. Evil can only be experienced as irreconcilable if it does not strike man as being *fateful*. This means that it may not come across as being natural, as being a kind of destiny derived from a natural source. Indeed, if that were so, man might become resigned to the situation and acquiescent, so there, too, exaggeration intervenes. It must become clear that evil has *human* origins. It can be blamed upon someone; a finger may be pointed at a guilty party. This, in turn, makes it possible to translate good and evil into the good and the evil, into culprits and victims, into the oppressors and those who are the chosen ones. Exaggeration must make it unmistakably clear that concealed behind the misery is a *perpetrator* upon whom all the blame can be pinned. The people must realize that the exodus serves to deliver them from a perpetrator and from the evil that he has caused. But that is not where it stops. If the road back is to be completely cut off, it must be made impossible for the perpetrator to still turn to the victim. The separation of the two must be absolute and radical, above all else in the interests of the victim. All that is relative in the relationship between the wrongdoer and the victim must be eradicated. To that end, exaggeration creates a *malicious* guise in the form of Pharaoh, who is portrayed as a deliberately resentful wrongdoer. The malice is subsequently transferred to the victims. Among those who have been repressed this must cultivate so much *resentment* that they must yearn to be freed forever from the wrongdoers, from those who have been responsible for such an unbearable existence.

This aspect of metaphorical exaggeration also somehow anticipates later radical revolutionary tendencies. To seal off the road of return, even Marx posits that human misery must somehow be channeled into a *victims'* category, in much the same way that criminality has to be attributed to an unmistakably apparent and recognizable oppressor. Only that will activate a decisive longing for redemption, only that will reinforce the belief that there is no other road to be followed than that of the exodus. Lived through oppression must be backed up by the identifying of an unmistakably guilty *perpetrator* who carries all the blame. Hence the reason that God informs Moses that Pharaoh will not simply let go of his people, not of his own accord. What remains curious in all of this is that the hardening of Pharaoh is something that is instigated by God himself. He, the redeemer, needs to have a guilty party from whom the victim seeks to be freed. The perpetually active hand of God himself is therefore needed. God it is who shall harden the heart of Pharaoh "and he will not let the people go" (Exod 4:21). That is why Pharaoh will not listen to Moses (Exod 7:4, 13); he is *not allowed* to listen. It is this hardened attitude that also prevents Pharaoh from springing into action. He refuses to let the people go and reacts by showing harshness. He saddles his people with an unbearable kind of repression.

The "game" of harshness and non-acceptance has a deeper kind of significance. It amounts to more than just the reinforcement of an acute longing for redemption. Such yearning must take a radical hold on man. The road back must, as it were, be *internally* cut off. The exaggerated misery must direct human will. The will must become creative, culminating in a determined *no* to the existing situation. Only an inner, thoroughly experienced, "no" cuts off the road back. In order to realize this "no" the exaggeration has to radiate in two directions. On the one hand the people will be subjected to unbearable repression, while on the other hand Pharaoh will bear witness to a series of plagues that will, for the time being, harden his heart. The contrast between perpetrator and victim is pumped up to the limit. On both sides it is not only estrangement that grows, but also a bitter, irreconcilable aversion to each other.

The plagues visited by God upon Egypt do not yet therefore serve to galvanize the Pharaoh, nor do they serve to punish him because of his hardened heart. Pharaoh *may* not take action, definitely not. The fact that the plagues will help him to gain greater insight is only true in relative terms, as becomes apparent from the effect of the plagues, Pharaoh is not even given the chance to gain greater insight. With every plague rained down on Egypt by God, it is not so much Pharaoh himself who hardens his heart but rather God who manipulates this. What is the real reason for this cycle of misery and hardening? Why does the omnipotent not make Pharaoh compliant? Why does God seek the reverse? To him it is about more than the pinpointing of a demonstrable guilty party for all the misery. It may, in fact, be expected that the repression will make the people rebellious. It may be expected that they will want to free themselves from the repression and from all its root causes as speedily as possible. And it is precisely this that God forbids. He has two main reasons for that. In the first place, he wants to settle matters with the wrongdoers, with those who are indisputably guilty. To let the Egyptians know that he is the Lord, he strikes them with "mighty acts of judgment" (Exod 6:5). This is noteworthy to say the least, because, after all, it is he himself who first turns them into stubborn perpetrators! Does God himself have a need for the cycle of guilt and retaliation? Does he himself have a need for wrongdoers? Where, indeed, does the resentment begin? The other reason is that the people are not able to liberate *themselves*. He, the almighty Lord, will redeem the people. Both the Egyptians and the people of Israel will have to understand that he is the Lord.

What kind of a people are we talking about here? To whom does the redemption apply? Through the cycle of repression and intransigence, God also wants to arouse something in the people. God not only transforms the hardened repressor by changing him into a new individual but he also makes the same thing happen to the repressed people. The utter evil of repression also has a great impact on them, all in the interests of creating a specific effect. The inner cutting off of the road back and the act of redemption may not be affairs affiliated to the *old* style of person. Through exaggeration and alienation it becomes necessary to dispense with man's free will and with the yearning for self-redemption. Redemption is only something that can be bestowed upon a changed, *compliant* person, cooperative under divine guidance. The repression and the longing for redemption must also guarantee, all at once, the security of the position of God. Before that can happen, though, man has to lose his own will. The redeeming has to be placed in the hands of God and occur at his will. Hardened repression thus serves to *make* human will internally compliant. In order to support this entire process, God appoints a *servant* in the form of Moses. In him something of the messiah already becomes apparent.

The ever-harder repressing of the people has amazing consequences. Generally speaking, one negative effect of the hardened circumstances is to be seen in the less accommodating attitude of the people of Israel. The people do not listen to Moses, they become impatient (Exod 6:8). In conjunction with God's position, this situation has to be changed. To that end, hardened slavery must not so much repress as create internal *Verelendung*. Pure repressing allows the repressed to exist, albeit without freedom. That which is repressed may no longer actually exist, it must in fact change. It is all about *breaking the spirit* of the Israelites, rendering them defenseless and unresisting. For that reason they have to be even more firmly *shackled* to their own misery. It would even appear that they have been robbed of the chance to reflect on their own situation (Exod 5:9). It amounts to a complete fixation on the workload, to a perpetually frantic existence devoid of will and reason.

Pharaoh's intransigence, the *exaggerated* misère of the people and the all-embracing nature of evil serve several purposes. *Existence* as such loses all sense of purpose. More to the point, man in effect loses himself. The people undergo a complete kind of *self-estrangement*. Ultimately, it is not so much about being liberated from a cruel kind of repression as about experiencing a radical redemption. God wants to make the former type of person die before the exodus can begin. Rather than being bothered about re-creating mankind and blocking the road back to the old way of life, God is concerned about his own position. In the past he had presented himself to the patriarchs as "God the Almighty," but now he also wants to be made known to the people as "Lord." People will have to realize that it is he, the Lord, their God, who has redeemed them (Exod 6:1). People will have to come to understand that he has given them everything; people will have to make themselves dependent upon his redeeming *grace*. Exaggeration, repression, and self-estrangement: this is what must give an obedient people unconditional belief in he who makes them a promise and provides redemption. Only a total submission to God will bring them salvation.

Just how laborious the process of inner change really is for man clearly emerges from the events that follow the exodus. The long *journey through the wilderness* seems at first glance to be a kind of *passage* but in reality it is more of a continued *catharsis*, a perpetuated process of self-estrangement. The process of losing the old identity, first initiated during the period of repression, has to be completed during the course of the long journey. After the exodus it becomes ever more evident that the people are not yet ready for the promise. The fact that the old identity has not yet been completely discarded is demonstrated by the discontentment, rebellion, and doubt that are displayed. In the process, people again show too little confidence in the divine partner in that covenant. The perpetual leaning towards idolatry makes everything quite clear. The journey through the wilderness that takes many years is necessary if the process of self-estrangement is to be accomplished and a true belief in God is to be realized.

The journey through the *wilderness* must therefore not only be seen as a dreadful reality, but also as a kind of metaphor. It does not constitute a challenge and a period of testing; it is rather a setting where former man can die prior to being resurrected as a new kind of being. For Jesus, the time spent in the wilderness was very much a period of *trial and tribulation* designed to make him strong. That, at least, is also how Nietzsche later reads the metaphor: being deprived and challenged serves to steel the will. As far as the people of Israel are concerned, though, it is more about *catharsis*. Man of the past has to be dispensed with in order to facilitate a completely fresh start. The journey makes it clear just how very difficult it is for man of old to surrender to redemption and to the new life. Being delivered *to* that which is new demands redemption *from* all that is old, and man does not seem to be basically inclined to go along with that. It is in this vein of recalcitrance that the real problem resides: man has insufficient trust in the Lord. The proof emerges when the Promised Land is finally reached. The fight that the people then have to put up proves to be too much for them and so once again they are overcome by doubt and despair. They cannot conceive that the Lord will really give them that land and so they even start to yearn again for their past life of oppression in Egypt (Num 14:1).

It all once again becomes clear to God. It is essential for man of old to internally die and for the whole process of self-change to commence but that is not sufficient. Catharsis on its own, the effect of all the repression and the journey through the wilderness is not enough for the people to allow redemption to be theirs. The most important ingredient that is missing is the absolute confidence that the people have in their Lord. The people still do not really believe that he is the Lord who will give them what has been promised. The people are still not *religious* enough; they are not yet truly *willing*. He therefore leads the people into the wilderness again, for forty years and what he is waiting for is a new, compliant type of man, but this takes time. Old-style man therefore has to physically die out: it will only be his children who will be able to reap the fruits of the promise. The gaping chasm between the old and the new existence can also be applied to man himself. That which is new requires a complete break from the old with its inclination to always perpetuate itself. The new can only surface once the old type of person has *died*. The metaphor of the long trek through the wilderness thus also turns out to be an extremely harsh reality: it is that of death, of the actual dying off of what once was.

It is a process that is unthinkable without the unconditional and recognized leadership of God. The process of death and renewal is unthinkable without the unconditional *belief* of man in divine providence. It is only God who makes it possible for the other side of the chasm between the old and the new to be reached. Hence the reason that man will have to come to know and recognize that he is the Lord and then freely come to serve him. This is the conviction that dying and reborn man has to gravitate towards: without such belief man cannot receive redemption.

6.2 RETRIBUTION

We return, then, to the matter of the *ordeals* to which God subjects his people and Egypt. These trials bring into sharp focus two kinds of *divine justice*: those pertaining to punishment and to reward. The hardening of the Egyptians is followed by God's legitimate punishing of their recalcitrance. He not only wants to eradicate them as representatives of the old world, he also wants to punish them for their part in all of that and for the responsibility they hold. They fall prey to God's *avenging* justice. The kind of justice that awaits the religious ones is justice of a totally different nature, involving *mercy* and charity, provided that they accept God's position as Lord. If they fail to believe, this people runs the risk of being at the receiving end of God's wrath. God's justice is designed to lead to an uncontested recognizing and establishing of his position as the almighty architect, as Lord. It must be eminently clear that he has led the people out of the house of service with "the strength of his hand" (Exod 13:3, 9). That must be firmly engraved in the collective memory of mankind.

The exodus is designed to eliminate every possible road back. The backward-orientation is synonymous with ruin and so needs to be prevented, as must the remnants of longing that linger. The retrospective glance must serve only to trigger shock. In ancient times it was thoughts of the future that incited shock, but now that must be banished to the past. In stripping the past of all positive value, the *experiencing of time* must gain an implacable forward orientation. The evil of the old existence must incite a level of shock that is sufficient to finally banish it to the realms of an earlier and, indeed, past era. In the forward-looking direction it is therefore the prospect of a good and perfect existence that beckons. The new time perspective is thus distinctly *linear*. All that therefore merely beckons, in contrast to the severed past, is the way ahead and the prospect of a favorable existence. The *certainty* of what is still to come—of what in other words does not yet exist but is only promised—does demand unshakable belief. There is, however, something quite paradoxical in all of this. The future perspective not only forces people to believe in what God has promised but also in God himself, as the omnipotent one. The strange paradox is this: the people that has been *freed* from alien powers once again has to *subject* itself, this time to an omnipotence, while simultaneously remaining faithful and compliant. What succeeds the *loss* of the old-style man, who has been subjected to tradition and slavery, is the *regaining* of a new kind of man who comes *under* the omnipotence of God. How truly liberated and redeemed is man beneath such omnipotence? After all, it is about an unconditional and willing kind of submission! The price that has to be paid for the redeeming God and for his promise is great indeed. But does faith really deliver man from God's avenging justice?

It has already been asserted that the omnipotent one is the God of justice. Such justice reaches out in two directions and has its own time perspective, extending forward and backward and embracing redemption *to* and deliverance *from*. The forward-oriented kind of redemption thus has a reverse side. It forces one to dispense with everything that might distract one from the promise, with the *powers* that bind people to what exists and with all that is engineered by these powers. The God of justice therefore has to liberate himself *from* all that may challenge his power, in other words he must *undo* whatever threatens to oppose his power. The plagues preceding the exodus are not sufficient to achieve that. It is ultimately justice that determines the final fate of the Egyptians, even after the exodus.

It is not enough to just defeat the backward-working forces. *Justice* also has to be done to such forces. But why should that be so? Because in the eyes of almighty God they should not really have been allowed to exist in the first place. The mere fact that they exist is a blemish upon God's omnipotence. The mere fact that God is unable to deny that such hostile powers exist is a provocation in itself. What is worse is that in his omnipotence he is unable to forget the mocking and vexing nature of these forces.

Hence the reason that he needs to go back and contemplate what was effected by these powers, he needs to look at what was. This answers the question posed earlier, which asked where resentment really begins: we now see that omnipotent God himself also suffers from resentment. He is unable to forget what the forces did that tormented him. That is why he seeks retribution, compensating *revenge*. Avenging the enemy must not only dissipate his power, it must also render his deeds undone.

The true justifying of revenge lies in the safeguarding of omnipotence. Revenge does not therefore so much avenge the deed as the wrongdoer. Revenge thus undergoes an *ad homoniem* metamorphosis. It is not enough to defeat Pharaoh and strip him of his power. The Egyptians in fact *embody* evil in their deeds; as *individuals* they are therefore *declared guilty* and are punished. The hardening of Pharaoh's heart must therefore also justify God's revenge. Pharaoh stands for a crime, committed not so much against the Israelites as against him in his capacity as omnipotent God. If the *crime* is to be avenged then the *criminal* must be dealt with. Omnipotent God is relentlessly *reminded* about what *has come to pass*. This means that he does not have a moment's peace. It is a curious image: whilst the people are forced to fix their gaze on what lies ahead he himself remains imprisoned in the retrospective glance. This forces him to seek a solution or answer in hindsight in an endeavor to *still* redeem himself from the troubling memory. But all to no avail because the memory will not disappear!

What is perhaps most striking about such avenging justice is the fact that it all has to do with a reaction to the intransigence that God himself brings to bear in Pharaoh. The conclusion is thus that creative resentment actually *gives rise* to such perpetrators. The hardening process—together with the subsequent reaction—demonstrates how the guilty are created, the only justification for that being to confirm God's position. In "hardening" the Egyptians and "exalting" them in the eyes of the hardened Pharaoh, the Egyptians will discover in no uncertain terms that he is Lord (Exod 14:17). Through this *exaltation* on the basis of the powerful action of the Lord, even the people of Israel come to fear and believe him (Exod 14:31). Resentment destroys benevolence, it recognizes no other but sees only itself and goes on to seek its own recognition at the expense of the other.

Everything therefore converges: God's justice as a struggle for redemption, omnipotence, and the self-exaltation of God, the universal recognition of his exaltedness, the inevitable pursuing of the exodus and the belief in God and his promise. God's covenant is through and through hierarchical; nothing remains reciprocal. Doubt and discussion are excluded. There is not even any *considering* of the promise like in the time of Abraham; that is out of the question. The promise is now *fulfilled*. The promise becomes a matter of God's unconditional decisiveness. In the case of Abraham, the covenant was more or less imposed by God. Now the position of the partner in the covenant is marginalized yet further. The partner, the people chosen by God, is merely required to follow: without questioning, without any own freedom of will and in obedient recognition of the omnipotent Lord. The partner in the covenant is the people who have been *made* submissive. Any invasion of this submissiveness or doubt concerning the exact intentions of the Lord will lead to retaliation. Even the covenant gives rise to hostility.

That is what makes the promise of redemption so frightening. With the promise, the other side of the coin is bitter enmity. In order to make his promise come true, the omnipotent not only needs to be exalted, but he also has liberated himself from what opposes his omnipotence and what pursues him. The fate of the Pharaoh shows just where omnipotence can lead. It is a destiny that can also befall the chosen people as was illustrated when the people bowed before the golden calf after the exodus. Embittered God ascertains that this people is more obstinate than he had thought. He thus becomes enraged and wants to destroy the image. It is only with great difficulty that he is kept from doing this. The *unfathomable* division between good and evil and between past and future has disastrous consequences. Everything that is relative disappears, including in the covenant. What is so fatal is that such a total subordination of the people does not really make them submissive, but sooner unresisting and therefore uncontrolled (Exod 32:25). On the other hand, the omnipotent lapses into arbitrariness. On both sides the sense of the relative disappears, as does moderation, balance, and the capacity for self-control. Time and again the omnipotent Lord expects too much faithful steadfastness and submissiveness from his people, and time and again he is disappointed. Time and again he threatens the wavering people with retaliation and destruction. He becomes entangled in the fatal consequences of the omnipotence to which he aspires. His position as Lord is not only at odds with the traditional equality between God and man but it also makes it impossible for him to interact with man in a balanced way. The covenant demands to have a person who has relinquished what is *human*. The God of this covenant still speaks of forgiveness but does not really grant this to mankind (Num 14:20). He is not able to react benevolently to what is evil in his eyes. He does not compensate for the evil, does not react to it with good but reacts rather with evil.

6.3 THE ETHICAL REMAINDER

Does God therefore turn away from his old *ethical* qualities once and for all? Is the ethical fulfilling of existence now a thing of the past, just like the accompanying discrimination between good and evil? And is the eradicating of the evil forces sufficient for the exaltation of him, the omnipotent one? It is not quite that simple. The destroying of the evil forces seems to open up the *way* to what has been promised, but in reality that is not how the promise can be fulfilled. When it comes to the matter of fulfillment it is not an easy question, and that is not simply because the road to the Promised Land is a long one. The matter is complicated by the fact that the people prove to be *stubborn*, even after having been liberated from oppression. The exodus and the long journey through the wilderness do, in effect, reveal something of the messianic conflict to come. Such a struggle is inevitable; it is born of necessity. A people that has been *estranged* from its old core may, in a certain sense, be freed *from* its captivity, *from* the dark forces that kept it shackled. This is certainly not just a liberating *for* the good life. The world that has to be conquered is far away, the journey there long and man is not always compliant. God has not yet been really exalted by his people.

During the journey, the first thing that happens is that the liberated people can hardly be kept in order. There is constant chaos and disorder. Each time there is a setback, the people not only start to grumble but they verge on reverting to longing again for the repression from which they have been freed. Any thankfulness that is shown is extremely short-lived. The belief in what has been promised is just as fragile as the confidence in the God of the covenant. The authority of the omnipotent proves not to have been randomly established. Even when God ventures to initiate a welfare state, when he provides food enough for everyone in line with the utopian ideal of meeting each individual's needs (Exod 16:21), the dissatisfaction remains. It is all crystal clear: a freed and disoriented people is "uncontrolled," it lives stubbornly in "great guilt" (Exod 32:22). Here the following words of Rousseau spring to mind: "how would a blind multitude, which often knows not what it wishes because it rarely knows what is good for it, execute of itself an enterprise so great, so difficult, as a system of legislation?"[1] Since the people of Israel, with all its willingness, still has to learn to discover what it wants, the need for a *lawgiver* also comes to the fore with this group. Or, to put it another way, the people do not spontaneously adhere to God's promise; they do not seek out what is good of their own volition. For the time being, there is a substantial need for leadership and order.

Hence the reason that God intervenes in what, for all intents and purposes, is a traditional fashion. In the first place, the people are given a legal system. Only the major issues—the terrain that still has to be covered by the people and the work that still has to be done—are left directly to God whilst leaders are appointed for the maintaining of order in the general sense (Exod 18:19). That is how God creates order from the general chaos. In the process he gives the people, via Moses, a legal structure in the form of the Ten Commandments and the many accompanying rules. People have been severed from the order from which they derive and there is no road that leads back. Regardless of the fact that they are on their way to the Promised Land, things cannot be achieved without an obligatory ethical order. The law of the Lord has to endorse belief in him.

But can God restore his *traditional* ethical qualities in this way? Is it not, once again, all about the ethical differentiation between good and evil, is it not about an

1. Rousseau, *Social Contract or Principles*.

enduring ethical order and a society of people? And then we come to the crucial question: does the people find meaning and *essential life's fulfillment* in such an ethical kind of life? These are questions that need to be answered. When it comes to the introduction of the Ten Commandments, this is preceded by an impressive manifestation on the part of God (Exod 19:3). He asserts himself in a way that befits his omnipotence, as one who is indeed *awe-inspiring*. In an overwhelming fashion, he conveys to the people that they must listen to him and keep *his* covenant. *His* covenant: once more we are reminded that there is no equality here between God and man. What ensues only serves to reinforce this observation. If the people carefully listen to him and adhere to his covenant then eventually, on the part of all peoples, they will become his *property* because the entire world belongs to him. The distance between God and man becomes immeasurable; the inequality complete. There is no longer any talk of *walking with God*. In effect, God has a free hand throughout the entire world and concerning all of mankind. It is only the recognition of that situation that gives the people of Israel an exclusive position within God's covenant. That explains why the commandments are accompanied by a certain *fear* of God (Exod 20:20); it is not *authority* but enforced *devotion* and a meek acknowledgement of the uniqueness of that one God. Devotion instead of authority: the omnipotent is also sometimes termed awe-inspiring. Small wonder that God manifests himself as an *envious* God who will strictly *maintain* the observance of his status. Only within the rigid framework of devotion and through the firm maintaining of power will the ethical rules of the Ten Commandments come into their own, like rules relating to ordered human relationships.

More to the point, the commandments and precepts would appear to have eternal and intrinsic value. They are actually embedded in a higher order value: that of the covenant between God and his people. Within this covenant, the commandments turn out to be a *condition* for the entering of the Promised Land. This not only tells us something about the ethical value of the commandments themselves but also about the position of the omnipotent. It is the subordination required by God that stands at the forefront, subordination that is given an ethical *form*, but this does not mean to say that observing God's commandments has true ethical *meaning*. That would lend the *good* of the Promised Land and a fulfilled life a relative kind of character. In such a case one would also find a certain life's fulfillment in the good of the ethical commandments. That, in turn, would give the commandments a value in themselves, an intrinsic, ethical value. Then, in both word and *deed*, the people would gain pleasure from *doing* ethical good and from leaving behind evil. At such a stage, organized society would become meaningful in itself.

It is precisely this latter point that really proves to be extremely relative. Not only of lesser *value* than the promised good life, ethical good remains at the same time subordinate to another even higher value, that of serving God. Above all else, ethical good is a *basic requirement* for the highest good, the submission to a jealous God: that is where ethical life finds its true meaning. The ethical sins of the people do not in the first place lead to the disruption of society; they represent more the challenging of God and the transgressing of his covenant. That is why after the trespass with the golden calf there is no *action* on the part of God that is aimed at maintaining ethical order: he *reacts* with wrath and threatens to destroy the people. A *jealous* God must become reactive. It then becomes difficult for him to honor his own covenant; it is only with difficulty that he is prevented from wasting and destroying his own people (Exod 33:3). The fact that God keeps to his covenant is nothing other than an expression of mercy (Exod 33:13). When the covenant is reinstated it is, in the first place, the position of God that is reinstated "for the Lord's name is the Jealous God" (Exod 34:14).

On the basis of that ruling value, space is allowed for yet another similarly *false meaning* concerning the upholding of the commandments. God promises, namely, to perform miracles, "as have never been performed in all the world or in any nation. All the surrounding peoples shall see the work of the Lord, for fearful is that which I will do for you" (Exod 34:10). Yet again, the upholding of the commandments, on the part of the people, turns out to have no inherent meaning. The true purpose is to show respect for omnipotent God; upon that hinges not only his promise of wealth for the people but also the awe-inspiring effect of the driving out of peoples, of the evacuating of the Promised Land (Exod 34:24).

The promise of fulfillment is once again reiterated before the people enter the Promised Land. Obedience to God is *rewarded*, whereas disobedience is met with *damnation* and with the threat of destruction. Obedience is rewarded with the chance to enter into and occupy the Promised Land and with the prospect of being able to lead a life that is blessed (Deut 11:8). If the loving of God is rewarded, all failure to sustain that will make the jealous one irate (Deut 11:13). "Understand that this day I offer you the choice of a blessing and a curse. The blessing will come if you listen to the commandments of the Lord your God which I give you this day, and the curse if you do not listen to the commandments of the Lord your God but turn aside from the way that I command you this day" (Deut 11:26). A covenant full of promise is ratified with the threat of damnation (Deut 29:14). The jealousy of God is perpetually palpable. The jealous one continually issues threats which are accompanied by fury and cursing. As far as God is concerned, the *greatest good* consists in the subjugation of the people, from the inner, totally experienced recognition of his omnipotent position. Only when the people prove to be subservient to that God will the own *good* come into the picture: the blessing of reward (Deut 30). This perspective reflects the tainting of the real ethical meaning of the commandments. Their only purpose is to see the fulfillment of God's enterprise.

6   Moses: Between Law and Promise

Everything that the God of Abraham revealed is repeated, despite the fact that the *deed* is now also added to the word of the promise. God is starting to make *true* or substantiate his promise. It is true that the promised good life cannot be realized if there is no ethical order, ethical good offers no fulfillment in itself. The fact that the omnipotent presents the people with the prospect of an awe-inspiring miracle helps to justify the utter subjugation that is required to him thus, as it were, redressing all else. Ethical subjugation is already given *ideological justification*. Small wonder that not only the people, but also the jealous God himself gains little joy from the ethical commandments that he has imposed. He definitely realizes that the enticing blessings fall short; that the commandments evoke *aversion* and that it will sooner be the threat of punishment that will make the people bend to the commandments than anything else. This makes him embittered in advance. The punishing of transgressions seems to draw more attention than the keeping of the promise.

Not *being able to* observe the commandments is, to start off with, already a blemish upon *wanting to* observe them. Even before anything else happens the moral will of the people has been too provoked to still be able to provide any joy. The ethical leanings of the people are pre-emptively overshadowed by the rigid upholding of the commandments, and, indeed, if the ethical life offers no own life's fulfillment then there is no alternative. Man therefore lives trapped between subserviently serving God and longing for a reward for such service. It is that double clamping action that ruins the ethical orientation of man: why should he cheerfully submit to an ordered life if the iniquity is ultimately too strong and, on top of that, if this order is not meaningful?

The stringency and inflexibility of the commandments imposed by God has yet another extremely disheartening effect: they *make* man sinful. They must make man so convinced of his sinful existence that he comes to feel completely *dependent* upon the grace of God. It is not really about concrete sins, about evil emerging from identifiable deeds; indeed such evil could be countered by the desire to do good and by actually doing good. Now it is the doom arising from another form of evil that gains the upper hand in relation to the total *sinfulness* of man: the incapacity to even *want* to do good let alone *be able* to do good. The *significance* of the ethical differentiation between good and evil is supplanted by the fatal *madness* of the whole *anger* of the human state. The whole existence is permeated with evil, however one might interpret that. This means that man is, by definition, placed at the mercy of God's justice. It therefore also means that the Promised Land comes to stand in a strange perspective: that of needing to be delivered on the basis of sheer *mercy*, it is deliverance engineered by a God who has complete and utter control over man.

Does this God truly love? When he is not threatening to destroy or to bring damnation he merely shows his clemency and such *mercy* amounts to a punishment that has not been cashed. But he can only show mercy if he himself is redeemed from his unabating burning *jealousy*. This, then, is the destiny of a God who tolerates no *equals* in his presence, be they other gods or man himself. It may be the case that he sees to it that man is placed *under* the great order to love, but this is a one-sided kind of love directed *towards* him, a kind of love couched in the falsity of form, of fear, of awe (Deut 6:13). God's order to *love* is also fed by an unceasing envy; the envy persists *obsessively* in the love. He is incapable of forgetting anything, which is why he demands that people do not forget him for a single second (Deut 8:11). The jealousy of the omnipotent and the omniscient makes it impossible for him to *forget* any last detail of what sinful man thinks and does. The fact that recalcitrant man does not leave him in peace for a minute is also to be blamed on him: for that matter he does not even allow himself a minute's peace. How can a God, who is unable to experience any joy in himself, be expected to gain any enjoyment from man? Both the omnipotence and the omniscience are disastrous for God and man.

The God of Abraham and Moses provides the impetus for a new phase in history, the era of *ethical atheism*. The image of this God puts an end to the equality between God and man as far as ethical life goes. Good and evil gain a dimension that is diametrically opposed to that inherent in the old ethical meaning; it is a dimension that hollows out ethical life. A new history is embarked upon that is, above all else, characterized by the unfathomable and which has to do with the inequality of God and man, of gods amongst themselves, of peoples amongst themselves, of past and future, of existence as it is, and of longed-for fulfillment. Ethical good can survive without having to long for a completely different life, without the need for an exodus and promising horizons. It is ethical atheism that ruins such meaning.

How drastic is this ruin? How pathetic does the belief that accompanies this atheism become? How much imagination does it spawn? It is imagination that gives rise to the illusion that the story of creation can be reversed. Amid all the expectations for the future and all the hope, man searches to find the road that leads back to a paradisiacal existence. Though the old God has forbidden it, man wants to eat from the tree of *life* and dwell in *eternity*. The apocalyptic pathos seeks to undo what, in *his* goodness, the God of creation had given man. What then becomes apparent is how *godforsaken* the world, as it is turns out to be, really is. The fateful facet of justice is then given free rein. Messianic longings take control of man.

7

Paul's Zeal

In the doctrine of Paul, the apocalyptic image of the age was overpowering. Any attention that might otherwise have been devoted to ethical matters was overshadowed by a sharp awareness of the futility of ethical life. There dwelt in him the conviction that this earthly existence is temporary. Life on earth was seen as a mere phase, as an affair that would speedily draw to a close. Man would inevitably testify to the final departure from this existence. The old world and the old life would cease to be. But why? Or undoubtedly more to the point: what would give rise to that? It would all be attributable to man of old lapsing into *sinfulness* and it would be because—with such people—the world itself would come to be governed by *evil*. The *Fall* was seen as the cause of such ruin and so human existence was also thought to be characterized by decline, a factor borne out by the final phase that was meanwhile underway.

The passing of that which was old was no fateful occurrence, but rather something integral to God's justice, a kind of divine *act*, a *fulfilling* of the ancient promise. God will intervene in order to again give man and creation some kind of prospect. Within the foreseeable future, everything that had been promised would be fulfilled. Paul's view of the existing world was clouded by an all-eclipsing prejudice. The image that the human world was dark and futile colored the view of the entire cosmos: it was a world that was not worthy enough to exist, the true and good had to be sought elsewhere. All that existed could only be tolerated in the light of the redemption to come.

The vigorous belief of Paul was radical and capable of instigating unbridled zeal. Incidentally, this was not the zeal of a zealot. He did not convert his assiduousness into political or social action. His zeal was displayed in the proclamation, in the spreading of the belief in the God of judgment. The number that could possibly be saved through a belief in this intervention of God's and through their belief in God had to be as great as possible. Indeed, perhaps such successful proclamation would even bring the end of time even closer. This vision of faith therefore spurred him on to reach all the peoples of the world as quickly as possible. It was no longer a matter of having a chosen people, nor was it about a promised earthly resting place or finding fulfillment in this terrestrial life. It was now about the chosen sector of *humanity*, selected for a totally different and liberated life. Beyond that all was lost.

7.1 THE BELIEF IN EVIL

Meanwhile, all that one could do was wait for the decisive *contest* between God and the powers of evil. In that struggle it would not only be creation—which had succumbed to evil—that would be destroyed, but judgment would furthermore be cast upon the contingent of mankind that had been lost. The exodus was thus seen as a redemption *from* depraved existence and as a deliverance of the chosen ones *to* an eternal life. This not only represented a rift with the eschatological expectations detailed in the Old Testament, the prophets included, but once again a breaking away from the realism of the story of creation. After the Fall, the prospect of eternal life was something that God did actually want to rule out.

There was hardly any longer any real ethical interest in concrete sins. Human sinfulness, the fatal tyranny of evil over everything and everyone, had now come to completely dominate belief. What had then also become crucial to salvation was the *belief* in the sinfulness of man, the recognized and fully experienced awareness of that. This awareness did not, however, prevent Paul from mounting an attack upon concrete, identified sins. It was a battle that Paul really did urge people to engage in. The real crux of the matter, though, was that such a struggle had precious little impact upon the decline into sinfulness and ruin. The crusade against sins was therefore deemed *futile*. In conjunction with the utter depravity, the departure from existence had to be radical and complete. It was something that had to do with the entire creation, with all of humanity and with the whole of mankind.

Following the exodus from a transient and *futile* existence it was a completely different, *spiritualized* existence that was to make its entrance. In the process, Paul thus explicitly distanced himself from human existence and from the story of creation. He referred to Adam, the *first* human being, as being worldly and tangible, thus transient and mortal; the second type of human being that was still to come, the new Adam, would be divine, spiritual, immortal, and everlasting (1 Cor 15:42). Hence the reason that Paul reverted to the tree of life, to the tree from which the previous God had forbidden people to eat. Again, we have to remind ourselves that belief did now carry the promise of eternal life.

7 Paul's Zeal

His God of eternal life was not therefore the *same* God as the one of the past, the one who made an ethical differentiation between good and evil. Similarly his God was not man's *equal*. The new God was not so devoted to separating good and evil from each other in an ethical sense. His God differentiated between good and evil on the grounds of their fathomless contrast. That which was differentiable was utterly rent asunder: all that remained was the division between what had to be *lost* and what could be *preserved*, albeit in a totally different form. God was a party to the radical contrast between good and evil. The totally good God rose above the powers of the comparably equal total evil that was so distasteful to him. This radical contrast is then conveyed to man in order to separate those who are destined to be lost from those who may be preserved in faith and mercy. In eliminating the ethical significance, it no longer remains possible to bring together good and evil as differentiating factors. In terms of *time*, the sharp contrast will also lead to a radical division, just like the transient, time preceding judgment as opposed to the eternity that ensues. The futility of ethical life is represented in the radical divide between good and evil, between the chosen and the lost, and between the future and the past.

Paul's limited interest in ethical matters and in the whole issue of ethical order not only emerges from the relative value that the handed-down rules, laws, and commandments have for him but, above all else, from the appreciation that he has for *Jesus*. The fact that he never actually knew Jesus is of secondary importance. What is crucial is the extremely minimal interest he attaches to the morality proclaimed by Jesus and upheld for mankind by the way he lived. Jesus' lifestyle and principles remain virtually out of the picture, they do not enter into what amounts to Paul's doctrine. This corresponds to his convictions concerning the futility of ethical life. What remains of Jesus is the echo of the Christ who was crucified, who died and was resurrected. What remains is the fact that he *died* because of man's sinfulness and the *belief* in his resurrection in conjunction with eternal life. This image of Jesus forms the model for man, for humanity, for creation. This Jesus is exemplary for man in a very different way than from an ethical *life*. This Jesus shows man the way through redeeming death and resurrection. The *new* life is not one of ethical introspection but rather an existential resurrection. For the man of *old*, Paul has but one message, one *doctrine*. His creed orders man to believe in the evil of sinfulness and in judgment, to believe in being redeemed *from* depravity and in being delivered *into* eternal life. His teaching commands a belief in the God who will cast judgment upon man and in whose hands salvation will lie. His doctrine demands that there be faith and attaches to that salvation the notion that without faith there can be no salvation. The *doctrine* of belief is invested with infinitely higher value than ethical *life*.

The appeal that Paul makes to ethical correctness is thus merely of relative value. It is ethical life that binds the community of believers together during their earthly existence, but it has no intrinsic meaning. It is the decay of sinfulness that makes it futile. The law and the keeping of the law is something that cannot save man: the sinfulness is too great, the evil too overpowering, God's wrath too full of fury. Man of old and the creation of old *must* therefore face destruction. Once again, the fact that this must happen is no disaster, it is simply included in God's justice. The intervention of God tolerates no doubt: it is totally integral to his providence.

Beneath the belief in redemption, therefore, lies the belief in the inevitable sinfulness of man. This is what gives *belief* a dual orientation: that in the direction of an existence *from which* one has to be redeemed, alongside that of a future life *to which* one has to find deliverance. It is belief that makes it crystal clear that this world, this type of person, this old-style Adam cannot be saved. That which was once molded in the likeness of God changes into a sinful and lost Adam, a God that is absolutely not equal. Belief places everything that exists, man and the world, at the mercy of a *categorical* moralizing judgment, a judgment that is actually presented as reality itself: the reality of the evil that is present everywhere.

One is once more reminded of the moralizing nature of this judgment. Ethical judgment gives direction to a person's will and deeds: it points ahead. A moralizing kind of judgment is retrospective: it allows an appreciation of the reality that has to be discovered to go ahead. Such judgment ruins the purpose of truth. In fact, moralizing judgment sees evil as something that exists, as an objective fact, as an essential feature of what is. Such judgment rests on the *belief* in the worth of the verity of this judgment. This belief makes moralizing judgment true beforehand. In effect, cognitive insight is made redundant. Even knowledge is dangerous in conjunction with the tenability of this judgment: it may actually only be confirmed. It is therefore only possible to believe in an unconditional type of judgment. Belief is not just directed in a *forward* direction, towards the anticipated salvation, it also has a *backward*-oriented facet in which the existing evil is *condemned*.

The moralizing belief turns itself against the old Adam of self-knowledge and ethical differentiation; this sort of belief also turns away from its God. The ethical God cannot be saved, he is lost or, more to the point, he is damned. Paul's God is the omnipotent one who wants everything to submit to him. In all that resists him he sees enemies that have to be destroyed. He is the God that wants to be everything to everyone (1 Cor 15:28) and so will intervene in creation to that end. With complete devotion, Paul testifies to the *apocalyptic* vision that predicts the imminent downfall of the world, the coming of the messianic kingdom and the ultimate kingdom of God. What was for Moses the *exodus* of the *people* of Israel from the *land* known as Egypt has become for Paul the marking of the *end* of *mankind*, a universal extinction. This death leads not so much to the entering of a similarly promised *land*; this death must make it possible for a new kind of *man* to enter into a new kind of *life* and a new *reality*. The new existence is totally devoted to the glorifying of God. It is related to the glorifying of the omnipotent, whom shall ultimately have dominion over all rule, power, and control. The thirst for power gains an apocalyptic dimension and is allied to a final struggle, to a final contest that must reward the omnipotent with a final victory.

7.2 THE FINAL CONTEST

Paul's apocalyptic vision was messianic. He awaited the coming of the Messiah by way of preparation for God's final intervention in the path of history. Such kind of vision spawns human devotees. Like so many others who have adhered to the apocalyptic perspective, he was not inclined to leave this Messianism solely in the hands of the coming Messiah, he also allowed it to pertain to himself. God intended that this special task would also partly be his responsibility. His position in world history was therefore indeed unique; he was one of God's *chosen* ones, if not *the* chosen one. Once again there was belief, now in an own decisive duty, an own position at a crossroads, at a juncture between ruin and salvation. He had to announce and warn. He was expected to save what could still be saved before it was too late. He called himself a *zealot*, a person with pathos, with the passion that was so characteristic of zealots. Up until the time of his conversion, Paul was described as a "fanatical devotee" of the ancestral tradition (Gal 1:14). He was thus subservient to the God of the law, to the traditional ethical order, and he subsequently devoted himself with "the zeal of God" (2 Cor 11:2) to his new vocation.

Zealots know no middle course, no compromise, no balance, and they find no rest. They are not, in themselves, able to provide any kind of standard. In their enthusiasm they lose themselves in extreme views about what is true and untrue, about what is good and evil. Their fanaticism prevents them from leaving their fellow humans in peace. Their views on any matters instantly extend to their views about mankind. Opinions about anything are also directed at people and a negative opinion inevitably leads to condemnation. The verdict is dominated by aversion and so seeks culprits; the complaint is translated into an *accusation*. The opponent becomes an *enemy* that needs to be rigorously combated. No judgment without *exaggeration*: it is always a matter of all or nothing. Exaggeration tolerates no restraint. Whether the zeal is channeled into the proclamation of a belief or into political action, the essence is that it remains a type of activism that is directed towards or, more precisely, *against* someone. The zealot may maintain that such activism will ultimately lead to something or will benefit somebody, but the initial impulse remains destructive rather than creative. The fanaticism of the zealot is reactive. The zealot lacks the capacity, though, to react sympathetically to challenges. With Paul, the opinion about good and evil thus permeates to the struggle between the good and the evil.

He did not, however, maintain that he was speaking for himself, but rather on behalf of a higher power. Paul testifies at God's behest. In other words, his assiduousness formed part of his service to the omnipotent and to the coming of his kingdom.

The fact that he wishes to leave the final judgment to the Messiah and to God does not conceal the great danger that lurks in this zeal. *Overzealous* activists are only too easily tempted to take the law into their own hands. Does the zeal of Paul therefore cast a shadow ahead in anticipation of the activism of the deeds of Marx?

This thirst for zeal also explains the transformation undergone by Jesus: he becomes the long-awaited *Messiah*, the savior who contributes to the realization of the kingdom of God. It was not a name that Jesus chose for himself, it was a name that was bestowed after his death. Jesus, who was himself averse to *great stories*, gained world-historical significance as Messiah. He was to put an end to the dominion of evil, to the reign of all power external to that of God. It was the Messiah who conformed, suffering vicariously, to the notion of divine omnipotence and victory. In this respect, Jesus' death and resurrection serve as a model for an event of world-historical proportions. He was to lead that event in his role as Messiah. His death demonstrates how uncompromising God's wrath really is and how unrelenting God's justice. It was in conjunction with God's wrath about the sins of man that Jesus was required to vicariously suffer and die. This death treaty does not help to dispel the lot of those who are subject to God's final judgment. This final judgment incorporates a paradoxical component that conflicts with Jesus' doctrine of not casting *judgment*. The implication is that, as Messiah, he will come again and execute judgment over the powers of evil. Jesus, who taught others not to judge, will return to *pass judgment*, to root out evil and to target evildoers.

The judgment will not only affect God's declared enemies but all the sinful people of old. Jesus' death and resurrection also serve as a model for individual human beings. The old-style, sinning person must die. Only then will God's wrath abate and will a new and sublime life be possible. All in all, it is quite amazing. Why does the omnipotent not conquer his wrath himself? Why is there no divine justice without avenging justice? As long as man possesses an *own will*, he will remain at a certain distance from the omnipotent and God will therefore be forced to become enraged. God thus has to impose his omnipotence by conquering man. As long as man fails to unconditionally subjugate himself to God, he remains sinful.

This is where a turnaround is seen in the idea of God. There is a shift from the God of creation to omnipotent God. God's own creation, made in his *likeness*, now angers the omnipotent; man who has been created in his own image now forces God to revert to retaliation. The God of the Messiah is also a different God from that of Jesus. He does not appear to be interested in the Jesus of the ethical doctrine. The omnipotent does not hold creation and mankind dear but rather himself. The divine justice that follows the final judgment and death not only represents a victory over sinfulness but also over everything that makes man human. The new *Adam* of eternal life is no longer the flesh and blood Adam of the differentiation between good and evil. The triumph over sinfulness and death lies in the unity of those who have risen from the dead together with the omnipotent. The spiritual rebirth of the new Adam and the communion with God must establish his omnipotence once and for all.

The Messiah triumphs over Jesus. The Messiah proves the futility of Jesus' ethical doctrine. There is thus conflict and judgment instead of compassion, and mercy takes the place of forgiveness. The Messiah marks a departure from the familiar Jesus of love and forgiveness but also from a Jesus who was not only adept at forgiving people's *sins*, but who even went as far as to dispense with the paralyzing notion of man's innate *sinfulness*. The individual who rises from the dead is a different being from the one who died. The forgiving *of* concrete sins makes way for the ultimate battle *against* sinfulness. Instead of the God who propagates peace, it is now the omnipotent that emerges to descry enemies everywhere and seek conflict. This is what turns the messianic dominion into a world-historical catharsis. In terms of serving to purify sinfulness, this *catharsis* is truly an *ad hominem* turning point. The disappearance of man of old also demands that judgment be cast over all those who cannot be resurrected from sinners' deaths.

Did the death of Jesus therefore also mark the demise of his ethical doctrine? Had sinfulness prevailed over sinning? Had justice triumphed over forgiveness? There is yet another question that is prompted by Paul's letters. No matter how futile ethical life might ultimately turn out to be, he devotes plenty of attention to the keeping of the laws and commandments and to the value of love. Could this value perhaps in the end prevail over disastrous futility? In reality, what significance does Paul actually attach to the honoring of the laws and commandments?

The eschatological perspective incorporates a twofold *redemptive* interpretation. There is, on the one hand, the redeeming *from* a life steeped in sinfulness and, on the other hand, deliverance *to* eternal life. Such a prospect is only possible if the person of old dies, only to be reborn as a totally new kind of individual. This amounts to an accentuating of the former exodus. Redemption now touches all facets of the person of old. This redemption commences before the actual triumph over sinfulness and death: in fact it is bestowed upon those who become faithful in God's grace. Faith in itself, even that constitutes a kind of salvation because it represents a detachment from worldly life. Belief makes the essence of the value of the laws and commandments relative in the wrong kind of way. The *thirst for zeal* that was designed to convert man of old and make him faithful was something of much greater weight than the mere *observing* of the commandments. It is faith that is at stake; laws and commandments cannot be soul-saving.

The vanquishing of man of old is decisive for the position taken up by ethical life. Ethical life is inextricably linked to this *man of old*. It is therefore nothing other than a temporary and ultimately futile correction of a lost cause. The ethical differentiation between good and evil becomes entangled in the conflict between good and evil forces. This ethical differentiation between good and evil that was especially designed to safeguard the life of people and their living together and to help combat enmity degenerates into a battle between adverse powers. Paul's creed of salvation amounts to a ruination of the true essence of ethical life. Even before the final contest, the *religious fervor* actually in fact robs existence of all its ethical substance. His doctrine has an ethical atheistic core. The doctrine includes the recognition that ethical life is futile, brings no salvation and thus possesses no enduring inner meaning. It is not ethical life but faith that must generate good. Even worse, he who seeks the greatest good in the good of ethical life lives in sin and is therefore lost. The sinfulness of man is indicative of the futility of ethical life. It is in the very recognition of this that the ethical atheistic core of belief lies.

Old-style, ethical man dies. The death of this old Adam was a peaceful demise, it was *dignified*: he was allowed to return to dust after having lived a life that had, in ethical terms, been *fulfilling*. Such a dignified death was not the preserve of sinful man, nor was the satisfaction of a fulfilled life. But that is not where it ends. Even redeemed man has to relinquish this dignity. The evil of leading a sinful existence and the good of a redeemed life reflect each other: in both cases it is ethical atheism that triumphs, in both cases, leave has to be taken from the ethical meaning of life. The good that will fall to the redeemed amounts to the fulfilling of God's complete omnipotence. It is only that which clarifies the significance of his goodness and redemption: he is everything in everyone. This goodness is far removed from the old ethical dignity. Ethical atheism is something that is perpetuated in heaven.

7.3 THE ATHEISTIC DANGER

This, however, is not a conclusion that explains everything. The sheer weight of ethical atheism did not detract from the fact that Paul most certainly did devote attention to life's ethical dimension—temporary though the terrestrial existence remains and futile as all the ethical efforts ultimately may prove to be.

In this connection, Paul's religious doctrine contains a striking kind of modernity from the point of view that it advocates the complete and radical emancipation of man. He liberates man from the old, crushing constraints and declares that all people are, in one specific sense, *equal*. With him, universality is elevated to a higher order than that dictated by special bonds or by what is traditionally distinguishing. *As human beings* all people are equal in that they are chained to sinfulness. They are all, in principle, also equal *as human beings* from the point of view of grace and redemption, in terms of justification through faith. In that way, he cuts across the *inequality* between people justified by previous gods. He knows no chosen people, no exclusivity in relation to rank or status, be they tribal, ethnic, or national entities. He orients himself to man as such and, by extension, to mankind in general. Sinfulness and hostility towards God are not, by definition, linked to any people or groups that can be concretely identified, and therefore not to those who are predisposed to being hostile to Paul. In

7 Paul's Zeal

this respect, all are *equal* in the eyes of God and Paul (Rom 2:1–11). No man is *a priori* excluded from redemption.

This does not alter the fact that he, once again, immediately draws an unfathomable dividing line of *inequality* through the world of equals. The human population of equals is divided into two camps. The intention is to draw a dividing line between those who have seen the light and those who refuse to be converted, those who will be redeemed and those who will be lost, and finally those who benefit from God's grace and those who are condemned by him. On top of everything else, what is added to this unfathomable division is the perspective of *strife*, a contest between good and evil, a power struggle, a final contest between life and death. In that struggle, divine power and the forces of unbelief come to oppose each other. It is a struggle that divides those who are equal, making them more *unequal* than ever before. Paul's involvement with the ethical dimension of life cannot be considered in isolation of this inequality and conflict. He displays indifference towards the finite, earthly, *worldly* existence that has lapsed into sinfulness and to its ethical order. He is much sooner prepared to concentrate upon the ethical side of life within the *religious community*. There, too, the only significance attached to ethical life is that it serves to bridge the gap while waiting for the arrival of the Messiah. Ethical life therefore has no intrinsic value and meaning. In the light of sinfulness and finiteness it is all in vain: that which is really meaningful has, indeed, to be sought elsewhere.

The stage on which the sinfulness and faith battle is staged thus has far-reaching consequences for the human environment and for its ethical links. Such connections are destroyed. Those who were, in principle, equal are separated into two segments that come to be totally detached from each other: those who have been lost and await judgment as opposed to those who have been redeemed and will be rewarded with eternal life. Ethical atheism creates an irreconcilable contrast from the point of view that on either side of the dividing line everything and nothing become diametrically opposed. In temporal existence, order and balance conceal the underlying antithesis which—sooner or later—will culminate in a final struggle.

The way in which significance is attached to good and evil simply confirms this very point. The ethical *relativity* of good and evil is, in the final instance, over. The inherent danger of this has already been indicated. Good and evil disappear from the ethical orientation of man and are transferred to man himself, to his whole being. Good and evil are no longer differentiating terms for ethical actions; instead they now come to segregate people. The God responsible for such a divide demands faith from man. Instead of actual sinning, it now becomes lack of faith that elicits God's wrath and judgment. This judgment envisages no ethical adjustments to be made to evil deeds; it is rather a settling of scores with those who embody evil. Regardless of how much Paul appeals to people to live according to the laws and commandments, the unconciliatory facets of good and evil continue to predominate the worldly life of individuals. Already during their temporal life the spirits are divided.

What then awaits the lost souls is the prospect of eternal doom, but what is terrestrial life like for those awaiting redemption? How do they prepare for the coming salvation? Do they have anything other than religious fervor to fill their transience? Ethical atheism also touches on the temporal, worldly existence that remains for believers. The *existential* expectation of a fulfilled, glorified life (Rom 8:21) does not release them from their ethical obligation, but it does somewhat ruin the pursuing of any kind of ethical life's fulfillment in the *existing* world. Creation—which has succumbed to sin—and, therefore also, present time, are not only subject to suffering but also to fruitlessness (Rom 8:18). The only comfort lies in transience, in the anticipation of deliverance from the present existence. So futility and hope, once again, go hand in hand. In the light of the nearing and perhaps even accelerated end of time, it becomes pointless to work on man's earthly coexistence. The only remaining ethical thing that makes sense is that of deciding how the final era in which man lives should be spent: that is the task that rests on the shoulders of believers, and so that is why they may not transgress. The prospect of a completely new life tends to fuel the feeling that it is pointless to expect any hope in this world. It is therefore not only the wisdom *of* the world that amounts to foolishness (1 Cor 1:20), but also the wisdom *towards* this world that is foolish and futile. How is it possible to offer anything good to a *world* that has lapsed into sinfulness? If even the wise are unable to sincerely communicate with each other, if all their efforts are doomed to end in shamefulness how can others ever hope to succeed? The God of creation was able to look back on his work and benevolently, happily, and conclude that it was *good*. This goodness becomes inapplicable. The only true option that still remains is to radically and completely recreate.

The futility of this earthly existence and the dominion of evil in terms of original creation has fatal consequences for ethical life within the religious community. The fact that alongside belief everything else lacks substance makes all the laws, commandments, and precepts extremely tenuous. This not only affects the laws and commandments of the Old Testament but also those of the New Testament. No matter how much order is created, the fatal sinfulness of man cannot be cured. Just like mankind and everything that exists, ethical good can therefore be completely written off. It is a kind of fatalism that strips ethical good of its real meaning, so God's justice must be seen as something completely divorced from life's ethical purpose.

Yet despite all of this, Paul tells believers to do good and not *repay* evil with evil. Does this then have no real ethical significance? No, that is not the case: restraining from retaliating is only meaningful in a relative way. In doing good one cannot conquer the spirit of revenge. Man is given the impression that justice, thus also avenging justice, is not a matter for man but rather for God. Human good is only able to meet the demand to refrain from that to which God is entitled. "My dear friends, do not seek revenge, but leave a place for divine retribution, for there is a text which reads, 'Justice is mine says the Lord, I will repay.'" (Rom 12:19). There is ethical gain: human revenge remains out of the picture. What is awaited is divine retribution. Just how relative human restraint is emerges from the appreciation shown for the justice that the ecclesiastical authorities obtain. It is justice that reflects divinity. It has no ethical foundations but is based on revenge and retribution. Regarding the authorities ". . . it is not for nothing that they hold the power of the sword, for they are God's agents of punishment, for retribution on the offender" (Rom 13:4). Instead of constraint there is justified retribution, instead of forgiveness there is revenge. Already the *image* of God does have *exemplary* power in people's terrestrial, earthly life. Restraining from adopting an own course is not something that stands alone when it comes to the matter of the comfort of divine avenging justice. It is a type of justice that can only be hoped for.

There are, therefore, definitely laws and commandments that apply, but abiding by them has no real ethical perspective in terms of meaning. In everything, in the light of the end of time, it is the battle against the darkness of earthly existence that persists. Laws and commandments must not therefore be so much *obeyed* as *fulfilled* in a coming and eternal life (Rom 13:9). Doing ethical good in the present life serves as a preparation for the true good of later and elsewhere. What remains of ethicality can only really be said to be negatively charged within the context of faith. Belief is all about justice, it is about the staving off of God's wrath, and it is about the grace bestowed by redemption.

But what about one's *neighbors*? And the love for one's *neighbors*? Surely that is something that Paul explores in depth. Even that love provides few answers to the ethical atheism question. The purpose of loving one's neighbor is again linked to the *fulfilling* of the law (Rom 13:10). One's neighbors may receive love, but what is the use of wanting to offer a person that has become sinful anything good in *this* life? It is all about saving one's fellow man from God's wrath. Real love for one's fellow man aims to secure such salvation. Loving one's fellow man should stimulate the conveying of hope and faith to that other individual: it must help to save and redeem him. To put it another way, love serves no ethical purpose but it helps people to put an end to sinful existence. Love serves to achieve fulfillment in *another* life. The sinfulness, futility, and redemption cycle is fatal in an ethical sense and has an oppressive effect. He who is truly conscious of his own sinfulness cannot really love himself. Such an individual cannot therefore love his neighbor *as himself*, nor can he transmit what is ethically good. The God of the ethical differentiation between good and evil has disappeared from the stage, just like man, his equal.

Religious love has no intrinsic ethical value. Ethical love of one's fellow man is sacrificed to a *spurious* type of neighborly love, a kind of love that only finds the way to being saved through faith, resurrection from the dead, and the hope of a fulfilled life.

Religious love kills off the old Adam and his ethical mission and purpose in love. Religious love therefore also has an ethical atheistic core. Religious love once again kills the Jesus of the Evangelists, the Jesus of ethical life. It is a kind of death that is more radical than crucifixion. The Messiah has no ethical message. What thus becomes essential is that he is made sinful—for us—so that he can subsequently be sentenced to death (2 Cor 5:21). It is not the *love taught by Jesus* that is of significance but a totally different kind of love, the kind of love that led him to die for others. His death has to make it possible for God's wrath not to affect all sinners. It is not about ethical love, it is about justice. The love displayed on the crucifix must lead to a situation in which God's justice does not reach everyone. This love certainly allows God's avenging justice to exist and so it may, in this respect, be said to be *in vain*. All it achieves is a mitigation of God's wrath so that believers may also benefit from God's righteous grace.

But does Paul not also want to hold on to the ethical good, to the institutional order, to the laws and precepts? Does he not frequently endeavor in his letters to do justice to the meaning of the laws of the Old Testament? This is only apparently the case. He does not actually live in two worlds, an ethical and an eschatological world.[1] The *law* is not able to give people life in the form of an ethical life. The law is not able to combat sin; it is the reverse. The law is no elaboration, no reflection of what may be found to be good. It is precisely the *sinfulness* of man that is made visible and evident by the law. If the law cannot bestow ethical life then it is not logical to uphold it simply in the interests of worldly justice. The letters to the Galatians are, in this respect, especially revealing. Paul asserts that justification cannot be found for man on the grounds of the law but rather on the basis of his belief in Christ (Gal 2:16).

The ultimate futility of everything should not prevent man from striving to live according to the law. In fact laws should help him to counteract his sinfulness; they should help him to curtail his sins, thus limiting the extent of human evil. Such a process would give the law positive and ethical value. Laws were, in the first place, created because of the human capacity to do evil, were they not? Laws should therefore be able to contribute to all that is good, to a balanced life, and to an orderly society. But this is not the value that Paul attaches to law. It is for totally different reasons that he appeals to the law. The law and the desire to observe the law have conflicting intentions and effects upon him. It is precisely in man's *endeavor* to observe the law or, more to the point, his endeavor to do that *in vain* that his sins become absolutely visible. The law helps man to become conscious of his sinfulness. It is an awareness that should ultimately lead man to God, not the God of law-making, not the God that helps man to observe the ethical good in the law, but the God of redemption and of justification through faith. "For through the law I died to law—to live for God." "On the other hand those who rely on obedience to the law are under a curse; for Scripture says, 'A curse is on all who do not persevere in doing everything that is written in the Book of the Law.'

---

1. Heyer, *Paulus: Man van Twee Werelden*.

7   Paul's Zeal

It is evident that no one is ever justified before God in terms of law; because we read, 'he shall gain life who is justified through faith'" (Gal 2:19, 3:10). Man must therefore certainly *try* to live according to the law: it is exactly that which reveals his sinfulness. The law turns the power of sinfulness into an unmistakable reality. The law makes it crystal clear to what degree man really is subject to death. In that respect he has little alternative than to turn to the saving God in faith.

The law is given to man precisely because it is *impossible to fulfill*. The *fulfilling* of the law is linked to an entirely different life. The law thus has no positive ethical meaning but above all else a negative connotation. But it is precisely this negativity that has, in fact, to be comprehended. The law does not actually *make* man sinful. Even before the Mosaic laws were laid down man had committed sins. It is because of the law that man is no longer able to *hide* himself from his sinfulness. The law exposes his sinful state; the law makes man unmistakably guilty. It is through the law that sins can also be *attributed* to man (Rom 5:13). Through the law the sins are even *increased*, thus making the sinfulness so evident that man is forced to come to fully understand the only possible escape route: the path of God's grace (Rom 5:20). The working of the law displays parallels with the *exaggeration* alluded to earlier. The difficult consequences of the law force man to believe in justification through belief. The law forces people to believe in salvation derived from God's grace and in the grace gained from redemption. The law has an *ad hominem* effect. It does not so much make man's concrete sins clear to him as his sinful nature in a general sense. The law is not given to man to allow him to curb the evil of his *sins* but rather to allow him to make his *sinfulness* and guilt apparent. It is not so much a case that the law defines guilt as that it *makes* mankind unmistakably guilty, and so he deserves punishment, falls within God's divine justice, and is forced to follow the only path that remains: that of belief. The law ratifies the belief in man's unworthiness and in the divine justice of God.

This throws light on the value of the Mosaic laws and precepts. It places them in a special perspective. The Hebrew tradition gave these laws sacred significance. They were held to be inherently good and had eternal importance. Now it is not so much the eternal value that Paul turns against as the *sacred* significance of these laws. It is from the sacred and traditional aspects that the value of the inherent good is taken away. The law undergoes a complete *revaluation*. The law has to make it clear that the tradition does not contribute any own worth or purpose, that nothing good issues from observing the laws that have traditionally been passed down. By demonstrating how great the sinfulness of man is, the law is able to prove that there is no way *back*—to the tradition, to the ethical world from which man has emerged. More to the point, the evident sinfulness refutes and prevents the sacred appreciation of any kind of law. New and better laws cannot replace the old ones. The fatal effects of the law prove that there is only one option that remains open and that is the road that lies *ahead*. The only way out that remains for man is incorporated in the belief in an avenging and redeeming God.

Just like belief itself, the law opens up *backward* and *forward* oriented perspectives. In the *backward* direction, the law forces one to believe in the sinfulness of man and in the death to which all of creation is subjected, the death which in terms of the messianic final era also awaited the law. In the *forward* direction, the law forces one to believe in the divine justice of God. It is not the ethical *reality* of the law that reveals God's blessing, nor is it through the doing of legal good that man is blessed by God. Man is blessed for believing in the *impossibility* of the law. "Does the law, then, contradict the promises? No, never! If a law had been given which had power to bestow life, then indeed righteousness would have come from keeping the law" (Gal 3:21). In former times the law was still viewed in a positive light. For a long time it actually operated like a disciplinary teacher and man was "impounded in safe custody" by the law. Now it emerges how relative and transient that was. The believer is enlightened. What becomes apparent to him is that the true meaning does not lie in the ethical order itself. It now becomes clear that belief is the meaningful aspect of the law. Now that, thanks to Christ ". . . faith has come, the tutor's charge is at an end" (Gal 3:25).

In this respect, Paul refers back to Abraham and Moses (Gal 3:15). In the interbellum period between Abraham and Christ, Moses had given man laws, thus ensuring that he remained in safe custody. Such measures were necessary for as long as the *actual* relationship between God and man did not reach fulfillment. It was a relationship that had commenced with the *promise* made by God to Abraham. This promise was to become God's true testament. It did not only apply to Abraham and to the people of Israel, but to mankind in a general sense. It was a promise that was of particular relevance to those who would find justification through belief. Moses' law made this old promise, this testament of God's, slightly redundant. Neither did the Law of Moses weaken the power of the promise, on the contrary: "If the inheritance is by legal right, then it is not by promise; but it was by promise that God bestowed it as a free gift on Abraham" (Gal 3:18). It would seem that everything now revolved around the promise, around the redeeming future perspective, around justification through belief. In this respect the intensely paradoxical nature of the law also emerges. The impossibility of the task to ethically fulfill the law forces people to believe in a completely different kind of fulfillment. Or, to put it another way: the proven *impossibility of fulfilling* the law liberates man, thus allowing him to revert to his original religious perspective while contributing to helping to *fulfill* the law in the way originally intended. Hence the reason that redemption must also free people from the law. To really become redeemed man not only needs to be liberated from his sins, but also from the law that reinforces this sinfulness, the law that chains him to his sins. It is an absurd, if not nihilistic *paradox*: it is a law that must prove that the true meaning of that same law does not lie in its ethical value. Paul gives *ethical atheism* a powerful impetus.

7   Paul's Zeal

This ethical atheism places the God of Abraham, the God of the promise, in a universal and radical eschatological perspective. Man now lives in the expectation that God will universally fulfill his promise once and for all. This God will make his position as the God of ethical life superfluous. The redeeming God *takes his leave from* the ethical God. He gives substance to his earlier, ethical being in an extremely strange fashion: by seeing to it that he no longer needs to operate as lawgiver and maintainer of the law. In order to live up to this divine fulfillment he is also forced to *bid farewell* to the creature created in his own image, to the old Adam, the person of the differentiation between good and evil. It is no longer the old God that breaks this covenant. This God himself also disappears.

Paul's radicalness knows no limits. His God of justice breaks the covenant that the former God had entered into with mankind after the Flood. This type of man also no longer exists. Not only must the old world become a thing of the past but also man of old and the God of old must die. Death reigns everywhere in the interests of fulfillment. The new God that arises from this death has to wipe out the final reminders of his ethical predecessor.

Paul's religious doctrine signifies the *death* of the God of creation: that God is replaced by the God who makes the radical promise to the people to recreate. *The ethical God is dead* and thereby also the ethical significance of good and evil. What was once hailed as good loses that qualification and undergoes radical reform. Man who was previously described as very good also has to disappear and make way for new-style man, for a new Adam. In the *backward* direction everything is ruined. With his promise, hope, and faith, the new, omnipotent God not only propels man *forward* but also himself. Now it becomes apparent where his envy is pushing him. He cannot rest until an end has been put to all the gods who taught man to live, to live together with others, and who gave him ethical life for that purpose. The nihilistic fulfilling of the law is the final blow for those gods. It becomes clear how much the envy is possessed by a revolutionary spirit. "And so it was with us. During our minority we were slaves to the elemental spirits of the universe . . . Formerly, when you did not acknowledge God, you were the slaves of beings which in their nature are no gods. But now that you do acknowledge God—or rather, now that he has acknowledged you—how can you turn your back to the mean and beggarly spirits of the elements?" (Gal 4:3, 8–9).

This jealousy makes the old gods, the God of creation included, sinful and, with them, ethical life. Even their after-effect is now seen to be negative: they merely serve to magnify the ruin. This nihilism even made Jesus himself a sinner and, with him, the ethical doctrine. They who expect justice from the law and from ethical life forfeit the grace of the almighty (Gal 5:4). The omnipotent cannot find any peace until he has become everything in everyone. God and man have become *unequal*, but they must become just as absurdly equal again. Was man able to hold on to this apocalyptic dream when the end of time did not occur?

8

Luther's Bitterness

Little actually came of Paul's apocalyptic vision. The failure of a final judgment to materialize not only moderated the perspective on death but it also forced the prospect of redemption and eternal life to be similarly modified. Believers have to learn to wait. The eschatological *doctrine* has to exercise restraint and provide space for a *life* that needs to be ordered, first within Christian religious communities, then in Christian churches, and ultimately in the world at large. The church cannot be confined to pure religious witnessing and to conversion zeal. Instead, it expands to become an institute that once again advocates enduring ethical maxims. The church gains significance for the world. Christian maxims do not, therefore, only relate to life within the church but also to the wider world. The church again gives meaningful significance to the *law*, which Paul merely finds good enough to speed up the coming of the end of time. The *doctrine* of redemption seems to have to be restrained for the benefit of the *life* of the church that is establishing itself throughout the world. The church also emphatically focuses upon ethical life.

Does this therefore mean that the God of the covenant with Abraham and his descendants repents and, despite himself, adopts his old guise? Does he again become the God of ethical life? The Catholic Church appears to seek this path. The fact that late-medieval *nominalism* exhausts itself in its endeavor to prove the omnipotence and omniscience of God does not detract from the fact that the church also has other matters which need attending. What is important is the establishment of the ecclesiastical *institution* as a preserver of the hallowed ethical tradition, one that was initiated by Christ and the apostles. The church views itself as a divinely inspired, sacred institute and as a protector of human life and human society. No matter how much evil is visited upon the world, one also recognizes in the church and in the world God's goodness: one dwells in the best of all the possible worlds. Here, the discussion is not just about the church as a sacred institution but also the human world in the broader sense and the cosmic order. God's providence offers so much justification for evil that it cannot ruin all that is good about creation. The world has been well created afresh, good enough to be preserved as such.

For a long time classical thinking seems to succeed in keeping Paul's apocalyptic doctrine at bay, or even, perhaps, in repressing it. The *cosmic order* proves the perfection of a God who gives man a haven. Though God may be termed omnipotent, this omnipotence is not implemented to establish a totally different order. The appreciation for the established Christian order is so great that the church seeks to protect that tradition against a too great urge to modernize. The visible world, dismissed by Paul as finite, sinful, and ungodly, is reinstated as something created that needs to be valued, and as evidence of God's benevolence. The visible natural imperfections that are seen all around and human evil cannot detract from this perception. It is a perception that provides space for the development of culture and science, for the wisdom labeled by Paul and later Reformers as foolishness.

8.1 THE FATAL FALL

Does this mean to say that established Christendom once and for all elevates an ethical, earthly life to a higher, if not to the highest echelon? Does *life* prevail over eschatological doctrine? Or, to put it another way, does Jesus triumph over the Messiah? The developments show that this conclusion does not hold. This does not, however, detract from the fact that down the ages the Christian *church* has perpetually made a point of establishing an ethical tradition, of teaching the ethical values and of upholding a legally regulated society. Its contribution to institutionalized society and to everything that emanates from that in the form of civilization and culture may not be underestimated. No matter how contrary the *wisdom* of man is, such folly never prevents the church from contributing a great deal to the integration of own and received wisdom in terms of terrestrial existence. So the church does not radically turn *against* the world just like that, but it proves, in its own way, to be in search of what is good *for* the world.

Yet the *doctrine* propagated by Paul also proves to be powerful. Undoubtedly, it is a doctrine that corresponds well with what is so innately *human* in man, namely: the tendency to moralize, to see evil everywhere and to subsequently seek good elsewhere. Hence the need to appeal to a certain higher value behind *belief*, to appeal to what is *possible*, to what God is said to have promised, to what could still possibly come about and to what may therefore rightly be hoped for. A moralizing kind of belief sullies the benevolent attitude. The more intense the experiencing of decline is, the less relevant good deeds will be. A moralizing experiencing of *belief* provides an incentive for a moralizing religious *doctrine*. This interplay of experience and doctrine not only damages respect for the cosmic order, but also for the ethical significance of the sacred tradition. It furthermore undermines the authority of the church, which stands as proof of God's goodness.

The Reformer *Luther* is an example of the renewed breakthrough in religious doctrine that appeals to the imagination. His radical faith was a sign of the times. The religious doctrine revived *ethical atheism* not only within the Christian community but also outside that community. His doctrine took moralizing judgment to extremes. Again there was the belief that hopeless sinfulness had ruined all existence. Again there was the perception that all of reality was steeped in evil. From this point of view, the ethical tradition was impossible to maintain. Not only did it lack eternal substance, but it was, like everything, finite, futile, and ultimately subject to *death*. All that man can surely do is to resign himself to omnipotence. What else remains? What else can he do than believe in the speedy intervention of the omnipotent? Death once again becomes overpowering. And again there is the crucial significance of death as a punishment for sinfulness. In the process, even Paul's cheerful visions of redemption are dragged down by such destruction The religious experience is given a depressing spin. It emerges that death penetrates the imagination much more deeply than the prospect of redemption. Death no longer simply marks the end of life but it becomes a *hellish* sequel to life. It is only for the few who are not subject to God's avenging justice that belief offers another perspective: that of justification through belief. But who can be certain that this perspective is his due?

Luther's doctrine is governed by a sombre-inducing undertone. Creation is completely riddled with *sinfulness*, the *fall of man* being the catastrophic reason for this. The mistake made by Adam has world-historical significance. The optimistic, ethical interpretation of the Fall is completely crushed by the discouraging existentiality in the form of man's ruin. Endless blame can be attributed to the Adam of old. His deed has plunged the whole of creation into wrack and ruin: mankind, the human cosmos, the physical world, and even history that traverses this history. Just like Paul (Rom 5:12), Luther maintains that one person is responsible for the arrival of sin in the world and, in its wake, death. Indeed, he is obsessed with death to an absurd degree.

Man stands powerless in relation to sin and death. What has actually negatively affected the Fall more than anything else is man's *will*. The will has lost the capacity to choose between good and evil. In reality, it is because of the Fall that the will has been deprived of its freedom to choose. In the process, the will has been written off in moralistic terms. Insofar as the will may still be termed *free*, it *inevitably* leads man to commit sin. This concept of freedom is obviously paradoxical: all that is left to man is a compulsive kind of freedom of choice. The one-dimensional freedom makes it really possible to declare man guilty of perpetually repeated sinful choices. Man is thus incapable, through his own failing, of doing anything good of his own volition. Even under the influence of an ethical order man is incapable of doing anything good. The ethical life cannot rectify sinfulness. The Fall and sinfulness draw not only traditional but also every other possible ethical order with them into the realms of destruction. Since the entire cosmos has been ruined by the Fall, God is no longer recognizable in the early, human, visible world. Luther even makes the depths of destruction more poignant by pointing out that it extends to everything, including the visible, institutional church, the Church of Rome. Even within the established church it remains impossible for good to be upheld. Since creation, man and the institutional world are permeated with evil it has become impossible for ethical good to exist.

Luther's true church is the *religious community*. This is no visible, enduing institution, but rather a community of true believers that is in reality invisible. True believers must not only withdraw from the world but also from institutional connections, the established church included. All in all, Luther was not working on the reforming of the church but on a withdrawal into *belief*, a belief that was entirely founded upon the word or the Bible. The sacred ethical tradition that was expected to protect people from evil and to preserve the Church of Rome was radically rejected by Luther. It was not a rejection that was determined by deviations to which the church and its representatives had surrendered. Precisely at that moment it would have been possible for him to reform the church and purify the ethical tradition. The deviations are nothing more than an extra reason for wanting to reject the institutional church. The institutional church binds belief too strongly to a tangible order here on earth and within the present timeframe. It implies that good can also be found in this world. It binds man too much to wisdoms and truths concerning the world that has descended into sin: it can offer nothing good. Or, to put it another way, there is no single ethical order that is capable of saving man, neither the traditional order nor any kind of modern order. No modern world order can save man, but neither can a religious order. Man cannot save himself; likewise, in this world man cannot be saved.

The notion that God's justice might attain its apotheosis through social justice, in other words, by socially recreating the world order, is alien to Luther. Hence the reason that he was so violently opposed to the social radicalism of Thomas Müntzer. Everything is, after all, subject to sinfulness and death, thus, certainly also the reputed salvation that belongs to this world. Only the *word*, the belief in the truth of this word, opens the door to deliverance, and not by man but by God. God's *redemption* demands justification through belief. Redemption is a matter of God's justice and therefore lies entirely in the hands of God. The prospect of redemption requires unconditional faith in him and in his word. In fact, an outlook is really all that a belief has to offer. It has already been established that even true belief provides no guarantee of redemption. What comes first and last is God's providence and justice, both of which far exceed human wisdom. That which is good is therefore a matter of redemption, salvation, a matter of a new person entering into an entirely different life. Goodness does not belong to this world that is so immersed in evil.

From this point of view, it is not strange to see that Luther also adheres to Paul's reading of the *law*. Laws do not contribute to the salvation of man in a positive way. Having true belief is a prerequisite if man is to be saved since only true belief holds the prospect of redemption. The believer cannot attain redemption simply by abiding by the laws. It is a realization that leads Luther to a sombre view of the Old Testament. For him, that part of the Bible is not so much about God's *promise* as about the *law*. It is precisely this law that makes him sombre. The essence of the law is that it makes the sinfulness of man explicit and unmistakable. Again, the paradox lies in the fact that the law reaffirms that man cannot possibly comply with it, he cannot fulfill it. The *fulfilling* of the law does not therefore lie in its being observed or in any endeavors in that direction but in redemption, also in the redemption of the law. The fulfilling of the law is not to be found in what is good in ethical life, but rather in what is good about a future, redeemed life. It is the road to this fulfillment that brings the *Messiah* into focus. The evident impossibility of the law points urgently, as it were, to the Messiah and to messianic intervention in world history.

Luther's *religious doctrine* is through and through *apocalyptic*. He once again turns the world into a battle scene for the *forces* of darkness and God's power. The doom of sinfulness and the fulfilling of God's promise, death, and eternal life stand diametrically opposed. He breathes new life into the anticipated Second Coming of the Messiah. The end of time and the return of the Messiah are near at hand. Apocalyptic visions lead to the belief in the battle between light and darkness reaching a new high point. As the end of time is nigh, it again becomes a matter of urgency to as quickly as possible make as many people as possible *believers*.

8.2 THE POWER OF SIN

What is striking is the extremely pessimistic way in which Luther deals with sinfulness and the inherent active force of darkness. It is a force that has much greater impact in him than in Paul. This means that he is more reserved and deals less cheerfully with the potential solution offered by finding justification through belief and, therefore, with the possibility of redemption. The cautious, anxious mood is partly prompted by the place that *providence* comes to occupy in him. It is seen as a mixture of God's *omnipotence* and his *omniscience*. The already melancholy view of man and the world is given additional emphasis because of the extremely nominalistic image of God that develops. The image of God becomes filled with doom. Everything lies in God's hands, he has foreseen everything: the lot of man, mankind, and the world. It is impossible for man to comprehend all of this. Even man's own lot is concealed from him. The omnipotence of God takes on a threatening guise since it is based upon a type of *arbitrariness* that is incomprehensible to man. How can man even begin to come to understand the paths of God? For man and his intractable wisdom, the ways of God remain incomprehensible and therefore also frightening. Providence ruins the cheerfulness testified to by Paul. The promise, hope and justification gained through belief can no longer make the uncertain and frightened believers happy. After the cosmic order ceases to hold, the future becomes enshrouded in darkness.

The time perspective comes to resemble a kind of future-oriented tunnel, and it is not so much light that shines at the end of that tunnel as God's *judgment*. For man, this judgment is incomprehensible and therefore again dark and frightening. What remains is a fatalism that extracts any joy from religion. What remains, above all else, is the frightening *final* question as to whether the faithful are really and truly justified through their belief. Luther cannot believe that man, who has become sinful, can so easily be eligible for the redeeming justice offered by belief. Such an interpretation of belief would offer man too much; it would unjustly offer him religious certainty. The combination of the total *sinfulness* of creation and God's providence is fatal to belief. Similarly, the combination of sinfulness and God's justice is equally demoralizing. What is true is that everyone has simultaneously lapsed into sinfulness and is thus subject to God's wrath. On the other hand, it is not true that everyone is automatically preserved by his or her faith. Such supposed certainty fails to take into account God's unfathomable *providence*. That folly defies the incomprehensibility of God's *justice*.

That, in turn, makes Luther sombre about the possibility of salvation. What is certain is that definitely not everyone who claims to believe is eligible for that redemption. Religious certainty is, in effect, a type of *hubris*. Belief is not rewarded with guaranteed redemption. Only a few believers will receive God's grace through their faith. For Luther, God's justice has *fatal* implications. He attaches God's omnipotence to unconditional freedom and *arbitrariness*. If man is unable to *fathom* God's wondrous ways, how will he be able to *intervene* in those ways? The true religious community is invisible but it is also thinkable that it is small.

The fact that this fatalistic image perpetually sows doubt, anxiety and despair must not perturb man for that is a state of mind that accompanies true belief. Fear and doubt not only reveal sinfulness to be a human *reality* but they also attach to that a—beneficial—existential *experience*. The experiencing of fear and doubt fuels belief, strengthens it, and protects man from unbelief, the worst of all sins.

This corresponds to the true nature of *sinfulness*, which is not so markedly determined by the discovery that the law is impossible to fulfill. It is this unattainability that makes the sinfulness so readily apparent. Neither is this sinfulness determined by concrete definable sins. If that were so, man would be able to do something about that—with the help of a discerning consciousness and a guiding will. The sinfulness of man does not so much emerge from his wicked *deeds*: man as such *is* sinful; he *embodies* sinfulness through and through. What is thus decisive is the *ad hominem* turn about. Being human is equated with *being sinful*. The existential experience corresponds with an *existential* fact of life. Sinfulness is not primarily an ethical question, a matter of forming judgment, of will and actions, or of detrimental interaction between individuals. All of that amounts rather to a *consequence* of man's sinfulness. It is not so much the case that man *commits* evil as that he *is* evil in all his fibres. That is what also makes his consciousness and knowledge, as well as his will and actions so sinful.

Possessing a better conscience or doing good works cannot therefore help to dispel sinfulness. Hence the reason for Luther's urge to reject Catholic doctrine on the matter of good works. There is no ethics that can cure man's sinfulness and evil. Divine *forgiveness* does not therefore apply to concrete sins. Forgiveness applies to sinfulness in an existential sense, to sinful man. Forgiveness really does have a very relative kind of scope. God's forgiveness does not actually take away man's sinfulness: it simply ensures that it is not ascribed to him. In this earthly life man cannot be liberated from his sinful nature. That is something that demands redemption, death and resurrection as a completely newborn person. Redemption is a matter of God's *grace*. In effect, the *inequality* between God and man could hardly be any greater. *Ethical atheism* could hardly penetrate belief in a more fatal way.

The fatalistic interpretation of *sinfulness* destroys what ethically defines man: the *zoon politikon*, the being who is so familiar with society and who draws from the goodness therein his whole life's purpose. He who is able to do good is not driven to despair by evil. That which is fatal in sinfulness destroys life's purpose. The fatalistic experiencing of an existence that lacks purpose is what forces man to have to make the absurd choice between nihilism and a desperate longing for salvation, redemption, and preservation. A person who is possessed by sinfulness, fear, and desperation is forced to become totally self-reliant. Sinfulness summons up dispiriting *existential* experiences: the fear of being lost, the fear of death, doubts about the possibility of being preserved, a pathetic longing for redemption. Sinfulness that is truly lived through makes the fear of death abyssal and condemns those who are shackled to desperate loneliness.

With Luther, all these experiences have a *negative connotation*; they are in fact designed to force man to believe, to turn to God. As has already been asserted, this belief offers no certain salvation for man. In the first place such faith pertains to God, to the ensured position of God. Belief is not, then, so much a reaction to sinfulness as a reaction to God's wrath in relation to man. This therefore gives belief a completely *reactive* status, but it is also precisely this that perfectly illustrates the incredibly reciprocal nature of the relationship between God and man. No matter how *unequal* the position of God and man is, the reaction to sinfulness displays striking *similarity*. Even omnipotent God proves to be reactive, even he can do nothing other than react to what presents itself to him in the form of sinful man and creation that has been ruined. His wrath is not so much directed at human sinfulness as at man himself. It is a kind of wrath that man is unable to eradicate. Ultimately God's wrath is not aimed at concrete, demonstrable sins that man could attempt to rectify. Furthermore, it is not seen as relevant that, since Adam, it is due to circumstances beyond his control that man has been received and born into sin. Man *is* simply sinful and guilty, that is all there is to it. God is therefore wrathful and all his wrath is directed at man. This wrath is unable to eradicate the *man of old*. Through faith, through the recognition of sinfulness and the justification of God's wrath, man does, to an extent, do justice to God's wrath: he recognizes the rightful position of the unequal, of the almighty.

It is a remarkable idea to think that the real cause of human sinfulness lies in the *original sin* of the old Adam. It is therefore not exactly the fault of all his descendants that they are born into sinfulness. There are two main reasons why such a situation as that may be said to be *fatal*. From the causal point of view, there is little that man can do to change matters but, by the same token, he can undertake no corrective action. Even if there is no blame that can be pinned on man he is, by definition, guilty, and so deserves to be punished. It is not so much that he needs to be punished for his sins—in that case punishment could have a chastening effect so that sins could be forgiven and forgotten—but rather as an individual. Man is doomed to be punished regardless of what he undertakes to combat his sinfulness. The helplessness and benevolence of man cannot eradicate God's abiding wrath. Instead of sincere forgiveness there remains only the solution of deliverance from the fatal human existence, at least for those who receive God's grace. Such grace is, of course, preceded by judgment. Does this then mean that only God's judgment can take away his wrath? Does this mean that God is unable to conquer the doom of avenging justice in himself? Does it mean that this is where he comes up against the borders of his omnipotence? Does the lack of leniency display God's incapacity to sincerely forgive and truly forget? Is it proof of God's inability to overcome *himself*?

That is how it seems. Luther's image of God has absurd, if not dangerous implications. The omnipotent is *unable to forgive* man for his sins; he is unable to take away the sinfulness of this being. By the same token, the omniscient one is unable to forget. He *cannot* leave what has been done behind him: he forgets nothing. He does not *want* it to be like this. He does not want this type of person or this creation, he wants *everything* to be *different*, also this type of individual. He wants old-style man to die, he wants all of creation to die off, he wants to subject everyone and everything to death. He wants to lead everything right through death and deliver it as something *totally different*. Since forgiveness is unable to take away the sinfulness of old-style man, redeeming death is necessary. In a fatal sort of way, God's *omniscience* extends *backward*: he forgets nothing and is therefore unable to forgive. God's *omnipotence* also extends *forward* in a fatal kind of way: he will have to make everything *different*. God is just as chained to man as man is chained to God. The death of old-style man must also save God. In that way the omniscient and omnipotent God makes it only too clear just how much the God of ethical life really is *dead*.

In Luther's doctrine ethical atheism persists still further. In his case, he does not place the essence of redemption in God's hands just like that, but rather in the mystery of God's *grace*. Instead of forgiveness—as taught by Christ—God knows only grace. God's grace still always has fatal consequences for man because grace simply on its own cannot dispel God's wrath, neither does it remove the necessity for God's rightful avenging justice. What is so unfathomable about God is the fact that some people do benefit from the grace of redemption, while what awaits most of humanity is avenging justice. One might therefore imagine that this is a kind of judgment that only affects those who have been lost and that only they are thus condemned. However, it is not only God's vengeance that affects man but also his grace. That grace robs man, who is already so sinful, of any remaining human dignity. In order to be able to qualify for grace, God lays down the already mentioned requirement of unconditional *belief* in him and in his justice, but this belief also has a fatal reverse side to it, a facet that destroys human dignity. It is ruined by the unconditional recognition and complete experiencing of human sinfulness. God's wrath and grace, his avenging and redeeming justice, have much in common: both are devastating for man, for his freedom and for his dignity. God's *exaltedness* is reflected in man's human *unworthiness*. His exaltedness demands more than a general recognition of human sinfulness: the *own* sinfulness and unworthiness must be so intensely personally felt that God's majesty can in that way be proven.

The *inequality* of God and man in that way goes further than being merely a contrast between an *everything* as opposed to a *nothing*. The recognition of human insignificance does not go far enough. The unworthiness has to be realized, recognized, and experienced. But even then it does not lead to God's grace: whichever way one looks at it, man does not deserve this. It is entirely the arbitrariness of God that determines precisely who may receive his grace. This involves the utter subjugation of man, who is unworthy, to God's majesty. Faith offers man no certainty, no joy, no pleasure in life, in fact it denudes man of all of this, it serves not to conquer evil but rather to create it. On top of that, it generates its own kind of evil: that of human unworthiness. Moreover, human belief gives God no joy or lust for life. It does not in actual fact liberate him from his insatiable longing for justice. He cannot conquer himself. In this respect, God's redeeming love becomes somewhat relative. After all, God's love transfers human sinfulness to his son, but this does not alter the fact that only a mere few will receive his grace. Even what remains of love pales into insignificance as it is overshadowed by an irrepressible urge to retaliate.

8.3 UNCONTROLLED RESENTMENT

As far as the time perspective is concerned Luther stands close to Paul. No matter how invisibly God works on his plan, the time of his intervention in the world and in world history is nigh. Luther is convinced of the imminent arrival of the Messiah and his judgment. He experiences an extremely apocalyptic time vision. He believes that such judgment will conquer the forces of darkness once and for all. That salvation will be preceded by a double kind of *death*: the death of sinners and sinfulness will be followed by actual death itself. That final type of death has the power to unite God with those who have been chosen through grace. Through actual death itself, death will be conquered, at least for those who are to be saved.

Luther's theology is particularly focused on the final stage, upon death and the ensuing redemption, rebirth, and recreation. In the light of the end of time, everything that is anchored in this world becomes finite, transient, and futile. God's coming justice makes it already clear that nothing in this world is of lasting value; nothing in it exposes anything that is intrinsically good. Again, this also reveals an opinion about the value of ethical life and institutions. Hence the reason for his heavy attack upon the Catholic Church and the value that this church attaches to tangible institutions and to the relationship established with tradition. The notion that *Christ* might conceivably be felt in the tradition of the institutions is something that he perceives to be utterly contrary to the idea of the coming *Messiah*. For him, Jesus is the Messiah and no ethical leader. The notion that man himself, in imitation of Jesus, might be able to work on what is good through institutions, laws, and commandments is something he finds to be totally in contravention with the belief in redemption through God's grace. He takes that to such extremes that he even goes as far as to declare any kind of attachment to tradition a sin. The apocalyptic perspective prohibits the positive valuing and wishing to preserve of anything of the visible world.

It may be asserted that Paul's revaluation of the *law* already had dangerous consequences. The law is indeed given to man but it has no intrinsic value. The law makes the inevitable sinfulness of man evident as well as the unattainability of the law. The unattainability of the law is proof of human sinfulness; it thereby anticipates the coming Messiah. The law therefore has no ethical meaning but rather a messianic perspective. The dangerous aspect of this is the temptation to recklessly deal with the ethical aspect of the laws.

Luther's radical stance only further emphasizes this interpretation. Real believers do not live in a visible religious community but rather in one that is invisible. Such a community requires no laws. God's real work is not, after all, directed at the visible world and at society. His work is not even apparent in the church as uniting institution. The death encountered at the end of time therefore not only holds for the law but also for the institutions. This is why Luther does not show any real interest in social or institutional reform. In effect, he is really even against that as it derives from the orientation towards a redeemed life. This anticipates the later Marxist opposition to social or political reform. That is something that only prolongs the death-struggle in which the existing world is entangled. It thwarts the redemption that has to be realized by the all-embracing revolution. This radicalism leads to a reckless attitude towards the institutions.

The central position occupied by the Final Judgment, by death and by God's justice, makes one wonder to what degree Luther's religious doctrine might emanate from *resentment*. Is the doctrine and the taskmaster not perhaps possessed by an aversion to what the world has to offer, including all the good of the world? The core of his doctrine might contain some hints. Is it possible that concealed in the conviction that nothing *can* be saved there is perhaps the view that nothing *may* be saved? That would explain how in submitting to death, guilt and punishment dominate. It would explain why the hope of salvation is overruled by the longing for the Final Judgment. Does this not give the messianic perspective an evil slant? Does Luther dedicate to God that which man himself *does not yet* quite legitimately dare to undertake? That is clearly how it seems. His enthusiasm is uncontrolled. He does not abide by the endlessly repeated conclusion to the effect that all that exists is of no value, that it is worth allowing everything to go to ruin. His religious doctrine is not only fatalistic and reactive, but it also includes an activistic impetus. He runs, as it were, to the aid of his God.

Religious doctrine cannot leave the death of creation that has descended into sinfulness entirely in the hands of God and the Messiah. The doctrine also fully intercepts here as well as beforehand. The referred to experiencing of sinfulness testifies to this. It is not enough to recognize that in the sinful world nothing good is possible and that all is futile. The sinfulness and futility of everything must be so intensely felt and internalized that it ultimately leads to self-condemnation. The experiencing of own sinfulness and guilt may not end in a fatalistic complaint, but must lead to an accusation. This judgment, this accusation affects man, the faithful. The real believer is convinced of his own unworthiness: I am sinful, I form part of the evil, I am unworthy and thus deserving of destruction. Luther's doctrine arouses among believers a kind of resentment that has a *self-destructive* twist. The resentment turns *inwards*.

He does not leave it at this though. He extends his tried and tested doctrine of sinfulness and guilt to include people whom he not only sees as extremely sinful, but whom also thwart this awareness of sin, to the non-believers. His doctrine of sinfulness also seeks its way *ad hominem* in an *outwardly* oriented direction. He not only sees sinfulness but also sinners; he sees not only unbelief but also non-believers. He not only applies this doctrine to himself but also to others. Such a kind of doctrine justifies personal resentment, resentment that seeks to anticipate God's justice. His aversion is not only directed at the Church of Rome and its preoccupation with tradition but in particular at the *pope*, at the church, as it were, *ad hominem*. That

8 Luther's Bitterness

is the reason why he sees in the pope, as institute and as incumbent, the Antichrist. The pope becomes the personification of evil, an object of justified ill will. His aversion also includes those who endeavor to reform the Church of Rome, thus in effect hampering the approaching final conflict between God and the powers of darkness. *Erasmus* is thus bitterly resented. A similar kind of resentment is also leveled at Jews and at those who are perceived to be witches.

The specifically angled directing of resentment gives the hammering away at the sinfulness of man an extra dangerous dimension. The doctrine of sinfulness does not stop at an *inwardly* directed kind of resignation; it also turns *outwards* in an aggressive fashion. Resentment is creative. It searches for the other and, to that end, is always able to find *justification*. Why had it not then anticipated God's judgment? Why not then already combat the visible forces of darkness oneself? What is questionable is Luther's differentiation between the beneficial, purifying suffering of those who are preserved and the justified suffering of those who fall prey to God's wrath. The incomprehensible providence of God does not alter the fact that he himself knows only too well who is susceptible to God's wrath. Was it not the Jews who were responsible for Christ's death? They must therefore be at the receiving end of God's wrath. Why should not Christians anticipate that? Much the same goes for witches. Why wait for God if his invisible plan is already so visible? Why not support God?

This demonstrates the implicit danger of the ethical *atheistic* basis of this religious doctrine. If ethical values have no significance, if laws cannot be upheld, why not then make a virtue of necessity? If real belief basically requires no law then religious doctrine can surely simply merge into a proper religious life? That justifies its own kind of justice. The justification through belief *in* sinfulness in that way nourishes justified action *against* sinners.

8.4 THE TOTALITARIAN PERSPECTIVE

As *aggressively* as the justification pathos can be disseminated, so *resignedly* can it turn inwards. The belief in God's providence has fatal consequences for human wisdom and for freedom of will. The fact that human fate is known to him beforehand seems to almost naturally lead to the doctrine of *predestination*: everything has to be preordained. God's omnipotence already forces one to conclude that everything is determined by his implicit power over man's will. His omnipotence furthermore ensures that such power over the will also remains completely transparent to him. That makes God a fate-governed factor for man: how can man exert influence upon God's will, how can man salvage some of his own destiny? Even having a minimum degree of freedom of will constitutes an infringement of God's omnipotence and omniscience. God's providence and omnipotence ensure that human fate lies entirely in his hands.

This notion of fate diverges from that of the Greeks who viewed it as a force to which not only man but also the gods were subjected. Luther's concept of fate is diametrically opposed to that of Nietzsche, who sees human destiny as something inevitable that is based not only upon what is, after all, unforeseen and impossible to steer, but also upon the implicit potential for *a change of course*. The unforeseen must be especially viewed as a *challenge*, one that man must actively take advantage of but in a wise way, with sober *reflection*. By reflection he means here also: incorporating meaningful change for the better. Such meaningful change totally contravenes God's omniscience and omnipotence: the very idea that man might be able to influence God's will is absurd. Providence makes the inequality between God and man, the widening of the gap between the two, infinitely great.

God's providence and omnipotence make human freedom of will unthinkable. If everything that occurs in this world really emanates from God's will, how then can evil or sinfulness be comprehended? Is even evil preordained by God? Is human sinfulness and sinning also preordained? Luther is consistent. He also attributes evil to God: that is also ordained by him. Since evil is included in God's plan it really does not detract from his goodness and justice. A further point of consideration is that it is not man's place to pass comment on God or to want to influence him. Man must not therefore seek to do this. He may not even attempt to understand God or to comprehend him in his omnipotence and omniscience.

Anyhow, how can the *unequal* possibly succeed in fully comprehending the unequal? How can the foolish wisdom of man possibly even come anywhere near God's elevated wisdom? It is therefore not even man's place to appeal to God about the evil in the world. At the end of the day, God is fair in what he does: man must observe a modest distance. God is just and good in all that he does, in all that he ordains be that good or evil. God's majesty is so endlessly divorced from man that there only remains one option for man, the option to *accept* the belief in this elevated God, to recognize his own unworthiness. God's exaltedness reflects the utter *humility* of man. *Belief* demands a willing acceptance of what passes all understanding. Belief places full trust in God and demands complete submission, even if man is in danger of being lost or is actually lost. True belief therefore leads to acceptance even if God does *not* allow man to benefit from his grace. Belief leads to voluntary fatalism.

The dichotomy has gone full circle. God's omnipotence raises him high above all that is mundane. Man who is subjected to that is obedient and accepting. Does this image not then point us forward to the arbitrariness to which the human God of totalitarianism subjects man? Is totalitarian evil not perhaps justified in a similar fashion?

Luther's religious doctrine is *insincere* to an absurd degree. The value of human wisdom, of the possession of self-knowledge, is destroyed. All that remains is eternal sinfulness and a belief in the complete ruination of creation starting with the human cosmos. That which is true is lost in fatal religious perspectives. It is trapped between a backward and forward-oriented perspective. In the backward direction, it is the holding to be true of the total destruction of all that is that predominates; the forward orientation has to do with holding to be true what should be possible but what has been withheld from man. In the retrospective direction the gaze is clouded by evil. When glancing ahead, it is that which is good that beckons, even though it might be concealed and confined to the terrain of God's will to which everything must be consigned.

The inequality of God and man also taints *sincerity*, not only between God and man but also between people in their relationships to each other. The ethical life is ruined. God is justified in everything that he does, even when that involves evil. What might then be termed sincere is in an ethical sense utterly impossible to differentiate. For God all that he does is good and righteous. This is also transmitted to the relationship between individuals. In fact, man is no longer capable of doing anything that is *ethically good*, which is why it becomes hopeless to even aspire to that. Good and evil are completely forced apart. For a few, all that remains is merely their own sinfulness and an egoistic longing for their *own* salvation, their own grace, preservation, and a good life of their own. Even the redeemed person has lost his ethical lust for life. The doctrine of sinfulness sullies ethical life as a reality but also as a future prospect.

How does all of this pan out if man further pursues atheism? What happens when man no longer sees a need for divine reflection? What if God becomes man? What if man appropriates divine providence and will? How, then, does the dangerous combination of inwardly directed resignation and an outwardly directed resentment further unfold?

9

From God to Man

The question now is how modernity can detach belief and the inherent longing for omnipotence from God. Modernity provides an image of a kind of man who pushes back his own barriers, a kind of man who discovers himself and his own *capabilities*. Man maintains that he can switch to self-determination, self-development, *self-creation*. As a perpetuation of that, the interpretation of meaning shifts: from celestial to terrestrial existence; it is a kind of existential fulfillment that can be realized here on earth. What lingers in that view is the hint of a utopian transfer to a totally different existence. The truth does not reveal goodness in the here and now and so both those aspects have to be sought elsewhere. That is why, even without God, man retains his belief even if the religious content changes to something metaphysical. Once again it is belief that fulfills a *metaphysical need*.

This need makes belief undoubtedly stronger and perhaps even more cynical than it was in its religious form. More than ever before it is not only the *traditional* ethical world but also the whole *idea* of ethicality that is viewed in a negative light. Belief that excludes God not only places the desire to be liberated from the traditional ethical urge in the hands of man himself, but also the subsequent arrival in the Promised Land of peace and fulfillment. He discovers himself and believes in himself as well as in his human capacities. The self-discovery of man means that he no longer sees himself as part of a traditionally inherited cosmic and ethical order. Just as with the extreme sophism of bygone times, it is the image of man as a natural creature that again comes to the fore, as one who is able to give substance to that natural facet himself. Society must be instrumental to that. More and more, man maintains that he is able to take his destiny into his own hands. To that end the old idea of omnipotence has to be transferred from God to man. God becomes man. Man conquers the divine image. The reality that is known and that has to be discovered then becomes a human affair. Hence the ultimately openly confessed *vérité à faire*, a truth and a reality that is to be created by man. Even that which is known is incorporated into the new creative reality. The faith in man makes the *recreating* God more human. What applies to the question of truth can also be applied to the issue of good and evil. That which is good is held to be as possible to create, in any respect, as evil is to abolish. In that way, what is good loses its ethical tie but evil does not.

The disappearance of God from the human stage is termed the *death of God*. However, with his death the associations with his name do not die. It is precisely the omnipotent God who becomes man in line with man's metaphysical requirements. The omnipotent and the belief that is linked to him are given a vital human guise. The God who dies is the one who was the source and protector of sacred ethical life. Though modern atheism may embrace the death of God, it does, in the process, in many respects perpetuate ancient *ethical atheism*. In effect, it continues on a human level something that has a long history in religion itself. But the comparison drawn goes even further. Modern atheism turns against God but not against his omnipotence, something that man now makes his own. It is precisely at the ethical image of God that the atheistic conflict is directed, at the ethical bond and the institutional unity of man.

The religious content that maintains a line of contact with the omnipotent does not therefore fade. The *incarnation of God* declares that man has to prepare to take the place of God. It is the erosion of the *sacred* value of the true and good that tempts man to independently free himself from the constricting ethical bonds. The trust in human omnipotence represents the manipulability of the true and good. The ideas surrounding the true and good lose their sacred status. What will become apparent is just how overconfident and cynical the belief in the ability to manipulate matters can *make* man. This kind of belief makes man recklessly *wayward*. To create meaning for himself, he is under the impression that he is able to recreate existence. The new greatest good is life fulfillment, which threatens to ruin sincere auto·*nomy* Self-determination spoils real self-knowledge, self-control, moderation, and proportion. The story of human omnipotence demonstrates how belief is allied to the deed, to an immoderate deed that is shrouded in justice. The yearning for omnipotence makes man discontented, restless, driven, and unprecedentedly *decisive*.

In order to gain a good impression of the incarnation of God we must first return to the God of creation. To oppose radical forms of contemporary modernism, Hegel wanted to cleave to this God. That makes clear to us exactly which God modernism turns against and in which God it certainly recognizes itself.

9.1 A FINAL FORM OF PROVIDENCE

It is incorrect to presume that God's assessment of his creation should imply that everything is *good* in the sense of being perfect. In a general sense creation amounts to a world in which man can and must feel at home as man, a world in which the human cosmos can be further extended. To that end, human capacity has to distinguish between good and evil. By eating from the tree of knowledge man made this capacity his in a willful way. Because he had made this first very human choice himself, the blame could not be placed on anyone else. Man is thus able to brightly and enthusiastically embrace existence. He is consciously able to differentiate and *is* therefore as man—other than as a living creature—*conscious*ness. This thus distinguishes him from everything that is "of nature." Consciously he is able to know in both senses of the word, direct his will, and act. This being human is an eternal fact, it is eternally reciprocal, it is never complete. Good and evil, true and untrue, cannot in a definite sense be interpreted as *the* true and *the* good: to that end man would have to elevate himself above that to which he is drawn by his discerning judgment. Similarly, the notion of truth cannot be termed a type of existence. *The* true does not exist; it is an absurd concept. Truth requires of man authenticity, an honest search for *what* is true. Neither can good and evil be termed a type of existence in the sense of *the* good and *the* evil. Good and evil are differentiating factors and cannot therefore be seen in isolation of the relative nature of judgment. *Man* can therefore no more be termed *true* than good or evil.

The road ahead, or retrospectively, to paradise is closed off to *man*. He who seeks it no longer wishes to be a human being. He who accepts what is human in man will not only have to endure eternal searching and eternal differentiation but will also have to want this as a purposeful challenge. What we are talking about here is the challenging of human freedom. This freedom is incidentally not compatible with arbitrariness or with the anarchy of the will. He who is able to freely distinguish controls himself *in* such distinguishing, in such own good. That links autonomy to freedom and to living within one's own *nomoi*, according to one's own ethical rules. Man owes what is good to his autonomy; however, the relative nature of his *nomoi* is attributable to human society, to people's shared cosmos.

It is also incorrect to interpret what is human in a strictly individual way. Both the true and the good are relative. The idea that each individual can freely determine his own truth, from his own perspectives and on the basis of his own interpretations, has dangerous consequences. No matter how many roads lead to true insight this truth is always relative and linked to the given world that is there to be discovered and to be known. The true not only reflects *what* is given, about which something can thus be said; such openness to what is also binds people. The true is shared. Much the same applies to good and evil. As the free expression of will brings the other into focus, the *nomoi* of human auto*nomy* remain a matter of human interrelations. It is through the *nomoi* that man meets the other.

Freedom is therefore a characteristic of human individuals, but it has no strict individual significance. What is meaningful and relative about what is good emerges from the etymological link between the Germanic words free and friend. In Old German, they and "vrede" (the Dutch word for peace) share the same root, *fri*, meaning something like to take care of, to treat lovingly. Viewed from this angle, one might assert that freedom and autonomy are unthinkable without the relative component or without the other. The *doing* of shared good presupposes a *knowledge* of what that is. That which is *typical* of man can only then in this way be *meaningfully* typical. No autonomy without *nomoi*; no good and evil without ethical meaning, without a collectively managed cosmos. No autonomy without a genuine recognition of the other, without sincere involvement with the other. Should the God of ethical life fail to make a sacred contribution to what is true and good then all that remains for man is to interpret former sacred meaning in his own unique way.

This human intractability is central to the philosophy of Hegel.[1] How must man cope with the world as he finds it if he discovers that he himself is the source of knowledge, if he discovers that he himself is able to and, indeed, must steer his own will and actions? Is it possible to reconcile free autonomy with an ethical world order and an ethical attitude to life? Or, does autonomy lead to a turning away from what is? To put it another way, can ethical autonomy be upheld if the sacred substance of ethical life is lost; if it becomes clear to people that it is not God but man himself who is the source of his own *nomoi*? Can man respectfully manage the divine legacy that he has claimed for himself? The first Fall made man *equal* to God in his knowledge of good and evil: this equality introduced him to the ethical world and made the ethical task possible.

However, can man cope with a second Fall? Is a more extensive *incarnation* of God, incorporating the traditional ethical challenge, thinkable? Is the ethical reality still acceptable if man discovers that this reality also has so much evil to offer? Can man still feel comfortable in a world where evil has human origins? Can man tolerate a brand of evil that is so very human, or must the idea that a kind of divine providence is still at work be salvaged? Must it be possible to justify evil in the interests of what is good? Is such justification still possible if man can be blamed for the evil, man who could possibly have organized the world differently? Is it not so that unjustifiable evil makes man desperate, indignant? Does this not make the given ethical order *relative* in the wrong sort of way? Does it not make it seem finite and negative, pointless and futile? Can modern man still adjust himself to a world that is not perfect? Will the yearning for a totally different world, now to be created by man, inevitably return?

---

1. See Hegel, *op. cit.*, 6vv, 14vv.

Hegel maintains that, thanks to the capacity to *reflect*, the justification question can be answered: when orienting *backward* man can recognize himself in the ethical world that he has given himself. He thinks that it is precisely modern, autonomous man who is able to benefit from the far-reaching realized fulfillment of the ancient task. Thus it is that the true always reveals the good, albeit retrospectively. This is comforting when man encounters evil: it is not everything. Modern man *cannot* start afresh but *does not* need to do this either, on the contrary in fact. The result of the creation task now becomes obvious to him after all. Man is able to *recognize* himself in his works. He can arrive at the conclusion that what he has done is *good*. He therefore proves, even more, to have become God's equal. Knowledge is all about self-knowledge, *recognition*, discovery, and *reflectively* comprehending what his *own* human world reveals to him. Such things make people grateful. It makes reconciliation with the human world as it is possible, also in the light of the ever-present evil.

The term Hegel uses to describe this is *Eigensinn*, or own will. What does he mean by this? In the light of grasping this in an ethical sense, it is somewhat surprising that he links obstinacy to belief and to the testimony of Luther. How can he make Luther's apocalyptic belief and messianic expectations correspond to the *reconciliation* with the given ethical reality striven for by him, all its evil included?

Hegel presumes that there is a line of continuity between religion and philosophy. In an intrinsic sense they overlap and are equal to each other. Though they may have a different form they do not in essence pose a contradiction, they do not refute each other. Both support the ethical life of man, both reveal the truth. Hegel wants to ensure that modern philosophy is not caught up in the wake of atheism and that it, as he puts it, does not have to turn against God. He places the value of God and religion in ethical life, in what man has built up in terms of ethical reality and life's purpose. If this legacy is to be preserved and further expanded, then philosophy has to make a connection with the ethical content of religion. Philosophy may not detach itself from all the historical achievements which are felt in the ethical world of the present. Without such connectedness thinking will lack substance, it will amount to knowing better and therefore to destruction. Philosophy may not create its own truths or elevate itself above the truth. It has to seek what is true in the given reality.

All the while man has been in his cosmos, active in his world, and has brought about much good. There is already, thus, a great deal of human reason that has reached fruition in the world. That is why this reality also shows itself as something human and that is why its good is recognizable. It is certainly not the case that man is confronted with a world that is alien to him. Evidently an own world stands open to him. Hence the inner unity between reality and reason. That is why philosophy is able to discover an own dynamic reality, and that is what makes it *submissively* creative. It works further on what it is given. It steers clear of knowing better, avoids casual opinions and seeks rather to detect the further design in the existing world. This makes it at once rational and enduring.

Here, Hegel sticks to a happy presumption drawn from the old enlightenment thinkers. They viewed nature and the cosmos as a rational and ordered entity; they even saw it as an *example* of ordered, human society. In comprehending the physical cosmos, man obtained a mirror for his own good life. In conjunction with its rational ordering the natural cosmos could be construed to be godlike; a cosmos with ordered laws. Since nature naturally strives for perfection, knowledge of its laws automatically brings the perfection of human life closer. The question relating to truth therefore directs itself towards an *exemplary* order and can thereby support the organization of life in the ethical world. Ethics, too, is averse to just *thinking up* rules, norms, and laws for society. In order to be able to live in an ordered fashion, man must learn to *contemplate* the divine cosmos that has been given to him. He is aware of its imperfect elements, he justifies the evil of this world. Above all else, the understanding of this cosmos is shared, which gives knowledge interpersonal, inherent ethical significance. Subjective opinion forming and ethical arbitrariness are absolutely rejected.

Hegel seeks to find again in human reality what the first enlightenment of the natural cosmos believed it was able to determine. This world is also rational and knowable; it contains what is good. Just as natural laws have to be discovered from the mass of apparently chaotic phenomena so philosophy, in its scientific *know*ledge role, must penetrate the apparently chaotic nature of the human world and *discover* its rational substance. This discovering brings together the knower and the known. Knowledge therefore *reconciles*, also if reality and the included existing human existence is hard and difficult to bear. It is not so much philosophy but more the rational core of the human cosmos that makes reconciliatory knowledge possible.

The substantial core reaches deeper than the immediate and actual. Reconciliation is therefore not nullified by the evil that is always present. Man *and* human reality do, after all, incorporate both good and evil. This evil *may* not be denied, but such denial is not necessary either. The inner rational core of reality makes it possible for man to repeat God's judgment of his creation: the present interplay of good *and* evil is also good. The true reveals the good. The—virtually literal—discovering of the ethical substance of reality makes knowledge normative for ethical life. Hegel's dynamic enlightenment philosophy thus corresponds to the first enlightenment. What must be avoided is that the now existing evil leads man to view reality in a sombre light. *Enlightening* knowledge must prevent man from developing a moralizing aversion to the world, from being skeptical, discouraged, and from possessing inappropriate irony.

So man again has at his disposal a mirror, a mirror for the true and good, a mirror that endows the human cosmos with something divine. This mirror must ensure that man and God do not stray too far apart. In other words, God is near at hand, he lives among his people; the divine is inherent in human existence. This must be properly understood. God and man are each other's *equals*. God is not man just like that; he is active and recognizable in the ethical substance of the human cosmos, in human society. This demands of the knowledge of human reality a similar kind of respect and awe as the knowledge displayed in the previous enlightenment. Just as this started with reverence for the divine cosmos, so knowledge now also supports the ethical life of man. Also, now that it is about the dynamic, human cosmos man is situated *beneath* the truth. Philosophy may not moralize, it may not seek its salvation in looking ahead to the future as though by knowing it better it will become knowable or possible to manipulate. The value of philosophy lies in being able to *look back* on what has been given. Only that makes it *true*. It always really arrives—by definition—*too late* to create an own world; it is not self-creating. The true knowing can only really begin once the human cosmos has been formed: only then does it become truly transparent and show its true face. Philosophy reflects backward, it is retrospectively oriented and that is the only way it endows life with meaning. That is where it differs from religion. Philosophy may not have what religion has been given as its task: the order to *move* people, to activate them. Hence the reason that the first person, at the beginning of human development, received his orders in religious terms. Because religion moves people, it takes precedence over philosophical wisdom. Does this mean that philosophy can do nothing other than accompany religion?

Hegel asserts that true philosophy leads to God. Also therefore, for philosophy, God is a reality. Also, philosophy must be directed at God if it is to arrive at true knowledge. But what does this divine component consist of? How does God appear? How does he reveal himself and allow himself to be known? What is essential is that God appears *in* the world, *in* the human cosmos. The divine is the substantial, enduring core of the world, the world formed by man's hands, man's very own world. This substantial aspect is what is permanent *in* the manifesting, temporary, passing, *in* the apparently coincidental, *in* the visible exterior of things. Philosophy must not allow itself to be blinded by appearances, instead it must penetrate the divine substance: that will facilitate the *joy* of recognition. Such knowing has *direction-giving* purpose. True knowledge does not ignore evil or conceal it but extracts from it everything that is good. That is how true knowledge gives direction to the will and to actions. The divine has ethical content that is to be discovered in this world. God and what is divine do not therefore refer to another promised world. God joins the present; he remains in man's midst. True knowledge helps to preserve the divine good. By honestly and respectfully reflecting on what is, it becomes possible to give direction to man's will. True philosophy helps man to become *sincere*, to be open to ethical society, open to the other. Philosophy helps man to find his way in the ethical universe that has been bestowed upon him. He recognizes himself in the world; that makes true knowledge also *self-knowledge*.

9 From God to Man

Hegel is opposed to the notion of a transcendent (*jenseitige*) God, to the God of the promise, the expectation, and the hope. He objects to the idea that the divine is still to come and that it is, at best, promised. There is no promised land. The cognitive and ethical efforts are both directed at the present, not at what is still to come. He is especially opposed to the idea that the good is still to come because what exists is supposedly permeated with evil. No promised land, no exodus from what exists, and no God who, in that respect, leads the way for man.

How, in this respect, can Hegel's philosophy be related to the theology of Luther? What is the significance of the fact that he seeks to finish what Luther began in the form of a belief? His doctrine is surely through and through apocalyptic? Is it not the case that—for him—the existing world is permeated with evil? Does he not fully displace the good to a heavenly reality that is still to come? With him man is expected to learn to detach himself from the existing world and to place all his hopes in what is to come, is he not? As for the ethical substance, the law: surely that merely serves to make apparent the sinfulness of man, the evil?

It is striking that Hegel seeks to find the link with Luther in the *Eigensinn*. It is indeed obstinacy that characterizes the modern age, the tendency being to accept nothing directional that cannot be justified by thought. It is a type of stubbornness that he sees as a typical feature of Protestantism and of Luther. Hence his hypothesis to the effect that what started with Luther as belief in feeling and in the testimony of the spirit comes to be adopted by the mature spirit as *understanding*. The ripened spirit wants to feel at home in the present. No word is mentioned about Luther's doctrine and the apocalyptic visions. All that is emphasized is his stubbornness. It is thinkable that Hegel does want to preserve the relationship between philosophy and religion, but simultaneously to render Luther's doctrine *harmless*. He positions his doctrine at a safe distance; he emphasizes only its typical Protestant identity. It is also thinkable that he attributes greater value to the Lutheran *Church* than to Luther's original doctrine. The Christian *life* could, as it were, conquer the doctrine by establishing itself as an institute *in* the world by—in spite of the apocalyptic doctrine—becoming a part of the world and participating in the enduring ethical life. Philosophy is then able to attach itself to this life. Even if the doctrine is obsessed with evil, modern Protestant *life* is able to realize much good *in* this world: that is where philosophy comes into the picture. Regardless of how untruthful and insincere the doctrine might be, Protestant stubbornness is able to make a truthful and sincere life possible. From this juncture, Hegel connects the revealed divine with the good and finds in that way peace.

Hegel's *Eigensinn* must be taken quite literally in both senses of the word. It is all about the discovering of the own human world, a world that is so *familiar* to man that he is also able to discover it. It is this familiarity that offers man real *meaning* in life. This life's purpose provides joy and even makes knowing an enriching activity. The perceivable evil of the emerging world is reason enough for wanting to persistently resist this evil. The manifesting evil does not therefore have to be fatalistically undergone. This should be no cause for taking radical action against evil as such, against the world in which evil occurs, let alone against the ethical good of this world. Such activism is even dangerous in view of the fact that taking radical steps to banish evil can bring down the good with it. Even though it constitutes an incitement to action, evil can also be borne, it does not detract from the meaningfulness of life. Reconciliation not only means that good can be recognized and can be experienced as meaningful, but it also makes it possible to bear evil. Good justifies the existence of evil; it liberates man from a fatal aversion to it.

The reconciliation inherent in philosophical recognition liberates people from the one-sided perception of the negative aspect of evil. Philosophy is also able to reconcile even if the temptation from one-sidedness is great. Such temptation is actually a latent component of philosophy itself, with its stubborn endeavor to only attribute value to something if it can be justified by thought. It is only too easy for thinking to be negatively critical; philosophy is thus perpetually threatened by the danger zone of moralizingly knowing better. The fact that retrospective thought can only be activated once a development has progressed to a considerable degree only reinforces this threat. The conceptual ideal is only able to detach and distance itself once the reality of things has matured. Philosophy is not exclusively an internal matter; it is also externally engaged. It is this quality of being distant that provokes the inclination to moralize. With philosophy, there is the underlying temptation to want to profess to know better what is good for people. This temptation is dangerous. The stubborn *recognizing* therefore also has a therapeutic effect: that of restoring the connectedness with ethical substance.

There is another striking point to be made about the position occupied by *belief*. For Hegel, belief is no unconditional certainty that triumphs over the relative nature of understanding and knowing. With belief it is just as little about the totally other, possible or promised: belief provides no certainty in conjunction with non-being. Religion and belief may not lose themselves in *Jenseits* (transcendence).

There is therefore no intrinsic contrast between belief and understanding; both have to stay together. That is what is meant by the clause that follows the referred to stubbornness. Belief is especially active in the phase when developments begin: belief makes man internally active; it galvanizes him into action. However, belief must do this in a credible fashion. That is why belief may never turn against the *relative* facet that is also submerged in knowing. Belief, too, is involved in *what* is in a positive sense. The internal activating of man thus begins with belief, as a testimony of the spirit. The *what* of this testimony, its essence, returns again later in the *what* of philosophically knowing. By holding together belief and the understanding surrounding this *what*, Hegel is endeavoring to avoid a wrong way of testifying to belief. He turns himself against a kind of testifying that aligns itself with radical hope, with the longing for what is totally different, with the possible as opposed to the actual. Such testimony ruins the life's purpose of ethical life.

In the *spirit*, Hegel sees the equality of God and man: the spirit is two things in one. At the time of the Fall, God terminated his equality with man. This equality in the knowledge of good and evil is given added topicality after a long history. In modern times it becomes clear how man has deployed and continued the divine process of creation, how throughout the process he remained God's equal. In this respect, Hegel alludes to the testimony of the spirit (*Zeugnis des Geistes*). What does he mean by this?

In the ethical world, it turns out that man is moved by a creative force equal to that of God at the time of creation. In the human cosmos man perpetuates God's creating power. In that way he demonstrates how the divine component is still present, how what was begun in Genesis is continued. This is where we find the first interpretation of what Hegel understands by *zeugen*: to *create*, to produce, notably in a spiritual and ethical sense. With the complementary useful characteristics of feeling, perception, devotion, and submission, this producing is a matter of the spirit; creating embraces reason.

Just like God, man can recognize the good, *in* his creative activity and creativity, *in* his own works. Creating man can also therefore constantly look back and conclude that what he has done is *good*. In his contribution to the human cosmos he is able, in a genuine way, to implement the capacity to differentiate. This makes man able to recognize himself in his own work, or to put it another way, man *bears witness* to his own creative deeds, to the work of his own hands. In his knowledge he mirrors himself. It is in this position as witness that the second meaning of the term *Zeugnis* of the spirit is to be found. The fact that man can bear witness to his work at the same time turns such openly expressed knowing into a shared kind of *witnessing*, a common, public understanding. That is therefore why the godlike in the ethical results of human labor can also be understood to exist. Even though philosophy, unlike religion, is unable to stir things into action, it is able to discern such activity, justify it, and subsequently perpetuate it. What it does share with religion is the position of witness and it testifies, with religion, to the good that has been brought forth by the spirit. It shares with religion cognitive joy. It involves the intractable spirit in its own meaningful work. This three-pronged *Zeugnis* of the spirit prevents man from escaping into a yearning for recreation and an entirely other perspective on meaning. Reconciliation and ethical purpose in life guarantee that belief and knowledge, God and man, future and present do not grow apart.

The testimony of the spirit places man beneath the truth. He can look back on what has been bestowed upon him and is yet the product of his labor. Looking back—in retrospect—he learns to see *what* is good in what he has done. In retrospect, a testimony can be deciphered from God's words at the time of the Fall, the full significance of which only now becomes clear. This unravelling is a careful and respectful kind of discovery. But why now? Because in the modern era, the creative human power produces a result that corresponds to God's original intentions with creation. In perpetuating God's creation like a process of self-creation, and by taking the time to do that, the intended result is divulged. The content of what is true in religion has a somewhat concealed character with a secret *meaning*; when it comes to rationally understanding through philosophy it is revealed to man in the most *unique*, specific way. It becomes clear to man as it is a matter for everyone. The divine has become a *public* matter. It can be publicly known and recognized. It is everybody's property and recognizable to all. God now first truly *reveals* himself to man.

In this way, Hegel opposes the idea that the world is godforsaken and that the divine has to be sought elsewhere. Religion is characterized by a sense of reality that is devoid of transcendental hope. The fulfilling of meaning does not lie in the future, in the hope of what is totally other. The godlike is of this world and has, itself, materialized in this era in such a way that it has become recognizable *in* this world. In discovering the divine in ethical reality, man becomes indemnified from the dangerous *atheism of the ethical world*. This atheism not only robs the ethical world of God but also—with God—of its ethos, its ethical purpose, its binding element, its mutually shared good life. Ethical atheism is not only dangerous because the good is sought elsewhere; what is much sooner dangerous is the refusal to find the true and good here and in the present. Ethical atheism not only ruins the purpose of truth but also public life in the broadest sense of the word. Ethical atheism leads to cynicism. In expelling the good from the existing world, man lapses into contempt and *unrest*. It is the time-honored type of unrest that seeks its escape in hope. Hegel's doctrine of reconciliation seeks to conquer this perpetually threatening unrest.

Hegel resists the danger of ethical atheism. After the divine order had disappeared from the natural cosmos, this atheism also expelled the divine order from the human cosmos. Modernism declared the ethical God dead. Does God then completely disappear from the scene through this death? Or, does he perhaps return in another guise? Does the death of the ethical God perhaps once again pave the way for the *other* God, the God of belief? Does the modern era once more exhibit the ethical atheistic change? Does man revert again to the God who had previously revealed himself from the time of Abraham to Luther's day? Does modern atheism demonstrate—with sinister cynicism—the old double standard: that of declaring the ethical God dead whilst breathing new life into the new God? Again we see the omnipotent, but this time, perhaps, in a human guise? Is God who has become man now resurrected from the dead?

That would amount to a dark kind of irony: a modernist *incarnation of God*. That would involve modern atheism breathing new life into the old belief: now in the form of belief in human omnipotence, to, in that way, substantiate the promise within the realm of human capacity. The question which then arises is this: does man want, of his own volition, to bring about recreation? Does he maintain that he now has the ability to do that? Does this mean that to achieve that he now appropriates the name and characteristics of the omnipotent? What are the implications of this for the old idea of divine providence? Does man still want to clamp to efforts made to justify the evil of this world? Is man still able to benevolently look back upon the good that has been extended to him in the past? Is he still able to distill the good of his world from the true description of what is, or does he perhaps perceive evil to be too overwhelming so that he seeks good elsewhere? Does this make the view of what is, of what man has been given, again sombre? Then there is the most gloomy question: does the realization of good again *justify* a redeeming final contest with its own evil? Does modern atheism become *messianic*? Does it produce its own messiah, one that has *become man*?

With his announcement of the death of God, Nietzsche warns of the danger of the nihilistic incarnation of God. Atheistic modernism demonstrates how apocalyptic longings seek instant fulfillment. It was for that reason that the *Messiah* becomes man.

9.2 THE RETURNING GOD

God's disappearance from public life was labeled by Nietzsche the *death of God*. This thesis—more an observation—must be properly understood. He is not, in the first place, alluding to a failing belief in the existence God or gods. He is more interested in the particular effect that God's name has had: its significance for human society, for institutions, and for culture. The loss of such an effect is thus followed by his signaling of the consequences. With the death of God, the connecting forces and the balance within man and within society then threaten to give way. There is, therefore, the threat of disintegration. The disappearing God is the ethical God, the God of the human cosmos.

The belief in God tells us something about the ethical relationship between the two important commandments. The significance of the love shown for God is linked to the ethical *value* of the love for and solidarity with the other. For Nietzsche, this is seen as an important facet of traditional religions. Any private and internalized religion is empty and of little importance to the culture and society. The death of God triggers the pressing question of whether an internally connected coexistence of people is possible, of whether man still wants to invest in his future, in the full spectrum of culture. Is man still capable of spanning the bow and aiming at a distant target?

Nietzsche typifies himself as a *truthful* atheist. What he means by that is that he no longer finds it possible to believe in the impact of God or of gods. God disappears from human life and religion loses its impact. This applies both to the *true* and the *good*, both to knowledge and to ethical life. Slowly but surely, expanding scientific knowledge eliminates God as an explanation for what had, in the past, been impenetrable facts, occurrences, and processes. God is no longer needed to answer the question about truth. The separating of religion from the question of truth is something that occurs gradually; it does not need to give rise to great and permanent excitement. What actually also seems to disappear with the exiting of this God is the contribution that religion makes to the ethical life of man; the laws, rules, and commandments lose their *sacred* connotation. Nietzsche maintains that both developments amount to things that cannot be changed, even if the full weight of the implications still has not sunk in. The diminishing sacred basis of ethical life thus has to be replaced by a human equivalent, difficult as that will prove to be. He does not therefore opt for a life without ethical values, even less so, for utopian prospects. He really fears that modern man will not be able to cope with switching in this way from the sacred to the human. He recognizes everywhere an *untrue* atheistic reaction to the death of God. The death of the ethical God is also, as a matter of fact, seen to occur within the church. He thus foresees catastrophic consequences for cultural and institutional life. He foresees far-reaching consequences regarding the question of good and evil. The best part of religion disappears whilst the worst is given a new impetus. Religion is given a radical twist and effect; it disseminates *untrue* values.

Twice Nietzsche produces penetrating analyses on the matter of the loss of God. The *fröhliche Wissenschaft* tells of the behavior of *foolish man*. He endeavors to impress upon the crazed crowd that God is dead and that it is present-day man who is responsible for this deed. The fool warns the crowd of the consequences: he describes an existence and a cosmos from which balance and sense have vanished. Nietzsche regularly presents the prospect of such consequences. Balance, moderation, and a sense of proportion disappear. The death of God leads to the threat of atomic chaos, arbitrariness, and degeneration, short shrift on the part of man, lack of restraint, resentment, and animosity.

In the introduction to *Thus Spoke Zarathustra* this emerges more explicitly. After a long, lonely period in the mountains, Zarathustra wends his way back to civilization, to godforsaken modern man, to the type of person found in market squares—the meeting places for individualized human crowds. On the way, he meets an old saint who passes his days in isolation in the forest and in praising God. The old man is not aware that God is dead; the consequences of that have not therefore got through to him. For the old man, God is anything but dead: he still loves him and can still happily praise him. But what kind of a God is it that in fact rules his life? The old man is set on glorifying God in isolation because man is much too flawed for him: loving his fellow man would lead to his demise. So the lonely individual experiences the joy of a personal relationship with God. He therefore warns Zarathustra not to go to the people. There is, after all, nothing more to *give*. The old saint only still observes the *first commandment*. He still loves *his* God; his God continues to give him joy and purpose in life, but it is a love that is experienced in total isolation. His belief has become a completely *private* affair. He keeps far away from his fellow man, from his neighbor who would jeopardize his belief and the joy gained from that. In other words, the value of the second commandment may be said to have completely escaped him. Involvement with the other is of no further value to him, certainly no sacred value. The lonely life in the forest is a blessing to him, a private blessing. Though his personal religious experience is lively, the ethical significance of God has disappeared. In an ethical sense, the lonely one thus demonstrates a *godforsaken* life.

The old man, who really symbolizes a modern believer, dwelt in the ethical atheistic world that Hegel had so emphatically warned everyone about. All that remains for that believer is a private experiencing of belief, an internalized belief, a belief lacking cosmic order. The old man is a cheerful modernist: he lives in a world in which God has lost his ethical value. Despite all of that he has managed to retain his optimistic attitude to life. Far from the madding crowd, he demonstrates a happy kind of religiousness and spends his days laughing and singing. Nietzsche has a degree of sympathy for this lonely soul and grants him the love he feels for his private God. This does not mean to say that he accepts a privatized brand of belief. The old man lives far away from others; the death of the ethical God does not really affect him, the danger of it is not immediately manifest to him, but for others that death is a reality.

This *danger* becomes manifest in belief as it lives on in modern man, in the belief obsession that becomes more powerful, *also* in atheistic circles. It is all about the atheistic believers, those who follow Paul and Luther in their aversion to the modern world and in their longing for the end of time and a new world. The messianic interpretation of belief not only dominates modern religion; such belief also lives on in those who turn their back on God whilst retaining the essence of their belief. Are they still able to sustain such a joyous attitude to life as that displayed by the old man? Alternatively, does the danger of the death of God become evident in them?

The fool in the market square holds up a mirror to the crowd in relation to the root of this danger. The danger lies in the modernistic crowd itself. It wells up in these individuals, with them it can so easily find a way out. The fool warns of the consequences of the godforsaken cosmos for man. With the diminishing sacred core of ethical life, order and equilibrium are also lost in man and in society. The fact that tradition is losing its ethical significance not only disrupts the tie with the past but it also makes the purpose of the future problematic. In short, his metaphors are only too clear. The earth has broken free from its sun and is plunging through the void, devoid of direction. There is no way ahead and no way behind, no above and no below, no horizon, merely an endless nothingness without light, without generative light. For man, the ethical God was a great inspiration, a force that set him in motion and gave him equilibrium. That danger for man becomes evident in another way: the foolish crowd does not understand the fool. With the inner equilibrium, what slips away from man is his *self-knowledge*, what he loses is the old adage which states *know thyself*. It is notably that which makes man foolish. He does not understand the implications of the death of God. Man does not understand what he has brought upon himself. He does not see the consequences that await him. The full significance of this deed is thus still to be felt. It will take time to comprehend the consequences and to come to terms with them.

A same type of incredulity is apparent when Zarathustra—again in a modernistic market square—addresses the crowd and urges the people to accept the present earthly existence as a challenge and to give it *meaning*. He warns these people to be wary of the old but still very relevant religious folly of surrendering oneself to a sublime or utopian hope. He warns them to be wary of developing an aversion to life. He warns about the spiritual poverty of the *last man* and his resentment. The warning is to no avail. It is sooner the case that it proves to be a danger in itself: no understanding, no insight, but instead derision and hatefulness. People want to be left in peace in what constitutes to their minds a fulfilled life, a life in which nothing more needs to be achieved. It is not so much the case that people yearn for a sensuous, aesthetic form of happiness that is still to come, because that has, they maintain, already been achieved. Zarathustra expresses this perfectly: people maintain that they have "*erfunden*" happiness—that is to say—that they have thought it up, invented it. People experience a figment of happiness, a semblance of meaning: a meaning that has to be *believed* in if something of it is to be experienced. It is the happiness of the land that has been promised them. People deny every doubt, people believe they are heading in that direction and that it *must* be possible to achieve, or at least to believe, that they have already achieved that goal. People prove to be very motivated. As a matter of fact, these people believe that they *must* also be able to achieve, over again and to an increasing degree, the apparently achieved happiness. People *must* believe in that now that the ethical significance of life has been lost. The happiness that has been invented is also an escape and an obsession.

Foolish man poses in this connection yet another notable and really rhetorical question. The question is not so much directed at the crowd as at man in general. After having established that it is man himself who has killed God, he asks himself if the enormity of this deed is really not too great for man. He then wonders whether people should not themselves be elevated *to the position of gods* to be worthy of such a deed. He is of the opinion that *man* could never achieve a greater deed and those who are still to come, in conjunction with this deed, are entitled to a greater history than the whole of history until that time. Zarathustra proposes something similar: man has no alternative than to conquer himself *as man*. He will have to be capable of suprahuman deeds. Does this mean that man has to make something that is divine his own?

9 From God to Man

What does Nietzsche actually mean when he talks of this supra-human attribute, this notion of becoming gods?

Is Nietzsche thinking here of *God's becoming man* in the sense that Hegel intended? No, that is definitely not the case, on the contrary in fact. To Hegel, there is evidence of a transition from God to man. In the course of history, exalted God and man have become each other's equals: what the God of creation asserted to be has become a reality. The distance between both has been bridged. A liberating ethical spirit endows man with a divine life. Hegel is thinking here of the modern, differentiated civil constitutional state with its free consciousness and ethical liberties. He wants man to recognize and know this so that ethical life becomes his own. He has to learn to understand this life just like his own work, as a work of art that gives him an own world, a cosmos in which he recognizes himself and which gives him joy and a zest for life. Hence the need to emphasize that modern and idiosyncratic facet of man. The fact that it is actually like this only becomes clear to man in retrospect. Without any kind of creative religious impulse, man could never have realized this. Without any sort of religious, sacred core, ethical life cannot maintain itself either. God's becoming man may not be allowed to destroy the ethical content of anything divine. If God is to bind man, then the *essence* of this *individuality* must remain sacred and hallowed. Man cannot manage this without stopping to *reason*. God's becoming man may not make man overconfident either; ethical life is not equipped to deal with so much *hybris*. That which is sacred in ethical life must be preserved if its essence is to be fully appreciated and if it is to be benevolently accepted. The social order may not be an arbitrary *product* of private individuals with complete freedom to do exactly as they please. A meaningful order cannot be founded upon *unconditional* freedom. The *value* that life buttresses in society must be enduring. Hence the reason that this divine aspect of man's innermost core must be preserved. It is therefore in an ethical sense that God has become man. In this way, Hegel hopes to be able to fend off the threat of modern atheism in the modern world.

Just half a century later, Nietzsche asserts that this endeavor has failed: the God of ethical life is dead. With the sacred heart, society loses its old ethical substance and that is precisely where the nub of the problem lies: the *ethical aspect* of ethical life is not able to cope without the divine component. Without the sacred aspect it becomes too human, it loses its authentic, sacred nature. That is why the answer *does* now lie with man, it *must* lie with man, and man must *want* it to be that way. God is dead; God remains dead so man cannot revert to God. Since society really cannot manage without enduring order, man will have to give shape to this order in his own *unique* way. Man *himself* will have to be the *condition* for his own purpose in life. The ethical substance is in this way transferred from God to man. He himself will have to invigorate his institutions; he himself will have to deliver the required cultural tension. The sacred core of these institutions has been lost to man, in that respect religion can no longer support man. Man therefore has to take over the divine work in his role as man. It all revolves around man: he himself now becomes the standard for things. Nietzsche has therefore turned around the orientation behind God's becoming man: since the divine can no longer be adopted and preserved as a sacred tradition, man has to develop it as man—in whatever guise that might turn out to be.

He adds something to that, though, he makes it plural. People will have to become *gods*. What was intrinsically essential to the one and omnipotent God can and may not be retained. It seems that man has to revert to the idiosyncratic of the pantheon. The divine must once again assume a versatile guise. The world will display an interweaving of divergent ethical competences, including the competitive aspect. For Nietzsche, the death of God also represents a *departure* from the enticing element that dwells in the one omnipotent God. This divinity must not take over man but rather win him over. In this way he notes resistance to the greatest danger lurking in modern atheism, that of holding on to the hope and expectations that are invested in the name of God. Where the old placed belief in God, the new—atheistic belief—hopes to be able to ascribe that to man. That is what makes this atheism *insincere*. God is *humanized* in the wrong kind of way. Modern atheism confirms, in an activistic way, the death of the ethical God, but it certainly does not turn against the omnipotent. Passionately it seeks human omnipotence in the same way and with the same longing that divine omnipotence was once sought. It now finally *wants to* realize a fulfilled existence and so it disseminates belief so that this fulfillment *can* become a reality. The new belief is presented as a new ideology, as a human doctrine of ideas. No matter how great the similarity is with religious belief, the new belief also takes a dangerous turn. The activist forgets how to wait, he forgets about *humility*, he forgets how to resign himself. Impatient and driven, he gears himself up to realize his doctrine.

In this atheistic danger Nietzsche recognizes active nihilism. The death of God not only goes hand in hand with a *revaluation* of the highest values, but also with a driven desire to realize these values. The true becomes a *zealous* proving, the good a *jealous* coveting. The activistic last person experiences life as oppressive, heavy, and troublesome. He forgets what is challenging about it, he forgets how to span the bow; he wants to be liberated from that. Every burden becomes too heavy for him and incompatible with the demanded *fabrication* of happiness. He becomes possessed by a passionate belief in the fulfillment of that happiness. He is perpetually pursued by an impatient and immense *not-yet*.

However, this is not where this revaluation of values stops. The gravity of existence does not leave the final person in peace. This gravity chains itself to evil, a kind of evil that cannot be justified. The fabrication does not just point ahead but it also has a *backward*-oriented facet. The contrived also creates jealousy, an aversion to what is, to what is too heavy to still bear. What has been contrived therefore gives rise to aversion. The invented gives rise to a two-way directed representation of power: a jealous desire for happiness clamps itself to a jealous urge to retaliate. That which has been contrived fuels resentment and turns itself outwards. Evil that cannot be justified can no longer be borne. The time-honored longing for *justice* is activated. Now that God is dead, this justice is justifiably transferred to man. Justice will now finally have to be done, redeeming and avenging justice. The longing for justice brings about unprecedented illusions of power, the illusion of human omnipotence.

The death of God plunges man into an *ethical* vacuum in which he unleashes *nihilistic* fury. This rage will have to conquer man *as man*. He wanted to be *like God* but he will have to become *like gods*.

How did the atheistic belief gain its stature? What kind of redemption doctrine did it develop? How did it seek liberation from an existence that was no longer bearable? Unless the omnipotent becomes man there can be no justice. This is also a story that can be told. It is the story of one who practices what he preaches; it is the story of believers who seek to realize the impossible. It is the story of a final contest in which also the Messiah becomes man.

10

The Imagination Unleashed

Here, modern atheism is examined within the context of God's incarnation as man. Man prepares to take the place of the omnipotent. But why? Because the godforsaken ethical cosmos no longer satisfies him. Because he wants to re-establish a world. Because he has come to believe afresh in miracles. Because he imagines that he himself can realize such a miraculous thing. No godlike omnipotence is any longer required for the certainty of this belief. Just as the belief in God's omnipotence gradually gained ground and was slowly linked to apocalyptic perspectives, so also God-made-man presented himself, first modestly and somewhat hesitantly but, in the process, apocalyptic prospects were nevertheless developed. It was not to be a process that would culminate in messianic *expectations*, but rather in the *realized* final conflict. Man no longer awaits God's intervention: Messianism becomes practical, revolutionary, and political. The revaluation of good and evil leads to a justified struggle. The question that arises, though, is this: how will man's own evil be justified in that battle? Imagination can lead to fabrication. Can such figments of the imagination also justify the madness of evil?

The story commences with the animosity towards the world of Plato, and ends—for the time being—with the totalitarian heirs of Romanticism. Plato's *doctrine* of ideas seeks to build a *bridge* between the old, objectionable world and the new, heavenly world. Modernity demolishes the old world.

10.1 PLATO'S ANIMOSITY TO THE WORLD

Plato's philosophy cannot be considered in isolation of the diminishing authority of the mythical gods. How can things continue with the cosmos, with the city-state, if the gods are no longer there to lay down standards for human action? His philosophy is also, in fact, a reaction to radical sophism which held that man had to take the place of gods; become a type of individual guided by his own instinct. Human nature thus becomes the criterion. Plato fears for the fate of policy if such thinking finally gains the upper hand. His doctrine of ideas must help to restore the ethical order.

His doctrine of ideas unmistakably gives shape to human modesty. For man, those *ideas* are, after all, a sacred fact of life: an original, eternal cosmos and directive for man's praxis. He has to see this divine teaching and act accordingly. These guidelines have nothing to do with free will as far as man is concerned, nor are they instantly available to the connoisseur. The phases of discovering and following amount to a *learning process* in two respects: man has to learn how to see ideas and he subsequently has to be taught how to act in accordance with those same ideas. The ideas may be recognized through introspection, by contemplating them and by discovering what has truly been given to man. This places man firmly *beneath* the truth. That which is good may thus be claimed to be founded upon a divine maxim that is to be revealed through memories.

Since ideas are of a divine origin, this does not make it easy as far as human knowledge is concerned. It is possible to have knowledge, but then a huge chasm between man's limited human capacities and the divinely celestial has to be bridged. That which is not instantly accessible demands patience and effort. Man should be grateful that he, in his role as finite being, may contemplate and participate in that which is absolute. Theoretically knowing about and practically adhering to what the idea generates demands reverence, respect, the ability to listen to that which is *true*, and to then, with that, do ethical *good*.

In that respect, Plato makes an effort to preserve what is *sacred*, even if it is no longer a part of the everyday apparent world. After all, the gods are dead: the sacred and divine therefore loses its innate manifestation. Knowing the divine idea thus becomes more of a philosophical affair than a religious matter. That which is sacred is therefore transferred to *people's* inner being and can only be discovered through human *knowledge*. Without man and his wisdom the *divine* no longer suffices. It is always necessary to really discover what man has originally been given; it is always necessary to *contemplate* precisely what precedes man. Human thought is thus active provided that it remains modest. No matter how essentially human thought processes may be, it is not man himself who creates the truth, he remains beneath the truth. Neither does man imagine that he is omnipotent. Indeed, that which is good is not subject to his will, it does not arbitrarily lie at his disposal. Does this make him authentic in his knowledge and sincere in his deeds?

One may criticize Plato's contention that man can be placed *beneath* the truth because he deviates from the basic condition laid down by the virtue of truthfulness. In fact, he does not tolerate what is *actually* given to him, what the world that is apparent to him has to offer. It is a world that scares him away. The city-state is corrupt and thus lost. He can no longer remain faithful to such a world. He fails to recognize the value of the traditional world that has been handed down to him. It has become a godforsaken world lacking in value and one that certainly has no ethical worth. The existing world no longer complies with the divine *example*. Since the true and the good can no longer be discovered in the manifest world, the knowledge related to that is also subject to ruin. As far as the existing and apparent world is concerned, there remains nothing other than the Socratic *prejudice of not knowing*. Such knowledge does not constitute a basis for existence. The world as it appears is so dominated by *appearance* that it is not *worth* getting to know it. This forces Plato to totally cut himself free from the existing world and to switch to something *completely different*, something that is not subject to untrue appearance and to the related knowledge.

In a cognitive and ethical sense Plato therefore bids farewell to the world as he knows it. He turns his back on the ethical tradition, no longer recognizing its value. In this respect he is an ethical atheist. His wisdom is false because his moralizing prejudice prevents him from becoming acquainted with the world as it is. In this respect he elevates himself above the truth. In the face of all the cognitive and ethical modesty incorporated in the doctrine of ideas, this turns man into a *judge* of the world. Philosophy embarks on an exodus from the land where one no longer feels at home. What *is* is worth allowing to go to waste; such moralism precedes the promised re-creation of an ethical cosmos. The *going to waste* is of a radical and skeptical nature. It is not so much the case that the divine tradition *is dead* as that it has been *declared dead*. Philosophical wisdom begins its revolt against the existing world.

The fact that Plato justifies this revolt by deferring to a higher order does not alter the fact that philosophy is beginning to impose its own kind of truth and good upon the world. On the basis of this justification, the philosophical god elevates himself *above* the truth and simultaneously above mankind who is imprisoned in life's mere semblance. Mankind is *unable* to know the truth but *does not need* to know it either. Mankind is required to *believe* in the truth that philosophy has to offer. Mankind resides *beneath* the credibility *above* which philosophy stands: the truth of *holding to be true*. Little remains of the apparent epistemological modesty. The faithful must adapt to what the elevated, philosophical god *commands*.

Early in philosophical history a similar religious doctrine was proclaimed to that seen in religious belief. From the very start, however, philosophical doctrine was given a more *human* dimension: man now made sure that he counted. In conventional religion man does not have the authority to express anything absolute without God. In philosophical religious doctrine a turnabout is perceptible: man maintains that he does now have *the power* to utter the absolute. This change does not alter the fact that religious doctrine still hinges on the same principle. The yearning for fulfillment still continues to be fed by the rejection surrounding what man is given. This rejection fuels a longing for the total other and an urge to recreate. The benevolent view of man and of the human world that he has inherited again becomes tainted.

The question is, how long can such cynicism about faith lay claim to the divine in a quasi-modest fashion? Surely the divine can also be replaced by human superiority. Why should human will not create its own apocalyptic perspective? Why should man not conquer religious modesty? With Descartes, it becomes clear how man overcomes his modesty. He achieves that by freeing the will and by imagining that he is omnipotent.

10.2 GOD AS AN OBSESSION

Modern subjectivism is a step in the direction of God's becoming man. Man's discovery turns omnipotent God into a challenge, possibly even an obsession. How can power be gained over this God? How can man claim omnipotence for himself?

The probing question posed by Descartes is this: how can man resist the omnipotence of God? For him, as man, as a being with limitations, God's power is taunting. God constitutes a perpetual confrontation. He cannot shake himself free of the exasperating human constraints. Surely it must be possible to surmount such human restrictions? It seems as if God's omnipotence has been unquestioningly accepted as a fact of life, a certainty which, as such, is not questioned for a moment. He unthinkingly adopts all the extreme nominalistic definitions. In so doing, he creates an image of God that has a taunting effect upon him and which thereby becomes a target for his human ambition. He creates an image of a creature that he as man would like to be. The obsessive question that resonates in his image of God is whether man can be *this* God's equal. But is this really feasible; can man be *equal* to the omnipotent?

For the sake of comparison one may consider an earlier parallel drawn between man and God in the story of creation. In terms of their knowledge of good and evil, God and man were each other's *equals*, in their awareness of the relativity of this discrepancy. The equality between the two was sustainable as long as the notion of omnipotence was not allowed to penetrate. The relative nature of matters to which that God was resigned also empowered human ambition. The whole idea of omnipotence destroys the capacity to live with what is relative and moderate. God and man become unequal. In religion God is annoyed with man who is not his equal but atheism turns this relationship upside down. Because man cannot be omnipotent God's *equal*, he seeks to appropriate for himself what is characteristic of this God. *Conflict* therefore becomes inevitable. Naturally, the whole idea of omnipotence rules out equality on the part of the omnipotent to start off with! God and man cannot both be omnipotent.

If the position of God starts to torment man and if he wants to be *like God*, then God's omnipotence will inevitably have to yield to that of man. The power has to fall to one of the two parties. *Equality in terms of omnipotence* amounts to a logical impossibility. Religion resolves the question by ascribing omnipotence to God. Man has to accept his *inequality* in relation to God. For him God's omnipotence is something fatal, its arbitrariness forces him into submission. All that remains for man is to hope or trust that the omnipotent will have his best interests at heart. The submission will fade if man jealously reacts to the divine omnipotence, if the omnipotence challenges him and the image of God becomes a tempting prospect. Why should man not be able to be *like God*: as man, as mankind, as a representative for mankind? Then the full implication of the contradiction *becomes apparent*: the two *cannot* be equal. With the former equality, the mutual *love* between God and man is once again lost. Previously omnipotent God had shown himself to be jealous: he was irritated by human *unwillingness* to bend to his will. It was this reluctance that drove him to threaten recalcitrant man with the prospect of his avenging justice. As a matter of fact, the temptation of omnipotence almost automatically leads to *jealousy* on the part of man. Why, then, should he any longer bow to God's will?

The image of God's omnipotence now turns against God like an *example*: like an example that man wants to emulate, that he *wants* to make his own. It is not only so that the image of the omnipotent challenges man, it also taunts him because it makes God unpredictable. He is, after all, able to perpetually change everything, he is *arbitrariness* itself. This arbitrariness makes human will and human knowledge uncertain in a fatal way. Hence the reason that Descartes seeks *certainty* above all else: human certainty. Hence his longing for human autonomy. He does not want to be subject to the will of another: to stand *beneath* it. He wants no knowledge that has simply been handed to him; he does not want to abide *beneath* the truth. He does not want to be compelled to follow.

Hence the reason that he places man opposite the divine example with the double capacity of being in possession of absolute *free will* and *ego cogito*. It is such will that liberates man and makes him autonomous. Free will makes man a self-satisfied being. He positions himself and moves as he wishes. Such will puts an end to human lowliness. Man must now also *want* to liberate himself, from the heteronomous, from everything that from the point of view of autonomy may become a *shackle*. There is no longer any peace. The paradox of the omnipotent turns autonomy into an obsession. He is constantly aware of the constricting ties of heteronomy. Man is *forced* to make his own omnipotence *a reality*. The longing for freedom and omnipotence chains man to the perennial *having to want to* of freedom. Inevitably it is something that leads to human brutality. Humility disappears, and with it any respect for that which is different, for what has been given to man, for the relative, for the sacred. All that remains of God is a concept, one that is useful for boosting human certainty. All the barriers are broken. Man turns against everything that threatens his freedom and power. It was a change that governed the thinking initiated by Descartes.

The certainty derived from *free will* and *ego cogito* was to form the basis to modernity. It now revolved radically around *man*. Man presented himself as the originator of things, as an endlessly active, self-liberating, and self-creating force. He does not want to depend on anything or anyone. Modernist man portrays anew the image of the exodus from an unbearable world and the entry into what is now a self-promised land. Even free will is dominated by the ancient double urge for redemption. On the one hand there is the longed-for deliverance *to*, a longing with a forward, recreating orientation. On the other hand, however, there is an even stronger and reactive longing for redemption *from*. Above all else, free will seeks to be liberated *from* all constraints, from all the chains. Man is in search of unrestrained self-liberation. From the time of Descartes, man has prepared to throw off the chains that have been holding him back. This craving for freedom is inspired by the self-created image of God, the human example. This God is no longer the God of the ethical world, the God who reveals himself in ethical life. In the Cartesian concept of God, it is the re-evaluation of the ethical orientation of man that is unveiled. The Cartesian God is ethically atheist. It is this atheistic image of God that is further elaborated.

Though this image of God may present a godforsaken world, the *ego cogito* registers, for its part, resistance to this world. It heralds the ruin of this world as an object of radical doubt. The godforsaken reality turns out to be ill-equipped to deal with a kind of dialectics which makes everything that exists relative in the wrong sort of way: changeable, transitory, superficial. The godforsaken world is eliminated. The *ego cogito* is the self-assured beginning *and* the insatiable result of the dialectics of doubt. Dialectics destroys what it wants to destroy, that is how radical its spirit of freedom is. The *ego cogito* is the self-satisfied foundation of human knowledge and actions. What it in fact wants to do is prove itself through the certainty of being able to create what it wants to create. This self-satisfaction has the power of *belief*, a belief that must perform a miracle. The miracle works. It makes man a creator, in actual fact a re-creator, simply because the liberating *from* must, by definition, precede the liberating *to*.

The dialectics generates, as it were, a power-crazed notion of truth. With knowledge it is not about the representation of fact, of what is the case and what has to be discovered. The God who has become man eliminates the entire existing cosmos with all its susceptibility to doubt. This gives the free *ego cogito* the opportunity to constitute its own knowledge. It is now man who answers for the certain validity of his truth. What is decisive for the truth is a kind of *certainty* that is devoid of dependence or of anything that is relative. The truth is merely what man himself reveals, understands and declares to be certain. Knowledge does not direct itself in a *representative* way to what is given, but *presents*, instead, a world of its own. The *ego cogito* imagines itself to be the autonomous creator of its world.

The old, one-time divine cosmos is therefore no longer a goal for man. It is man himself who becomes the foundation of creation. However, there is still a problem. Unconditional, certain knowledge also proves to be a constraining factor. All *determination* is in reality *negation*, and so it is confined and finite. Does this not make human freedom again limited? Does man remain subjected to something that is insuperable? Descartes recognizes this limitation but he places it in a totally human perspective. If certain knowledge is seen as a form of self-limitation on the part of man then all external limitations must remain out of the picture. Is it possible to continue to assert that self-limitation does not again tie man down? Does the self-constraining not again affect the newly acquired freedom? Recognition of this will lead, at the very least, to acknowledgement or resignation.

Almost automatically, man is challenged to strive to also overcome this problematic self-limitation. It is difficult to bear this outlining of human omnipotence. How can this be justified? Why should one even try to do that? Why should the longing for omnipotence be tempered? Why not completely capitalize on the longing to be like God? It is Descartes who instigates people to explore the full breadth and depth of this radical longing, the longing to allow nominalistic God to become man in all his various facets. His *ego cogito* is self-satisfied; it not only turns against external limitations but also against self-limitation. Why not adopt even greater *belief*, the kind of belief that such limitations can be ended by the will itself? Why should this unleashed and unleashing God be reserved or inhibited. Why is there not even more impertinence? Why is there not a remorseless attitude towards everything that opposes unleashed man? Descartes' *ego cogito* does not only place man explicitly above the truth but also, implicitly, *above* ethical life. Where what is known no longer, in a cognitive sense, goes before the one who knows, it is only too easy for the other to also no longer precede the own ego in an ethical sense. One is thus, once again, reminded of the paradoxical implications of the pathos of freedom, a paradox to which the religious all too happily surrender: the *enmeshing* of the will in the yearning for redemption. It is not only the *different* that does not fit into this picture but also the *other*. The unleashed urge for freedom has a fatal reverse side to it, the urge to chain the *will for power* to own power, a chaining that makes everything seem false and insincere in relation to what opposes own power.

It was an entanglement that had already started with medieval nominalism. The sheer notion of there being an omnipotent God does in fact imply a certain arbitrariness. This arbitrariness makes it hard to hold on to a God that can be recognized in a cosmic order. At any given time the omnipotent can change this order to suit his will. Arbitrariness similarly ruins the image of a God that precedes man in ethical life and is, in that respect, his equal. The omnipotent does not give love, he demands it; he wants to be loved. He only tolerates believers who blindly adhere to the good of his will, whatever that good may be. It is an arbitrariness that man now wants to adopt.

In his self-satisfaction he now only recognizes himself. The ethical atheistic *ego cogito* becomes entwined in envy and the perverted enjoyment of power.

This, then, is the reverse side of unleashed freedom of will. It robs man of the virtue of giving, of the ability to give. It is the lot of anyone who places himself above the truth and above the ethical order. God who has become man gets himself tied up in an endless struggle for redemption. He wants to be liberated from everything that stands in his way, in himself but also in the other.

This dual urge to seek freedom returns in the thinking of Kant. In founding human will in what is *noumenal*, he renders human will, in principle, unconditionally free. In fact, he instantly makes man's will free *of* all limitations: not only those inherent in the causal urges of physical reality, but also those latent in the ethical urges imposed by society. The newfound basis therefore ensures the unlimited possibilities of this freedom. *Possible* does not mean to say *real* or, more to the point, *actual*. Man has to make use of and *want* to make use of this opportunity. Only then can there be evidence of freedom *to* do something. Unimpeded freedom of will tolerates no imposed ethical ties, but the fact that such a thing exists surely cannot be denied. Does this make Kant revolutionary?

In a certain respect, that may be said to be the case even though it might not ensue from physical violence but rather from the machinations of fundamental criticism. In a negative-critical way, he eliminates the heteronomic validity of the given ethical or political curbing of freedom. Man must, in fact, see such constraining as self-sought. Whatever man might have wanted, he is free to change his mind. The world of ethical experience does, in any case, fall within what coincides with his will. That then leads to his *sapare aude*, in other words, to the appeal to man to make use of his reasoning powers and to free himself from all *self-chosen* and self-blameworthy inarticulate states. To put it another way, man cannot reason away the *a priori* facet of freedom. He *is* free. What he can do is ignore such freedom or negate it; he can leave the inarticulate situation for what it is. He himself can then actually be the reason for not making use of what inevitably belongs to himself. This turns the a priori aspect of freedom into a *hermetic* type of *reasoning*: even the denying thereof becomes an act of freedom. This must therefore make it logical to *really* accept and implement freedom of will. If the very abusing of freedom is an act that is born of freedom of will, even if it constitutes a wrong deed, then man really has no other alternative than to turn such freedom to good use.

One might then presume that man is perfectly free to randomly make use of his freedom of will, as though use of own powers of reasoning and own understanding were instantly possible. But it is not quite as easy as that. To that end, one will first have to willingly rectify the incorrect deeds. The actual enlightened use of freedom therefore commences in a negative, critical way, as an act of liberation. The creative freedom *to* act thus starts with a radical liberating *from*. The active, free implementation of the capacities to reason and understand thus begins in a *reactive* way. True articulation thus starts with the eliminating *of* all that perpetuates lack of articulation. Does this also include the liberating of the constraints inherent in ethical society and therefore also in fellow man? How does *withdrawing* from an inarticulate state bring the other aspect into focus? What exactly is that inarticulate state? For Kant, where do the other and the ethical relationship to the other reside?

The actual cause of inarticulacy lies in man himself: in his lack of courage, his *laziness*, his *cowardice*. Hence the reason that Kant views the inarticulate state as something that is *self-chosen*. If, in freedom, man him*self* opts for constraints, if this is something *self*-imposed, then man can also free him*self* from such limitations. Man *is* after all free, and therefore needs only to liberate himself from his own inarticulateness if he is to give a correct interpretation to his own freedom. An inarticulate individual is part of an ethical, political, or moral order that is not entirely peculiar to him, that he would not voluntarily have created. It is essentially incorrect to think that such an order is strictly heteronomous. Apparent heteronomy may not be seen as a constant, as externally imposed: heteronomy may be blamed upon people themselves. The first and most fundamental cause lies in man himself, in his incorrect use of freedom. That is why Kant accuses the inarticulate person of *laziness* and *cowardice*, not of lacking sense or of being *stupid*. Freedom is unconditionally given and therefore possible. Human *incapacity* would spoil such an unconditional state. It would not only make heteronomy insurmountable but also, undoubtedly, welcome, as it would prevent worse things from happening. Laziness actually defines heteronomy as *unwillingness*, the unwillingness of oneself to work on an order that corresponds with what human reason dictates. Kant leaves no space for what is confining or relative, for what in an ethical sense precedes individual man. In conjunction with the unconditional, it is only *the* individual, *the* will and reason that count in a universal respect. In everything that man is and in all that concerns him, Kant anticipates that the *withdrawal*, already completed beforehand, will be radical. It is still merely about *actually* executing this so that the promised world of freedom can really be *realized*. Thanks to this liberating *from*, man becomes conscious of what it is he really has to *do*. The direction in which reason steers human knowledge and human will and dealings is evident. Nothing may be taken for granted; everything must be justifiable in terms of reason. This not only applies to the act of redeeming, but also to the way in which articulate man organizes the world promised him.

The indicators for such organization are the universal, regulative ideas of reason. The conversion into the justice of will and dealings offers the *categorical* perspective. Only self-chosen universality justifies moral rules. The articulate and thus autonomous individual finds himself in an incredible predicament: he is at once man and mankind. Any space between the two disappears, and therefore also the traditional, ethical, or political order that has to be conveyed. The withdrawal is unrelenting: anything that cannot stand up and be justified in front of the tribunal of universal reason is rendered invalid. This would imply that in terms of the new order that has to be created, the position of man is entirely free. But is this order still ethical? The individual *must*, after all, surrender voluntarily and unconditionally to a universal order. Everything is founded on the free *will* of the autonomous individual. This individual then finds himself devoured by in a universal *must*. At the same time, the other one to which the will must, in a moral sense, direct itself, disappears—vanishing into humankind, into universality. The *other* in terms of fellow man is sacrificed up to *the* other as such, an anonymous category. What remains of the justifiable ethical order falls within universalistic panoramas such as humanity, the world, and world history. After the articulate stepping aside from the handed-down, traditional ethical order follows revolutionary panoramas, those of a recreated human race.

In order to strip ethical reality of all its sacred worth and affinities, God himself is even humanized: he is *turned into* a notion that suits man. The significance of this idea has nothing to do with discovering and knowing; it has more to do with a regulatory, practical idea that can be *realized*. The God of *before* the departure from inarticulacy is a very different God from the one of *after* the departure. It is freedom of will that dethrones the old God, and with him, also are destroyed: his creation, tradition, and ethical order. The new God is articulate; he is the self-creating and thus omniscient and omnipotent mankind. Kant completes a similar kind of revolution to that completed in the time of Abraham. Through the exodus, the traditional, ethical God changes into the omnipotent, into a God that assures man of his promise. With Kant, divine omniscience and omnipotence turns into human reason. It then becomes man's responsibility to create his own human cosmos. *In the beginning* there is now the unconditional freedom of the will that stubbornly creates an own world. Even though knowledge-style reasoning might find itself up against what is relative, unconditional free will promises itself that it will conquer this relative side of matters. Reason is radical and revolutionary. What has been given to man is robbed of its intrinsic value. Will and reason make man all-powerful.

In the case of Kant, there is no evidence of a doctrine for two worlds; there is no phenomenal world alongside a noumenal one. Theoretical reason may not attach itself to what is *given fact*. Knowledge does not help man to find a niche for himself in the existing world. Truth does not serve to support ethical good. That would denude good of its foundations in unconditional freedom. From the point of view of human freedom and autonomy, reason works, in a theoretical sense, in a *self*-restricting fashion. But reason may not simply leave it at that. Free, articulate, and practical, reason is moreover able to release it*self* from its own self-constraints. One only needs to want this, one can want this, one should therefore *have to* want this. If man unconditionally ascribes this freedom to himself then there is nothing that still stands in the way of his own freedom. No theoretical *explanation* is needed for unconditional freedom—such an explanation would even amount to a contraction. Salvation is sought in the practical explanations of articulate people when they propose that they themselves are the unconditional, free creators of themselves and their own cosmos. Man merely therefore needs to actually *proclaim* his freedom.

Can a philosophy that introduces the notion of truth to an unlimited kind of substantiation subsequently be termed *truthful*? Does an activistic type of philosophy remain true to the earth? Does not that which *is* in that way lead to resistance that has to be conquered? Does the will, that wishes to be unconditionally freely creative, not turn itself against all that is given and that resists it? Can an unconditionally free will ever detach itself from anything? The appeal to, as man, *recognize* nothing unless it stems from human freedom is surely obsessive? This urge for freedom makes the *antimony* of freedom and causality unbearable. Since the drive for freedom wants to secure the miracle of freedom, at whatever cost, the will becomes even more doggedly determined if such a miracle does not become manifest. The pathos of freedom makes the will a *prisoner* of always wanting something else, of wanting more, of *having to want* more. The actual antimony lies in the desire for unconditional freedom itself. By experiencing all that binds as a heteronomous sort of chaining, the will is forced to seek *act*ual sovereignty. That will must strive for omniscience and omnipotence.

10.3 THE PATHOS OF FREEDOM

It later becomes clear how provocative the consequences of Kant's doctrine of freedom legacy could be. This is not only illustrated by the philosophy of Fichte, but his philosophy was also, in its turn, to become influential. The ideologies inspired by him demonstrate the totalitarian consequences of the freedom pathos. Fichte's philosophy unleashes a power-seeking wanting-to-fulfill. Whatever resists the new omnipotence is not only stripped of its value, but also becomes an object of *animosity*.

For Fichte, everything starts with an *I* that presents itself. This *I* is united and it *does* want to unconditionally assert itself as being free. That is why this *I* wants to turn outwards: it wants to be everything, recognize itself in everything. In turning itself outwards, this *I* comes into contact with what is different and with what cannot, as such, be borne: it encounters the obstinate *not-I*. Even that is, in fact, posited by the *I*, by the power of *imagination*. By providing something recalcitrant in the perspective of the infinite *I*, the imagination has a restless effect upon the *I*. The *I* which presents itself is as being unconditionally free is thereby unable to find peace until it has made everything familiar to itself: a vicious circle. This *making familiar to itself* has nothing to do with the repressing of what amounts to the other self, but rather a complete disowning. Everything that is unique to itself is destroyed. The real basis of things is, after all, the own self or *I*. Restlessly, expansively, and intolerantly, the *I* searches for the way out but tolerates nothing external to itself. Obsessively, Fichte's *I* wants to integrate what is different, break what resists, eliminate that which refuses to integrate.

Through its imagination and struggling, the *I* is therefore one ball of energy, of endless power and duration. And just like Rousseau, Fichte bases all of this on the *one I* and the one, *universal will*. How, in fact, could this *I* otherwise be able to become infinite?

Whilst Descartes still wanted to pitch himself against the arbitrary nature of omnipotent God, the *strivings* of Fichte's human *I* intrinsically carry the pretense of divine unconditionality and omnipotence. If there is unconditional freedom of will, this would imply that there is arbitrariness. This *I* cannot therefore bear to reside under the truth and to confine itself to representing what is given. From the point of view of the freedom, omnipotence, and arbitrariness of the *I*, truth operates like a constraint that has to be surmounted. Fichte's free and indomitably active individual not only keeps God at bay, but also wants, at the same time, to aspire to divinity—to be an extremely *jealous* god.

This god is possessed by an unrestrained desire for freedom. His "wanting to" really amounts to "having to." Time and again it emerges that he is unable to break free from what stands in his way. He is perpetually assailed by the not-yet and the not-enough sentiment. He is not actually so obsessed by the irresistible aspect of *what is*. He is much sooner influenced by the own, irresistible, impossible to control and impossible to restrain *power of the imagination*. Through his own imagination the human god turns against everything that does not belong to him, that is given, that was there before him, that is different, that he cannot fully control. He lacks any kind of respect for the own value quality of the other. But that is not where it ends. Imagination moreover makes him *hostile* to what is different. Restlessly this god pushes himself on. Nothing is allowed to be left in peace, least of all himself.

This gives a rather dangerous twist to the issue of imagination. It is only too easy for the imagination to reinforce the impression of being threatened by a hostile outside world, whatever exterior force that might be. That is what the *I* reacts to. That exterior is not so much the outside world itself—what is other or different—but a constructed outside. Man reacts to his own construct: he creates his enemy himself and turns against his own *image*. In the words of Nietzsche: the creative resentment turns itself against the self-created exterior. In the philosophy of Fichte there is plenty of space for the power of imagination to unfurl itself.

In actual fact, everything that resists becomes problematic by being presented as *not-I*, as the creative product of a profoundly irreconcilable type of imagination. Such a creation can be randomly dealt with. Creative arbitrariness eliminates beforehand hesitancy, moderation, respect, esteem or—once again in the words of Nietzsche—fearfulness. All that is different is rebuffed with no show of respect. The *not-I* in effect says that, in an initial deed, the *I* expels itself from all that exists: nowhere *is* it at home, it does not *want* to be at home anywhere. The outside world that is created on that basis is, as it were, in conflict with the *I*, and therefore unbearable. This leads to restlessness and fanaticism. Every exterior becomes an unbearable self-restriction of freedom. The self-constraint which, in Kant's theoretical reasoning was given a certain degree of flexibility, is now apparently a too great provocation.

When Fichte gives the absolute *I* the guise of a *concrete* intersubjective whole, this does not change. He seems to accept a certain degree of self-restraint. Indeed, he places the universality of the *I* in perspective by allowing man to be integrated into a mystical, organic, national common unity. Within this common unity there is a restless kind of activism that prevails. Even in nationalistic or patriotic respects, the *I* turns fanatically against what is different. It shows no respect for what has been traditionally handed down and what presents its own values. Institutions, social structures, and existing moral rules are all subject to the grip of the imagination and its pressure. The *I* demonstrates a driven type of *jealousy* from which even omnipotent God could not free himself. Meanwhile the human god loses his patience and humility. His jealousy becomes more *decisive* than ever. There is nothing that any longer holds him back from converting jealousy into action. Imagination makes decisiveness powerful; it fuels a reluctance that unrestrainedly wants to assert itself. This is also apparent within the common unity.

In linking the *I* to the notion of a mystical, organic common unity, it appears that man is incorporated into an original oneness that unites everyone as equals. In that way, the mystical idea of a united kind of *humanity* is dispelled, at least for the time being. For now, universality is sought nearer to home, in an all-uniting common idea, or at least, in the impression of that. What is particularly striking is that within this suggested kind of unity, he then goes on to distinguish two types of people. The people have to be at one with each other, but it is not that simple. It is not only the *I* but also the *not-I* that takes on a concrete, distinguishing guise. Those who *allow* themselves to be controlled, who show themselves to be subordinate to what is characteristic of the *not-I* are negatively assessed. They live, as it were, in an *unreal* state. Worse yet, they have resigned themselves to their non-identity, they are passive. Since their *not-I* is no product of their own imagination, they are unable to overcome their improper identity. Their powers of imagination fall short. Opposed to them are those who do possess unconditional freedom and who are therefore capable of creatively imagining. They refuse to resign themselves to an unreal existence. They therefore constitute the original foundation of the common unity. In reality, the passively content type also amounts to an opposing force that they have to break down.

In his *Reden an die deutsche Nation*, Fichte dubs the unreal types strangers; they are not able to participate in the creative activity of primitive society and therefore have to be removed. Not only does the power of imagination prove to be envious, but it also gains a *messianic* form. It looks for conflict: not only between good and evil but also between the good and the evil. The power of imagination moralizes on good and evil, which therefore justifies the battle between man against man. Those who resist and are not able to enter into the mythical unity, anyone who cannot submit to the decisiveness of the most unique I is declared an enemy and can expect his deserved fate. The choice is simple: either one is incorporated into an all-overpowering unity, or one is removed.

Disruptive obstinacy has to be quashed. The only justifiable position for the *not-I* is one of resistance that has to be conquered. That which resists may only temporarily oppose; it has to show itself prepared to transform, to be *made* one with the mystical *I*. He who wishes to become a part of the *I* and to give expression to the vigor of that *I* may unrestrainedly give free expression to the required power of imagination. It is his task to bring about the miracle of the successful synthesis, over and over, even if the promised miracle appears to be an incredibly far-flung objective. In other words, we are talking about uninhibited *zeal*. The *I* is goaded on, it propels itself forward. The creative imagination continues to find new forms of opposition that it needs to conquer. Where *resistance* cannot be beaten and where it evokes *repulsion*, envy threatens to degenerate.

It takes very little to make insatiable zeal and envy turn excessive and violent. More to the point, what is there to prevent the hyperactive power of the imagination from becoming totalitarian in its scope? The mystical dichotomy in people is a handy justification for taking a firm stand. Anything that does not fit into the mystical popular idea can be given a *face*, one that evokes revulsion and prompts activism. The *I*-god also tolerates no other gods, as that would destroy his uniqueness, omniscience, and omnipotence. God may become man, the *not-I* much sooner becomes a *monster*: it is dehumanized. It is not so much *what* but rather *who* resists that provokes the jealous god. He is unable to detach himself from *who* it is that resists him. As a matter of fact, the resentment is at its most creative when it is externally identified in person by turning *the* other into a problematic *not-I* and giving that a face.

The absolute *I* makes concrete strides towards becoming omnipotent, a state formerly attributed to God. Apocalyptic belief finds its continuation in ideology that places belief in the hands of the human will to achieve power and human vigor. Man gets tired of waiting and so aspires to put his words into action, above all else there is the actual fulfilling of justice. The danger behind this ideology is great. It justifies activistic violence after evil that has been made visible everywhere has undermined *truth*, the ability to bear truth. The moralizing extends to being reactive, to a furious *making true*. All that then remains is the choice between changing and destroying, together with the apotheosis of violence in aid of the mystical synthesis. The miracle must at last occur, at the expense of all else. The mystical common unity shares nothing in common with the ethical order. It pretends to be the fulfillment of an *existential* goal in life. This atheism seeks the fulfillment of the promise that dwelt in the name of omnipotent God. The death of ethical God persists in the omnipotent's becoming man.

This god can find no peace. He gets swept up in a type of strife that is just as unleashed as it is endless. Whatever this god achieves, it is never enough, never complete. He is never truly everything in everyone. Where envy does succeed is in the creating of enmity. To become free he is forced to endlessly conquer, to overpower, to appropriate, to absorb. It is impossible for him to love his enemies: his desire for justice compels him to destroy them. Good and evil separate irreconcilably. If, in the divine *I*, that which is good is illuminated, whoever opposes it *embodies* evil. The self-creation of man becomes the setting for the justified struggle between good and evil. Where such justice has become a goal in itself, it does not need to perpetuate the failure of the miracle of what is good. As an end in itself, this conflict becomes a devoted struggle, endless in time and space. In utter dedication, envy is able to throw all its energy into a battle against evil that is always to be rediscovered anew.

10.4 BETWEEN NOSTALGIA AND PARANOIA

Fichte's thinking fits in with a wide movement that commenced in his time and still persists today, namely that of *Romanticism*. It is not the intention to analyze the Romantic Movement here. What is interesting is to see how Romanticism contributed to *God's becoming man*. What is clear is that the Romantic mood formed the basis for the thinking that was to further elaborate Fichte's legacy. The romantic power of imagination tied up with the questions about good and evil; the ideologies were able to build upon this.

The Romantic period saw a break with the basic idea adhered to in the early age of enlightenment. It was a notion that saw the cosmos as some kind of divine order and as an example to ethical order. The whole order-idea lost in the battle against the idea of *nature*, which was envisaged as a compelling force. God's voice now spoke through nature and primarily through human nature. This nature reflects no ethical order, not to speak of virtue, prescripts, balance, and proportion. New nature shows itself to be an unbridled force able to inspire human imagination. Instead of the ethical example, it is now the irresistible *aesthetic* effect that dominates. The natural forces inspire and legitimize the opposition to the old order, to everything that represents the existing order. Nature asserts itself with the power of unleashed imagination, demonic, titanic, revolutionary. Nature releases dark and compelling forces in man, forces that must and want to be let out. The natural forces activate a will that seems to be opposed by nothing. The more that ethical good disappears from view, the more powerfully evil comes to the fore.

There are new heroes that develop around this evil. The battle that they have to stage displays parallels with the fate of that of the mythical figure *Medea*. In her struggle against evil she displays the full scope of the power of imagination. She feels betrayed and suffers intensely from that. She is a victim, not only of her husband but also of the order that he represents. She therefore starts to rebel and seek revenge, filled as she is with passion and vengefulness. Through her passions nature remains active, impossible to resist, and justified *as nature*. This nature not only *seeks* all the space it can get but it also occupies it as well. Driven on, the heroine gives free rein to her nature and justifies that: *because* it is in fact nature that is working through her, because nature *wants* this space. When she contemplates this in the interpretation made by Euripides, there is a voice that interprets the logic of this will: "I know that it is nature that compels me but nature does not heed either the law or nomos." The sophistic contrast between *physis* and *nomos* is taken to extremes.

Nomoi represents the ethical order, the laws, the morals, the traditionally applicable commandments, the written and unwritten law. When the Greek culture found itself in a time of crisis, this old ethical order became very brittle. The order was seen to be fabricated by man and was thus a thing of chance, changeable, even superfluous. Whatever way one looks at it, the *nomoi* lose their sacred quality and eternal validity. The relative nature of everything has a fatal effect. What had been created by man could, in fact, have been different! Just because a thing is valid for some, that surely does not mean to say that it has to be valid for others? Why then cleave to this accidental order, why hold on to any order? It is this awareness that leads man to free himself from what once applied; he starts to experience the ethical order as something imposed and constricting. He therefore rises up against this order. This final point can be presented differently. Whilst rebelling, man feels *another* force welling up: he detects a more original type of life, one that comes across as *truly* divine. He experiences the power of his *physis*, his nature, a nature full of needs, longings, passions, a nature full of compelling urges and full of the power of imagination. This nature seeks space and wants to escape, also where the old ethical commandments wave a corrective finger at it and where it contravenes the laws. The extreme degree of sophism passionately takes sides; it takes the side of *physis* against *nomoi*. Nature is the primeval force, not a force instigated by man but something eternal. Why then should such nature be repressed by the *nomoi*?

Some sophists perceive human *physis* to be essentially moderate and peace seeking. Living according to nature would therefore automatically lead to a peaceful cosmos and to a peaceful human world. Small wonder that later utopists were wont to harken back to this particular movement. Others were, by contrast, inclined to perceive of nature as wild, passionate, full of craving, and thirsty for dominion. Living according to nature thus leads, virtually automatically, to the hegemony of those who possess strong characters. The prevailing of the "order" of nature is nevertheless good since it subjects those with a weak character to bow to the dominion of those endowed with stronger characters. Without power and dominion there can be no sense of purpose in nature, which is so fluid and changeable. This movement points less to the *laissez faire* attitude of later market liberalism than to extreme movements such as fascism and Nazism. The power of nature is inherently good, and therefore also the actions unleashed by nature. The natural way of the world thus clashes, seemingly automatically, with the artificial ethical order, which curbs nature. The *nomoi*, the laws, ethics, and morals stand in the way of nature which has to be liberated; the *nomoi* repress in a way that cannot be justified. Power seems to be naturally good.

The fact that *physis* brings with it evil—evil in a moral sense—is no argument: morals do not count. The awareness that nature is an irresistible and compelling force does not need to instill fear. The boundless power of nature is a force that liberates life. The fact that the Medea's revenge is born of passion and vengefulness should not frighten people off either. What is at stake here is natural passions and they have a purpose, not the *nomoi*, which tends to curb such passion. Despite the evil she dissipates, the Medea is right. After all, she gives free expression to her true nature. It is her husband who is in the wrong, as he represents the evil of the repressed policy order.

The myth makes crystal clear what ethical atheism can set free. The counterforce inherent in ethical life now fully comes into its own. Insofar as the ethical gods maintained that they represented some kind of primeval value, the powers that subsequently declare these gods dead claim to be even more original. Is nature not older than culture? Was it not unjust that the *titanic* powers were beaten and repressed by the cultural gods? Now that culture seems to be corrupted and now that its divine origins have been superseded, nature must surely regain its full freedom? Does the same not apply to human nature? Should mankind not submit to its inexhaustible power? Should man not also *wish* to have such powers? Should he not subjugate himself to such primal forces? What is wrong with allowing these powers to discharge themselves? Why is no battle waged against the corrupted *nomoi*?

Nature is all about strife, urges, and will; *what* precisely such will elaborates and where it leads are really of secondary importance. It is sooner about human will being led by nature, really *as* nature, and tuning in to its orientation. It is especially the fact *that* it works and seeks direction that is of importance. Nature is movement that is full of promise. And no matter how amazing it is, this promise also demands *belief*; nature commands man to believe in it and to follow it wherever it goes. In the words of Euripides' Medea: *knowing* that nature implores is reason enough to justify following in its footsteps. What we are talking about here is an active and activated type of following. Nature is able to offer itself, but it is subsequently up to man to actively and creatively *invest it with experience*. It must be converted into a lively force that is able to transport man. Inevitably, man himself does not really act and nature is not steered by a controlled will. It is sooner the case that man is aware of being propelled by an irrepressible natural force that needs to be further developed. Man *has to want to* be one with this force; man himself *has to want to* become this powerful force. That is what is so *paradoxical* about liberated nature: the unity of having to and wanting to, the surrendering to creativity, passive and active experiencing, obedience and omnipotence. Its *omnipotence* is worshipped and glorified in the face of reputed good and evil.

Berlin shows how it is that Romanticism *wants to* and *must* go on to embellish this paradox.[1] He describes the Romantic experience as an obsessive kind of engagement. People allow themselves to be transported in a movement that is perceived to be original, more original than cognitive human knowledge and thus impossible to really comprehend with appropriate knowledge. The active power remains, in the final instance, concealed. Knowledge about this movement is not therefore based upon certain cognitive insight, but rather upon the capacity to empathize and upon belief. Hence the prevalence of metaphors concerning *depth* and *darkness*. One not only has to surrender to this coercive force but one also has to actively want it, actively bring it to life, in other words, literally: *invest it with* life.

In this engagement he recognizes two directions. The romantic experience and imagination possesses both forward and a backward orientation, both of which are obsessive. The *forward* directed kind of obsession seeks expressive space with a certain degree of optimism: he labels this experience nostalgia. The *backward* directed experience is similarly dominated by a pessimistic mood. One is preoccupied with the feeling of being pursued and hunted: he labels this experience *paranoia*. People are propelled in both directions without being able to avert or control the process. More to the point, people should not want to resist this movement. The matter of "where to" is just as incomprehensible as the matter of "where from."

He typifies *nostalgia* as *Sehnsucht*: an unquenchable longing to be a part of the original and infinite aspects of the movement, to absorb that and become a part of it. In that way, man himself becomes a creative natural force. One becomes one with this god: a god of nature, a universe in infinite motion. There is no single way in which this god of nature resembles the ethical gods, those of the *nomoi*, of organized culture and institutions. They fall under the moralizing judgment of evil. With them, everything that exists is filled with evil. Deified nature that raises itself above all of that does not have an ethical voice but rather, an aesthetic one. It is glorious to give this god a human voice. But why should this divine voice have a permanent nostalgic effect upon man? Because this expressive voice may never be termed perfect, never absolutely fulfilling. Because the infinitely divine never finds complete expression, finite man is doomed to be eternally driven on in efforts to achieve such expression. But divine nature compels. Man *has to* be steered onwards; man has to learn *to want* this. Man therefore suffers from what is impossible and is tortured by longing. Man loses himself in submitting to having to want to. The blessed experience does not liberate people from the ever-recurring nostalgic feeling, the feeling of not having succeeded.

---

1. Berlin, *Roots of Romanticism*, 104vv.

Faith does not therefore actually reward people with the Promised Land and a blessed existence. Nostalgic belief gives man eternal strife.

The only real permanent comfort is the fact that deified nature is an inexhaustible source, one that will always challenge expression. The unity with deified nature makes man therefore simultaneously excited, optimistic and dispirited, pessimistic. He wants so much, also has to do so much. He knows that there is no road to redemption. There is an endless number of roads, none of which are capable of truly leading to redemption.

Romantic nostalgia is something that has already possessed the soul for several centuries. This spirit is ethically atheistic because it seeks no ethical connection but rather aesthetic fulfillment. Man goes in pursuit of the Promised Land, man bears witness to his belief in that and subjugates to that his entire power of imagination. Man seeks but cannot find. Promise, hope and expectation cannot take away the awareness that such fulfillment is a distant and nigh on unattainable goal.

It cannot be otherwise. As has been mentioned, Nietzsche terms the anticipated aesthetic fulfillment of man a *fabrication*: the mere semblance of meaning, only lending itself to belief with no prospect. But why is it so hopeless? Because the aesthetic fulfillment of human existence is a delusion: a tempting and sickly delusion that always races on, tainting a balanced and purposeful life and society. The fabrication always demands more and constantly finds escape in other fulfillment. Belief and fulfillment cannot be drawn close together; there is always a gaping chasm between the two. So the once so *optimistic* religious delusion of a promised life changes into *pessimism* as soon as actual fulfillment is supposed to come into view. It is the pessimism of shortfall, of futility. In the final instance, atheistic belief has little other to offer than a "trotzdem," a kind of "despite-all-anyway" sentiment, a melancholy or possibly even pent-up "Sehnsucht nach dem ganz Anderen." Belief in existential fulfillment must be able to turn *hope* into a *principle*, albeit it perhaps a futile principle, one with which one perpetually begins but is never able to finish. It does not, therefore, stop at doggedly striving and hopelessly seeking for fulfillment. What unavoidably remains is the danger of which the ancient Greeks were so afraid: that of surrendering to excess, to the extreme, to extravagance.

The belief system is therefore not only overshadowed by nostalgia but it also induces *cynicism*. This brings *paranoia* into the picture. Camus' *Myth of Sisyphus* reveals something of this mixture of nostalgia, cynicism, and paranoia. His modern Sisyphus demonstrates the fate of man who feels hunted and who is oriented towards fulfillment. His whole existence is marked by an apparently in every respect, challenging, but in actual fact, impossible task. He has to carry a heavy stone up a mountain and throughout he is preoccupied with the one goal of reaching the top. It is not a freely chosen goal, but one to which he has been condemned. The tragedy of it all is that he is possessed by this objective and passionately wants to fulfill it but simultaneously realizes that it is unattainable. All endeavors to reach the top fail, but every time this leads to renewed attempts, again and again, interminably.

What should have been a challenge is sketched by Camus as a "having to," devoid of any prospect. Sisyphus toils even in the absolute awareness that the goal will never be achieved. The word *challenge* thus becomes anomalous: he is trapped in a hopeless destiny and endures it as a condemnation. Undoubtedly, given the freedom to choose, he would not have opted for such a life. Undoubtedly he would not have opted for human existence at all. But he was not given the choice. He does not therefore feel truly at home in his existence. Everything around him is experienced as a *not-I*: his whole environment, the life he has been given, his challenges. The fact that his *not-I* so exasperatingly opposes him is not only what goads him on, but he also experiences it intensely. He toils on, against his better judgment. Cynically he undergoes his condemnation, and it is that selfsame cynicism that goads him on to reach the top.

But why should he want to reach the mountaintop? Why such an unfeasible and endlessly distant goal? Why such an over-ambitious longing? What is so typical of the romantics is that they are only ever satisfied with the highest possible achievement. They cannot help longing for the impossible, even in the knowledge that it is unattainable. It is, therefore, not strange to see that they in that way get caught up in cynicism. Proportion and feeling for proportion disappear; balanced judgment has to give way to excess and extremity. The unavoidable "having to" spills over into futile "wanting to." Man experiences existence as though he has been *thrown* into an eternal conflict; he always wants more, something different, something new. Even an apparently ironic mood brings no real joy. In the light of the fateful occurrence not even hope is to any avail. The fateful fails to challenge but instead makes people grimly determined.

Camus also narrates that tale. Each time that the greatest good is not achieved, Sisyphus is overwhelmed by a vindictive mood. He realizes that the gods have punished him with this existence. They have imposed upon him this hopeless fate, hopeless from the point of view of the top that cannot be attained. Futility and discontentment ruin even the illusion of purpose. The only thing that should be able to give a feeling of purpose, a complete existence, cannot in fact be achieved. That not only makes his efforts pointless, but also his whole existence. His fate is not perceived as a challenge for a single instant, nor does it give him any sense of purpose. Since it is only the final goal that counts, the challenge is ruined. Camus changes the tragic myth into an absurdist, existential drama. The romantic power of the imagination does not stop at the personally experienced futility. For Sisyphus, the final experience is reactive: it amounts to *contempt*. What, in the forward respect, might have remained in terms of illusory hope evaporates. The cynicism reinforces a retrospective trend: the element of illusion is more likely to heighten the bitter, rancorous reaction, but it is precisely there that he seeks a feeling of triumph, of superiority over the gods and the fate that they have imposed. Contempt is therefore the final reaction, contempt as an absurd kind of bliss.

What does such bliss indicate? How can one enjoy it? Without the power of the imagination such a switch is impossible. "Il faut imaginer Sisyphe heureux." You have to want to imagine, you have to want to *believe* that Sisyphus is happy. It is the experiencing of happiness as a belief, a belief to which imagination *has to want to* transport people. An absurd kind of happiness is sought in the imagining of purpose, an absurd purpose in the form of contempt. What is absurd is that the contempt does not so much apply to destiny but much more to the perceived instigators of this fate. Gods are the objects of contempt. These gods provide no uplifting meaning but rather the bitter bliss of *aversion*. Now that Sisyphus seeks his salvation in a grotesque and illusory fabrication, he is not only overwhelmed by the futility of it all but also by the bitterness it brings. It is the fate man imposes upon himself through his romantic belief: never feeling at home, always wanting too much, always the nostalgic longings, thus always again the futility of it all. And futility spawns bitterness, hate, *rancor*. Imagination brings together illusion and disillusion, hope and bitterness.

Imagination ruins truthfulness. One is unable to be open to what is, to the reality of things. What *is* comes into focus as what it is *not*. Imagination also destroys the integrity of the other. Futility tempts people to go ahead and pin the blame on guilty parties, such as the gods of Sisyphus. If the illusory *purpose* turns out to be unattainable and if the nostalgic longing is smothered by futility then paranoia opens up the door to a creative twist. Why, then, cannot the victim of the gods become the one in pursuit? Why should not the victim deploy his creativity and powers of imagination to show *aversion* to those who may be held responsible for his fate, for his futile striving?

In the belief in God, the promise offered God's certainty and comfort. Amid all the futility and despair it was possible to fall back on a God who had made the promise and in whom justification could be found for the failure of the promise to materialize. This could prevent too much bitterness arising. Camus demonstrates what the human reaction is like if this God disappears from the scene and the justifying confidence is shaken. Futility then turns into cynicism and undisguised rancor. The cynicism is not directed at anonymous nature, which is *exonerated*, as a fatality, in advance. Cynicism creates perpetrators, guilty parties and does not *appeal to* them but *stands against* them as an accusation. Surely somebody must, after all, be blamed for the futility in which man has become imprisoned? Why, in the retaliation, is the final, only remaining bliss not sought? Why not seek revenge against those who have to be blamed for the illusive hope? In the retaliation, it is imagination that can well be justified that seizes the *power*? Nostalgia extends to become paranoia. The figment of the imagination known as happiness rolls over into the cry for justice. All that then remains is the power to do justice to that appeal.

Paranoia turns out to work in two directions. Only too easily the romantic falls under the spell of a persecution complex: followed, chased, and spurred on himself, he, in his turn, resorts to following. How easily this disposition gives Fichte's *not-I* an *ad hominem* twist.

The creative imagination gives evil an identity. Man is under the illusion that he is surrounded by enemies to which he is, *of necessity*, forced to *react*. Though the fabrication of perceived good may prove illusive, evil is present everywhere. How, in this mood, can one feel at home anywhere? This mood is emphatically worded: not only as *contempt* but also *disgust, anger*, and *Angst zum Tode*. Such a mood turns existence into a dark emergency situation. In the forward direction, the futility of the utopian prospects lead to despair, in the backward direction the vigor can be boundlessly released, in repayment for the futile.

Since the differentiation between good and evil has been denuded of its ethical value, the backward-oriented energy can even mercilessly assert itself. Man becomes compliant to what the darker powers dictate. Why should the ethical atheist not be able to tackle the evil present everywhere by implementing his own justified evil? Why should he not be able to glorify his own evil? Why not enjoy the *sublimity* of this evil? Why not willingly adhere to what nature, human nature, this unbridled and immoderate *omnipotence*, wants? This not only gives evil but also omnipotence an identity, a dark, human identity. Omnipotence that has taken on a human form elevates itself above good and evil. Why not take the justice of the Last Judgment into one's own hands? Why should there still be a *heavenly* Messiah? The modernist belief in a utopian heaven paves the way to a hell on earth. The ancient belief prepares itself to manifest itself in an earthly finale. The atheistic belief breathes new, earthly life into Messianism.

In the twentieth century, the messianic expectations are fulfilled. Romantic obsessions prove to be a good source of nourishment for the plea for justice, redeeming and avenging justice. The belief in God is translated into a radical belief in human all-powerfulness.

Meanwhile, religious Messianism also proves to be resilient and vital. Generally, this brand of Messianism stops at a restrained type of apocalyptic belief: people maintain that the end is near at hand and that the signs of this are evident but, for the rest, they passively wait. When the Messiah returns it will become apparent what kind of salvation awaits the believers and the non-believers. Now, also within religious circles, people are prepared to support the awaited Messiah. Religion also politicizes, within the church, in political *evening* prayers. As soon as one maintains that one knows about God's plans for man and for the world, as soon as it is clear which way God's justice is going to go, it becomes tempting to judicially support God. Apocalyptic faith can easily turn political and is thus, from time to time, inclined to flex its religious muscles.

Such practical display of strength pales in significance alongside the activism of atheistic ideologies. Atheism suits the action to the belief: it wants to see the apocalyptic visions fulfilled. Now it becomes evident what kind of miracles faith can perform, what kinds of mountains it can move. Even if atheistic ideologies endeavor to scientifically legitimize themselves, their effect is down to their sheer power of imagination and their own vitality. What is seen as essential is nothing other than a matter of the *deed* performed. That is the purpose of human power. The exodus of old is now coupled with furious energy. Hence the reason that *totalitarian* zeal can be stamped out. It becomes clear that the *vérité à faire* can be unleashed and is able to implement the ancient call for justice.

It is *Nazism* and *Marxism* that finally give form to god in the shape of man. Man adopts for himself the messianic visions, in doctrine and in revolutionary practice. In the interests of justice omnipotence is coveted. In the interests of justice, resentment is also given all the creative space it needs to unfurl itself. Marxism constitutes a clear example of the danger that lies encapsulated in the yearning for omnipotence. In closely affiliating avenging justice to that which redeems, this ideology legitimates its own evil. That, then, was how Marxism was able to gain the support of so many believers. In other words, Marxism is a *demonstratio ad absurdum* of the longing for omnipotence. It is Stalin who, like no other, demonstrates for us the full extent of such absurdity. Like no other, he puts into practice the pretensions of an ultimate type of philosophy.

11

The Messianic Unburdening

Stalin, Stalinism, and all its totalitarian variants cannot simply be dismissed as a degeneration of what was, in essence, well-intentioned Marxist idealism. One may indeed question whether Marxism seeks to achieve anything other than what can in fact be realized by means of totalitarian violence. Stalin converted doctrine into *anticipated* deed: he breathed life into that *doctrine*, a revolutionary type of *life*. Inspired by him, many were to bring a similar kind of vigor to that same doctrine.

Neither can communist totalitarianism be dismissed as the tragic upshot of deviant infirmity of mind on the part of Stalin himself. It is much more likely that the doctrine and reality of communism dovetailed with what may, in a more general sense, be termed the sickly aspirations of man, and that Stalin was merely an extreme exponent of that tendency. The knowledge that he was a psychopath and that he came to suffer from dementia helps to explain the fact *that* he was so receptive to totalitarian doctrine. It was that doctrine that prescribed *what* he did and indicated *from where to where* he wanted to lead mankind. What Marxist doctrine and Stalinist lifestyle demonstrate for us is just how an unleashed plea for justice can be converted into action. The required omnipotence comes within reach; the judgment can be accomplished.

In ideological terms Stalin was *a real believer*. He even saw in himself, as an individual, the fulfillment of the promise to which religion and philosophy had so long borne witness. This belief now not only came to experience its ideological climax, but it was also made, in the most literal sense of the word, flesh. The realization of that belief was executed in a considered, calculated, and rational fashion. The totalitarian catastrophe throws light on the thinking that facilitated it. The *praxis* of the totalitarian spirit translates a driven brand of *thought*. Man demands justice. Now, finally, it is time to *put paid to* what has for so long stood in the way of the promise. Stalin thus constitutes a perfect example of *man* as a problem.

He fulfills the insatiable human longing for omnipotence: he pursues the goal of God's incarnation as man. In the interest of the road to salvation, he claims omniscience and omnipotence. And here again the omnipotent requires that man place implicit belief in him. What is, perhaps, rather remarkable is the fact that he hardly seems to become enraged when the faith of his people wavers: he *makes* the people believers—in the way that he maintains that everything can be engineered. In the interests of the promise of salvation, he acts, as an atheistic Messiah, as the one who prepares the way for God's earthly kingdom. The final judgment falls to him; it is his task to abolish evil. He is able to do everything for the sake of justice: he elevates himself above good and evil.

Stalinism places totalitarian imagination in the seat of power. He believes that mountains can indeed be moved and sets about performing that very miracle. He knows that his time has come; all that now needs to happen is to see that everything that has been said is put into action. His religious fervor makes the time-honored resentment more creative and decisive than ever before. It seems as though he is proving Nietzsche's genealogical analysis of resentment in a very practical way. What had once *started* as reactive negation, as imaginary revenge wreaked upon a too strong outside world, finds *fulfillment* in totalitarianism. The imaginary revenge is translated into an actual rage of retaliation. Scores are now settled with the exterior that was once too strong.

Stalin's zeal links up with a long tradition. He makes concrete a type of pathos with which Marxism is preoccupied. For its part, Marxism provides an ideological interpretation of romantic yearnings and of Fichte's imaginative power. This ideology not only inspires activistic zeal but it also justifies an unleashed type of envy. How then does Marxism contend that this activism and envy can be justified?

11.1 UNLEASHED ZEAL

In all the comparisons that are made, Fichte's absolute *I* deviates from the omniscience and omnipotence of God: with him the humanized God does not in fact channel itself into a single individual person. Just like Rousseau, Fichte wrestles with the unity of that which is general and individual in the *I*. Their escape becomes that of the general will which is able to *present* itself as an *I* that is one and indivisible. In both philosophies it is the *unity of the people* that expresses this one indivisible will. He who does not recognize himself in this presentation of matters *is* a major problem: he after all resists everything that is somehow valid. That which resists must therefore be broken down by being totally absorbed or abolished. Complete integration is intrinsic to the

11 The Messianic Unburdening

notion of this one *I*, to the unconditional will and to the ceaseless struggle implied by this notion.

The pretense of the *I* is not only intrinsically totalitarian but it also creates aporia. How can the anonymous *I* extract itself from the original unity and switch to thinking and doing? How can it translate its will into action? How can it change endless spontaneity into concrete or, in other words, finite activity? Then there is a further point. The presentation of unity cannot exist without representation. The pressing question then becomes *who*: the question being whether a concrete person could *represent* the *I*. Can a concrete person masquerade as the humanized God and be everything in everyone? Is such a person also bestowed with the promise that the *I* presents? Is such an individual also rewarded with the road that leads there: with the breaking of the resistance of the *not-I*, with the clearing away of everything that stands in the way of the promise? Does this person represent everything that previously automatically came to the personal God? Does this person also receive messianic pretensions?

It is not only in the presentation of the unconditionally free *I* that the philosophy of Fichte and Rousseau becomes entangled in limitations. Much the same also applies to new man and to the world in which this *I* must become a reality. The longing for the unconditional and for the infinite really tolerates nothing finite, limited or relative. Nevertheless, both thinkers content themselves with what is relative. When presenting the *I* they confine themselves to separate states or peoples, which always thus have a particular own identity in relation to other peoples. In that respect, Rousseau is too French and Fichte too German to be able to fully realize the discrepancy that exists between idea and reality. The zealots of the French Revolution are unaware of the discrepancy between their universal idea and the desired realization. From the perspective of their extreme nationalism they are so overzealously preoccupied with breaking, overwhelming, integrating, and destroying the periphery, the tradition, the independent institutions, that they hardly construe the self-chosen limitations as resistance, an annoyance, or as a challenge.

In the light of the utter infinitude of this idea, like humanity or the world, the ideas of people, nation, or state become inadequate. Just as the God of faith once had world-encompassing pretensions and wanted to be God of all mankind, so one may expect to see in the humanized god a similar world-encompassing urge to be recognized. The yearning for omnipotence seems to automatically force one in this direction.

Now, also, the limited popular idea can challenge itself to surmount its own relativity. A separate people can, after all, become possessed by an irrepressible desire to prove itself. It can get carried away with the longing to conquer the world and become humankind. The popular idea can also forcefully direct itself at the outside world. The people, as a folk, can turn against other peoples, at which point they have little alternative than to fully assimilate—and thus lose own identity—or be destroyed.

Nazism demonstrated the challenging pathos of this idea. It made clear exactly what such an activist urge can lead to. It demonstrated how much power such a shameless will can unfurl, how resistance can be broken. The popular idea proves to be able to pour itself into a fury of destruction, a fury that seeks to be all-embracing and can thus find no peace. The popular *I* appears to be able to be taken over by an overwhelming longing to elevate itself to become a world *I*. The *I* utterly consumes, as the popular *I*, all the space in the world and chases after its own eternal life. It searches for omnipotence in order to be able to realize this will. Nazism has proved to us how the popular *I* can come to *believe* in itself and in its own promise. It shows how a people is able to furiously submit to the *making true* of its own totality and boundlessness. To become humankind for all eternity it puts into practice what it preaches. In order to be able to become mankind it becomes messianic.

The yearning for the realization of totality and endlessness can also lead in another direction: towards the individual person himself. He can then, essentially, in a very immediate sense declare himself to be an individual who is just a direct part of universal mankind. The belief in the fulfillable nature of one's own identity and that of everyone can be so great that only one immediate actual making true still remains. As soon as man learns to *see* himself as detached from everything that keeps him away from his pure individuality, it becomes fairly natural for him to want to *detach* himself from all of that. What may happen to apply to a single person only then needs to take on a universal dimension; that is how unity between the individual and mankind comes about. Such radicalness must free man from all *attachment* to a group, tribe, folk, or nation, and also from attachment to institutions or ethical connections. He is no longer a part of any particular traditional, ethical, or cultural identity. He redeems himself from that and imagines that all he has is an existential identity: "I am a person and nothing more than that." As physical beings all individuals proclaim to be each other's equals. This makes every historical and ethically evolved differentiation not only irksome, limiting, or repressive, but also superfluous. Modern liberalism tends towards such a perspective.

It is in this way that *Feuerbach* also emancipates man. He declares him to be a sensual being, a being with sensual needs. No further substantiating analysis is really required; a confession of faith is sufficient. The sensuality of this being needs only to be recognized, as it is already so self-evident. Again, now there is the unity of belief and promise: that of the fulfillable satisfying of sensual requirements. His atheistic belief promises man a universal identity. Because everyone, in the sensual sense of the word, is each other's equal, people form together humanity. All that remains is the exodus of the compelling, constraining, and repressive nature of ethics, institution, and culture. All that remains is the realization of what is avowed to be unrestrictedly

11 The Messianic Unburdening

possible: the satisfying of people's sensual human nature. The Promised Land of freedom and happiness suddenly becomes easily attainable. One only needs to construe the old, imagined heaven and one will know what may be expected of life and what can be made to become true.

In order to make the transition from theistic to atheistic belief plausible, Feuerbach creates a radical and depicted image of theistic God and of belief in God. Whatever lay incorporated in the image of the old God, no matter how ideal and supra-human the doctrine, all of this was now hailed "in truth" sensual. Since religion—in the words of Marx—is an expression of "illusory happiness," it is only really the actual core that still has to be revealed: the actual, sensual happiness. *Man's* whole existence becomes sensual; he has sensual desire and is driven by a longing for physical satisfaction. The totality and endlessness of this sensual craving of man is illustrated by the difference between animals and man: the animal as a *limited* sensualist as opposed to man the *absolute sensualist*. Feuerbach developed a refined interplay of imagination and decisive action. He dethroned ethical God from religion and from Christendom by first *humanizing* him—to become a utopian projection of man—and then subsequently *sensualizing* him. Viewed in this light, religious projection may naturally be said to provide, seemingly automatically, surrogate satisfaction.

Feuerbach developed a virtually perfect kind of *ethical atheism*. Almost perfect because his atheism in fact very immediately takes effect. Imagine that the ethical world were to offer resistance, imagine that the traditional God were to resist being represented! Imagine that man were not to spontaneously be carried along by the representing. How would the atheistic belief then be able to make true its promise? What kind of religious fervor would then be needed to make the whole of humanity a party to this promise? This is the cue for Marx to appear on the world stage.

11.2 DESTROYING WHAT RESISTS

Feuerbach's *image* of man has something immediate about it; *Marx* emphasizes more the process of man's *emergence* by tracing historical and social developments. Society is the entirety of inter-human relations, which, in the final instance, is determined by the method of production. The method of production determines the tapestry of relationships, including the institutions, the culture, human consciousness, and man's knowledge and world of ideas. The social integration of man is no static process but rather a dynamic one, the ultimate upshot being that of the worldwide integration of people. The process of man's development therefore not only creates power relationships—political, cultural, and spiritual forms of repression—but it also opens up the prospect of liberation. There is, in the process of man's evolution, an emancipatory potential that opens up: on the one hand that of a liberating from physical constraints, and on the other hand that of the redemption from the duress of tradition and institutions as well as from power inequality. The *emergence* of man thus follows what is, in the final instance, a global social process. This process makes it possible for people to develop as equals and to be integrated into the *human race*. Without a social process there can be no humanity, without humanity, no actual emancipation of man as man.

Throughout his political-economic analyses, Marx perpetually gives one the impression that this is a process that adheres to the forces of *natural laws*. Just as in nature everything is subjected to natural laws that work in a causal way, so in the human world everything must surely follow a path governed by historical and social necessity. Nothing can escape from this naturally dictated law; nothing can halt its historical process. Here, Marx seems to adhere completely to the hypothesis of Euripides to the effect that even insight into the force of nature can change this state of affairs. *Conscious*ness—awareness of being—does not, after all, free one from being subjected to the state of *being*.

Yet this is only true in a relative sense. Determinism only at least holds *within* the historical process—within what Marx terms *prehistory*. It is therefore different from the natural laws. Whatever happens, these cannot be abandoned. Man can, however, deploy them technically; that is what the whole production process is based upon. The laws that determine the social process can really be abandoned as soon as man is aware of them and circumstances allow them to be controlled. They can, like a *not-I* created by man, be bequeathed to the *I*. Man himself can in the end uncover the prospects of emancipation. He can give the natural force within the social process a liberating *twist*. He can bring society into line and reign over it on the basis of will and consciousness. He can gain *power* over nature, over the natural and social circumstances under which he had, until then, been forced to live. Even if such power cannot be instantly seized, man is able to work on that politically. He can possibly make that come true *as man*. He can acquire liberating power over his own circumstances.

Does everyone participate equally in this process of liberation? Does such power fall to each individual? Can all people free themselves from the doom that kept Medea hostage? That is certainly not the case. The active process of liberation has to be delegated, as too must the power that it brings with it. The liberating is laid in the hands of a body that must take care of that, the revolutionary, communist party. This movement not only *presents* man and mankind which has to be liberated, but it also *represents* it—for so long as emancipation has not been fully realized. The *communist* party takes over the position of the absolute *I* of Fichte: now as an *I* with a world and mankind-spanning perspective, liberated from the confining people's identity. As a party, thus as part of humanity, this universal *I* also actually has something paradoxical about it: it is a component that really wants to be all and everything.

As long as social liberation is not complete, the oppressed cannot become absolute individuals or mankind. As long as what is possible has not become a reality, the

11   The Messianic Unburdening

communists will form a *party*. This party will hostilely turn itself against all resistance, against every power that stands in the way of the complete liberating of man and of humanity. The party develops a universal power against all the forces that resist it. The *resistance* is formed by everything that is understood to fall under social relationships. It is all about the institutional framework, the church and its ethical pressure, the cultural bonds that keep the people imprisoned, the repressive ideas and ideologies, incorrect human consciousness, and even the not emancipated person himself. Marx amounts to a radical, *unleashed* Fichte: all resistance has to be broken down, all boundaries overstepped. The communist party has to free man from a country to which he does not belong, from the existence that is *strange* to him. The party has to lead people into the Promised Land, a totally different world, a whole new existence. The party gives the people another name, another being, another identity.

To make all of this possible, the party first activates a radical ethical atheism. Contained in this activism is the party-*I* consciousness, will, and deed, all rolled into one. At the core of all the vigor is the *revolution*, which is directed at totally emancipating and altering man and mankind. The revolution cannot, of course, spontaneously happen just like that. This is where Marx lets go of the immediateness of Feuerbach. What also has to be considered is the fact that the revolution may not be a partial or hesitating turnaround but it must rather be a far-reaching process penetrating everything and everyone. Not only society but also man is stubborn, he does not easily allow himself to be changed and that is precisely why both his consciousness and his will will have to undergo a profound change. The opposition does not thus only come from outside but also from within. The revolution filters in at both levels.

It would seem that Marx is trying to somehow re-enact the *exodus* of the people of Israel, not now under the leadership of omnipotent God but under the leadership of the equally powerful communist party. Even now the entry into the Promised Land does not seem possible without catharsis, without an inner changing of man. Even now the entry demands something akin to a long journey through the *wilderness*, a revolutionary journey that must redeem the new individual from the old type of person. The modern journey demands not only the material but also the spiritual degeneration of man. He has to undergo *estrangement* from all that is unique to him, from all that ties him to the old person and the old world. Estrangement has not so much material significance as something that extends deeper. It has in view the redemption of man, a total liberation *from* all that is old: only then will the liberating *to* the new be possible. The new person is man who has been liberated for sensuality and who forms part of a united humankind. The *proletariat estrangement* is thus the historical journey through the wilderness of modern man. During this journey, man is doomed to leave all that is old behind him, also what is old about man himself. This journey is still made from the point of view of the old promise, the perspective of a life in peace and the satisfying of the person to whom such peace falls. The nostalgic mood keeps the glance firmly fixed in a forward direction.

What is crucial to the revolutionary process to be led by the communist party is the deed: the critical deed, the *struggle*. It all has to do with an integral struggle against the *external* enemy—the existing powers—and the enemy *within* in the form of man of old. It is a struggle that cannot be anything other than absolute and definite, that is only satisfied with complete victory. This struggle breaks down all resistance to the entry into the Promised Land. In part this resistance can be broken down within the civil society itself by the hard laws of the free market. This process leads to the deterioration and estrangement of the worker and the majority of the small business owners and capitalists. Again, what is characteristic of the proletariat is not so much the long working hours and the low wages, thus leading to material deterioration, but rather the accompanying estrangement, the total *expropriation*. The proletarian not only loses all that he *possesses* but also everything that is typical of him, what he *is*. In this loss of self he utterly distances himself from his old being, from the historically determined ethical and cultural identity. Much the same fate falls to most of the owners of capital: after having been defeated in the process of competition regarding their business property, they too have to face up to complete self-estrangement. The social process can therefore generate its own wilderness, an own catharsis.

The expropriation, the complete self-*estrangement* may not only be negatively perceived: the total self-*destruction* is in fact a precondition for total self-*recovery*. The social process does not only therefore raze external frontiers, such as those of institutions, peoples or nations but it also turns inwards. It revolves especially around this latter point: around the breaking down of man's old identity, the breaking down of everything that resists the emancipation of man and mankind. As proletarians, all individuals are freed from the inner galling bonds. The radical self-estrangement of man is the modern exodus from the old world and the old existence. The self-estrangement not only liberates from the institutionalized shackling but it also signals the end of the inequality of those who are, in principle, equal. As proletarians all the people are unconditionally *equal*. At the end of this probationary revolutionary course of events *within* the social process, the communist party elevates itself *above* this process and takes responsibility for the unconditional revolutionary leadership. It leads the revolutionary apotheosis.

Marx was not, however, inclined to leave it at this economically dominated theory. From the worldwide point of view, the social process was, after all, divergent and unmanageable, invariably too pre-modern. He distinguished two deviant situations, situations in which the social process is not dominated by modern economic developments. What was remarkable was the fact that it was precisely the irregular, not so modern circumstances that were to produce successful communist revolutions. This

11   The Messianic Unburdening

proves that it was not in fact the economy but rather the *ideology* and the *politics* that determined the revolutionary process. Marx had definitely foreseen this in his analyses and had angled his revolutionary concepts in that direction. His *Frühschriften* bear witness to this very point, especially his *Zur Kritik der Hegelschen Rechtsphilosophie*. Apart from the economically developed kind of society, there are two other types of surviving societies that he describes. On the one hand, there are circumstances in which the revolutionary process will have to be entirely triggered by political intervention on the part of the communist party, whilst, on the other hand, there are political situations that absolutely do not lend themselves to revolutionary change.

In view of this latter point, it needs to be mentioned that Marx and Engels maintained that certain groups and populations could be typified as incorrigibly counter-revolutionary; for them there was no future. They did not form part of world history and thus deserved no place in the emancipated world. They were furious about the Czechs, Croats, and Russians, and that was a judgment that was also reined upon other *reactionary* or *historically backward* peoples or dynasties. Because of their unhistorical or anti-historical status, they would have to face denationalization or destruction. He who is not chosen is doomed to face judgment, the *Final Judgment*. *Man* and *mankind* can tolerate no deviations. He who fails to adapt or who cannot adapt is condemned, lost, doomed. Those who are not tolerated by the revolutionary fury are also lost. Any opposition that is too problematic must be conquered in a revolutionary fashion. That is how the revolutionary will must frantically spread, randomly and charged with pathological zeal. The appeal to approach such peoples in a *rancorous* way is actually not all that surprising. Hatred is a revolutionary type of pathos. The *hatred* of races can easily be presented as a motivating factor. The *not-I* that does not allow itself to be integrated by the merciless party-*I* falls prey to a bitter fate. In addition, Marx also throws *imagination* into the arena. His dividing of humanity elaborates on that of Fichte. In order to break down the *resistance*, revolutionary *revulsion* is stimulated. Romantic paranoia is endowed with revolutionary purpose. This will be further explained in the pages to come.

Then there are the circumstances that demand *political* intervention if they are to qualify as revolutionary. It was clear to Marx that a successful revolutionary process could not always be left in the hands of naturally necessary developments. There are situations that demand a thorough support of the process. For them, *Germany* could be seen as a pre-eminent example of a social situation where, in an economic sense, things were under-developed but which nevertheless offered a promising revolutionary perspective. He was not so much concerned about how special that nation was but more about its circumstances in a more general sense. Marx turned the apparently bleak situation of backwardness into an advantage, or to put it another way; he turned need into a revolutionary virtue. Instead of having a phased revolutionary process, he developed for this situation the concept of total revolution all at once. Revolutionary *political* action would have to *make* the impossible *possible* after all. The backward situation made it necessary to take a great leap forward. Apparently impossible circumstances made it imperative to kick-start the revolutionary process in an *artificial* way. The revolution had to be forcefully organized and imposed top-down. To that end the communist party was required to usurp all state power, thus effecting the revolution. Through such seizing of power the concept of self-loss and the reinstating of man could be fully accomplished.

The accompanying revolutionary recipe was that of a forced Verelendung. Marx sought artificially created poverty (*künstlich produzierte Armut*). Enforced impoverishment would be deployed to wear people *down* and to prepare them for meekly submitting to the further revolutionary process. Marx introduced the formula of compelled self-estrangement imposed from above. Compare this with the logic behind revolutionary starvation politics as practiced by Stalin and *Ceausescu*. The perceived natural necessity has to be ensured by means of merciless revolutionary action. The absolute *I* of the party forcibly leads politically created proletarians through the wilderness. The *I* creates, where, and insofar as that it is necessary, its own proletariat: through political power and state-instigated terror. Those who cannot or do not want to join the ranks of the proletariat will be met with the fate of objectionable resistance, the destiny of being removed from world history and from all humanity. Such activist state terror corresponds with the revolutionary *messianic fervor*, which, after the political seizing of power, the party must at all costs elaborate upon. This needs to be further elucidated. What should be clear is that where the self-estrangement, the loss of self of old man does not automatically occur, the process has to be helped along. In such cases, the pressure of social natural necessity has not been coercive enough. The terrorizing *plagues* that the God of Israel once visited upon the Egyptians now affect *reactionary*, backward, and unhistorical factions. The period of *testing* to which the people of Israel had once been subjected now affects the *chosen* proletariat, in this case to prove whether they have really been chosen.

The ownership relationship was used by Marx as a lever to bring about people's self-estrangement. This not only pertained to the *ownership* of real estate or capital but also predominantly to the legally anchored *private* legal personality, to the proof of ownership of body and members. The corporate personality had released man from the old slavery situation, from being the physical property of another. In terms of the ownership relationship it had been supplanted by a new slavish integration into society. As a private individual, as an egoist, he became socially trapped in this law. Private man therefore remains a *shackled* individual, chained to his own interests and to the maintaining of his position. This ruined his possible fulfillment as man and as a part of humankind. Hence the reason that man also needed to be liberated from this private ownership title: the owner has to be disowned. The private position stands in

11 The Messianic Unburdening

the way of self-fulfillment, this resistance must therefore be abolished by means of social and human self-change. This is really a practical question, a Fichtean *making* true, a matter of revolutionary praxis. The practical *solving* of everything that stands in the way of man's self-fulfillment is simultaneously the *solution* to history's secret. What is crucial is the revolutionary fervor, the will to conquer everything that estranges, to abolish and resolve it. The revolutionary fervor must run like a thread through all peoples, classes, and cultures; every differentiating identity must be finally resolved. Marxism knows its own, revolutionary *Endlösung*.

Revolutionary zeal must break down the resistance of the old world and man of old. Thanks to the expropriation, the self-estrangement, and the loss of self, man is able to regain his true self. As has been asserted, the expropriated *I* is really already at the same time an individual-*I* and a world-*I*. The revolutionary loss of man of old—and of the old world—in that way incorporates the equally revolutionary perspective of regaining new man and the new world. The complete and thorough loss precedes the total regaining. There can be no Promised Land without an exodus and conflict, no fulfillment without revolutionary, political, and spiritual estrangement. Marx's definition of what is proletariat expresses this very well. He speaks of a politically impassioned class that screams out to the opposition, passionately and ripe for the revolution: *I am nothing but I should be everything*.[1] This is the pathos that expresses the revolutionary recipe. The revolutionary violence begins with the creation of what is *nothing* and it is from this *nothingness* to *everything* that the whole, all-embracing revolutionary process proceeds; a process that must make everything and everyone different. But does Marx leave it at this? Is nothingness a good enough precondition for everything?

11.3 THE REALIZATION OF PHILOSOPHY

The revolution has to break down everything that is hostile and resists. Actually, this hampers what *has to* emancipate as well as what *must want to* emancipate. What resists is, above all else, the old, ethical impulse, the attachment to the culture and the institutions. What Marx means by the *shackles* that the proletarians have to lose is the tie to *ethical* compulsion. On the other hand, the proletarians have a world and a life to gain. Marx's pretensions are grotesque: they can win a *world* by changing the *world*. That which is possible has to become a reality; the promise has to be fulfilled here on earth. The topics of previous metaphysical speculation—man and the world—are brought back to the earth and made a matter of decisiveness.

This pretentious vigor cannot, however, be left to the proletariat. How could a completely estranged mass be able to lead, change, or regain itself? Here, Marx

---

1. Marx, *Frühschriften*, 221.

encounters the same dilemma as the one Moses was once up against when he had to lead a people, groaning under the yoke of repression, out of Egypt. Moses recognized the abyssal problem: how could he get the people to believe in him and listen to him? Hence the road of hardened oppression and amplified misery. How can the *right will* be inculcated upon one who is unwilling? How can it be made clear to him that he can become a part of that promise? It is the unwillingness that forces him to embark on the therapeutic journey through the wilderness: all of the old must pass away before new man can inherit the Promised Land. In more modern times, Rousseau recognized a similar problem: how can a people lead itself and manage to steer the own will in the right direction? Marx accentuates this by coming up with a radical conclusion. An utterly estranged proletariat is able to do little other than militantly unite with humanity. There remains, for the time being, the proletariat: an indignant and recalcitrant *mass*. This impassioned mass is merely a *material* weapon. This unguided missile must therefore be placed in the hands of a *power* that can oversee the long march. This power is the communist party: it has at its disposal the correctly directed kind of *will* and is thus able to lead the revolutionary process. The communist party possesses the *spiritual* weapons, the right insight into the circumstances within which the struggle has to be fought, and the objective that has to be realized.

If communism is the goal of the battle in terms of world history, then it is the communist *party* that will have to provide the necessary leadership. The goal and the means are inextricably linked. An amorphous mass of militant beings can fight for the fulfilled existence of mankind. The perspective of this struggle may be labeled mankind, but where does this mankind dwell other than in its existence as a mass? Throughout the conflict, the party possesses power over the impassioned mass, over the material, proletarian force; it determines the will and the direction of the proletariat. The party-*I* conducts the battle against the *not-I*. It is a battle that has to be thoroughly fought out. In order to dispel man of old, the old institutional world also has to be destroyed. The *not-I* is especially tenacious in an institutional sense.

The material force of the revolutionary process is therefore led by a spiritual-political power. This gives rise to an ensuing question: *Who* within the communist party is in possession of the correct philosophical insight; who has the legitimate power? Who is able to maneuver himself into this position? As long as the proletariat masses are nothing other than fodder for violence, they have to be represented by the communist party. But *who* is it that leads the party? Who represents the world-historical active *I*? Who can present himself as the will and the consciousness of the revolutionary modernizing man? In the words of Rousseau: who must lead the blind masses and teach the people to learn to see the right kind of orientation, who must teach the community to discover what it wants and thus give shape to the unity of reason and will? Should the thorough emancipation of man also not be placed in the hands of a universalistic individual within the party? Should the world-historical atheism thus

11 The Messianic Unburdening

not create a god of its own, a god who becomes a man? Should this final god not lead man through the wilderness for a final time? Must this god elevate the divided masses to a common humanity? In that way, this god could become a linchpin connecting old and new man, the old and the new worlds.

Does this final god modernize and radicalize the old doctrine in any other way?

The terrestrial twist presents itself as a world-historical final judgment. The final contest is in fact the definitive contest between good and evil. Does this, then, put Messianism into the picture again? Does the revolutionary struggle between good and evil take on the guise of a contemporary *messianic judgment*? If this were indeed the case, it would give rise to certain questions. Does the communist party recognize its own revolutionary Messiah? Does it create such a person itself? Would this individual be able to dispose freely of the spiritual *and* the material weapons? Does such a revolutionary Messiah have the power and the insight to drag mankind through the final phase in what is *his* correct way? Does a human now claim to possess divine omniscience and omnipotence? If all this were so, how would revolutionary Messianism deal with good and evil? How does it deal with its own revolutionary evil? How can the revolution bring justice into focus? How does man who has become god deal with avenging and redeeming justice?

As far as the question of power is concerned, what is important is the Marxist interpretation of the *spiritual* weapon. The omnipotent cannot manage without omniscience: Marxism brings both those aspects together. Philosophical insight must get the revolutionary process moving in a *fundamental* way. This insight guides and directs the process. We are not talking here about an introverted and speculative type of philosophy but about a kind of philosophy that becomes practical, a philosophy that seeks its own realization. Finally, practical philosophy ultimately makes itself redundant: it raises itself up in its realization. A kind of philosophy that becomes practical gives guidance to the definitive estrangement of man, creates the proletariat masses and gives leadership to the process of abolishing the proletariat. It leads mankind to its destination. It works in the sphere of the perfect uniting of man and nature. It unites naturalized man with a humanized type of nature, it leads man towards a state of peace and fulfillment. The communist party and its philosophy, the insight and the power, the thinking and its exponents are seamlessly linked. This applies to the final perspective but also to the road leading up to it.

Without philosophical insight the party cannot work on the revolutionary process, on the completing of the final judgment and the opening up of the way to salvation. In this process, philosophy keeps open the perspective of redemption and fulfillment. In this respect Marx speaks of the *realization of philosophy*: the philosophy has to realize itself—as a philosophical idea and as a revolutionary activity.[2] Communism *is* not just the resolved riddle of history but it *understands* itself as that. Marxism

---

2. Marx, *op cit.*, 224.

secularizes the age-old divine *providence*. In the accomplishing of the communistic process, utter fulfillment and total transparency can in fact come together. In terms of the process and the result, communism makes clear what the *path* is. It offers the prospect of a fulfilled life and *makes* this *true*. The path, the truth, and the life come together in a modern fashion. The party leader embodies the universal *I*, it makes the path, the truth and the life its own. He gives the party, the struggle and communism unity of person. He gives the party an *I*, a provident god. It is up to him to realize his omnipotent philosophical insight. Can he find peace without man and the world becoming one in him?

The task to *make* true in the final, practical philosophy gives rise to pressing questions about the notion of truth behind philosophical knowledge and know-how. What, then, is Marx's interpretation of the idea of truth? His analytical works imply that he respects what is given, the factual reality that should underlie the theory. Other works of his deal with the idea of truth in a much more normative and prescriptive way: one almost gets the impression that image and theory should precede the factual. Whether Marx's practical theory is in any way hindered by the facts is therefore very questionable. His philosophy is much more based on metaphysical concepts pertaining to matters such as man and society, history and the world. The scientific, in his case, is much more based upon theoretical speculations wielded for the purposes of practical processes of change.

The question thus becomes more specific: does an own-realizing philosophy accept something that ideally has to be viewed as a given fact? Does Marxist philosophy recognize something conditional or does Marx follow in the footsteps of Fichte, and does he subject the opposing, the reality that needs to be recognized, to his *power of imagination*? Is it the case that he cannot rest until the *not-I* no longer stands in his way and all is completely one with *his* idea? Does this mean that his analysis of the old world and of former man, of history and of society, of repression and estrangement is largely a product of his imagination? Is the supposed analysis nothing more than an image? Does he dictate the facts; does he create them? Can a final, practical philosophy be named authentic? The philosophy that emerges does indeed prove to have totalitarian pretensions. To that end, it first manipulates the old and corrupted man and world before then, leading humanity on to a new existence. The revolutionary process recreates past history so that it can freely dispose of man and the world, in order to act in a freely creating fashion.

Any practical philosophy that is in the hands of one individual will inevitably lead to arbitrariness. That is unavoidable. The realization of such philosophical thought means that the actual image of reality can be randomly manipulated. Philosophical omnipotence merges with arbitrariness and we are talking here of the randomness of an omniscient and omnipotent leader. *His* imagination becomes the bridge between

11 The Messianic Unburdening

idea and reality. *His* imagination has to realize the world of ideas concealed there within. What emerges from the first of his truths is the realization that if facts cannot be subsumed in the idea or in the theory, then that is just too bad for the facts. This throws some light on the earlier-mentioned unhistorical situations: what cannot be changed, what cannot be realized, can only be eliminated. Anything that cannot be made to correspond with the idea is granted no future. This throws some light on Marx's *real* solution to the *Widerstreit* between the human *essence*—imagined by him—and their (again imagined by him) concrete *existence*.[3] What remains for existence is the fatal choice either to adapt to this kind of essence or to submit to defeat.

Philosophical providence justifies unprecedented revolutionary energy. Through that *contrast*, this vigor seeks to eradicate all that would differentiate. Atheistic providence feels able and justified to break down all *opposition* to what stands in its way. In the revolutionary mode of self-change it is also man that is destroyed. This *destruction* is presented as a fatality. The new providence justifies its fatality by calling it historical and social *natural necessity*, by seeing it as the voice of nature. It is all about a voice that does not listen to *the other* or to *what is different*. The divine word *knows* what nature wants because it *dictates* its voice and then presents this dictate *as* nature, as irresistible power. In the revolutionary recreation, the providential word speaks out as an unfathomable voice of nature.

11.4 THE SPIRIT OF ANIMOSITY

The question which then follows relates to the mood in which this voice of nature pursues its work. Is it matter of fact and objective or is it tinged with something of the romantic mood? The nostalgic imagination clearly does its work. But does this also extend to the paranoia? Is the revolutionary battle fought from a pure and providential angle or does natural necessity involve more than just legal force on its own? Does the necessity also activate spirit and pathos? Does nature also reveal passion? Is the effect of the spirit of Medea still felt in nature? Does the atheistic god show himself to be zealous or is he also enraged, jealous, revengeful?

Marx's revolutionary spirit does not avoid the pathos. Assentingly he alludes to the unrelenting appeal of George Sand to: "fight or face death; the bloody war or nothing."[4] Fichte's *I* becomes brutal, aggressive, furious. The revolutionary *I* not only disdains the *not-I* but it despises it. This contempt is a slight repetition of the earlier struggle between God and the gods, but now the conflict is between the party god and the existing ethical and political powers. The fight is not only directed at all who resist the omnipotent but also against those who do not receive salvation. Once again the finger is pointed at those who oppose the classes and who decry the people. That contempt unleashed more, though, and demanded more. The fury of destruction also

3. Ibid., 235.
4. Ibid., 524.

demands a furious mood. The battle is fought from the same ethical atheistic perspective that it also wants to project: *beyond good and evil*. The revolutionary philosophy liberates itself from good and evil. It recognizes only *contemptuous* and *despised* enemies. The omnipotent *I* reveals itself as an executioner, driven by revolutionary hate. It places the despised and hostile *not-I* beneath the level of humanity. Hate and revenge conquer unlimited space. The final judgment does not therefore only bestow power on arbitrariness, it does not only seize the weapon of terror, but it also mobilizes paranoia, hatred, and the urge to retaliate. The party mobilizes and justifies the entire war, the "merciless confrontation of man against man,"[5] the revolutionary *Endlösung*. Is such fury really necessary? Could history not be created in a rational way on the basis of will and consciousness?

Marx's epistemological notions not only revolve around the *vérité à faire*, but also around the question of to whom this *making* true falls. The object to be examined, society and all its processes, is itself a product of human activity. Man forms his own world, albeit not always in an adequate and conscious fashion. The raw materials of such knowledge emanate from a producer. This is the subject of Marx's *Thesen über Feuerbach*. The question of objective truth is not something he sees as a theoretical matter but rather as something practical. In the praxis man must prove the truth, that is to say *his* activity and power. The problem, though, is that the generator of this reality is no objective clear reality: also that still has to be created. The practical truth that is to be realized also demands a practical and to be realized person who therefore has to be changed. Just like Abraham of old, the modern creator of the truth will also have to undergo a change of name. In a fundamental way he will have to become another person. The producer himself still has to be produced by means of revolutionary praxis. This extends much deeper than simply changing the social circumstances: man also has to become essentially different.

This logic does not detract from the fact that what we are seeing here is something quite peculiar. Whilst social man is given the prospect of a revolutionary process of change in order to really become a producer of the truth, the philosopher and those of his ilk maintain that they are in a position to partly reveal this secret. He elevates himself above the social turbulence. What emerges in the *Thesen* is a sharp social *division* between human beings. Above man—who is subjected to natural forces—rises another, extremely small portion of humanity, in the form of those who are able to see through the social process and lead the revolutionary changes taking place in people and in the world. Marx broke down Kant's *antimony* of freedom and natural necessity. He divided people into two types and made one superior to the other. This is unprecedented cynicism! Those who would have to throw off their chains were first of all completely chained to a naturally necessary process. It is not social relations that shackle people but Marx himself! In order to throw off their chains these shackled

5. Ibid.

individuals have to undergo a drastic change. Also, this revolutionary change falls to those who elevate themselves above chained humanity. They feed off those who are chained down.

He who is elevated places himself above the truth. He holds the key to the truth in his hands, the key to processing the raw material. He demands that theoretical questions are resolved through revolutionary praxis. The *vérité à faire* hallows no frontiers. Not only the interpreting of the *world* becomes part of the change, but also *man* has to be changed in a revolutionary way. Also, man becomes part of the reality that can be constructed and thus beneath those who possess the *power* with which they can give direction to this process. Not only *Truth* is fabricated but also power, power that possesses human raw material. The apparent loss of self of the shackled man of old amounts to turning him into raw material for man that has to be rediscovered. The *recalcitrance* of the chained material makes it only too clear that this process of loss of self and regaining cannot spontaneously take place. It is therefore neither a matter of coincidence or of accident that the revolutionary processes that occurred continued to gain a totalitarian tinge. Totalitarian practice is, after all, part of revolutionary theory. It is not so much in the proletariat that revolutionary omnipotence *finds* its *material* weapons. It is rather, that such omnipotence *turns* the proletariat into *material that can be manipulated.*

The final, practical philosophy of Marx creates a new god that is human and re-creative. This god manifests itself at the time of the completion of history in order to close the period now known as past history. The completion not only promises man that the former heavenly promise will be fulfilled, the period of completion will also force people to subject themselves to extreme processes. The inferno that religion held before people as a prospect for the final judgment is realized in an atheistic fashion, and that is coupled with fury. But why should that be so? Why does this omnipotent being not pass on his promise to all involved in a loving way? Because he *is* not and does not want to be a god of love. Because he has other plans for the people. He is moved by something other than a positive realization of reality, the creation of a utopian world. He does not love mankind. The ethical atheist despises man, this man, the man of old. He does not want this type of person and cannot tolerate him. For him this person is an annoying and objectionable being. Neither does he want this human world; he wants to get rid of it. This person and this world make re-creation impossible. The new, *jealous*, god not only banishes other religious, political, or ethical gods, but his jealousy is also directed at man. He tolerates no equals at his side. What his repulsion prevents him from seeing is that the object of his hatred is a product of his own imagination. The once sinful man is now known as socially corrupt. Just as Camus' Sisyphus despised the gods, so the new god despises this corrupt kind of man. He thus preaches a revolutionary, unsparing *battle* against him. Whatever resists him must be overthrown. Hence the reason that everyone and everything is promptly declared changeable.

The new god renounces his love of man and so Marx calls people up to go to war, but this is not a war against a respected enemy. He knows only hateful objects. He propagates a fight against an enemy that resides below the level of history and under the level of humanity. The war mounted against chained man is a war against subhuman beings. Philosophical insight, power, and pathos all come together. In his *Zur Kritik der Hegelschen Rechtsphilosophie*, he terms the philosophical component the head of passion. Passion is then the weapon that has to be used to destroy the enemy, the enemy as a contemptible and despised being. As has been stated, it is a struggle that extends beyond good and evil. The new creator is therefore in no way held back from freely making use of human material. With unbridled arbitrariness, revengeful resentment can be activated. Without vengefulness, without having a free hand in an ethical and atheistic way, the revolution cannot be successfully seen through. In the effort to combat the evil of chained man, everything is acceptable. This means that own *evil* can also therefore be employed in the conflict. In order to be able to do his work, the new creator becomes an ethical atheist. That is where this creator distinguishes himself from the previous one. This new creator no longer wishes to share what is ethically good with man. He no longer wants to be his *equal*, he wants to be elevated, he wants to glorify his immorality. He seeks evil and wants to be able to implement it in an exaggerated way. He even conquers the Theodicy: he no longer needs to ask the question that relates to evil because he has positioned himself above good and evil.

The old creator saw man as his equal in terms of ethical differentiation. His creation ended with this eternal task and challenge. The becoming man of man amounted to the exodus of the natural state. The human state was the eternal returning challenge to seek ethical good. No other future would be added to that, no heavenly or utopian panoramas, no promise that everything would once again change. For this person there was no way back to paradise, but also no way to a future paradise.

The moralizing *revaluation* of good and evil began with Abraham. It was a revaluation that ultimately empowered the imagination. Forward beckons the image of the good life, and backward the image of an existence doused in evil. An imagination that sees everywhere the signs of evil makes people bitter. Guilt and retribution are therefore sought. The revaluation of good and evil reaches in Marx its apotheosis. The image of world-historical exodus and fulfillment is linked to an appeal for animosity and hatred. The paranoid power of the imagination creates a type of human nature that is monster-like. It is not dramatic to see that utopia has become something unattainable. It is much sooner dramatic to see that the evil aspect of human nature has been able to swing in a grotesque direction. It is especially this evil that has sought to endorse the theory.

11   The Messianic Unburdening

This drama cannot manage without a fixed *belief*, a belief in revolutionary wonders. The miracle of heavenly fulfillment gains a sensual earthly revaluation. In addition to that an attack is opened upon another value of religion, the value of ethical life fulfillment. Marxism departs radically from the ethical meaning of life that religion champions. Hence the reason for the sharp rejection of the church as an *institution*. The church is classified as an institution that stands in the way of progress: its resistance has to be broken down. The communist party takes the place of ethical institutions. Its ethical atheism and depicted pathos is designed to release people from their bonds. The God of creation is relieved by the natural god that has become man.

Marx's judgment about religion creates an exciting conflict with *Luther*. His criticism is diametrically opposed to the twist that Hegel gives to Luther's doctrine. Marx offers what, in his eyes, is a sobering appreciation of what appears to him to represent the essence of religion. He lays claim to what seems to him to be the real purpose of religion, after which follows the atheistic direction taking. Religion is there to give suffering man the prospect of a fantastic heavenly reality: this implies that in a *wrong* world his needs will thus be alleviated. Man escapes into an imaginary world while he should have sought a terrestrial solution. That, then, is how religion sustains and reinforces a *wrong* awareness of the world. Marx wants to turn the gaze back from spiritual, heavenly appearances to sensual earthly reality.

In *Zur Kritik der Hegelschen Rechtsphilosophie*, he asserts that religion offers man the prospect of the imagined realization of human substance because man can find no *true* realization. A wrong world gives rise to an incorrect consciousness. Here it is the concepts *true* and *wrong* that Marx juxtaposes. He moralizes about the term *truth* in the above-mentioned way. That which is true points to the realization of what is in a sensual sense a good life; an existential fulfilling that takes the place of ethical life. Also, the *wrong* religious consciousness is given a moralizing interpretation. The wrong is an *expression* of actual human misery whilst at the same time being a *protest* against it. It is opposition, the demand for real happiness, the demand to put an end to all situations that cannot manage without illusions. Religion gains immanent critical significance; that is why it is not without meaning. This critical element is inherently *atheistic*; to be precise, it is ethically atheistic. What *is* inherent to religion is the opposition to human misery and all its causes, thus also the reference to the good. Religion provokes, as it were, the modernist turning of attention from heavenly reality towards earthly reality: from theology to politics. The immanent critical impulse *from* religion lies in its criticism *of* culture and the various institutions: this in fact perpetuates a wrong world and a wrong life. Does religious criticism not in that way really allude to aspects of the Old Testament? Does Marx not in this way distance himself from the heavenly-oriented Luther? Does he not reinstate the terrestrial perspectives of Abraham and Moses? What, then, is the basis for his appreciation of Luther? Marx searches for a combination.

Despite his harsh criticism of the law, the state, and the church, Marx expresses great appreciation for German legal and state philosophy and for Luther's theology. It has already been demonstrated that Marx wants to use politics as a lever to make the backward German situation revolutionary. It is intellectual progression that makes political action possible. A communist party can therefore be organized. This party will not actually be recruited from the proletariat masses but rather from educated circles, involving those who were emancipated in religious, philosophical, and political respects. As a Reformer, Luther had anticipated the leading position that would be occupied by philosophy. The German revolutionary past is of a *theoretical* nature and was activated by the reformation. Here, Marx is alluding to the liberation from the anachronistic, ecclesiastically based ancien régime. In this liberation he acknowledges a revolutionary impulse. Luther reformed the traditional, ecclesiastically oriented theology. This theology supported the quashing of the peasants' revolt, the most revolutionary occurrence in Germany until that time. What Marx admires in Luther is his breaking away from belief in institutional *authority*. Through him man begins to become liberated from the institutional chain, through him begins the conquest of servitude. What Luther is, however, guilty of is putting the authority of *belief* in its place. He replaced it, in other words, with a new type of servitude or enslavement.

Why does Marx view the authority of and the enslavement brought by belief in such a positive light? Because he sees the *humble* attitude of the masses and their unshakeable *faith* in the revolutionary liberation as crucial to the revolutionary plan. Luther's steadfast religious binding of the humble masses to the perspective of *apocalyptic* development serves for Marx as a model for the attaching of proletariat masses to an equally apocalyptic revolutionary process. In his book, humble is not defined as retiring and accepting but rather as meek and submissive. His apocalyptic philosophy amounts to a worldly continuation of the apocalyptic religion. In this respect the communist party will take over the role of the church. It is now up to the *party* to show shackled believers the route they have to follow to the terrestrial Promised Land. It is an *earthly* Luther who in that way leads the party in the right direction of revolutionary process.

Just as with apocalyptical theology, so also in apocalyptical philosophy, evil must be absolutely conquered by good. In order to fight the battle in a dynamic, passionate, and effective way, things cannot simply remain with *the* good and *the* evil. The philosophical mobilization of man likewise makes it imperative to give good and evil a *face*. Marx therefore gives the chosen ones a face, all of which is vaguely reminiscent of the Christian tradition. The oppressed, impoverished, and estranged are permitted to leave the old face behind. All that is good comes to them. After turning *the* good into a substantive so that it could be *separated* from *the* evil, both good and evil are given a

11 The Messianic Unburdening

face. This face would have to make it possible to *separate* the good ones from the evil ones once and for all.

The good ones will be preserved, albeit in a totally altered human form. Those who have not passed through *death* will not be entitled to rebirth and a fulfilled life. Evil also gets a face: the face of enemies. No rebirth awaits such individuals but rather destruction. Marx is completely open on this point. The chosen few can only unfold to embrace humanity if evil and the evildoers disappear. That turns the conflict between good and evil into an apocalyptical final judgment. In this struggle everything revolves around justice. There can be no redemption without avenging justice. The final judgment recognizes a messianic apotheosis.

Who attributes to Marx the messianic position? And against whom does this Messiah turn? In the case of evil, is it really a matter of actual, definable culprits and proven guilt? His recipe is captivating. He urges that all that is negative, all social defects and all evil should be concentrated in one specific class. Evil has to be pointed out in *certain* people. It is not a matter of analysis but rather of attribution, of declaring guilty, of placing blame. In the interests of the revolution, one social stratum must be made responsible for *all* the misery in society, misery that is branded as *criminal*. The elimination of this criminal factor will be seen as the self-liberating of man. Revenge will be a revolutionary virtue. Redeeming *from* is a more powerful force than delivering *to*, or to put it another way, avenging justice is a much stronger *recruiter* than redeeming justice. Hence the strong emphasis on animosity. The longing for own liberation unites and binds the chosen ones too little: it does not really make them revolutionary. To mobilize and give direction to revolutionary willpower, evil has to be ascribed to others, those others must be declared guilty and evil has to be their reward. The revolutionary mobilization of the masses requires that evil be given a face. Revolutionary action can only be a success if the crowd is *seized* by a hostile pathos and becomes obsessed with collective rage. In order to be seized by such intense anger, the masses have to be edged into the *grasp* of the omnipotent designer. A great deal is therefore asked of the power of imagination. It is really a very willing servant.

That is how the aesthetic god gets man to bend to his will. Man is made so rancorous that he starts to thirst for avenging justice. Whether the supposed evils are the real cause of the misery hardly seems to matter. Whether the alleged evils bear even the least blame for the attributed evils does not matter. It is all about manipulating the masses and getting them to rally round and unite in the struggle against evil. It is thus legitimate, indeed necessary, to exaggerate. Only through blaming, accusing, and condemning can the revolution be a success. After all, there is a certain history and logic to Sartre's *j'accuse*. There can be no revolution without pathos and rancor. The revolution makes it necessary to turn the mass into something dangerous: to cultivate a raging will of the people.

In order to mobilize this will of the people and the required revolutionary power, Marx maintains that it is precisely German situations, with apparently little chance, that lend themselves better to the cause than situations in countries where the revolutionary process progressed in phases. In countries where the ground seemed more fertile for the revolution to get a foothold, it was necessary—time and again—for general representatives of evil to be identified and cited. In France this had once been the fate of the aristocracy and the clergy. By making them the universal representatives of all social crimes, the bourgeoisie was able to develop a universal consciousness. Such a consciousness was merely able to achieve a revolution completed in phases: only as a phase did it become part of the world-historical process.

In socially backward *German situations*, the revolutionary process really has to be completed in radical and sudden ways. In such countries there is really a lack of a class with pathetic enthusiasm and revolutionary courage; what is also missing is an unrelenting will that stops at nothing, a will that detects representatives of evil and settles scores with them. How does Marx think that he can resolve this problem? Such will must at any rate be alien to any kind of reservations and moderation. The storm that Protestant apocalyptical powers of the imagination had unleashed had not been enraged enough because of the excess amount of morality and honesty. People remained too scrupulous in their dealings with each other; people were not embittered and revengeful enough to hold a particular group responsible for all the misery. In short, the preconditions for revolutionary rage had not been met. Hence the reason that Marx is anxious to abolish such kinds of *anachronisms*. Hence the rise of militant ethical atheism: the determined will to root out the normative core of such institutions.

Marx's proletarian motto is this: *I am nothing and should be everything*. In this motto it is not the *everything*, the hope of the *possibility* of the possible, that is the revolutionary essence. Also, the *nothing*, the *impossibility* of the whole thing, is really not enough for the revolutionary élan. It is not even about the cause of this nothing, actual or perceived. It is all about the unleashing of a revolutionary pathos: the unrestrained *anger of the people*. This is what is shamelessly evoked. The revolutionary hate of the Russians is therefore angled more at the fight against an unhistorical people. It is about the *hate* itself: that must actually, in *deed*, make things revolutionary. The chosen segment of mankind must be united through the cause of hatred. The rage of the people must unite. In the interests of the *omnipotent* the creativity of the party goes to the limit: it must make his blinded and subjugated masses *possessed* with a common rage. Imagination does wonders. The jealous omnipotent one on earth, who tolerates no other at his side, eclipses not only the view of existence but even more so the view of fellow man. As vague as the forward glance is—which hankers after redemption—so sharp the backward glance is which hankers after revenge. The apparent impossibility of revolution appears to be a provocation of the revolutionary desire for power.

11   The Messianic Unburdening

No omnipotence without an omnipotent. Justice asks for the willpower of an *I*. This *I* must become one with the social body, the people, mankind. Hence the reason that revolutionary conflict is necessary. The world-historic final conflict is *messianic*. This task falls to the communist party. That party *represents* mankind, it *presents* itself as an omnipotence that galvanizes the revolutionary battle forward. It *presents* the perfect insight into the conditions and the progress of the revolutionary process. It has to gain political power if it is to manipulate history in the way that it wants. By *making* its *ethical* atheistic mission a worldwide thing, *sensual* atheism can then be realized. Again, there can be no omnipotence without an omnipotent. The messianic conflict is unthinkable without a Messiah. It is not only evil that is given a face, but also the communistic Messiah gains in this judgment a face, a human face. The task is for him to mobilize the will of the people and keep that particular show on the road until the judgment has been accomplished.

The revolution may declare *man* to be the highest of all beings, but this communistic Messiah claims that he is the most superior *person*. Without this elevated, sublime individual, the party is unable to meet its revolutionary brief. The revolution has brought forth many sublime representatives of mankind. They have made the revolutionary fury theirs in a merciless way. Their task legitimates the most terrible evil. Also, god who has become man demands unconditional *faith* from his people in what he thinks and does. He is the human incarnation of the old nominalistic God; he maintains that he is capable of *making* true the ancient theological *promise*, that of *salvation* and justice. In the words of Marx and Adorno: philosophy prepares itself for the realization of its promise. It realizes itself—in Stalinism.

12

The Stalinist Final Contest

The communist revolution was the endeavor to realize Marxist theory in relation to the changing of man and the world. The revolution was no longer prepared to wait and see the historical results of the social process: natural necessity was given a helping hand. The apparently impossible was made possible and, what is more, by an unhistorical people. Historical destiny cannot manage without the *compulsive* changing of man and society. After a hesitant warming up with Lenin, it was Stalin who was to demonstrate real revolutionary zeal. With unprecedented power of will, this persevering *I* saw the revolution through.

The power of Stalin's ideological belief was indeed unprecedented. He believed in the miracle of recreating man and the world. This miracle may have been presented as a necessity but what was inescapable was that, for Stalin, it was a matter of sheer will and power of deed. He was the *nominalistic god* made man; he proved that omnipotence worked. His belief did therefore move mountains. It gave him the willpower and the strength to persevere in order to effect this miracle, to cynically and practically take to task the Marxist realization. He certainly had fully comprehended and applied Marx's analysis of the *German situation*. The perspective that appealed to him was that of a sudden radical revolution on a world-historical scale. But he remained practical. It in fact soon became clear to him that the final contest could not be completed all at once and on a world scale. The proletarians of all countries would not simply allow themselves to be swept up and united in a worldwide revolutionary movement. He therefore developed a calculating strategy of *phasing* the revolution in, country by country. Cynically, he took advantage of the circumstances that hindered the revolution occurring *all at once*. This had nothing to do with the phased revolution also criticized by Marx. The phasing did not occur within a given country but rather between

12 The Stalinist Final Contest

countries. It was still the revolution that came from above, still a political takeover of power.

Stalin's radicalism did not wait for economically engineered estrangement. He did not believe in a revolution that filters up *from below*, from the material circumstances. He radicalized Marx's concept of a revolution *from above*, instigated and directed by the party and by the state power that it had seized. The estrangement—the complete loss of man—would be artificially imposed from above by this power. He gave universal scope to Marx's concept designed for German circumstances. The revolutionary process would be entirely placed in the hands of the omnipotent communist party. The revolution gained messianic stature as a *dictatorship of the proletariat*. Centralized dictatorship would have to realize total estrangement, the precondition for winning back man.

12.1 THE JUSTIFYING OF EVIL

It is indeed ironic that Lenin and Stalin both found the revolutionary concept, intended for German circumstances, suitable for a people that Marx and Engels had written off in terms of the world-historical process. Within the framework of the revolution, they had in fact wanted to tackle Russia—perceived by them as backward and counter-revolutionary—in a resentful and warlike fashion. In the end, though, things can sometimes turn out differently. It seemed that Lenin and Stalin were much sooner inclined to place Russia in the same situation as that ascribed, in Christian eschatology, to the Jews: the state of being a *chosen people*. They saw Russian culture as a very suitable operational basis for the world revolution. To their minds, the Russian population, composed largely of servile farming folk, constituted such an amorphous mass that it would be relatively easy to create a submissive, proletariat group of people. In Russia it would undoubtedly be relatively easy to dispense with the institutions that were so inconvenient for such a revolution. Stalin must have been convinced that a messianic party dictatorship would fit in well with this people and its spirit.

Stalin's practical notion of a world-historical revolutionary process corresponded in many ways with Fichte's philosophy. The scope of this mental legacy would now really become world-historical and totalitarian. The revolutionary process no longer tolerated any frontiers, restraints, or conditions: man and the world fell, in their entirety, into the recreation category. Everything derived from historical processes, which meant that things could be seen as relative or transitory and, therefore, as possible to change. The fact that nothing is eternal also applies to *history* itself: with the aid of a goal-oriented revolutionary process it will come to an end. The Romantic need to always have to and want to strive for things was construed by Stalin as a rational final goal. Being naturally necessary did not mean to say that the revolutionary realization could not be turned into a transparent process which thus fell within his omniscience.

He knew that the ancient kingdom of God was at hand in the form of *his* kingdom. That could no longer be devotedly awaited: it had to be worked upon. Not only his activism but also his nostalgic longing and unceasing paranoia had a rational facet. Nature and reason do find each other. That made the dictatorship of the proletariat a transparent conflict, at every stage. That was also what made it possible to conduct the revolution as a justified war.

The final contest demanded certain qualities of both the party and the leader that were nigh on divine. The characteristics of the nominalistic God gained a human guise. The divine became human, in fact, all too human. The longing for omnipotence and for omniscience was coupled with a pathological craving for uniqueness. His *jealousy* turned into a kind of paranoia that bordered on madness. Everything had to fall to him, all that exists: life and death, good, and evil. He had good and evil at his disposal in an utterly immoral way. That turned the ultimate evil of the revolution into a calculated and justified core. That, in turn, made the miracle possible. His jealousy gave rise to masses that were incredibly submissive. He created a folk that was submissive and blindly faithful. Out of conviction, out of fear, he made the masses devoted. He actually realized the Orwellian conversion. His revolutionary belief radiated among the either active or passively submissive masses. He engineered belief in himself and in his cause. He created the right conditions to win over the people: to make him and his people one.

Everything that stands in the way of this unity loses its right to existence. This applies in the first place to the *institutions* and the traditions as well as to the values and culture that make it sustainable. Obviously, the ethical God is also sacrificed to justice. It has already been asserted that atheistic salvation necessitates a long march through the institutions: a contemporary journey through the wilderness. As far as Stalin was concerned that journey should not last too long. His revolutionary undermining of tradition and ethicality was angled at driving man, at not leaving him in peace, at giving him no time to catch his breath. Not only all the remnants of attachment to the old structures had to disappear but also morals and conscience. The ease with which he dispensed with those closely allied to devoted party officials, the ease with which he sacrificed not only them but also those close to him all had a revolutionary purpose. They were not only sacrificed because they would stand up to his unrelenting will, but also in conjunction with the eliminating of institutional and moral solidarity. All had to bow to his will, a will that had conquered ethical differentiation. People not only had to bend to his will in complete belief and devotion but they also had to become a highly motivated aspect of that will, regardless of how utterly arbitrary it may have been.

The position held by the *state* and by state bureaucracy vis-à-vis the institutions that had to be eliminated was a curious one. Ultimately these would also have to be disbanded, but only when the worldwide revolution became a successful reality. Until such a time the state was badly needed, and did—in fact—even need to be reinforced. The dictatorship of the proletariat actually had to be effectuated by means of state terror. This terror would form the revolutionary core of what was known as *democratic centralism*, the institutionalizing of the dictatorship of the proletariat. This dictatorship was a form of state terrorism which really left no space for institutions to develop. At the point when the people were *truly*—that is to say intrinsically—convinced and actively and without any reservation merged with the one will to thus become humanity, the revolutionary state institution could, *de facto*, be allowed to die off. The revolutionary state was therefore no ethical institution but rather a totalitarian *anti-institution*. Democratic centralism served to make the revolution top-down successful; it left nothing untouched, it left nothing in peace, not for a single moment. Democratic centralism was *totalist* in its scope and *totalitarian* in terms of its approach. State terror sets everything in perpetual motion and changes everything until the final objective has been achieved.

In this respect, Stalin not only gives Fichte's *endeavor* a huge boost but also his *power of imagination*. Unleashed and with unabating creative arbitrariness, he searches for his *hostile not-I*, creates it, finds it. The romantic paranoia becomes extreme and possessed. Are enemies of the revolution not active everywhere? Are they not visible and recognizable all over the place? Time and again the sure-footed imagination points them out and they are attacked as malignant *not-I* phenomena and stamped out by being denationalized, deported, or eliminated. Stalin's paranoia and powers of imagination may be pathological, but that is not all that there is to it. That analysis fails to take into account the essence of his *revolutionary* obsession. The sickly aspect was governed by a kind of *resentment* that not only displayed willpower but which was brilliantly calculating. It was able to justify itself so rationally that it seemed that *providence* itself had come into play. This justification worked and attracted. The coercive power dragged along many with it in the wake of its revolutionary belief, many in whom, undoubtedly, an own kind of resentment was seeking justification. So it was not only incalculably many who fell prey to this creativity but also untold numbers that were swept up in the revolutionary pathos—almost as though they were waiting for that to happen and a yawning chasm of longing could now finally be satisfied.

The kind of creativity that comes with resentment is as old as man himself and seems to perpetually appeal to the imagination. Stalin's revolutionary danger not only dwelt in his *power* but also in the *power* of imagination unleashed by him. His hostile game with the *not-I* enlisted admiration. It responded to an incredibly deep human need: how otherwise could people so readily have believed in him and in his work? Stalin shows what resentment can do with people and how totalitarian leaders can mobilize this. It does not seem to be difficult to identify offending evil and mercilessly avenge it whilst in the process justifying one's own evil. The own evil can at the same time serve the ultimate goal. The *final*, ideological justifying of own good makes it less serious. More to the point, it can be glorified. Eschatological salvation excuses the urge for revenge. Nostalgia is an ideological opium for the paranoia. It is therefore not so strange to see that the *Communist Manifesto* openly and boldly ends with an appeal for justified war. Communists do not need to make a secret of their intentions. It is not so much that their intentions blind people, more that they fall on fertile ground and thus spur people on. These are dangerous words because they seek to summon people to attack evil with their own justified evil. Such armory appears to be able to be presented as a virtue, and that is reason enough to make one feel sombre.

12.2 THE DICTATORSHIP OF THE PROLETARIAT

Marxist ideology and the revolutionary process serve to assimilate people in many respects. As a social being, man is integrated into the naturally necessary process by which means he can be a repressor or part of the oppressed, that is to say perpetrator or victim. In the revolutionary process a similar kind of division exists, people can be perpetrators or victims of totalitarian violence. It is not so much the oppressors of the proletariat who are most guilty, but all those who put up resistance to revolutionary change; from that point of view it does not matter that they are randomly declared guilty. Man is simply blameworthy for the shackles that people are powerless to throw off and do not want to cast off. Stalin selects perpetrators, guilty parties, and victims of his paranoid animosity with calculated *arbitrariness*. This arbitrariness contributes to the establishment and confirmation of the omnipotence. Arbitrariness spreads *fear*, which in its turn makes people submissive, whilst deadly fear makes people slavish. That is why it works. Arbitrariness has to leave a permanent mark on people and that is what lies at the heart of Luther's *choosing*. Everyone is really lost: one does not after all become a part of the old and depraved world just like that, but rather through one's own sinfulness and therefore through one's own fault. The matter of who is chosen for a new life is the exclusive preserve of the unfathomable will of the omnipotent. The *providence* of the omnipotent is a fatality that man is unable to fathom. This makes people unresisting and subservient; the mass thus learns—in fatalistic faith—to adapt to its own destiny.

It is, however, the case that the *power of the imagination* gives this arbitrariness unprecedented possibilities. The imagination always finds some guilty parties; either in groups or individually they become part of the revolutionary fate. Marx's vindictive litany on reactionary dynasties and classes, historically backward peoples, or unhistorical and dark forces, is an endless source of inspiration for the imagination. Fate can always befall new victims afresh; there is plenty of evidence of that. Stalin emerges as a grand master in this field and also in the justification thereof. One need only look at the extermination of the Kulaks, the starvation politics, the great terror, the deportations, the terror of the Gulag archipelago, the anti-Semitic campaign: each time it was in the name of the revolutionary imagination. Here it was not about dispensing with—arbitrarily selected—guilty parties. It was about more than that, a more elevated sublime *objective*. It was about dispensing with the old and therefore guilty individual. The anticipated salvation, following the totalitarian terror, was of less importance. Above all else, it was about recreating man *in* that terror. Stalin and those of his stamp all effected the totalitarian recreation of man in an extremely refined manner. There is only one way to start with the recreating of man and that is by getting rid of the old-style individual. That was supposed to justify their totalitarian activism. Man of old had to pass through *death* because without taking that step it would be impossible for a new man to be born. Anything that has not passed through death cannot be saved. The justified dying off of old man was *categorically imperative* to the revolutionary process. This death was central to the dictatorship of the proletariat.

What should be mentioned is that Stalin continued his revolutionary struggle in a selfless fashion, thus in the process purging virtually all the other Stalinists. Totalitarian rulers are almost always interested in accumulating private wealth and establishing dynasties. They only too easily abuse their public position of power during the revolutionary process—also to establish private empires of power.[1] Stalin, though, was not like this. He was even able to carry along his family in his revolutionary devotion. The intended purpose behind the cult of the glorification of his person was to glorify the absolute, revolutionary *I*. When personifying the revolutionary process, it was *not he* himself who had to become immortal but the revolutionary *I*. His own devotedness at the same time gave rise to a similarly devoted and innately convinced human mass. Under his unquestioned leadership the revolution had to be internalized to such a degree that people would not individually accept being objectives of the process. In this particular unification man was seen to blend, as it were, with the *other*, but eventually even this unified whole would disappear as a concrete entity. Man was no longer a *person* in the old-fashioned sense of the word, a concrete self hidden behind a mask. Man as man had much sooner merged to become one with the universal mask. The *comrade* was not the private other but the impersonal self. In that way, the ethical relationship with the other was thus also resolved: sincerity had been superseded. The significance of moral love for the *other* disappears when no ethical value can any longer be attributed to the other. The other disturbs the creation of socialistic humanity. Universal comradeship hollows out the purpose of the *second* major commandment: how can a person, in an ethical sense, love someone else as himself if the self and the other have both been dispensed with? How can someone love another as himself if one cannot and may not any longer love oneself?

What does not disappear is the first commandment: in terms of Stalinism that commandment is fully exploited. People have to learn to love their human god above all else, above the other, above themselves. People have to become one with this god,

---

1. Ree, *Political Thought of Joseph Stalin*.

with his will and vision. Man has to completely merge with this virtually absolute proximate unity. To that end go betrayal, the offering up of the other commandments, and justice. This commandment therefore has to be devotedly played out. If man himself possesses no intrinsic value then the other certainly does not. Such amoral *unification* of faithful humanity must outlive the revolutionary process; this unity must be perpetuated in the successful, terrestrial fulfillment of existence. Together with the memory of man of old, it is man himself—the essence of the ethical differentiation between good and evil—that must disappear.

This unification should have become the utopian result of the dictatorial process. What one can really question is whether creative resentment would have disappeared after the realization of this nostalgic longing. The *anti-morality* of the totalitarian dictatorship of the proletariat could well have outlived the ideal state but it never got as far as that. Since everything had to be channeled into the revolutionary dictatorship of the proletariat, the realization of the utopian state remained suspended like a dream above the heads of the people and the world. What was built up in terms of salvation was especially used to reinforce a propagandist image. That was why the nonsense of this notion of salvation remained a more or less concealed promise behind the success of the revolutionary destruction of man of old.

The messianic nature of Stalinism has to be more fully elucidated if this latter point is to be fully understood. This Messianism became practical in the mold of the referred to *dictatorship* of the proletariat. It was a dictatorship that deviated significantly from what is generally perceived as dictatorship. Traditional dictatorship pertains to a coup d'état of limited scope. For as long as the dictator wields power the ordinary man is deprived of all his freedom, rights, and privileges. The population—or at least those against whom the dictatorship turns—is repressed. This *oppression* indicates that the repressed, even though situated outside the law, are still present. What is thus implicit in dictatorship is that the change or destruction in question is not complete. There is therefore, essentially, a *relative* side to the dictator: he is not totalitarian as long as he allows the other—the repressed—to exist. When the dictatorship disappears, those who have been repressed are released and are allowed to continue living as they did in the past: they are again allowed to come into their own right.

The communist *dictatorship of the proletariat* was really of a totalitarian nature. It was not so much directed at oppression but more at destroying or changing everything that resisted. In the first place, it related to that which resisted most; that which was most enduring in the form of the institutions and the spiritual and cultural property of the people. Hence the reason that the totalitarian approach led to life and death struggles, to an all or nothing mentality. The dictatorship *of* the proletariat was thus, above all else, a recreating of man *as* the proletariat: the eradicating of man of old until *nothing* remained. Such dictatorship did not *wait* for man to be reborn but *made* him be reborn. It wanted to realize what religion, by contrast, still placed in the hands of a divine Messiah. His intervention in history had to be awaited in suffering and with great longing. The proletariat dictatorship could not, however, wait any longer. Full of fervor it took the law into its own hands. In this respect, the dictatorship of the proletariat could be seen as a radical *journey through the wilderness*.

In order to be able to leave old-style man, the *internal* enemy, behind during the course of this journey, hostile powers that *externally* threatened the revolutionary process had to be dispensed with. From both points of view, the final contest amounted to a life and death battle. Whilst the dictatorship was underway, the alleged demonic powers of evil were also well aware that it was all a matter of life and death for them as well. Wherever the proletariat revolution booked success, the hostile evil would desperately fight to oppose the pending doom. As the counter-revolutionary forces would certainly do all in their might to hold on to their power and survive, the final conflict would have to mobilize all possible means. Alternatively, in this final contest—to put it another way—the necessary goal justified or even *sanctified* all possible means.

12.3 INSPIRING SALVATION

Regardless of how unbelievably evil it was, the revolutionary dictatorship did give some hints of what the Promised Land and a fulfilled life could possibly be like. Democratic centralism was, indeed, working to construct communism. The socialist entry into the Promised Land did not yet, as such, offer the guarantee of a complete and fulfilled existence: after all, the communist utopia still had to materialize. Only when the world revolution had been completed could the totalitarian dictatorship reach fruition. That would be the first time when the power of the party and of the state could be relaxed. Only when the need for it had gone would the dictatorship of the proletariat die off. Even the *paranoid* class struggle would then begin to reveal something of its fulfillment. There was even a glimmer of salvation in the persecution and vengeance. At any rate, man of old died off. The image of this salvation became stronger whenever the outlook was *reawakened* or grew nostalgic and whenever there was a prospect of utopian life.

The signs of salvation became perceptible in two activities that were linked to the revolutionary dictatorship—activities which proved to be supreme, and both of those activities worked upon the *realization* of what the imagination offered.

One of the revolutionary activities, the *processes*, amounted to the essence of the totalitarian terror. A degree of salvation was perceptible from its successful completion. The glance was fixed in a retrospective direction: at man and at the world as it should not have *been*. The processes therefore directed themselves not so much at the deed as at the *perpetrator*. It is not what he *did* that stands center stage but what he *was*. Just as sinfulness highlighted how wrong man of old was, so guilt underlines just how wrong the social being was. That wrongness had to be clarified. The accusation should not so much lead to *confession* of the deed but rather to the *conversion* of the wrongdoer. The accused must be made to repent and to thus make the accusation his own. Such people have to internalize the imagined guilt to such an extent that it becomes real. It must be experienced by them as very real, it must be made true in them. The repentance must thereby make them one with the revolutionary process. The representatives of the segment of mankind that has not been chosen must also totally give themselves over to the naturally necessary heart of the revolutionary process. They, too, must help to realize this process and prove the rightness and purpose of revolutionary dictatorship.

It should have become apparent that fictitious accusations and confessions can profoundly pervert the truth and authenticity of things. In these kinds of processes, it is about everything other than making known and recognizing what amount to the facts. It is all about adapting reality to suit the *arbitrariness* of the ideological precepts and political programs. The processes demonstrate extreme insincerity, but how, in such untruthfulness, can any sign of revolutionary salvation be traced? It can be traced or seen because reality, man included, proves possible to *fabricate*; because it turns out that man is able to get caught up in the revolutionary process; because man allows himself to be drawn into a world that transcends good and evil; because man is apparently able to stray from his capacity to discern. Making a confession gives revolutionary hope, definitely if such hope has also been internalized. The confession is proof of the belief that the victim has in his own guilt—just as in religious belief, it is not so much concrete sins as experienced sinfulness that is the matter of central importance. Traditional *dictatorship* oppresses and kills man as he is. Revolutionary *terror*, though, fundamentally changes man before then eliminating him. Before the execution takes place he has therefore already been killed *as man*. The confession shows how man has to be led through death before he can ultimately be saved.

The other enlightening revolutionary activity is more directed at those who have been chosen. The glance is therefore now fixed in the forward direction. In this particular case, it is much more about positively making visible the signs of actual change. Something can already be seen of the concrete fulfillment, it is already possible to anticipate the longing for the absolute other. Something is already revealed of what it is like to live in peace and to be satisfied, of devoted mankind and of *aesthetic* life's fulfillment. Convincing relevant images were produced by communist *propaganda* and by socialist *realism* in art—also a kind of propaganda. *Art* was thus given a new function. It had to draw attention to the real utopia that was unfolding. Its realistic images were designed to make the masses believe and subsequently comply with the revolutionary process. In a forward direction, the imagination also had a job to do: it had to, as it were, bring the worldly kingdom of the heavens so close that its signs could become visible and be represented.

12 The Stalinist Final Contest

For the uninitiated, *socialist realism*, as manifested in communist art, could perhaps come across as naive. It is an art form that seemingly has little other to offer than straightforward propaganda. And this art was intended to act as propaganda if not to mask a wrong, unsatisfying kind of communist reality. Throughout the revolutionary process, during the journey towards the promised final goal—but always in conflict with the reactionary forces—one *may* not expect to bear witness to the perfect utopian reality. Hence the reason that revolutionary man needs to be encouraged. The realistic *imagination* also serves to supplement the process: it supplies a nostalgic view of the communist person and world that is to come, a world in which the *signs* are already present, signs that can be displayed to man and learned. Realism brings closer something that is already taking place but which will only reach its full potential in the future: it shows the *sublimity* of the overwhelming process, but especially the beauty of a full, constructed existence. The image projected is that of the revolutionarily engaged, of those who are already sensually satisfied and living in peace. The propagandist image stimulates the nostalgic attachment of man to the beckoning perspective of the revolutionary process. The *sublimity* of the revolution and the *beauty* of the realistic art supplement each other. The sublime is overwhelming; the beauty impresses one.

The beauty of realism taints the truth. Realistic art brings belief and truth deceptively close together. As much as possible, the view of the facts is turned away from what is really the case; reality is hidden behind a fictitious image. Realism is false. It misleads. The real objective of realistic art is to change people and the world. That is why its image contributes to the changeability of man. What art already displays still has to be *made* true. To that end it therefore creates believers. It is a tempting and deceptive addition to the propaganda and the terror. Its realistic perspective makes it so much easier for socialist man to believe in what is to come. The introspective glance of Plato gains a prospective twist; the sights are now set on what is to come and on what is, as such, already recognizable and visible. In addition to that, realism makes this belief as blind as possible: it furthermore manipulates the sublime, inner unity between man and the process. Even in the face of the harsh dictatorship of the proletariat, realism has to keep the communist nostalgia alive. Communism thus preserves the promised purpose.

Socialist realism is thus the attractive supplement to terror, to the processes which makes man, in militant fashion, one with the revolutionary process. The whole arbitrariness of the terror—in the words of Heidegger, *Angst zum Tode*—is designed to inculcate *overwhelming* fear in man. Also in his terms, it is not about the instilling of *dread*; that would be too concrete, too deliberately directed, and it might even provoke resistance. It is about a paralyzing fear of the incomprehensible, of what for isolated individuals, is utterly impossible to control. Overwhelming fear makes man, as it were, negatively submissive. Fear intimidates, makes docile, easy to manipulate; the overpowering aspect of fear also makes man, in the end, unscrupulous. Fear makes people prepared to *believe* in everything and go along with everything.

What remains rather amazing is the fact that the nostalgic experiencing of belief of aesthetic realism is not destroyed by the paranoid fear elicited by the terror. Overwhelming as the fear may be, it does not rob all experience of purpose, it does not extinguish nostalgia. More to the point, even the most terrible evil manages to preserve its meaning. No matter how destructive the revolutionary conflict is and no matter how complete the evil may be, there is always a ray of light, even *in* the thick of evil. Is this perhaps because man already knows *that* this evil will turn to good, and *what* will ultimately be offered to man in terms of fulfillment? Alternatively, is it because the unity of the revolutionary process and the disappearance of the *overwhelming* whole gives rise to an experience that makes evil and fear more than simply negative? Does even madness offer an experiencing of purpose? Is that how the *sublime* operates? It would then appear that the sublime is able to internally procure the frighteningly overwhelming as well as nostalgic belief.

The deceitful truthfulness far exceeds that of religion, which Marx so sharply criticized, at least, as perceived in his own terms. He positioned the images of this religion alongside what he had described as a vale of tears. Religion covers up the real woe by offering man a fantastic reality, an illusory justice. Socialist realism takes this a step further. It trumps the illusory joy of the religious heaven by holding out an apparent real kind of justice. The fact of the matter, though, is that *heavenly* justice is merely a beckoning perspective that hovers above the clouds like a tempting lie; it does no more harm than that. The revolutionary lie, however, contributes to man being handed over a totally *different* kind of justice: meekly he submits to the overwhelming nature of *avenging* justice. In the process, though, the heavily criticized illusory happiness of religious justice is not abolished. The socialistic belief does not take away this heavenly illusion but makes use of it instead, also to justify the hard reality of the avenging justice.

12.4 BEING ONE WITH THE OMNIPOTENT

Stalinism gives the yearning for justice an extreme stimulus. No matter how much salvation shines, it is revenge that has the upper hand by far. As has already been asserted, it is an *ad hominem* brand of justice. It is not what has been done that is the matter aimed at but *who* has done it, man of old. This entity *embodies* evil and is subject to revolutionary judgment. He therefore has to *believe* in his guiltiness of being evil. Stalinism realizes ethical atheistic belief in an extreme way. The extreme side of it works, elicits euphoria everywhere, also beyond the dictatorship of the proletariat. People share a belief that *wants* to create an own reality.

What is so strange is that people not only believe in the truth of the guilt but also in that of the apparent deed. It is experienced as really having been *committed*.

Victims of terror only too often go along with such falsity. But there is some logic to that. Without the recognition of guilt, a non-conquered *not-I* disappears into the grave. Stalinism proves how successfully *ethical life* can be eliminated. The dictatorship of the proletariat is above all else an *unchained* ethical atheism. Good and evil undergo such a thorough revaluation that they are able to fit into the revolutionary process. That is what makes those who do not allow themselves to be converted and who refuse to go along with the belief so dangerous. Their destiny is to be dehumanized with the help of different means. In a human respect they are declared defective, seen as psychiatric cases. What awaits them is a different type of extraction from the human world, from the submissive masses, despite attempts to forcibly make them bend to the general will. For that matter, the signs of fulfillment tolerate no psychological and physical forms of handicap: it is also their fate to be removed from the realistic image of bliss. This removal is not done with a view to invisibility but rather with a view to non-existence. The picture of utter sensual happiness does not happen to tolerate any form of imperfection. Stalin proves that totalitarian unity is not a myth but that it can be successfully realized.

Such success is unthinkable without omnipotence. In the dictatorship of the proletariat the omnipotent raises himself above what is true and good. By manipulating truth and lies, good and evil to suit himself, he is able to allow everything and everyone to be swallowed up in his arbitrariness. Mankind prepares to unify with this omnipotence and omniscience, to vivify as one man democratic *centralism*. Even the executory machinery of party and state is completely absorbed into the omnipotence of this one will.

This unity of will and power deviates somewhat from *Rousseau's* concept. Also in his case, there is evidence of one will of the people, a will that unites everyone in complete consensus. It is a will that actually *mandates* the implementing task to bureaucratic organizations; in the event of friction such a mandate is instantly withdrawn. The will of the people and the power of the state are not, therefore, one and the same. What should be noted is that Rousseau's democratic centralism fundamentally deviates from the *bourgeois* democratic system. It is not only the case that the bourgeois system is founded on a division of powers, a multi-layered government structure and limited government competencies but the system does not furthermore demand consensus within a general will. The decision-making requires compromises. Any *compromise* acknowledges that everyone is to an extent right and wrong. So there is no omnipotence, no omniscience, no complete unity, no body that unconditionally stands above mankind and the truth.

In Stalin's democratic centralism, the will of the leader and of the people converge, which means that also this will and power have to be unconditionally one. Terror and socialistic realism are only necessary if man still has to learn how to understand this *own* will. He has to learn that this is completely *one* with that of the omnipotent. The dictatorship of the proletariat can be fully accomplished once everyone has become truly united with this one, omnipotent will and sincerely lives in accordance with that. The well-known *ovations* do not really constitute agreement on the part of individuals who might think or act in deviant ways. They also add up to more than an obligatory demonstration of unity and resigned behavior. The ovation is an expression of prior and internally experienced unity with the leader. Whereas romanticizing Christianity longingly anticipates the heavenly cheering before God's throne, Stalinism already realizes this state of bliss on earth.

12.5 RULER OF TIME

The conviction that one stands above the truth and that one possesses the power to realize everything that one wishes for creates yet another amazing pretension. It would seem that Stalin is attempting to prove that man has the power to realize the entire *nominalisatic* description of the omnipotence and omniscience of God. This even extends to his governing of time. He directs his will to have power at more than the manipulability of man and the world; he seeks more than complete dominance over the *future*. In his urge to achieve nominalistic perfection, he wants to make not only the future but also the *past* bend to his will. His will is also expected to be able to regulate retrospective matters. His will must also be able to *actually* change past history. In a retrospective fashion the will is expected to recreate what has been made and done. To put it another way, the will can also create a new past and at the same time make the old past disappear.

In the end, a substantial part of the revolutionary process has to do with breaking down the past, previous history. The aim is to achieve a new beginning, a new history, a communistically recreated man and world. The revolutionary process proved to be extremely successful in the domain of making the old disappear but there remained just one problem. Much of history prior to communism was preserved in collective living memory and a portion of it had been put down in writing and published. In the end, much of that history came to be ideologically reformulated, and with a degree of perfection that was sufficient to efficiently wipe out many of the real memories of the past. That, then, was how a large portion of the past was eradicated, banished from the human spirit and from living memory.

One might think that the new, socialist history—that started with the revolution and the dictatorship of the proletariat—could have been freely written and made part of living memory but that was not so. Such a move would put the relative nature of the unconditionally free will and the arbitrariness of the imposed omnipotence too prominently in the picture. Hence the reason that the rewriting and reshaping of history had to continue long after the revolution had been completed and extend into the time of the dictatorship of the proletariat and the building up of the communist individual and worlds. At that stage, unprecedented zeal was demanded. The rewriting of history had to be so comprehensive that it would virtually wipe out the former recounting of the past: the idea was to banish it from the human imagination. The retrospective reconstructions of contemporary history were then utterly devoted to the arbitrariness of the one omnipotent will.

There were very many writers, such as Gorki and Platonov, who were engaged in the activity of rewriting the past. They became known as *engineers of the soul*. Their *realistic* task consisted of relating the great communist wonders, including also all the grotesque works. The descriptions had to catch the imagination. Their stories of devoted communist heroes totally satisfied the will and imagination of the omnipotent leader. Everything was described in accordance with the rules of socialist realism: what was described *gave* the world the right image of socialist realism. In these images belief, truth, and reality were totally intermingled. That was how those stories protected a realistic image, which, in its turn, dominated the memories. The heroes described are images, *examples* really, of belief and devotion and therefore also of success. Stories and examples have to keep the experience of belief alive in new man and help to steer his will and effort in the right direction.

However, this was accompanied by a certain specific problem. The dictatorship of the proletariat could also witness successful occurrences and affect exemplary individuals. Adulated heroes could fall into *disgrace*, which tends to imply that it was only on the basis of *grace* that they had become heroes in the first place. Their exemplary status was merely bestowed upon them by the merciful omnipotent. Their fall thus indicated nothing more than that their given grace had fallen away from them. These people were only credited *afterwards* which meant that they were absolutely no longer *examples* of the salvation that was being realized. Endlessly many fell into disgrace during the period of revolutionary dictatorship, as they were unmasked as revolutionary traitors. A *recorded* official history of these heroes and their deeds would make the omniscience and unfailing will of the leader relative; it would emerge that he could make mistakes. It would also make the communist history of salvation that so appealed to the imagination relative, which would, again, taint the realistic credulity of the docility of mankind. Whole volumes of recountings of heroic deeds were therefore retracted so that history could be rewritten around new heroes. The old examples no longer existed, neither as examples nor as remembered reality. Like a suddenly disruptive *not-I* with an after-effect, they were still eliminated by the omnipotent *I*. They were removed as a reality and as an image; they were driven out of the memory. In this way, past history was able to perpetually revive itself and it did that with such perfection that even after communism it would prove hard to reconstruct the rewriting. The imagination evidently has great capacities. The engineers of the soul demonstrate that, even actually recalled and spiritually living history is, to a large extent, retrospectively manipulable. As a ruler, also over time, the nominalistic God proves that he is very easily able to convert to being man.

12.6 THE DIALECTICS OF POWER

Stalinist totalitarianism took the ancient apocalyptic vision and converted it into an extreme sort of reality. Regardless of the success with which the revolutionary pathos spread, the revolution was never to become a worldwide phenomenon. Outwardly the revolution came up against barriers, whilst inwardly it proved to trigger internal conflict. The fact that it did not turn into a world revolution and the fact that revolutionary Messianism had to confine its judgment to land by land revolution is definitely not something that can be attributed to the determination with which the rest of the world preserved its own ethical legacy and rejected messianic visions. The revolutionary unfolding of power and the dictatorship of the proletariat very much ran aground in their own processes. The problem lay in the internal *contradictions* that were inherent to the whole notion of omnipotence. It turned out to be impossible to consistently implement God's becoming man. Was that why a certain unwillingness might have arisen to adhere to the revolutionary changes to an absurd extent? Was this what might have turned communism into what Nietzsche predicted would become a *demonstratio ad absurdum* of belief in salvation? To put it another way, was the demonstration clear and effective enough to be able to learn something from history? In one respect Stalinism was definitely revealing: it showed that where success was concerned, there was a clear difference between redemption and revenge. Redemption did not occur or, more to the point, it failed, but avenging justice, on the other hand, was splendidly successfully executed.

The *paranoia* was to trigger endlessly much more than the *nostalgic* longings. The destruction of man of old and of the old world can also be termed a resounding success. One can also phrase it this way: the ethical atheistic pathos of the Marxist ideology turned out to be more successful than the salvation pathos. Of the traditional institutional connections, many of them were to become "history" and where they did not disappear altogether, they only retained a latent functional value. Can the fact that ethical life, morals, and conscience became brittle be evidence of what might be termed success? The fact that little was to come of the promised salvation, of living in peace and satisfaction, does not refute the impact of Marxist ideology. The utopian justification of the seizing of power chiefly served as a dishonest fabrication, as an opiate to hide the true nature of the revolutionary will to gain power. The *evil* of the resentment proved itself to be a much stronger motivating force than the building up of a supposedly *good* life. Profound discontentment and aversion proved to be capable of achieving much more than the utopian reverse side of the coin of expecting to find meaningful life's fulfillment elsewhere.

Due to the success of *ethical* atheism, the desire to wreak revenge could be exercised virtually unhindered. Throughout the world, revolutions have proven how such pathos is able to make its way and how it manages to justify itself. During the process, the revolutionary storm runs its course without too much ado and without ideological justifications. In conjunction with this, totalitarian omnipotence is hollowed out, as is the will to establish such power. How is this possible? The whole idea of omnipotence is now paradoxical and its realization carries with it absurd consequences. Was this what caused the messianic experiment to fail? Can something of this be deduced from the way in which the Stalinist process progressed?

What Stalin had in mind was that there should be utter and unconditional devotion to the revolutionary process and he would show the people or mankind the way. He was preoccupied with the complete *unity* of will between individuals, collectively and with the leader. His omnipotence was channeled into realizing this unity of will. This was what forced the dictatorship of the proletariat to continue until the process had been completely *accomplished* and unity had been realized. Only once this accomplishing had occurred could the old religious and philosophical promise be realized: the promise of man being reborn and the world being recreated. Only then could there be talk of history being completed.

This completion came to an early end in the communist part of the world itself. The process was never completed but stagnated instead and went into decline. It became ensnared in an unstoppable spiral of internal decomposition. Even before the process had had a chance to finish the omnipotent had lost all his ideological motivation and energy. The will to gain power appeared to lack the potency to conquer the *inner paradoxes of the omnipotent*. The will to do that proved to be insufficiently driven and dedicated to the task in hand to intrinsically keep people together. As soon as the pathos had blown over the dictatorship got itself caught up in the process of inner disintegration. Was this perhaps because through the success of the revolution, the hostile *not-I* had vanished from view? In the end, is it just the hostile *not-I* that remains outside the own barriers, and does this perhaps mobilize things insufficiently for the dictatorship of the proletariat to be pursued? This is a possible explanation. After all, as soon as the paranoid *envy* wanes and the unceasing pursuit of the *not-I* loses some of its enthusiasm, so the willpower and vigor of the *I*, its power of imagination and strivings, its will and tyranny will become deflated. If the *negative* fury of destruction passes then the revolutionary élan of omnipotence will weaken. The revolutionary pathos is intrinsically destructive not constructive. If the struggle against the *not-I* dies down then it is almost natural that man will subsequently refuse to place his personal destiny in the hands of this unity of will. The people and the leader grow apart as soon as the *I* starts to moderate his revolutionary pathos. The general *will* embodied by the omnipotent leader no longer proves to be precisely the same as that of everyone. Without furious effort the will to attain *omnipotence* is weakened, the will grows exhausted. Without a strong-willed *I* the revolutionary process is certain to stall.

What then emerges is that the *success* of ethical atheism itself also contributes to the hollowing-out of the revolution. The revolutionary morale decays. If the revolutionary devotion and fervor start to pine away then the institutionalized revolution will relapse, almost automatically, into a static and cynically employed type of *bureaucratic centralism*. The conglomeration of power that has evolved appears to easily be able to cut away from its internal affinity with the revolution and with the time-honored aims of the dictatorship of the proletariat. The lost ethical meaning of life and the established party power seem to have opened up the way for a curious *dialectical turnaround* in the revolutionary process: one that leads towards a privatized fulfilling of the revolutionary goal. In an ideological sense power corrupts itself in an absurd way. In a *private* way, the utopian promise is invested with meaning through the longing for and the chasing after own sensual satisfaction at all expense. The unethical world tempts socialist man to become materialistic, a pitfall that Marx disdainfully warned people about in his *Thesen über Feuerbach*.

The private attitude comes to prevail over everything, certainly within the power monopoly of the party and state bureaucracy. Everything starts to revolve around people's private positions and their projected purpose in life. Why should the new and, in an ethical sense, liberated individual really be preoccupied with what a true communist interpretation of real needs should be? Why should people not be satisfied with what is at least attainable? Is it not so that the leaders and members of the party shamelessly take priority over the people? In that case privileges, corruption, self-wealth accumulation at the expense of the collective, and the communist future becomes an everyday and poorly concealed practice. Who is hampered by public morals now that this also has been sunk in the ethical atheistic storm? The promised ideological *quality* suddenly switches to privatized *quantity*. The salvation doctrine is not therefore realized collectively or in a comrade-friendly way.

This should not really come as a big surprise. The *comrade* is not in fact the other with whom one is connected in an ethical sense. The comrade is the impersonal other, someone that one has nothing to offer. Ideological comradeship shows that shameless *egoism* is not only impossible to avoid but it even goes as far as to justify it. Where, in the communist world, there is still evidence of solidarity, then that is attributable to residues of the old ethical world. That is what supports not only the remaining moral connections, but also the new ones that are invariably small-scale.

Ethical egoism is able to spread its wings after the revolutionary will has been dampened, and its *instrument of power* can then be deployed in another practical way. *Democratic* centralism loses the battle with the own operational body, the centrally organized *bureaucracy*. Party members who should have been keeping alive the revolutionary will were then therefore able to fully benefit from their own positions of power within the system. What remains of the revolutionary dictatorship of the proletariat is a cynical abuse of power. Since will has merged with power, it is now the unity

12   The Stalinist Final Contest

of will and power that takes revenge. The operational body of the revolution turns into an impenetrable and uncontrollable power structure in the service of private interests. Once the revolutionary and power-thirsty will had passionately turned against a resistance-providing *not-I*, but now a *desirous* will gloats over the opportunities that the realized power is able to offer it.

In the light of Nietzsche's *will to power* theory this is no strange phenomenon. He asserts that the desire for power can develop in two directions by being either active or reactive. The *actively* oriented desire for power is forwardly directed; again and again the will seeks resistance and challenges. In this respect, the desire for power is a will *to* that seeks its challenges in the freedom *to*. The desire for power can sometimes be manifested as a lust for *power*. The will is then of a *reactive* nature and pitches itself, in aversion, against that which opposes or threatens it. This latter type typifies the revolutionary will: *ad absurdum* it demonstrates how inordinately *reactive* the will can become. The will perpetually entangles itself in a struggle *against* something; overzealously it seeks resistance that needs to be broken. This will searches for liberation *from* what resists. Without *power* the will is unable to realize such fervor. A chronic lack of active will is compensated by power that can be reactively implemented. The will seeks the power that will enable it to put up a fight against whatever *not-I* comes along. The power is above all else a force *against*. The revolutionary power of the will therefore fights in a reactive respect.

Nietzsche heeded the orientation *against* the danger of the weakness of the will. The weak-willed easily becomes obsessed with the external facet that is impossible to bear. A threatening exterior must be eliminated because it is really too strong. The weak-willed thus seeks compensation for his weakness: *he seeks power*. He wants power because opposition is not a challenge but a threat. He avoids competition because he is not capable of strengthening his will through his opponent. This orienting towards power in order to keep a threatening exterior at bay applies *in extremis* to the revolutionary weakness of the will. With exaggerated imaginary powers, it is thirst for power and power that develops in the case of these weak-willed individuals. Omnipotence must provide the certainty that every actual or imagined threat can be withstood. If revolutionary omnipotence draws strength from the opponent then it is only in order to eliminate him. What characterizes Stalin and the Stalinists is their unprecedented weakness of will. That explains their absurdly creative will to power. The creative *no* of their revolutionary dictatorship is driven by an immense craving for power.

The dialectic *turnabout* that has been sketched can take place if the power in question is established and if so much resistance is broken that the basis of power is no longer threatened. The restless, goaded on will can then restrain itself and the power can be capitalized on. Small wonder that such a will provides insufficient resistance to the corruption of the own utopian zest for the future. The bureaucratic power conglomeration becomes useful in another way. Those who have profited from bureaucratic centralism vegetate within the instrument of power, the precondition being that the fortress of power will endure. Hence the need to maintain a hard and repressive system but without totalitarian fanaticism. The vegetative existence is also no longer borne by *belief*—in view of the corruption that would also in fact be an impossibility. The old, revolutionary religious zeal lapses into complete cynicism.

Cynicism even leaves little intact of the own ideological truth; that of realizing. So even in the realizing or making true, a dialectic turnabout may be seen. Those who profit do not so much imagine themselves to be *above* the truth, but it is much more the case that they hide *below* the lie. Bizarre lies have to cover up an equally bizarre reality, even though that might be done with precious little conviction. The lie does not have to be believed in: it is enough to simply not contradict it.

The certain end of the communist Soviet Union is one of history's big examples of irony. The end was somehow reminiscent of a devoted and confessed faithful leader who is keen to inject new incentive into the *doctrine* in an effort to stave off corrupted *life*. Gorbachev was aware that the corrupt communist bastion was in danger of losing its basis of power and permanence. The doctrine of salvation was thus also destabilized. In order to salvage the communist promise, he reverted to the tried and tested revolutionary concept of democratic centralism. Whilst his *perestroika* was designed to reactivate revolutionary centralism, *glasnost* was aimed at attacking the bureaucratic and essentially counter-revolutionary *not-I* through the media. He remained convinced of the supremacy of the revolutionary will and vigor. Then there was the irony of the fact that his endeavor to reanimate this *will* was what finally knocked down the foundations beneath this ossified power conglomeration. The system collapsed. Perestroika failed to breathe new life into the communist *belief*. The doctrine no longer attracted people. It proved impossible to once more arouse revolutionary passion and encourage people to get whisked away in a world-historical *desire* for omnipotence. What the attempt led to was the eroding from *within* of the established communist power. In effect communism became a victim of its own success.

Following the will to power, it was also now power itself that was being eroded. Together with power, communism was now also wiping itself out as an ideology. Perestroika tore down the seat of power; in an endeavor to re-ignite the revolutionary process it simultaneously put paid to the death struggle in which the revolution had become engaged. The attempt to revive *democratic* centralism had put an end to *bureaucratic* centralism without even having had the chance to reanimate even the beginnings of the revolutionary spirit. Democratic centralism was thus also smothered. Without belief there can be no revolutionary pathos. After all, the *fight* against man of old and the old world had already been virtually fought: it hardly needed to be thoroughly re-enacted. The attack mounted against those who had profited from the established power did not again serve to make the revolutionary process *credible*, nor did it do anything to restore the revolutionary élan. Perestroika might still have preached utopia, but it could not for a moment create for anyone the illusion that there was a world to be won.

As a matter of fact, the system's power base was also given an external push, and there was a touch of irony to that too. This was to come from Reagan, a believer in the apocalyptic completing of history. In helping to bring down the *power of evil*, he was, in effect, going against his own religious convictions: the success was to contribute to the postponement of the Day of Reckoning. Ironic or not, some elucidation is required. Reagan's apocalyptic belief was religious, not atheistic. The ending of history, in other words, the anticipated kingdom of God and the messianic struggle, were to be left entirely to God. Even if man should see the signs of such a day, it would not be for him to take this exclusively divine matter into his own hands. What was most important was the confidence in a higher power. The two apocalyptic visions might somewhat correspond, but Christians and Marxists have their own distinctive ways of dealing with how they conceive of life during the final contest. The Christian doctrine requires man to resign himself to God's will. In that way Christian life always takes ethical responsibility for finite earthly existence.

By contrast Marxist doctrine always exhorts activist Messianism. This activism is predominantly directed against the whole sacred basis of the ethical outlook on life. Even though Marxism is perhaps inspired by Hebrew and Christian religious doctrine, the politicized radicalness of this doctrine goes its own way. Though Christian movements may perpetually be captivated by apocalyptic expectations, the *traditional* Christian *life* upholds alongside all of this a second big commandment pertaining to ethical love. In the *life* of the Christian *church*, attention is always devoted to the ethical interpretation of this commandment. In that way, the church also manages to counteract the danger of its own doctrine. The commandment to love tempers the longing for retaliation. It teaches people to live with evil and its exponents. Ethical God always has an after-effect. The church teaches people to also respect the ethical order and its laws, commandments, and moral prescripts. Where it fails to do this, it is always exposed to immanent criticism. Reagan would have known and respected the commandment to love. It would have restrained him from blindly submitting to apocalyptic visions.

How long will this ethical tradition remain intact and have effect? How long with the effects of the ethical God be felt after his death? Human and divine omnipotence may by now have been robbed of many of their illusions, but the ethical atheistic pathos still works. The question is to what extent we can still trust in the religious counterweight to these passions. Fundamentalist doctrinairism will not be able to revitalize the ethical meaning of life. Religions enlist, but does the same apply to their ethical significance? Alongside introvert religiosity, the credulous seem rather to awaken expectations of salvation.

Yet the demise of communism undoubtedly has far-reaching consequences. Now that we have witnessed the death of *ethical* God, it would seem that *omnipotent* God and man are now announcing their parting of the ways. In the process, man does not, incidentally, regain ethical meaning in life. The plea for justice can also resonate without omnipotence. Does man therefore still have to learn to conquer his longing for justice? Must he learn to come to terms with himself as a problem? Does he *himself* therefore still have to learn to actively take leave of the omnipotent and everything for which his name stands? In order to be able to *depart* from the omnipotent, must he learn how to overcome himself?

13

The Self-Conquest

The matter of the *incarnation* of the omnipotent turned out to be a disaster. The human omnipotence got himself entangled in a *futile* process. Would this futility lead to the omnipotent, in whatever guise, being forced to again *take his leave* of man? If the omnipotent is not able to realize his promises then he simultaneously loses his illusion and magnetic power. In the process, the will that strives for omnipotence also inevitably loses its impetus. Does this mean that in this way, an historical or perhaps a world-historical people's project is nearing its end? Do the atheistic deviations ruin the eschatological illusions? How could that still be believed in after having been historically refuted? Does atheism have a purifying effect? Does this seemingly automatically open up the way to other perspectives?

That is the question. First and foremost it can be stated that an *historical* interpretation of recent developments is unfounded. In terms of history, processes do not continue in a linear fashion—insofar as one can indeed speak of *the* history of anything. Why should the above-mentioned developments ultimately exhaust the longing for omnipotence? Why should this spirit not be brought back to life? The fact that the big ideologies might have lost their energizing force does not mean to say that the yearning for justice and omnipotence has also been extinguished. If such longing coincides with insurmountable human weakness of will, it can always be reawakened, and in many different forms.

Since the ideological and politicized will to secure omnipotence has not yet drawn much interest, it is even more important to bear in mind its religious roots. The appeal for justice has certainly not been silenced; it is an appeal that can always seek an escape via the will to *power*. The fact that man himself has not been able to fulfill the ancient divine promise is reason enough for the weak-willed to look to the religious origins of the will to power and its promises. A failed communist experiment does not necessarily need to signal the end of the eschatological panoramas of man.

In that case it is not enough for the omnipotent to take leave of man in his atheistic guise. It is sooner the case that man *himself* will have to learn to depart from the omnipotent. What he will have to conquer is the call for justice and the escape found in omnipotence that lies embedded in himself. Is man capable of doing that? If the call for justice proves to be an eternally recurring human longing is the conquering of this same longing not then also an infinite task?

If this is indeed the case, it will always be possible to provoke the ethical meaning of life and it will remain necessary to fight for that so very human facet of man. Through the personage of the *final person*, Nietzsche shows us how post-modern fabrications of the mind can also destroy the ethical meaning of life. This character makes clear how also without great ideologies, this decay can do its work: via the market, politics, and modernist religion. Hence the reason that man himself has to learn how to become resilient to this. In the process, he must make sure not to imitate the traits of his *opponent* by incorporating his revolt and resentment. He must not become, in that respect, his equal. Above all else, he will have to learn to see the human aspects of himself as the real challenge. That is the only way in which man as a problem can find himself in the sphere of a promise. In order to actually become a promise he will perpetually have to conquer himself as a problem. He will have to learn how to overcome the appeal for justice, both avenging and redeeming justice. He will have to learn how to *let go of* the longing for power and for the justice that can be fulfilled through such power.

The question that this immediately evokes is that of whether religion can, or even should, support such self-conquest. If so, religion would have to find again its ethical essence. Can ethical gods again become normative in religion? Must gods revive a sacred ethical interest in life? Is it possible, after the death of omnipotent God, for ethical gods to come back to life? Can these gods provide an ethical purpose to life that will be able to withstand apocalyptical temptations? In religion will ethical *atheism* not prove to be irreversibly stronger? With the death of God *all* gods seem to have died, also the ethical ones—and does not fundamentalism again prove this *ad absurdum*? Does this force man to develop a non-sacred ethical meaning to life? In that case he will have to conquer his all too human problem himself and, on his own strength, he will have to become a promise. He will only be able to succeed in that if he learns to see this human problem as a challenge. Is that possible?

13 The Self-Conquest

13.1 FROM HUMANS TO GODS

The story leading from Abraham up to the time of modern Christendom demonstrates to us how eschatological doctrine can affect the ethical meaning of life, also in religion. Atheistic heirs have given ethical atheism a radical twist, but their loss does not put an end to the enlisting power of ethical atheism and to the erosion of the ethical significance of life.

This gives rise to questions that are not easy to answer, undoubtedly *final* questions. This applies to the question posed above as to whether religion can rediscover ethical substance and can again bestow *living* content without lapsing into deadly fundamentalism. If not, then after the death of God, ethical life will have to manage without religion. That, in turn, gives rise to the contrasting question of whether an enduring ethical life is possible without a *sacred* basis. Using his own strength, can man give form to a true and sincere life? Then the *becoming man* of God will have to occur in a different way than the incarnation of the omnipotent. Is this what Nietzsche meant when he claimed that people must turn *into gods* if they are to live virtuous lives? If, solely on his own strength, man is to develop his own ethical purpose in life, then he will have to take over the ethical substance of the old gods. This was what he had in mind when he referred to the *self-conquest* of people, of man as a problem. How can man give significance to this promise? What we are dealing with here is final questions: questions to which no clear answers are possible, questions which, therefore, cannot be simply dismissed. They are open questions packed with contingency, undoubtedly *eternally returning* questions. They represent a superhuman challenge for man who is only too human. Will the call for justice cease if man finds peace with the *past* and opens himself up to a non-redeeming *future*? Is Nietzsche expressing what amounts to a challenge to religion?

Averse to optimism, Nietzsche refers to the departure from the sacred fundament of ethical life as a *fateful* occurrence. Thanks to human intervention, the sacred substance of ethical life disappears and the institutions become brittle. This own intervention is unavoidable. Fateful means to say that the departure from the ethical gods is *inescapable*. The sacred basis of laws and commandments, morals and institutions had to fall away and the road back was cut off. The death of God is also a *catastrophic* occurrence, one that heralds a period of destructive nihilism. With the loss of ethical life's definition, the restraining effect that culture and institutions had upon man also fell away, which led to uncontrolled resentment. The immense effect that this can have has been demonstrated by recent history.

In order to survive, omnipotent God even became man. Though omnipotence might have lost some of its luster, the omnipotent is not dead as long as the will for omnipotence lives on in man. That is why man will have to overcome his own *will to become omnipotent*. Only then will it be possible for people *to become gods* and to have their own ethical meaning in life. It is the challenge of human self-conquest that is at stake here. In order to say something about this we can revert to Nietzsche. The fateful death of ethical God may not only be seen as depressing fate; it should rather be perceived as *inevitability*. Therein lies hidden the opportunity for a challenging *turn*, a perspective inviting change: the need for man himself to invest life with some kind of ethical purpose. It is a turnabout that challenges man not to want to revert to what lies concealed in the name of the omnipotent. In that respect, Nietzsche appeals for a wholesome, *true* type of atheism, an atheism that does itself wish to *take leave of* what lies concealed in the name of omnipotent God. True atheism seeks not only to conquer faith and hope, together with promise and the expectation of salvation, but also jealousy and vengefulness. The atheist wants to interact truly and sincerely with the other and with what is different. His atheism does not therefore turn itself *against* ethical life. It turns itself against the brand of atheism that has possessed religion and ideologies. He does not therefore turn himself against religion and gods just like that. If *gods* are to regain significance in terms of ethical life, they will have to be different from omnipotent God. Where, then, does one go from here?

What is important is the answer that Nietzsche seeks to false atheism, its militant appeal for justice and its hunger for power. One would expect him to urge people to forcefully oppose this threat. Why should there be no hostile attitude to such nihilists? Why not arm oneself with one's own form of decisive action? Why not present an *opposing power* to counter these dangerous forces? Why not politically attack this danger? He is, indeed, keen on resistance, but to that end he seeks no political arena, neither does he declare outright war backed up by appropriate power factors. He does not want to take on the morals of the opponent, nor does he want to justify them. He does not want to become his *equal*. He does not want to start moralizing himself. He propagates no aversion to and hatred of ideologies that propagate precisely in this way. He opts for a moderate and *moderating* reaction.

This requires further elucidation. In his new course of action he does not wish to take a *reactive* stance, which is why he seeks to avoid *re*action in the true sense of the word. The reaction in fact binds itself to that against which it wishes to arm itself; it embeds itself in the logic of victim and perpetrator. It seeks out *controlled* action. It seeks a strong-willed answer; it thus seeks moderation, balance, self-control. This requires a life guided by self-knowledge. He wants to see controlled *force* of deed, no obsessive force of *deed*, not to mention *power*. Controlled *judge not* suits him better than casting judgment. In the spirit of Jesus or Lao Tse, he does not seek to conquer the *other* but rather *himself*. He wants to love his enemies, even the most dangerous ones: *as* enemy. He even wants to appreciate the enemy in an ethical respect. This enemy must challenge him and spur him on to do good himself. It is only in that way that man will have something to *give* the other. If one is to assuage danger, one cannot first adopt the essence of such danger. Revenge does not therefore even fit into socialism. One cannot conquer the adversary by becoming his *equal* and by asserting authority in *his* way. In order to be able to gain the upper hand one must first conquer danger, and to do that one first has to address and conquer the dangerous inclinations found in oneself. Only then will one have something to give, something that makes the other *different*.

At a first glance this might seem rather passive, if not blasé, resigned, fatalistic—but it is not. He who does not invest in himself and gain wealth on his own strength has little to offer the other. In his response to ethical atheism, Nietzsche takes Jesus' second moral *order to love* very seriously. People have to learn to love *others* as they love *themselves*. This is asking a great deal. One thus not only needs to elevate oneself above the animosity and danger of the other, but one also has to elevate oneself—full stop. In order to love the other one has to *be able* to do that, which means that one genuinely has to love oneself. Does this give another twist to the ethics of Jesus? One needs to elevate oneself in order to convey this sense of elevation to the other. Above all else, this edification is of an ethical nature and it demands an investment in the ethical capacity of the first individual. If one is to offer the other something and *sincerely* look him in the eye, then one also needs to be true and sincere with respect to oneself. This demands self-knowledge and self-control. To be able to love oneself, one has to be aware of one's own truth. Without the "know thyself" element, there can be no sincerity.

To that end, one has to want to be conversant with and to overcome one's own aversion and resentment. One has to steel one's own will and be able to direct it; one has to gain ground in the field of own *force* of deed. By becoming a standard for oneself, by becoming strong and abundant, one can also develop overflowing love for others. One has to learn to *give* instead of wanting to receive. One has to activate such *giving virtue* in oneself. One has to learn to gain joy from giving and to be able to actually give. To that end the will has to be strengthened, the *ethical* will. The strength of the will also conquers the will's desire to seek refuge in *power* and in the justice pursued by power. By conquering retribution, the longing for redemption can be given a *redeeming* twist. Revenge that has been released from will no longer needs to be redeemed *from* what is and *for* what still needs to be done. This redeemed and redeeming will is so strong that it no longer seeks redeeming power. This will no longer needs to love either divine or human omnipotence.

Herein lies the *answer* to the power question, to the longing in which both religion and ideology become hopelessly entangled. In order to be able to truly reflect on what is and upon what has been done, reflective man must be able to deal with everything in a light-hearted manner, even if this is a difficult thing to do and even if man as the problem starts to play up. For that reason, man has to unburden himself from the *weight* of what is, a weight that tempts one to *want* to undo what is. This weighted directionality of the will starts with bitterness and ends with the inevitable awareness of futility. The knowing aspect always comes too late. True knowing is able to optimistically recognize this. The will cannot simply want to go back, the will cannot undo what is and what has been done. In its *backward* orientation the will is only able to know. Only in the *forward* direction does the will have open orientation at its disposal. The matter of reactively wanting to undo cannot operate in a liberating way. Only actively, creatively wanting to do can work in a liberating way. The active freedom *to* conquers the futile striving, the reactively wanting to frees *from*. The *reactive* wanting to reverse matters therefore has to have been transformed to an *actively* wanting to do.

Retrospectively this places a demand on the virtue of truth, on honestly recognizing what is, on the capacity to interact with what is *different* in an enlightened and unencumbered way. In the forward direction it demands the virtue of sincerity: being able to sincerely want to interact with the *other*. These virtues should help to conquer the appeal for justice and to avoid fleeing in the lust for power direction. The will to have *power* is a *self-defense* born of weakness, a futile attempt to overwhelm that which threatens from *without*. He who, in this respect, conquers himself will experience the exterior not so much as threatening, but more as a challenge. He then becomes a promise to himself and to the other.

13.2 AN ETERNAL CHALLENGE

How, then, can Nietzsche conquer the *weakness of will* danger, the obsessive will to gain *power*? In general terms, *weakness of will* is a human fact of life. It is not something that is necessarily *by definition* dangerous. Not everybody is automatically able to openly acknowledge the reality of the world and to actively react to challenges. Problems are not automatically presented as challenges. Problems can always, of course, weigh heavily on people, sometimes too heavily. Problems can also, however, be *made* heavy and can serve to only reinforce negative opinions about life. All in all, it is not easy for man to remain faithful to his earthly existence. How difficult, indeed, it therefore is for the weak-willed when they are faced with such difficult facets of existence. Many subsequently experience life as a burden, as something *heavy*, which—in the words of Nietzsche—prevents them from flying.

The inability to translate challenges into something actively purposeful does not immediately need to give rise to resignation, aversion, and resentment. This is actually something that is very consciously apparent in the case of consciously experienced heaviness, in which case the longing to be released grows. As long as this can be influenced in a moderating way, weakness of will need not be dangerous. Nietzsche also termed such moderate weakness of will *mediocrity*, which need not necessarily be seen as negative; it can even be viewed as virtuous. Whatever the case, mediocrity cannot manage without external support. If it is to be virtuous this support must be *internally* felt. Such support is attributable to the ethical effect of culture and institutions.

13   The Self-Conquest

However, the ethical effect will not be felt if the culture has to keep man under control like a repressive *Über-Ich*. As soon as the pressure falls away, the enduringly virtuous also ceases to be. The internalizing and moderating tendencies somehow help to counteract resentment. That which is virtuous helps to moderate the heaviness of life; it makes the *awareness* of such weight less apparent and the burden thus more bearable.

Consciousness is not by definition a blessing; *self*-consciousness even less so. Having a sharp awareness can add wisdom to a person's whole existence. Without such acuity, consciousness can easily have an oppressive effect upon people. Focusing very markedly on one's own particular existence can culminate in the earlier-mentioned *unhappy consciousness*, whilst actively *undertaking* is much more likely to have a liberating effect. Openness to the *to what end* facet provides a challenge and creates meaning, whilst fixating on the why or *how it happened* aspect takes away meaning. Could everything not have been *different*? Continuing to inquire why makes people unhappy and reactive: the relative aspect of life then becomes heavy. An unhappy consciousness tends to fuel the imagination. Weakness of will, the question why and *being* conscious are just as intimately intertwined as strength of will, inquiring to what end and consciously *doing*.

Being moderate protects people against dangerous developments. People can be taught, given the opportunity or forced, to lead a controlled and balanced existence. Indeed, that was how traditional, ethical life gave people support, even though such support was often exaggeratedly heavy-handed. By internalizing matters, this kind of life could be made more authentic. The ethical permeating must be so strong and so convincing that latent unrest is combated. It is crucial that man learns to accept the ethical *good* that is offered. Even if it is imprinted in a hard-hearted fashion, it is man's possession.

Ethical good only becomes a problem if inner acceptance falls away. At that point, ethical life is seen to be forcibly imposed and discontent is activated. One may question whether weakness of will actually has an answer to that. Discontent almost automatically turns itself against the harshness of life and, in the first place, against hard ethical life. It is then experienced as a tying down, as an external thing. The weak-willed is not then so much someone *with* a problem but one who proves to *be* a problem in himself. As no element of challenge is seen in such an exterior, any lurking, latent resentment that might be present is only encouraged. Hence the longing to lighten the heaviness of life by eliminating the reasons for its being like that. The futility of all of this has already been examined.

If life does not prove to be challenging and if moderating ethical connections cannot be restored, how, then, can the danger of weakness of will be counteracted? How can a *supra-human* challenge work out for the best without having any concrete ethical ties? How can one prevent a *repressive Über-Ich* having to keep man in order?

How can man learn to become a standard for himself? In this respect, do the futile efforts of the big ideologies to bring justice to man have a cathartic effect? Does this disillusion lead to any repentance? Does the state of affairs help to make man stronger? Does it help to place the ethical substance of human society in man himself? Can man become a foundation for ethical purpose in life?

Nietzsche's philosophy provides us with no unequivocal answer to this. These are, after all, the *final* questions which still remain unanswered. His philosophy provides no direction. On top of that, it appears that he places the will for *power* in an historical kind of perspective; this remains an open-ended perspective and therefore one with no certain outcome. Historicism does not apparently correspond to his concept of time concerning the eternal returning of the equal. The pattern of events sketched by him therefore has a rather *ironic* undertone to it. He maintains that the paradox of the omnipotent could conceivably trigger developments that could also come to threaten the omnipotent one himself. By destroying so much, the omnipotent could find that he ultimately *destroys* himself as well. What does this mean? Is there also a compelling logical force operating in the will for *power*? Does the will for omnipotence undermine, in the process, its own creativity and energy? Does it mean that in this way revengefulness will also be exhausted? Will the futility of revenge thus become all too evident and will the appeal for justice in this way lose its *credibility*? For man, will the significance of the future gain a different and more open aspect if eschatological expectations prove to be false and therefore lose their significance?

Something of a changing perspective could possibly shine through in the image that Nietzsche sketches of the post-modern *last man*, the sensualist with all his dismal *fabrications*. The fabrications embrace a longing for salvation that makes eschatological hope somehow superfluous. People do, after all, believe that they can find happiness in the here and now. The problem, though, is that these fabrications ruin any active orientation directed at human self-control and self-elevation. The question that then arises is whether the recent human being is able to curtail the destructive danger of resentment. Will his resentment become so trivial that it will also hamper the longing for a redeeming omnipotence? In the future will the problem thus confine itself to a somewhat less dangerous type of resentment and to a depressing experiencing of meaning? Will the old thirst for power thus get stranded in a comforting kind of absurdity? This is not the conclusion drawn by Nietzsche, quite the reverse in fact. The last man will not stop at the meaning of life being absurd. His life will continue to be dominated by resentment that cannot be alleviated and this final human seems to be a worldwide, all overrunning phenomenon. The modernist last man disseminates a dangerous brand of susceptibility to the creative offloading of resentment. Though his longing for omnipotence may have become rather private, he still functions on the basis of a trivial will for *power*. This offers little opportunity for an active, energetic zest for life, let alone for any type of ethical interest in life.

13 The Self-Conquest

Again there is the question of the implications of omnipotence destroying itself? What exactly does Nietzsche mean when he talks of such *destruction*? To get to grips with that we need to examine more closely his legacy of texts that deal with how he expected the socialistic hunger for power to pan out.[1] This can throw light on the matter of whether, with a disillusioned omnipotence, the longing for such omnipotence will automatically disappear so that man will bid farewell to omnipotence. Alternatively, is more required to conquer omnipotence and its dangers? How, indeed, does he perceive that this departure from omnipotence will occur?

What is important when it comes to the matter of coming to terms with his perception of *destruction* is the fact that Nietzsche speaks of *Sollen*, not of an objective process. He furthermore perceives of *destruction* as a process involving the *destroying of oneself*: the weak-willed lapse into nihilism and a desperate urge to precipitate self-destruction as soon as existence becomes unmistakably devoid of purpose. The destruction signals the nihilistic final phase of the fury of destruction in which the call for justice becomes entwined. What now becomes unmistakably revealed is the hard reality of the thirst for power and just how futile that is. This could have a *purifying* effect whilst actively stimulating the wills of both the strong and the weak. He sees certain possibilities in the symptoms of this destruction. Nothing can be guaranteed, but despite that new challenges do open up. What is important is how he links the *will* for power to the *strength* of power.

Nietzsche presumes, with a mixture of fatalism, logic, and *irony*, that socialism will inevitably emerge. He wants to perceive it as a challenge, which is why he asserts that it should be given a chance. The ideology that is hostile to life provokes a challenge, which is why it will have a positive effect. That is why he even goes as far as to call the experiment *desirable*. The practiced doctrine of salvation could be *exhaustive* so that it would force choices to be made. The experiment might be able to *discourage* and *challenge*. None of this could, however, be *historically* interpreted as though the catastrophe might automatically lead to the adopting of another purpose in life. The experiment does, however, make one thing undeniably clear: it unveils the eschatological illusions, reveals the futility of the hankering after power, and it demonstrates just what the call for justice could lead to. That discourages, purifies, and undoubtedly also encourages individuals to conquer their only too human weakness of will. The experiment does nothing more than that. It creates no certainties, no reborn people, no totally different history. Though the grotesque experiment is indeed the result of eschatological longings, it does not, in itself, open up any eschatological perspectives.

What one should bear in mind is that all of this is what Nietzsche *expects*. The world-historical developments still had to take place. All he could hope was that it would unavoidably lead to something. In effect he endows this hope with activated

---

1. Nietzsche, *Sämtliche Werke*, VII.3, 312v.

content. Hence the reason that he anticipates that all of this will have a *discouraging* effect upon the weak-willed and that it might *challenge* the strong-willed. He expects something for both realizations of the will to power. In retrospect the anticipated *discouragement* is, to an extent, confirmatory. The revolutions were a failure; they were self-destroying. Marxist revisions were not really able to reawaken the eschatological hope and the revolutionary activism. Did this really and truly destroy the appeal for justice and the will for *power*? Did this really filter through to the ancient, *religious* longing for justice? The discouragement alone is not sufficient. It is, in fact, an inadequate answer to the actual origin of the experiment, that of man as a *problem*. The answer to that must much sooner be sought in the other dimension of man, the dimension of a *promise*. That is why the *challenging* aspect of the experiment must reinforce the promising aspect of man. In terms of the promise, man must see that he conquers himself as the problem, time and again and forever.

This brings us back to the other effect of the experiment, the *challenging* effect. Nietzsche believes that the curatively challenging will be forced upon humans. As the revolutionary doctrine of salvation no longer projects the claimed salvation into a heavenly future, the revolution creates a now or never situation. Revolutionary activism will rob good-natured, democratic, gregarious man of his lethargic peace. He will hardly be able to escape the fateful situation. People will have to defend themselves in their confrontation with the omnipotent. Nietzsche hopes that this situation will not tempt them too much to want to create a counter*force*. He hopes that there will be an inner activating of those who carry a promise within themselves. People must not so much be forced to take up this *challenge*; it should sooner be the case that they freely wish to enter into it. For them, the inevitability of the socialist experiment must take on the appearance of occurring *perforce* (of being a "necessary turn"); it must be a challenge that can provoke a *change*, a promise-filled change towards which the need of the problem drives them. Their promise is founded in the capacity for *self-conquest*. This capacity is something that Nietzsche presents as health. Those who are able to conquer themselves will also be familiar with struggling against resentment; they will really be able to control that, and in turn that will make them *moderate*. In such cases people can provide standards for themselves, people can moderate themselves and actively aim at elevated objectives. A healthy attitude to life makes it possible to contemplate the hard reality of life and not to flee from it. It enables people to be honest, also where self-knowledge is concerned.

Therein also lies the road to finding ethical meaning in life. What the healthy attitude to life also involves is love, people being able to love both themselves and others. People can give shape to what Nietzsche termed the *giving* virtue, the virtue that is primarily directed at wanting and being able to give something to others. With this giving virtue, it is the promising facet of people that comes into play. They have to help to conquer man as a problem. It is a virtue that asks no justice. It does not

13 The Self-Conquest

therefore need to seek refuge in the will for *power*. It is much sooner the case that such virtue will help people to *bid farewell* to the omnipotent *themselves*, even after the phenomenon of omnipotence has been destroyed. In that way, strength of will is able to conquer the thirst for power. The fact of omnipotence being destroyed may not be confined to taking leave of man. What is so challenging and meaningful about the whole thing is that it gives man himself the opportunity to depart from the omnipotent, to make use of this escape route. This final matter is an eternal task, not a definite twist in history. No matter how much omnipotence is phased out, the yearning for it remains. The socialist experiment ensures nothing. It only makes the challenge more imperative.

It is curious to compare Nietzsche's expectations to what has actually happened. Has the demonstration worked in a challenging way? That would not appear to be the case. It is sooner so that the skepticism has been justified. Europeans can hardly be said to have experienced the absurdity of the experiment as a challenge. How many really saw in this *external* provocation the opportunity for a spiritual power that strengthened itself? How much inner expansion force was developed? To what extent has a strengthened will been able to stand up to and respond to the doctrine of salvation and its call for justice? Without *external* help even free Europe could at some point all too willingly have submitted to the revolutionary absurdity. The secret or even open concession to absurdity often appeared greater than the opposition to it. In the light of the challenging effect anticipated by Nietzsche, what is much more surprising is the awareness that the totalitarian omnipotence was, above all else, *destroyed* by itself: by internal contradiction, by own futility. It was not the provocative challenges that gave rise to the demise of the omnipotent. Even the *destruction* of the omnipotent does not automatically prompt changes to occur. Does this therefore mean that the absurdity of the last man will become an all-predominating phenomenon? In the totalitarian world, ethical atheism was sustained on the basis of a violent and externally prompted seizure of power. Did it gain its victory in the post-ideological world in an internal way? So far there is little evidence of a spiritual power that has powerfully manifested itself through an activating culture and enduring institutions.

13.3 THE SUPRA-HUMAN

The failure and the evaporation of the totalitarian ideologies did not easily put an end to all the apocalyptic prospects. Man was not once and for all awakened from his dreams of redemption. In religion such dreams have already been revived, so why should ideological variants not follow? On top of that, nostalgic yearnings can also emerge without the need for apocalyptic fantasies; there are dreams enough. Why should happiness be projected into a distant future and a recreated world? Nietzsche's modernist or, if one wishes, postmodernist and last man seems to have become an omnipresent phenomenon. Even though his fabrications of salvation and his urge to avenge might well seem trivial, they remain an everyday reality. Hegel's *bad infinity* of sensual desires is what had become normative for him. Man had once been part of a sacred ethical world but now the world revolved around one person who lawfully claimed his justice. It is an unethical *legal principle* that is busy dissolving the *zoon politikon*. But why place vengeance in an eschatological perspective? Why not have a direct, militant call for justice? Why, for that matter, does vengeance have to be justified?

It would seem that *ethical* God is completely taking leave of man. Can the existing institutional structures maintain the social lines of contact? Can what is problematic about man be restrained? Is it perhaps not the case that what remains of cultural and institutional ties will more and more come to be experienced as a repressive and objectionable *Über-Ich* from which hasty *leave* needs to be *taken*? What is so challenging about all of this? Does the degeneration of man induce repression, or is this a problem that can be surmounted in another way? As has been asserted, Nietzsche connected this challenge to the self-conquest of man. He viewed it as an eternally recurring challenge. This challenge brings Nietzsche's *Übermensch* into the picture, so we shall pause to briefly examine that matter.

The term *Übermensch* can be interpreted in two completely contrasting ways, both of which have everything to do with the appraisal of the *will to power* concept. The difference in interpretation lies in the reading of the preposition *über*, which can be understood in its *dative*, third case usage or interpreted as *accusative* and fourth case. The fluidity of *over* in the accusative is demonstrated in constructions such as overwintering, overstepping, or crossing over. What is crucial in this kind of usage is that there is a certain reflection of progress or change but no hint of ending or termination, not to mention of triumphant apotheosis. The accusative points to an eternally returning and always challenging human situation. The accusative bestows upon *über* the sense of a process and development, a movement that passes on or through. The dative, by contrast, emphasizes the superior-seeking nature of the interpretation of *über* so that it comes to mean: hierarchically positioned above something else that is positioned lower down. The dative seeks or describes a static situation whilst the accusative reflects movement. The term *Übermensch* can therefore be interpreted in two ways depending on how one translates the preposition. Similarly, it is the preposition that lends interpretation to the word *power* in the phrase will to power.

The interpretation that *Nazism* gave to *über* in the word Übermensch was, of course, the dative-based reading. There was explicit evidence of a superior type of being that elevated or raised himself *above* an inferior type of person who was positioned *below* himself: an *Untermensch*. Insofar as there is evidence of a movement or process, what it concerns here is a battle between both types of people, a battle for the one type to gain *power* over the other. In this sense Nazism seeks a connection with Darwinism.

13 The Self-Conquest

In this struggle it is about more than survival, it is about power, about prevailing over others. In this conflict, the will to gain power is active in that it is directed at *power*, hierarchical power. The dominion over the other delivers evidence of superiority: that of the Übermensch and of the accompanying arbitrariness. The inferior other is sometimes worth overruling, but if not the road that remains is that of destruction. The will to power is ideologically justified as a struggle for *justice* in both senses of the word: by putting paid to what stands in the way of superiority and by redeeming the self to an elevated existence as a superior being. Also within the superiority, the hierarchical *über* persists in the *Führer* principle, in the urge for a battle for leadership. Everywhere, then, there is the dative reading; everywhere there is the justifying of omnipotence.

Although in an ideological respect Stalinism cannot be completely equated with Nazism, in both cases the party and the leader had a *super*human position, elevated above all those who were either worthy of rebirth or who were seen as unworthy beings and therefore had to be eliminated. Here again everything revolved around conflict and power. Also here, *Übermenschen* saw themselves as omnipotent, as called to rule and to take leave of all who stood in the way of their grand objective. Here again it is power and arbitrariness that reign supreme; it is not a matter of despotic power but rather of totalitarian power. It is therefore about recreating rather than oppressing those who are ruled over. That then situates the omnipotent above and opposite the other: both the chosen ones and the lost, rejected, unworthy types.

In the case of this Übermensch, an historical reflection of the age pertaining to the rounding off of history is of relevance. In this sense, the Übermensch must in fact be viewed as an extremely sickly and *weak*-willed exponent, as a person full of resentment. To compensate for this weakness extreme power is sought: destructive, avenging power. The superior kind of individual who is bent on gaining power loves himself just as little as the other. This Übermensch sees in the other no element of challenge but rather a threat; the other is a hateful object that has to be dispensed with.

Nietzsche's Übermensch has nothing to do with a notion of progress nor with any desire to rule or to possess power. He sketches no struggle for power out of which a redeeming, Übermensch should ideally emerge. For him the term Übermensch has no historical dimensions. For him the *über* prefix is accusative and stands for movement. Also, in this sense of movement the idea of *conquering* comes emphatically to the fore, not now as a conquest over the other but as self-conquest, as a surmounting of what is only all too human in man. The stress does not lie on the *power* aspect of the will to power but upon the active and controlled directedness of the *will*, an orientation towards the good, elevated, and sublime. Such a kind of orientation demands of the will the necessary power or strength of will. If, in the term Übermensch, there is an echo of the *above/super* definition, then it is in the sense of *supra*-human. Nietzsche regards the self-conquest of what is all too human in man as a supra-human feat, an eternally recurring kind of effort that is hopeful but does not have a guaranteed outcome.

Special, elevated individuals who could, as a kind, be typified as Übermenschen have always been around; such successful, happy strokes of luck will probably always remain. More than an Übermensch as a person, it is the Übermenschliche nature of the challenge and self-conquest to which Nietzsche refers in the general human sense. This brings for man the earlier-mentioned twist in the ever-recurrent human problem. The concept Übermensch thus has nothing to do with gaining power over or ruling over others. One has to become a norm unto or standard for oneself, one has to be able to control oneself and direct the will in an active way. It is about the ability to give oneself elevated goals to achieve and to then actually realize those same objectives. The exalted one does not recreate man and the world but, in creating, he does add *values* to man and the world, sublime values. What is central to this active appreciating is the term *ariston*, meaning good. This good is directed at virtuous living together. This virtue is not able to survive without the will to invest in enduring institutions. The superhuman *will* to power thus actively adds values to man and to his human context. This will has both purposes for the future and for authority.

Though the superhuman might start with individual people that is not where it ends, on the contrary. He who is able to create values, he who is able to achieve the sublime in himself can—and also wants to—convey that to others. He who is able to love himself, he who is able to deal openly and honestly with himself and can give direction to his own will also seeks the other. He is also able to give to the other what is valuable, not as a help-seeking and pitiable other but as another who is challenging and to be appreciated. There can be no sincerity towards the other if there is no foundation in truthfulness. There can be no integrity if there is not the ability to remain faithful to the earth: one has to want to invest in human nature, which needs to be valued. This Übermensch lives according to the life principles founded on ethical meaning.

The *übermenschliche* person is filled with a self-conscious and self-conquering will for power. What is really central to that is the elevating directedness of the *will*, not power, and therefore not any ambition to seize power. The *accusatively* construed Übermensch is thus diametrically opposed to the *datively* construed Übermensch. The one may not wait until the other is destroyed by his own desire for power: he has to conquer the urge for power and the will for omnipotence in himself. The omnipotent must not be beaten by omnipotence. The first takes leave of the second by conquering the will for *omnipotence* in himself and in others. He departs from the omnipotent by becoming *powerful over himself* and by allowing the other to share in this virtue.

Nietzsche's Zarathustra expresses this in a sublime fashion. In his struggle with his problem of the last man, he refuses to give in to the tempting instigation to lead the people, to become a good shepherd for a flock in need. He even refuses to address the people; his experiences have also helped him to deal with that impulse. He seeks instead another more ethical path. He goes in search of those who are similarly disposed, those who know how to follow themselves instead of seeking salvation in leaders and rulers. He seeks not to *shepherd* a *flock* but rather to entice fellow beings away from the flock, also the group of last men. He goes in search of creators, fellow creators of values. He does not wish to either rule or serve: his brotherly love challenges the other to become a creator himself, to be capable of such creating. Those who are capable of such superhuman activity will want no omnipotence or omnipotent. They will, in the old ethical sense of the word, become *gods* themselves.

Can gods assist them in any of this? Should they desire that? Does man have the final word or, to that end, must creating man also become a creator of gods? Can the final man be conquered without *final* gods? The first man was able to cheerfully meet the human challenge because a God that was his *equal* stood at his side. The omnipotent removed himself from man and became his complete *unequal*, which ruined the happy existence. Does renewed cheerfulness, a true and sincere life, once again demand gods that are equal to man? Alternatively, is the *final* word with man himself? This *last* question is open; it expresses a final challenge.

14

Faithful to the Earth

No unambiguous and definitive answer can possibly be given to *final* questions. The underlying challenges do not disappear, the inevitable will always again occur. Finding a way to escape is not desirable either: surely that would herald the end of what is human about man? What is most fundamental about man does not therefore have to make him feel sombre. This makes Nietzsche's description of man as simultaneously both a *problem* and a *promise* cheerful and challenging. In the case of *man as a promise*, it is all about something quite different than the promise of redemption and justice; what also belongs to him is the eternally recurring problem. Man is a creature that is consciously able to *differentiate* and has a will of his own. It is this human quality that distinguishes him from the rest of nature—with him not everything derives from nature. Good and evil, truth and falsehood, justice and injustice are unique to him. Man must not seek to be released from such human capacities. No matter how much evil has to be surmounted he must not seek to be liberated from the *phenomenon* of evil itself. Through this evil what is human about man could ultimately be lost. Totalitarian ideologies have tried to realize everything that the many utopian doctrines have promised: redemption, the undoing of what lies encapsulated in the emergence of man, the ability to differentiate.

What is inherent to any doctrines of salvation is the regressive recreating of man as a natural being. The blissful natural state is truly closed off to man—including also the heavenly or utopian variants. This is what the old, ethical God had already established and after the ethical God had died this did not change either. He who truly and sincerely loves man must even be able to conquer the longing for this natural state. Regardless of what—in this living being—remains to remind one of the natural state, the road back must always be declared irreversibly closed: *nature* is in its essence *non-human*. The yearning for redeeming nature not only fails to recognize the *problem* that comes with being man but it also ruins the promise that lies in *man*. It is up to man to supplement nature by contributing human values. He elevates nature, above all else human nature, and makes it sublime.

It is final questions that constitute the true recognition of the open nature of the human condition. They stand opposed to a final philosophy that sought, in a practical way, to force a redeeming answer to be given to this condition. That philosophy sought the abolition of man, of all that was human in him.

Man can only *be* a promise if he is able to bear this human condition and *want* to see in it a hazardous enterprise and challenge. This challenge gives priority to the matter of wanting to meet that challenge. This wanting to thus confronts the following apparently paradoxical task: to free man from the desire to be relieved of the human condition. The redeeming *from* must dwell in a liberating *to*. This will and its freedom are open matters. That is why man must accept this challenging contingency in a positive and light-hearted way.

The accepting of this challenge ties Nietzsche to the ability to remain *faithful* to the earth, the earth as a *human* social environment. Animals are naturally faithful to the earth, the natural earth, even where this proves fatal to them. With man it is more about a virtuous kind of faithfulness, it is more about the ability to contribute worth to the human social environment. In this faithfulness lies the answer to ethical atheism. Being faithful to the ethical social environment is the voluntarily accepted precondition that underlies meaningful human existence.

14.1 VIRTUOUS WISDOM

In his longing for omnipotence man proves to be decidedly reactive: he is unable to shake himself free of what obsessively possesses him. In providing the answer to this Nietzsche refuses to adapt to his antagonist. He does not want to be equal to him; his reaction may not be similarly reactive in the true sense of the word. He does turn himself *against* this power of the will, but then in terms of a challenge. He wants, as it were, to give something back in an active way to the one who has been challenged: he wants to strengthen his will. He seeks no sheer brazen *counterforce* to combat the omnipotent. In terms of *inner power* and where willpower and introspection are concerned, the answer lies in resentment, in turning against earthly existence, in the aversion to the other. This demands a charitable *recognition* of man as the problem. This recognition implies a conquering of one's own aversion; it is a precondition for the true *knowing* of man. True knowledge is above all else self-knowledge. It is therapeutic; it provides the road to man as a promise. How can an answer be given to the issue of man as the problem if things are not seen as they truly are? The fact that the truth of the all too human reality is hard is no justification for taking refuge in lies and fabrications. That is the reason why the truth must not only be borne but also accepted: as a challenge and as a risky enterprise.

Without cognitive openness there can be no virtuous loyalty to existence. Such virtuous loyalty reactivates a core element of ancient life, albeit without the old ethical *gods*. Nietzsche doubts whether man is still able to provide himself with gods that can support his ethical life. People will therefore have to become *gods* themselves. The answer to the issue of man as the problem is in that way immediately returned to man: he himself will have to become the promise, on his own strength and without any sacred embedding. If gods remain silent and disappear from the public domain then the *start* of virtuous life will be transferred to man. It is in this virtuous beginning that the answer to the challenge of ethical atheism lies.

Truthfulness has an *epistemological* aspect to it. It constitutes a special value and is a pre*condition* to cognitively interacting with *what is different*. It amounts to the essence of the ability to bear the truth, even if the truth is hard and inclined to deter one. It is indispensable as a *virtue* since man does not naturally possess this capacity. For man, it is not only not knowing and being mistaken but also denying and lying that are all too familiar, all too human. An honest attitude prevents man from fearing the truth, from being averse to what is a fact of life and from seeking refuge in lies. The knowledge that the truth always comes *too late* does not work as a deterrent: he can always look back without cognitive repugnance even if there is reason enough for such aversion. *Sincerity* has an *ethical* side to it too: it is an essential pre*condition* to getting along with *the other* and thus to organizing life and society. Sincerity empowers the capacity, the will to direct oneself towards what one would wish to impart to the world, to oneself and to one's fellow man. He who is able, in a cognitive sense, to take life as it comes is also able to be genuinely creative. Sincerity makes people benevolent; it makes it possible for them to make promises and to honor such promises. Whereas truthfulness maintains a benevolent *backward*-oriented glance, sincerity fixes its glance, in just such a benevolent way, in the *forward* direction.

Nietzsche's idea of truth was opposed to the *metaphysical* idea of truth, a notion that sought to unveil an unconditional *not* realized or *not-yet* realized reality. The metaphysical idea of truth sought to free man from the *façade* of a kind of reality that was experienced as hard, changing, and thus reprehensible. It was an endeavor that was doomed to be futile. The truth is always relative and therefore *conditional*: knowledge always needs to be fed in some way, something must always *precede* it, otherwise its existence is unthinkable. Knowledge does not create but follows on from what simply exists. It does not really aim to present anything new; it always comes *too late* and it wants it to be that way. Truth is insight, but it does not redeem from what is. It therefore carries no promise and is not a matter of belief. It does not point to what is yet to be but to that which could already be revealed in the idea. It is not elevated *in relation to* the relative nature of appearances. The literally *meta*-physical truth seeks to be elevated *above* what is the case and should be able to *foresee* what is still to come. This *moralizes* both the idea of truth and the given truth. The cognitive opinion is then predisposedly intertwined with the question of good and evil. What is so detrimental about that is the fact that moralizing preconceptions ruin the openness of the cognitive view. Like a *Sollen*, they imply that it is possible to be redeemed from a type of reality that is experienced as meaningless; like a *preconceived notion* they magnify the aversion and disgust towards what exists. So even where the suggested un*condition*ality of the metaphysical truth is concerned, this is still preceded by a *condition*, a moralizing *value*: what *exists* is rated as evil and the supposedly *true* is seen as good. The moralizing prejudice proposes that what *is* cannot be true. It is an opinion that constitutes a *contradictio in terminis*. The given reality cannot, as such, be true: only *knowledge* of what is given can be true or not true. True, cognitive openness wants to see things as they are: it *discovers*.

The truth merely discovers; it offers no purpose, it does not appreciate. The metaphysical truth offers only fabrication, a semblance of meaning, a purpose for belief. The greater such belief is, the more forceful the conviction will be and the more tempting all the accompanying fabrications. Purpose is not a matter of *being* but rather of human will and actions, of appreciation and creative activity. The truth really does not create any values or meaning; it only offers insight into what is given. It cannot therefore be allied to the truth, which is more powerful than everything in this world. That, too, endeavors to make *truth* and *meaning* identical. The idea of a promising, meaningful, or valuable truth is a mere figment of the imagination, a deceptive semblance of reality. Hence Nietzsche's conclusion to the effect that art is *worth* more than the truth. After all, art is an expression of creative values; truth only discovers what is, it creates nothing. The fact that *wanting to discover* the truth might contain a *value* does not mean to say that the *content* of such discovering appreciates or lends meaning. The *giving* of purpose is something different from the knowing of the *given facts*, the actual world. Meaning lies in the good of what is desired, in the creating directedness of the will and its vigor.

Therein lies also the experiencing of joy and happiness. Man gains his *happiness* from the directedness of his will, from what is good about his creating activity. Meaning and happiness lie like cheerful experiences encapsulated in the sublime directedness of the will. Both will and experience can have a liberating effect upon the unhappy consciousness and all its fabrications. This idea of the truth corresponds with Hegel's aversion to people's moralizingly knowing better: he too wants, above all else, to *understand what is* and keep a distance from the *pedantic* escape to a world that should have been.

This idea of truth may not give rise to the suggestion that knowledge can simply be acquired. The reverse is much sooner the case. The limited cognitive capacities of man make it undoubtedly impossible to ever fully and adequately grasp the whole reality. The fact that a stubborn, changing reality escapes the limited cognitive capacity of man is even more reason for wanting to cling to the *pathos* of reality in the idea of truth. This pathos prompts an everlasting search, the need to keep on testing and adapting the insight gained. This pathos is the beginning of truth, it is the *in the beginning* of truth.

This pathos corresponds nicely with Wittgenstein's *tractatus* hypothesis to the effect that "the world is all that is the case." It is a hypothesis that is everything barring tautological. It seeks to urgently link knowledge to what is given, to facts, phenomena, occurrences, or whatever. What matters is *that* man must be prepared to direct his cognitive capacities towards *what* is given. In a similar way, also after the death of God, Nietzsche seems to want to hold on to the old *sacred* relationship between man and his world. His *faithfulness* to the earth is particularly concerned with the ethical connectedness with the human social environment; it is a kind of faithfulness that must filter through to the cognitive relationship. True knowledge starts with *respect* for what is given, with amazement. Wisdom makes sure that something is added to this or detracted from it. What is known precedes the knower. Knowledge should really leave everything exactly as it is. Wisdom commences with recognition, the recognition that the truth cannot create or recreate. Knowledge is thinking *about*, not thinking *up* or thinking of *beforehand*.

The human capacity to know is definitely limited. One-sidedness and mistakes are unavoidable, which means that corrections perpetually need to be made. Nietzsche translated this necessity into an active virtue. He wanted to approach complex and changeable reality from as many as possible angles and examine it from all possible perspectives. Indeed, perspectives possess something intrinsic and *conditional*. They have a specific *value* that steers knowledge in a particular direction, thus implying a certain degree of *holding to be true*. The cognitive objective thus, as it were, makes use of direction-giving frameworks.

In his culture man gives shape to such values, consciously or not. The old ethical cultures more or less dictated such values: they were sacred and therefore had normative and binding validity. Human knowledge was linked to the ethical order; ethical values imperatively imposed *true* interpretation derived from *good* life. Even without knowing this the true became embedded in the good: the ethical framework of interpretation established the cognitive space. The conditional aspect of this sacred perspective was seen to be absolutely true. This did not mean to say that these cultures demonstrated an *untruthful* attitude, on the contrary. Regardless of the amount of *terror* that the hard ethical and physical world instilled, it provided little space for fatal disgust or a deceitful attitude. One was bound to the own, given world. One had to remain faithful to the own closed, ethical world. There was no alternative. One thus had to bear the hard reality, above all else the ethical reality. Insofar as one had any insight into reality, one *complied* with that.

The ability to comply lessens as the religious and cultural ties become looser: one then starts to find the hard character of the social environment unnecessarily repressive. The capacity to comply is reduced even more if knowledge comes into view that cuts itself loose from the ethical interpretation frameworks. It then becomes more difficult to give credibility to such a framework and to the relevant applicable knowledge. New perspectives ruin the traditional legitimacy. This not only means that there is a growing desire for freedom but it also brings with it uncertainty and confusion. Science has played a big part in all of that.

Nietzsche wanted to take advantage of the freedom of space that could be offered by the many knowledge perspectives. He wanted to implement the many possible aspects in an active and creative way in his quest for the truth. There is something relative about perspectives. That also gives the freedom won a hard side to it because it can lead to confusion and can come across as threatening. *Freedom* asks a lot of people. The loss of binding ethical frameworks makes the world, in a certain respect, *infinite*: it can after all be opened up from many different angles. This applies to the physical cosmos but even more to the already very changing human world. People must not be deterred by painful revelations and they must not fall prey to aversion and disgust. Precisely now it is important to remain faithful to the earth. The space provided for freedom actually makes it tempting to want to see things differently from the way they are or to want to make things different. The *lies* and the *need to prove* are untruthful reactions to the *shock* concerning infinity, which is experienced as threatening, and to the *hope* for something totally different. Freedom gives people the chance to choose between truth and lies, cognitive openness, and moralizing. Truthfulness demands an *open* attitude in a world that has opened up and which thus offers free, active, and creative use of perspectival space. The many perspectives must complement each other, liberalize, and correct. Cognitive openness not only demands that science be *buoyant* but it also makes that possible. The open world must prove challenging. Nietzsche narrowed the challenging aspect of this perspectival openness down to the individual: the aim must be to dare to unite as many as possible perspectives in one individual. The idea must be to dare to see things as they really are, and therefore consider matters with many eyes from many personal points of view. The more persons one can unite in oneself and the more discussion and competition one can process, the closer one will come to the truth. The more open and creative one dares to be *below* the truth, the closer one will come to the truth.

This is no carte blanche for perspectival arbitrariness. As if they were to one's liking, agreeable perspectives can be chosen whilst others can be ignored. The arbitrariness presumes that a position is held *above* the truth; this position is expressed in the ideas about omniscience and omnipotence. This *power* of the will is subsequently forbidden by many in the form of perspectival randomness. It is an arbitrariness that offers everyone their own truth, their own position of power and the presumed capacity to be able to elevate oneself *above* the truth. The perspectival will for *power* typifies the *post-modern* ruination of the idea of truth. The denying of absolute truth-making does not alter the fact that post-modern relativism perpetuates this idea. It proposes relinquishing the notion of absolute truth and omnipotence; it furthermore proposes introducing a similar will for *power* in its place. The one, lonely, all too human god makes way for many, still lonely, human gods. The power-crazed *each to his own* stance still amounts to a dangerous destroying of the ethical purpose in life. The new godheads once again dream that they are *above* the truth, their truth. The old uniqueness of power is dispersed over the still randomly appropriated power perspectives of many. The disappearance of the one omnipotence does not therefore put an end to the arbitrariness of the will to *power*. The post-modern arbitrariness accepts everything, whether it is good or bad. With Nietzsche there is no perspectival arbitrariness, nor is there a post-modern appeal for a battle between the powers. In his case there was no will to *power*, no situating above the truth, no arbitrariness attached to realizing. Truthfulness does not seek to stand *above* the truth; it does not randomly want to have it at its disposal. Perspectival openness is situated *below* the truth. That in itself is evidence of wisdom. That also, in fact, requires that one be faithful to the earth if its openness seems to have become infinite. This loyalty guards space against ethical sincerity. The truthful does not actually flee from man and the world as they stand. He *appreciates* man and the world; he wants to value them. Why, then, should he take refuge in redeeming power?

Perspectival openness inevitably makes the idea of truth clash with compelling cognitive interpretations that are formed on the basis of religious points of view. But why should religion get so dug into an *own idea of the truth*? Rigid interpretations of the truth in religious narratives and descriptions make religion vulnerable while at the same time destroying the richer, underlying tapestry of connotation. This thus makes the loss of religiously founded truth less tragic than it might seem. The diminishing pretension of truth does not necessarily have to affect the broader perspective of meaning in religion. Why hand over religion to own pseudo-scientific explanations of physical and human reality? Why choose this way to condemn its *ethical* meaning to destruction? Was it not so that religious stories invariably served as metaphors, were they not integrated to help people reflect on such aspects of meaning? In such meditations it is always about more than the strictly factual dimensions of the story in question. To put it another way, the stories are not intended to be taken to be *true* but they do tell us some important things about what is *good*. Descriptively informing about this good says something about the world to which such descriptions belong: the human world. The various reflections throw light on the purpose in life accompanying the stories told. Literally interpreting such narratives only spoils their real meaning.

In the first place, metaphors help to bring into focus a human cosmos. In holding the image, the metaphor, *to be true* in a strict and factual sense, the true thus comes to *ruin* the good. Being affronted about the scientific elimination of nonsensical or disruptive religious misconceptions is definitely detrimental to religion. The *judge not* maxim of Jesus is also highly relevant here: it could open up the way to lively ethical significance where religion is concerned. To actively orient itself towards what is good, religion should *free* itself from the true: undergo a real freeing. Undoubtedly, religion could then still be of significance to the ethical ordering of the human cosmos, the forming of the human spirit and the building of cultures and institutions. Such work could again be termed *good* but not *true*. In the mission to search for truth it would be better for religion to abandon that particular pretension.

The opening up of the world does not only have consequences for the truth. Once the world opens up, this likewise affects the ethical significance of human existence. In an open world, this kind of purpose is also unthinkable without freedom and *movement*. Leaning on a good sense of proportion and equilibrium, the danger of being held back by stagnation and arbitrariness must be prevented. It is not only the true that keeps man in motion but also the good. In the opened up world, the ethical *substance* must keep apace with unfolding human existence, though always in a restrained way, contemplatively, always rooted in culture and institutions. The true can be an affair of individual man whilst the good is always in any case a matter for people amongst themselves. That must make the individual more thoughtful, certainly if the private range becomes greater.

14.2 OWN EMPOWERMENT

What has been asserted above is presented in challenging terms; it is presented as a challenge to religion. This does not resolve the question of whether religion can keep one's own future open-ended. Is religion able to keep the true and good separate and hold on to ethical good in an open way? Is that what religion seeks to do? This is, once again, an incredibly complex question, which not only affects religion but also people in general. Can there be ethical order in a world that is opening up? To put it another way, how open can ethical order be? Having open ethical order involves no longer being attached to traditions, not to mention being attached to established, sacred foundations. There is even another way to put the question: can *enlightening* truth exist side by side with *enlightened* ethical *substance*? Does the liberated and enlightening true insight not seemingly automatically undermine the *obligatory* core of what is good?

The imperative, *substantial* component seems—in an enlightened world—to move from the good to the true. The question pertaining to truth does in fact draw man's attention to what is, to what is a fixed constant. After the death of God, after the cognitive opening up of the world—a world that thus appears to have become infinite—the truth directs man towards what is certain. Truth obliges man to do justice, in an enlightened fashion, to what the sacred attitude once commanded. The only question that then remains to be asked is this one: *what* is really the truth? No matter how much respect man is able to muster for culture and institutions, morality and legality; this imperative element of ethical good has been abandoned. Whilst seeking ethical good, what, in the final instance, slips away from man is a world that is familiar and intrinsically recognizable to him. He now has to want what is good, he has to want to do good himself but without an accepted and fixed target. He therefore has to be challenged to endow the world with ethical values himself. He has to want to impart such values to his fellow man. He has to make the human cosmos good without being able to give this good eternal and universal significance. Only on the basis of such an open and sincere point of departure can man then ask himself the true question by questioning whether what he has done was really good. This is, indeed, a fine sequel to the story of creation. The true and the good cannot and may not any longer become embroiled in each other, yet both questions continue to maintain their hold on each other.

Again we pose the interminable question: does the opening up of the world threaten man's willingness to seek ethical good? Does the true not threaten the good? Is it not the case that the openness undermines all ethical *order*? This final question is one that cannot be ignored, but no certain answers can be given. All in all, the questions asked are as open as the openness of the world itself.

Hegel thought it conceivable that the ethical purpose of religion could survive the opening up of the world, which, in his eyes, was synonymous with enlightenment. Ethical substance can remain vigorous if religion knows how to rejuvenate and activate this deepest core. In enlightened times religion would also be able to move and hold on to ethical meaning. Nietzsche showed more skepticism, even though for him skepticism was not the final thing. The ethical gods were dead; that put an end to the sacred core of ethical life. All the old ethical substance had been lost. In religion ethical atheism finds its negative apotheosis in ideological atheism and in post-modernism. He attached to this loss of substance what he termed *true nihilistic conclusions*. If the good no longer constitutes any original *given facts* then the challenge remains open. If the sacred substance of the *good* falls away then a human challenge emerges, one that man must actively *want* to take up. Insight into the human origins of the ethical world may have made this world relative in a cognitive sense, but now it is up to man to make the *relative* normative in an ethical sense.

At this point it is an old question that again comes to the fore, the question concerning the justifying of notably human evil. The openness of a world that has become human makes at least one thing very clear: man no longer lives in a sacred world nor, by the same token, does he live in the best of all possible worlds. Can he bear the hard human reality without receiving sacred comfort? How can he free himself from the pressure to want to justify the human evil of this world? Should he also, in this respect, conquer himself? Must he seek to overcome the justification question? Must he learn to equate human *evil* with all the suffering that the physical world brings with it? Such suffering cannot be justified and it does not need to be because it cannot be blamed on human beings. Physical suffering is pre-eminently a matter of inevitability; it remains a challenge insofar as man does not have to resign himself to it. Naturally, insight is able to explain evil and that, in its turn, liberates people from casting moralizing judgment.

Much the same applies to human evil. Here, too, insight can release people from the need to cast moral judgment. The command *not to judge* can somehow make the harder aspects of human existence more bearable. The true can free man from his malignant tendencies to want to see deeds in occurrences and guilty wrongdoers in deeds. Insight can contribute to helping people to respond to vile deeds with retaliatory deeds in which the offender is able to recognize something good. The true can help people to forgive by responding with something good, by adding value to the virtue of giving. The true thus not only makes it possible to bear the *other* and to perceive him as a challenge, but also to bear what is *different* and to see that as a challenge. The aspect of bearing extends into the risky enterprise of giving. The faithfulness to the earth, or to *the other*, therefore also involves being faithful to the human cosmos, or to what is *different*. This, too, can be appreciated in an active sense.

Nevertheless, there is one special, somewhat modernistic problem with which this challenge has to contend. The opening up of the ethical cosmos still leads to an erosion of all the traditional ethical values as interpreted in culture and institutions. In the loss of substance accompanying these values lurks the danger of ending up with disoriented and chaotic individuals: both internally and in their interactions with each other. Here one must be cautious of creating the picture of a history in decline that puts an end to what was once a harmonious and ethical cosmos. There has never been original harmony, so no end can logically be put to something that has never been. It is, however, the case that down the ages, man has put a great deal of energy into creating a somewhat ordered and ethical world. This ordering always gave good and evil a place, thus making it, in a certain respect, possible to contend with evil. When sacred tradition is lost, both man and society lose proportion and balance. That makes it harder to bear evil, let alone to *justify* it. How much more dangerous will this become if undisciplined human nature gains space or, more likely, claims space?

Hence Nietzsche's word of warning concerning the degeneration of modern man. He does not so much caution us in conjunction with man's *natural* wildness. He is more concerned that *anarchy* will take charge of the regulated spirit. He warns of a gone adrift type of *human* nature, one that will seek and find space in an opened up world. Such liberation is, of course, dangerous because it is reactive and allows plenty of space for the imagination to run riot. It is a kind of liberation that lacks active and internally directed will. It is a kind of freedom that cannot be reversed with the help of the old ethicality. The threatening degeneration must therefore be tackled in another way; this necessity will have to be given a change of tack in another way.

Repressing this degenerative nature is the worst possible solution. In such a case what has been repressed will continue to smolder, just waiting for a chance to again flare up. Suppression was also to be the escape route for *power*, rather than following the path of active orientation on the part of the will. One should, of course, remember that it was thinking in terms of power that encouraged degeneration in the first place: the will to *power* was also itself responsible for ruining ethical pleasure in life. That is why Nietzsche does not want to direct himself *away* but rather *towards* man. Now that sacred values can no longer support man, they will have to exercise and find autonomous control, balance, and direction. Man will have to bestow values upon himself and so establish the *measure* of things himself. The sacred values of the past will have to undergo a human and earthly *revaluation*. Is man capable of this? Is everyone able to do this? This revaluation does demand superhuman effort. The all too human aspects of the weak-willed will have to be conquered. This means that some will have to lead the way for others. Hence the reason for Nietzsche's plea for *aristocratic* values that can be disseminated and institutionalized by aristocratic segments of society. *Leading the way* is really something different from repressing; *disseminating* involves virtuously giving. Is the core concept of the aristocracy the right one?

This brings together the true and the good in a special way. In bearing and risking truth, man proves his faithfulness to the earth and to earthly existence. Through his creating of good he comes to appreciate this life. True knowledge is *necessarily* linked to *what is*, but it is really nothing more than that. Such necessity is not in fact the final thing. Through his will, man is able to take advantage of such necessity. The turning forward of the will can follow on from the glance that is cast backward. That is why Nietzsche sometimes also called the will an *inevitability*. The will can *give* a twist to what is *given*, including its need, its evil. That which is a given fact cannot, as such, be undone; it has happened, it has been done and so it is irreversible. In the forward directional sense the done is not definite. From this point of view the will is liberating. It is not about liberating *from* what is; such an attitude is reactive and futile. It is all about a challenged and directed liberating *to*. The driven will is not unconditionally free but rather liberating: what *is* gains, in that respect, an appreciating and a liberating side to it.

The will is the ability to view the necessary as *inevitable*. This also liberates people from drawing fatalistic conclusions. "What was" cannot be undone. The will can, in a liberating way, add to that how "it had wanted it to be" and how it "will be!"[1] The active *where to* frees individuals from the weight of what is, and also makes evil less

---

1. Nietzsche, *Also Sprach Zarathustra*, 177.

oppressive. Even though the truth may arrive late it will never be the last thing; the good can always be added to the truth.

The liberating will makes evil less oppressive. It is simply part and parcel of man and his capacity to differentiate. It is given in combination *with* the good. The fact *that* evil is a fact of life is a matter that is inescapable for man: it always returns. Precisely *what* evil is really is no fatality. Concrete evil is a need to which it is always possible to give a twist. Evil emanates from man and is therefore also a challenge for man. That frees him from the doom of evil. It also frees him from the fatal endeavor to *justify* the evil in the world. If the world as we know it cannot be declared the best of all the possible worlds then justification fails. One is then merely left with the conclusion that it is *not* possible to justify evil, a conclusion that has evoked too much own evil. If evil is not the final thing then man does not need to liberate himself from that, neither does he need to seek refuge in a power that should be able to eradicate evil. This frees man from futile yearning and it frees him from the futile call for justice. Man must therefore want to depart from the omnipotent.

Human *evil* is not exclusively negative. It comes with the good. Man cannot shake himself free of it without also ridding himself of what is good. There is another possible way in which evil can be *assessed*: it perpetually challenges. This therefore frees evil from the bleak chaining to sin and blame, hate and retribution, redemption and revenge. The challenging element makes evil lighter to bear or to contemplate risking. More to the point, man needs the negative to be able to wish and to give direction to the will. A strong will is able to bear what is necessary. A strong will does not immediately *react* to what is negative but comes to terms with it. A strong will seeks the negative and *risks* it in order to oppose, as an impetus for the benevolent answer. The appreciation turns into actively wanting to do rather than reactively seeking to undo.

A strong-willed individual is in that respect *powerful*: he has power over *himself*. He surmounts resistance, above all else the resistance in himself. He has confidence in himself; he dares to explore himself. Since he is able to be sincere towards himself he can also be open and benevolent to others, or *sincere*. He is able to see others as friends but also as enemies. These are enemies that he can appreciate: *as enemies* they are challenging so they need not be despised or hated. Evil is especially an excuse to do something in return without any need for retribution. Instead of retribution comes forgiveness, accompanied by the value of the *given*, an expressing of the virtue of being able to give. For the rest, the strong-willed are able to forget: what has happened or been done constitutes no objection, it does not poison the memory.

This active turnabout in events demands of man that he be restrained and calculable, for himself and for others. Having self-control makes it possible to supplement forgetting with another virtuous capacity, a capacity that will make "that is how I want it" directed and enduring: the capacity to *promise*. Promising involves the one who makes the promise—to himself or to others—keeping to the "that is how I want it" part of the bargain. Sincerely promising can take the place of old-style reliability born of ethical coercion. Forgetting relieves existence of its weightiness; it helps people to bear the truth. Promising then adds to that all that is good about active meaningful life.

Can there be any ethical purpose to life after all the ethical gods have died? Man once taught himself to cope with this life's purposefulness; it was a hard learning process that bestowed him with the ethicality of ethics. That ethicality was cruelly and painfully etched into his memory, an ethical memory. He learned to adhere to a promise that was imposed upon him. For a long time this memory formed the basis of society. However, after the death of the ethical God, man was left to answer the challenging question of how, as man, this promise could possibly be made concrete and how ethical purpose to life could be attached to the "that is how I want it" sentiment. This requires faithfulness to the earth, to life, and thus also to existing society. That has to be appreciated and that appreciating is something that man has to want to do. This is not compatible with will to *power* escapism that seeks good elsewhere in a totally different existence. To that end, man has to gain power over himself. Is he equipped to depart from the omnipotent? That is the question that has to provide the challenge; it is the final question.

Bibliography

Adorno, Theodor W. *Negative Dialektik und Jargon der Eigentlichkeit*. Gesammelte Schriften 6. Frankfurt am Main: Suhrkamp, 1973.
Berlin, Isaiah. *The Roots of Romanticism*. Princeton: Princeton University Press, 2001.
Čapek, Karel. *Gespräche mit Masaryk*. Stuttgart: Deutsche, 2001.
Hawking, Stephen. *A Brief History of Time*. London: Bantam, 1988.
Hegel, Georg W. F. *Grundlinien der Philosophie des Rechts*. Edited by Johannes Hoffmeister. Hamburg: Felix Meiner, 1966.
The Heidelberg Catechism.
Hejdánek, Ladislav. "Was ist Wahr." *Communio Viatorum: A Theological Journal* 43 (2001).
Heyer, Cees J. den. *Paulus: Man van Twee Werelden*. Zoetermeer: Meinema, 1998.
Marx, Karl. *Die Frühschriften*. Stuttgart: Alfred Kroener, 1968.
Nietzsche, Friedrich. *Also Sprach Zarathustra*. SW VI.1. Berlin: Walter de Gruyter, 1972.
———. *Sämtliche Werke: Kritische Gesamtausgabe*. Berlin: Walter de Gruyter, 1972.
Ree, Erik van. *The Political Thought of Joseph Stalin*. London: Routledge Curzon, 2002.
Rousseau, Jean-Jacques. *Het Maatschappelijk Kontrakt, of Beginselen van het Politiek Recht*. Utrecht: Het Spectrum, 1977.

www.ingramcontent.com/pod-product-compliance
Lightning Source LLC
Chambersburg PA
CBHW060311240426
43661CB00059B/2731